Protecting the human body: legal and bioethical perspectives from around the world

To Amy Gutmann
with kind regards

B. Feuillet

15

COLLECTION
DROIT, BIOÉTHIQUE ET SOCIÉTÉ

Protecting the human body: legal and bioethical perspectives from around the world

Edited by
Brigitte Feuillet-Liger
Geneviève Schamps, Kristina Orfali

bruylant

International Academic Network on Bioethics

This study was carried out by the *International Academics Network on Bioethics*, a network of academics from several countries whose aim is to promote international and multidisciplinary research on bioethics.

The international and multidisciplinary workshop which provided the impetus for this study was made possible thanks to funding and support from: French National Research Council (Agence Nationale de la Recherche), Institut Universitaire de France, F.R.S.-FNRS (Belgium), Centre for medical and biomedical Law (Université catholique de Louvain, Belgium), University of Central Europe (Hungary), Doshisha University (Japan), University of Tokyo (Japan), IODE, University of Rennes 1 (France).

Front cover: Michelangelo Buonarroti, Studies for the Libian Sibyl, 1511, book design Zsolt SANDOR

For all information, please go to our website; www.larciergroup.com

Éditions Bruylant
Espace Jacqmotte
Rue Haute, 139 - Loft 6 - 1000 Bruxelles

Printed in Belgium.

Dépôt légal :
Bibliothèque nationale, Paris : juin 2016
Bibliothèque royale de Belgique, Bruxelles : 2016/0023/115

ISSN 2033 – 3498
ISBN 978-2-8027-5165-6

Collection

"DROIT, BIOÉTHIQUE ET SOCIÉTÉ"

Directed by Brigitte FEUILLET-LIGER
Professor of Law at the University of Rennes I,
Member of the Institut Universitaire de France,
President of the International Academic Bioethics Network
Director of CRJO (IODE, UMR, CNRS no. 6262)

The life sciences and in particular, biomedical science, have considerably progressed over the decades to offer a multitude of new treatments. Going beyond its initial therapeutic goal, medical practice offers the unique opportunity to respond to society's expectations related to individual personal desires. Men and women are now able to access techniques which allow them to have children; to assert their social identity; to decide about their end of life... in all, to respond to suffering instead of merely treating disease. Recourse to medical technologies has become, at least in part, a social and cultural phenomenon.

However, despite the unquestionable benefits of such progress, it also brings with it clear risks for fundamental human rights and can even impact upon the structure of families. Faced with increasing demands, we can observe the emergence of a market of 'well-being' medicine. The fundamental problem is to find a way to reconcile individual freedom, based on personal autonomy with the protection of the human being. Legal norms appear to be one of the best tools to address this goal, even if we rely increasingly on ethical norms to regulate the area of biomedicine. However, different cultures respond to the challenges of biomedicine in different ways. Biomedical practices deal with issues related to life, to the human body, to sexuality, reproduction and death. Yet, there is no single understanding of these concepts: it will depend on individuals, on culture or on religion. If we agree that the law of different countries translates the different social options it should however be analysed through the prism of other disciplines, such as anthropology, philosophy, sociology, psychoanalysis, psychology... in order to enable us to understand (and to respect) the cultural differences and to reflect upon a possible (universal?) harmonisation. The "Droit, Bioéthique et société" Collection strives to contribute to the diffusion and promotion of multi-disciplinary reflection on these critical questions.

Books published in the same collection :

– *Procréation médicalement assistée et Anonymat.Panorama international*, sous la direction de Brigitte FEUILLET-LIGER, 2008.

– *Who is my Genetic Parent? Donor Anonymity and Assisted Reproduction: a Cross-Cultural Perspective*, edited by Brigitte FEUILLET-LIGER, Kristina ORFALI and Thérèse CALLUS, 2011.

– *Adolescent et Acte médical, regard croisés. Approche internationale et pluridisciplinaire*, sous la direction de Brigitte FEUILLET-LIGER et Ryuichi IDA, 2011.

- *Adolescents, Autonomy and Medical Treatment-Divergence and Convergence across the globe*, edited by Brigitte FEUILLET-LIGER, Ryuichi IDA and Thérèse CALLUS, 2012.

- *Les proches et la fin de vie médicalisée. Panorama international*, sous la direction de Brigitte FEUILLET-LIGER, 2013.

- *Families and End-of-Life Treatment Decisions. An international Perspective*, edited by Brigitte FEUILLET-LIGER, Kristina ORFALI and Thérèse CALLUS, 2013.

- *Principles of international biolaw. Seeking common ground at the intersection of bioethics and human rights,* Roberto ANDORNO, 2013.

- *Corps de la femme et Biomédecine. Approche internationale,* sous la direction de Brigitte FEUILLET-LIGER et Amel AOUIJ-MRAD, 2013.

- *The Female Body : A Journey Through Law, Culture and Medicine,* edited by Brigitte FEUILLET-LIGER, Kristina ORFALI and Thérèse CALLUS, 2013.

- *Le don de gamètes,* sous la direction d'Aude MIRKOVIC, 2014.

- *Les incidences de la biomédecine sur la parenté. Approche internationale,* sous la direction de Brigitte FEUILLET-LIGER et Maria Claudia CRESPO-BRAUNER, 2014.

- *Reproductive Technology and Changing Perception of Parenthood around the World,* edited by Brigitte FEUILLET-LIGER, Thérèse CALLUS, Kristina ORFALI, 2014.

- *Principes de protection du corps et Biomédecine. Approche internationale*, sous la direction de Brigitte FEUILLET-LIGER et Geneviève SCHAMPS, 2015.

- *La nature humaine, le donné et le construit – Approche pluridisciplinaire*, sous la direction de Clotilde BRUNETTI-PONS, 2016.

TABLE OF CONTENTS

OVERVIEW

LIST OF CONTRIBUTORS

Hassan Abdelhamid is a Professor of Philosophy of Law and Comparative Law in the Faculty of Law & Graduate Studies at Ain Shams University, Vice-Dean of the Faculty and Dean of the Law Department in French at Ain Shams University. He is also an associate professor in the Department of Law and Justice at Université Laurentienne, (Canada). He holds a PhD on Philosophy of Law from Université de Paris X – Nanterre in 1994. Dr. Hassan has published numerous papers and books on these topics in periodicals, scientific journals and international networks for research in Arabic, French and English languages in the fields of the search for justice in the era of globalization, biotechnology, bioethics science and law, the idea of universal law, the historical evolution of the phenomenon of organized crime, the phenomenon of reception of foreign laws in Egypt, the Islamic logic and practice of human rights, the State and religion in the Islamic East and the protection of human life in the Islamic legal culture.

Penelope Agallopoulou is Professor Emeritus of the University of Piraeus, where she offered courses on Civil Law (1969-2008). She has also taught Civil Law, as a visiting professor, in other Greek and foreign Universities. She has published several books and more than 100 articles (in Greek, French, and English), mainly in the area of family law and bioethics. She has been Member of Legislative Committees, as well as Member of the Greek delegation of the Committee on Matters of Civil Law of the Council of the European Union (also President of the said Committee during the Greek Presidency in 2003). The University of Piraeus published in 2011 a two-volume work with Essays in her Honour, containing 82 contributions in Greek, French, English and German.

Amel Aouij-Mrad is Professor at the University of Tunis (Tunisia), President of the Tunisian Association of Medical Law and was member of the National Medical Ethics Committee (2002-2012).

Thérèse Callus is Associate Professor in Law at the University of Reading (UK), Director of Postgraduate Research and member of the School of Law Research Committee. She is an expert in comparative biomedical and family law, with particular expertise in the regulation of new technologies, especially in the field of assisted conception. She has published widely in international peer reviewed journals and books, in English and French.

Anderson Orestes Cavalcante Lobato is Professor of Constitutional Law, Ethics and Environmental law at the Federal University of Rio Grande – FURG – RS (Brazil). He is Visiting Professor of Public Law at the University of Toulouse, UT1, 2004; and Visiting Professor of Public Law at the University of Rennes 1, 2013 (France). He has acted as a Government Consultant to the Ministry of Justice, Special Secretariat for the promotion of policies of racial equality – SEPPIR, 2010 (Brazil).

Maria-Claudia Crespo Brauner is Professor of Civil Law, and Biolaw at the Federal University of Rio Grande – FURG – RS (Brazil). Professeur visitant of Private Law at the Faculty of Law and Political Science, Rennes 1, UR1 (France) and a researcher at CNPq (Brazil). She has acted as a Government Consultant to the Ministeries of Health and of Justice and was a member of the National Committee for Research Ethics (CONEP) and the Commission on access and use of genetic material human, Brasília (Brazil).

Carmen DomÍnguez Hidalgo is Professor of Civil Law and Director of the Family Center of the Pontifical Catholic University of Chile (Chile). She has published three books and numerous articles on Civil Liability, Legal Theory, Family Law and Bioethics and has led several research projects in Chile and abroad. She is a practicing lawyer, a referee of the Chamber of Commerce, and was Alternate Judge at the Court of Appeal of Santiago (Chile). She is a permanent consultant to the Chilean Congress as an expert in Family Law and Bioethics.

Brigitte Feuillet-Liger is Senior Fellow and Professor at the Faculty of Law, University of Rennes 1 (France), where she specializes in the Individual, Family and Bioethics Law. She is a Senior Member of the Institut Universitaire de France, member of the Institut de l'Ouest: Droit et Europe (IODE, UMR CNRS 6262), Chair of the International Academic Network for Bioethics and awarded Erasmus Mundus by the European Union in 2005. She is Doctor Honoris Causa of University of Louvain (Belgium).

Françoise Furkel is Emeritus Professor of the Franco-German Center of Law at the University of the Saarland (Germany), and has been an invited professor in several French universities. She specializes in comparative German and French family law, bioethics and in biotechnology. She publishes regularly in German and French peer-reviewed journals.

Marsha Garrison is the Suzanne J. and Norman Miles Professor of Law at Brooklyn Law School, where she teaches bioethics and family law. Recent books include The Law of Bioethics: Individual Autonomy and Social Regulation, 2009 (with C.E. Schneider).

Dominique Goubau is full Professor at Laval University, Quebec City, for 25 years. Author of numerous books and articles in the field of family, persons and children's law, he is also past-president and active member of the Family Law Committee of the Quebec's Bar. He was a member of the Family Law Reform Commission of Québec whose 2015 report proposes, among others, to set up a new framework for parentage and assisted reproduction.

Shinichiro Hayakawa is Professor of Law at the Department of Advanced Social and International Studies in Faculty of Liberal Arts, University of Tokyo (Japan), Member of the Board of Legislative Council for Japanese Ministry of Justice. He teaches Contract Law, Torts Law, Family Law and Private International Law etc. His main field of research includes Private International Law, International Family Law and International Transactions Law.

Ryuichi Ida has been appointed Chairman of the Shiga University. He recently created the Institute for governance bioethics at Doshisha University in which he was previously attached and was vice-director of the International Institute for Advanced Studies. He was a member and president of the International Bioethics Committee of the UNESCO.

Francis Kernaleguen is Professor of Private Law at the University of Rennes 1, France, where he was also Vice-Dean for studies (1990-1998), Director of the Judicial Studies Institute (1987-2007) and Member of the Regional Ethics Committee (1990-2008). He is Co-Director of the collection "L'univers des normes" at the Presses Universitaires de Rennes since 2007.

Christine Lazerges, professor emeritus of the Paris-Sorbonne University and former member of the French Parliament, is president of the French Consultative Commission for Human Rights (CNCDH) since 2012; this commission being the body recognised by the United Nations for the promotion and protection of human rights in France. Christine Lazerges academic work covers in particular criminal law and criminal public policies. Among her recent publications, she in particular contributed to comparative law studies: e.g. *Figures du parquet* [about the *French Prosecution Service*] (2006); *La victime sur la scène pénale en Europe* [the place of the victim in criminal law in Europe] (2008), *La dangerosité saisie par le droit pénal* [dangerousness in criminal law] (2011), *La minorité à contresens* [legal infancy in the wrong way] (2015).

David Le Breton is Professor of Sociology and member of the University of Strasbourg Institute for Advanced Study (USIAS). He is also a member of the *Institut Universitaire de France*. He specializes in issues of anthropology of the body, anthropology of risk taking in youth, and ethics in medicine and is the author of *Expériences de la douleur* (Métailié, 2010), *Anthropologie du corps et modernité* (PUF, 2013) and *La chair à vif. De la leçon d'anatomie aux greffes d'organes* (Métailié, 2006).

Pierre Le Coz is Professor of Philosophy, and holds a Ph.D. in Life and Health Sciences. He teaches medical ethics and moral philosophy at the Faculty of Medicine of Marseille (UMR 7268 ADES/CNRS/EFS Aix-Marseille University). He was Vice chairman of the French National Consultative Ethics Committee for Health and Life Sciences (2003-2012). Actually, he is Chairman of the Ethics Committee for the French agency for food, environmental and occupational health safety.

Dominique Manaï is tenured Professor of Law at the University of Geneva (Switzerland). She was Chair of the Swiss Expert Committee which drafted the Federal Law on Research on Humans (2000-2006). She is the author of nine books and has published many articles in the field of Biomedical Law and Moral Philosophy of Law. She is a specialist in personal rights. For eight years, she was President of the Association of Professors at the University of Geneva.

Cosimo Marco Mazzoni is Professor of Law and Director of the department of Law and Economics, University of Siena

(Italy). He is editor of *A Legal Framework of Bioethics* (Kuwer Law International, 1998), *Un quadro europeo per la bioetica? (An European Framework for Bioethics?)* (Florence, Olschki, 1998), *Ethics of Biological Research* (2000), *Per uno statuto del corpo* (Milano, Giuffrè, 2008), *Psiche o la forma del corpo* (Milano, Giuffrè, 2013).

Saibe Oktay-Özdemir is Professor of Civil Law at the Faculty of Law, Istanbul University (Turkey). She currently teaches the Law of Persons for undergraduate students and BioEthics and Law at PhD level. She is the author of the book *Law of Persons* (Istanbul, Filiz Kitapevi, 15th edition, 2015).

Kristina Orfali, Ph.D. is a graduate from école Normale Supérieure and a sociologist; she is currently an Associate Professor of Bioethics at Columbia University Medical Center, Department of Pediatrics (USA) and a Fellow of the Institute for Social and Economic Research & Policy. She has been Associate Director and Assistant Professor at the University of Chicago. She has published work on patient's hospital experiences in a cross cultural perspective, on clinician and family decision making in neonatal intensive care units and on Bioethics in France and Europe in several books and international journals. She is a member of the Morgan Stanley Children's Hospital Clinical Ethics Committee and a clinical ethics consultant in pediatrics.

Verónica San Julián Puig is Professor of Civil Law and Vice-Dean for Research and Quality, Faculty of Law of the University of Navarre (Spain). She is also a Researcher at the Center of Research Society and Culture (ICS) at the same University.

Judit Sándor is a full professor at the Faculty of Political Science, Legal Studies and Gender Studies of the Central European University (CEU), Budapest. She had a bar exam in Hungary she conducted legal practice at Simmons & Simmons in London, had fellowships at McGill (Montreal), at Stanford (Palo Alto), and at Maison de sciences de l'Homme (Paris), at NYU (New York, as a Global Research Fellow). In 1996 she received Ph.D. in law and political science. She was one of the founders of the first Patients' Right Organization ('Szószóló') in Hungary, she was a member of the Hungarian Science and Research Ethics Council, and currently a member at the Hungarian Human Reproduction Commission. In 2004-2005 she served as the Chief of the Bioethics Section at the UNESCO. She published seven books in the field of human rights and biomedical law. Since September 2005 she is a founding director of the Center for Ethics and Law in Biomedicine (CELAB) at the Central European University.

Geneviève Schamps is Professor at the Faculties of Law and Criminology, of Medicine and Dentistry and of Public Health, at the Catholic University of Louvain (Belgium). She is President of the Institut pour la recherche interdisciplinaire en sciences juridiques and Director of the Centre of Medical and Biomedical Law (UCL). She' also a Member of the Royal Academy of Science, Letters and Fine Arts of Belgium.

Gülen Sinem Tek, teaching assistant at Bahçeşehir University (Turkey). She pursues her PhD studies at İstanbul University with Professor S. Oktay-Özdemir as her advisor. She has participated in the bioethics PhD seminar classes of Professor Oktay-Özdemir and assisted her with the teaching of the course on the Law of persons.

FOREWORD

BY

Christine LAZERGES

President of the French Consultative Commission for Human Rights (CNCDH)

Emeritus Professor at University Paris 1 Panthéon-Sorbonne

Between bioethics and law, between foreign laws, comparative law and international law, the research laboratory of the 'Western Institute of Law and European Studies' – the IODE – (UMR CNRS 6262) offers us, under the aegis of the *International Academic Network on Bioethics*, chaired by Brigitte Feuillet, an eleventh collective publication. A work that commands attention like an ancient fresco, given how much it brings to mind, how much it explains and tells us about a people, an era, or a subject. The subject here is one of those that raise questions for anyone, wherever they are, wherever they come from, whatever they think or however they live. *The principles of protection of the human body* in an international approach: what are they? How are they created or imposed? How are they protected or guaranteed? How are they violated? What about sanctions if they are not respected? What do they say about a society? What links do they maintain with the principle of dignity enshrined in article 1 of the Universal Declaration of Human Rights: "All human beings are born free and equal in dignity and rights." Numerous other questions are also raised.

There was an element of boldness, perhaps even recklessness, on the part of Brigitte Feuillet, Geneviève Schamps and their research team when they embarked on the difficult and fascinating journey of exploration of the protection of the human body in seventeen countries on four continents; in Europe: Germany, Belgium, Spain, France, Greece, Hungary, Italy, the United Kingdom, Switzerland and Turkey; in Asia: China, Japan and Taiwan; in North and South America: Canada, the United States of America, Brazil and Chile; in Africa: Egypt and Tunisia.

In terms of methodology this was a serious undertaking that commands admiration, whether for the collective definition of the subject in the difficult summary chapter of comparative law, or for the workshop presenting and debating foreign laws.

In scientific terms, the reader cannot fail to note the subversive nature of comparative law, the inescapable humility of international law, or of course the links required and formed with fundamental rights and freedoms.

It is an honour as well as a difficult task for the president of the French National Advisory Commission for Human Rights (CNCDH), to write a preface to this work, given how much the subject echoes the problems that our commission has attempted to study in successive steps and on numerous occasions, as demonstrated by a series of opinions adopted in the unenclosed field of bioethics. I will refer to just one contribution to the debate, presented in a plenary assembly of the CNCDH on 14 June 2007 under the title "Human rights, bioethics and their relationship to the body". Our commission sought to highlight the important questions that arose when the legislator, French in this case, chose to set out guidelines for a status of the human body to protect the person: by means of 'bioethics laws'.

This status, as defined by French law, is based on two complementary principles: on the one hand, that the human body is unavailable, and that, as a result, the elements that comprise it are "not for sale". Thus any exchange relating to the elements of the human body refers to a donation rather than to commerce. The European Convention on Biomedicine of 4 April 1997 refers to the prohibition of making the body or its elements a source of profit.

The most difficult debate, raised so well by Brigitte Feuillet in the excellent summary chapter of the collective research undertaken, appears to concern the issue of whether or not there is a distinction between the person and the body. This is also the central point of CNCDH's contribution to the debate. If the body has a status, it is that the law treats it as inseparable from the person. It is a matter of helping the person to preserve the integrity of his body, and to that end sheltering him from the pressures exercised by others to procure elements of the body that have become useful or valuable. The philosophy of our commission, which underlies the analysis, is based on the prohibition of all forms of slavery, from the most insidious to the most visible. The gravity of the issue implies that the person is protected against himself. The risk is that he might be persuaded to renounce control of his body or elements of it in the name of interests that are not his own and could be profitable.

However, it is impossible to ignore the question of whether one has the right to protect the person against himself in such a private matter. A logic that is individualist rather than universalist opens possibilities and lifts prohibitions, with the aim of giving each individual control over his body.

The debate at the heart of numerous CNCDH opinions on bioethical issues, or more generally on ethical issues, concerns the meaning given to the principle of dignity and the notion of informed consent, with regard to vulnerable persons, as well as to those who *a priori* are not. This problem is found in the research led and coordinated by Brigitte Feuillet and Geneviève Schamps on the comparative and international approach to the principles of protection of the human body.

As with any work related to comparative and international law, a certain unity concerning the principle of respect for physical integrity, albeit one that should not be overstated, emerges from a reading of the successive chapters of this book. Indeed, while the need for protection of the human body is recognised everywhere, and while it transcends cultural differences, as observed by Brigitte Feuillet, it nevertheless covers different realities. It is very interesting to note, along with the co-editor of the work, that “while the principle of respect for dignity, recognised in most countries, is not systematically endowed with a normative scope, in that it only confers subjective rights in certain countries [...] it is generally considered a founding principle for all other principles”.

When it comes to protection of the human body, as with other subjects dealing with the person, a subtle game of balance develops between dignity and autonomy. This game is perfectly illustrated in this collective work.

The publication of this transnational research, with all the difficulties that brings, is as pleasing as it is useful. The work carried out enriches our knowledge, while closing no doors; quite the opposite, in fact, as it opens up new areas for reflection on human rights.

This preface was offered to me on behalf of the French National Advisory Commission for Human Rights (CNCDH), the first independent national institution for the protection and promotion of human rights, created in 1947 by René Cassin. Robert Badinter described our commission as “a company of the vigilant”; this vigilance should only be exercised with modesty, albeit enthusiastically with regard to respect for fundamental rights and freedoms. To have approached the CNCDH is a strong sign that the magnificent undertaking of this collective publication, on the principles of protection of the human body in a comparative and international approach, is part of the long and winding road, often swept by contrary winds, of the universalism of human rights.

THE BODY AND THE PERSON: WHICH ANTHROPOLOGY(-IES) SHOULD BE CONSIDERED FOR THE LAW?

David LE BRETON

Professor of Sociology at the University of Strasbourg

Member of the Institut Universitaire de France

Member of the University of Strasbourg Institute for Advanced Study, (France)

I. – The body as the incarnation of a person

When all is said and done, it is less about protecting the body and more about protecting the person. Isolating the body from the person is a dual undertaking, a recent phenomenon in the history of our societies, as it does not oppose the body to the soul or to the mind, but to the individual himself(1). In this sense, the body is a question, never an answer. Certainly, the human condition cannot be conceived outside of the flesh that gives us a face. Both an individual and collective identity it is what is projected to be viewed and appraised by others. It is what enables us to be named, recognised and identified with a social group, a gender, an age, a skin colour and an appearance. Any relationship of mankind with the world is formed through the intermediary of the body (understood in the sense of the flesh). From the body's technical feats to expressions of affection, from sensory perception to body art, from hygiene habits to nutrition, from table manners to bedroom behaviour, from the ways in which we present ourselves to taking responsibility for health or illness, from racism to eugenics, from tattoos to piercings, the body is an inexhaustible subject of social practices, representations and imagination. It is impossible to speak about a human being without assuming in one

(1) D. Le Breton, *L'adieu au corps*, Paris, Métailié, 2012; D. Le Breton, *Anthropologie du corps et modernité*, coll. Quadrige, Paris, PUF, 2013.

way or another that the subject is a creature of flesh and blood, moulded by an individual sensitivity. The body is the "general key to understanding the world", said Merleau-Ponty[(2)]. The body is not a separate thing or object in itself, it is the matter or substance of the person, the person's 'being-in-the-world'; it is impossible for the individual to dissociate himself from it without disappearing, as he is no different from his flesh. The body is first and foremost self-transparent.

In social and historical terms, the "body" has not always been a foregone conclusion. It has a dual connotation and is not considered as such in all human societies. Some representations do not distinguish the man from his flesh. The body is more a question than an answer, a visible and self-evident fact with a multitude of different representations which accordingly assigns a specific position within the general symbolism of society. These representations are derived from a social status, a vision of the world and, within this vision, from a definition of the person. The body is a reality that changes from one society to another: the images that define it, the knowledge systems that clarify its nature and the feats it has achieved are innumerable and contradictory. From one society to the next, the images endeavour to reduce its mystery in cultural terms, or rather the mystery of the flesh that forms the density of the man. Dualism, in other words the designation of the body as a separate or virtually autonomous fragment of the person, presupposes a distinction that is alien to a number of human communities.

Biblical anthropology ignores this division between the body and the person. Unlike the Platonic or Orphic way of thinking, it does not regard the human condition as the fall of the soul into the body. "Hebrew," says C. Tresmontant, "is a practical language that gives names only to what exists. What is more, it has no word for 'matter' or for the 'body', as these concepts do not relate to empirical realities, contrary to what our old dualistic and Cartesian tradition leads us to believe. No one has ever seen 'matter' or a 'body' as these are understood by substantial dualism"[(3)]. In the Biblical world, man is indistinguishable from the flesh that puts him in the world. The Christian tradition also focuses on the

(2) M. Merleau-Ponty, *Phénoménologie de la perception*, Paris, Gallimard, 1945, pp. 271-272.
(3) C. Tresmontant, *Essai sur la pensée hébraïque*, Paris, Cerf, 1953, p. 53.

physical moulding of humans by God, the incarnation of Jesus, the Eucharist, the resurrection of the flesh, which illustrate the solidarity between the person and their body.

In many traditional societies, the body is not designated as separate from the man. On the contrary, it is a sign of inclusion in the world, through a close-knit network of connections. The flesh of man and the flesh of the world are mutually intertwined. The body is not the mark of a breach, of a difference defining the individual and separating him from the rest of the world. Although these societies recognise a relative personalisation of social relationships, the person is blended within a social and cosmic whole. This is exemplified by the Kanak people, studied in the past by M. Leenhardt, among whom the flesh of man is named in terms taken from the plant and mineral kingdoms. Depending on their shape or structure, the various body parts are designated by terms that also identify trees, fruit and shells. In its own environment, the body appears to be another form of plant, or a plant an external representation of the flesh. The same materials make the world work and feed the flesh. In addition, in Kanak cosmogony, the tree symbolises membership of a group by implanting man in the earth and according him a specific place in nature, and each individual knows which tree each of his ancestors is linked with.

In the Melanesian society described by Leenhardt, the concept of person structured around self, as held by our western societies, lacks substance. If the body is directly related to the plant world, there is no border between the living and the dead. Death is not seen by the Kanaks as a form of destruction. It marks the path to another form of existence in which the deceased can take the place of an animal, a tree or a spirit, or can even return to the village or town and mingle with the living in the form of the *bao*[(4)]. There is transferability between the living and the dead, rather than a radical breach. On the other hand, during his lifetime, each man exists only through his relationships with others; he is part of a social unit in which everything is interrelated. The person's substance stems from the sum of its connections with its partners; no one can be characterised as an individual in the modern sense, and no one draws his legitimacy from his person alone, erected

(4) M. Leenhardt, *Do kamo. La personne et le mythe dans le monde mélanésien*, Paris, Gallimard, 1971, pp. 67-68.

as a totem[5]. The concept of the individual in the western sense of the term is not, therefore, identifiable in Kanak sociability and social representations. The body does not exist, or rather it is not identified as an autonomous "reality", in traditional Kanak thinking.

Well-aware of the magnitude of alcoholism and distress affecting the indigenous populations in the first part of the 20th century and eager to assess how French society impacted on traditional Kanak ways of thinking in New Caledonia, Leenhardt questions an old man on this matter: heresponds, to Leenhardt's great astonishment by opening up an inexhaustible issue for the anthropology of the body: "One thing you have brought us is the body"[6]. The Melanesians, affected in a rudimentary fashion by these new values linked to their evangelisation, or destabilised in their traditional ways, have become partially detached from the web of meanings in which their existence was immersed, discovering their bodies as a result of their individualisation, which replicates, to a lesser degree, that of our western societies. The boundaries defined by their bodies now partially distinguish them from their companions. The community dimension has diminished. Some Melanesians feel more like individuals than members of a community, although this transformation has not become firmly entrenched. The shrinkage towards the ego resulting from this social and cultural transformation leads to a new perception of the self. This social and cultural transformation confirms an idea of Durkheim, according to which in order to distinguish one subject from another "there must be an individuating factor, and it is the body that fills this role"[7]. Durkheim rediscovers the principle of individuation conceived by Thomas Aquinas. The modern idea of the body is a result of the individualistic structure of the social field, a consequence of the failure of solidarity that blends the person into a collective and into the cosmos through a web of connections in which everything is interrelated.

In community-based, more holistic societies, where the meaning of human existence indicates a subordination to the group, to the

(5) C. Lévi-Strauss, *La pensée sauvage*, Paris, Plon, 1962, p. 285.

(6) M. Leenhardt, *Do kamo. La personne et le mythe dans le monde mélanésien*, *op. cit.*, p. 263.

(7) E. Durkheim, *Formes élémentaires de la vie religieuse*, 5th ed., Paris, PUF, 1968, pp. 386 et seq.

cosmos, the body, theoretically does not exist as a rigid boundary. It is not separate. Considering ownership of the body in this context is abstract. As an isolatable element of the person, it can only be considered in terms of individualistic structures in which everyone is separated from the others and relatively autonomous in their actions and values. The face then becomes the preferred indicator of one's intimate difference(8). The modern concept of the body involves externalising the world and other people. It turns the person into an individual, no longer merged into a "we-others" projection, but detached and left to its own devices, a self in a radical and reflective position face to face with others. The modern definition of the body, as it has been gradually developing since the Renaissance, involves a threefold withdrawal. Man is separate from others (the body as a demarcation point for the individual), removed from nature (nature is different from man, it is no longer cosmos but environment) and cut off from himself (the dualism between the soul or the mind and the body, or today between a man and his body). In our democratic and individualistic societies, the body is effectively the mark of the individual, its boundary, and what differentiates it from others(9).

II. – The emergence of a dualism

Since Vesalius and the first anatomists, the medical representation of the body has no longer been directly associated with a simultaneous vision of man. The publication of *De Humani corporis fabrica* in 1543 was a symbolic moment for this epistemological transformation, which led the way, through various stages, to contemporary medicine(10). Before Descartes and his philosophy of mechanism, anatomists founded a dualism that remains at the core of modernity (and not only in medicine); this dualism distinguishes man from his body. This brings to mind Marguerite Yourcenar's image in *The Abyss (L'Œuvre au noir)*, when Zeno, the doctor so similar to Vesalius, and his companion,

(8) D. Le Breton, *Anthropologie du corps et modernité*, *op. cit.*

(9) D. Arasse, "La chair, la grâce, le sublime", *in* A. Corbin, J.-J. Courtine and G. Vigarello, *Histoire du corps. De la Renaissance aux Lumières*, Paris, Seuil, 2005; D. Le Breton, *La chair à vif. De la leçon d'anatomie aux greffes d'organes*, Paris, Métailié, 2008; D. Le Breton, *Anthropologie du corps et modernité*, Paris, PUF, 2013.

(10) D. Le Breton, *La chair à vif. De la leçon d'anatomie aux greffes d'organes*, *op. cit.*; id., *Anthropologie du corps et modernité*, *op. cit.*

another doctor, are studying the corpse of a young man, the son of the later: "In the room steeped in vinegar where we dissected this dead body, who was no longer a son or a friend, but simply a wonderful example of the human machine"(11). Modern medicine has no concern for the man, only for the diseased body; it treats "the human machine", not the son or the friend, *i.e.* the man as a unique being. Medicine deals largely with the organism and its parameters. Historically, it has focused its attention on the body (on a certain representation of the body, transforming it into an organism). This dissociation of the person from its body is an old narrative in medicine; and the philosophical dualism that was set in motion by Descartes at the same time emphasises a division between the mind (or the soul) and the body.

Medicine has a minimal dependence on anthropology. The medical specialisations based on certain functions, organs and pathologies, or even the hospital infrastructure that treats the human body like parts on an assembly line, the use of ever more sophisticated imaging technologies in developing a diagnosis, and the reliance on increasingly high-tech treatment methods are among the numerous medical approaches to the ailing human body that place the patient in medical parentheses as an unimportant and occasionally obstructive accessory to a disease that alone is worthy of interest and care. The human body now sees itself divided up and parcelled out. In addition, through the legacy of the mechanist philosophy, it is understood to be a sophisticated machine.

III. – The fragmentation of the body

In western legal thinking, Roman law divided the world into "persons" and "objects". The body and the person become superimposed as the body existed solely as part of the person. Roman law considers the human being and does not see the body as anything other than the man it embodies. In this sense, it is difficult to say that it "disembodied the human being", as Jean-Pierre Baud put it(12). For these legal experts the idea that the human being was identical to its body was so obvious that they

(11) M. Yourcenar, *L'Œuvre au noir*, Paris, Gallimard, 1980, p. II-8.
(12) J.-P. Baud, *L'affaire de la main volée*, Paris, Seuil, 1993, pp. 48-89.

never considered establishing any difference by distinguishing the body from the person. In fact, in phenomenological terms we *are* our body, which is not categorized as a property but as one's identity. It is not an external thing that we can say we possess; the body is intertwined with the person. "Why is our body the mirror of our being if not for the fact that it is a natural ego, a given form of existence, such that we never know if the forces that hold us are the body's or our own, or rather that they are never entirely the body's nor ours"[(13)].

Since medicine has been using body parts separated from the person for collective purposes, it has completely overturned the traditional legal representations. In the second half of the 20th century, it was by no means only the body that lawyers rediscovered – they had never concealed it – but a previously unthinkable fragmentation. The Civil Code has been overwhelmed by medical advances since the body or parts of the body have been used for medical purposes distinct from the individual. An offshoot of Roman law, it sees the person as subject to the law and makes no distinction between the person and the body. By isolating the body, biotechnologies compel the law to consider a body as being detached from its environment. Detached from the person, the parts of the body cannot be treated as a person, although the person has some say in how they are used. The body imperceptibly takes on the status of an organism. The question now arises of ownership over the body.

With blood transfusions and, above all, the possibility of preserving blood outside of the body, there was for the first time concern about providing a legal framework for practices resulting in the removal of parts of the body in order to make provision for them in social changes. The first blood banks appeared in the 1940s and gave rise for the first time to the question of the independence of certain human components outside of the body. In 1952, when French lawyers established the first law in the world on blood transfusions, they introduced the principle of cost-free and profit-free donations of blood and blood derivatives. Following blood transfusions, there were the cornea, organs and tissues that could be taken from a corpse or a living person: sperm, eggs, placenta, etc. Removed from the person, these body parts enter a particular area

(13) M. Merleau-Ponty, *Phénoménologie de la perception*, *op. cit.*, pp. 85-86.

of understanding of the law. They are not liable to be removed from the person without consent, and only subject to certain conditions. Depending on each legal context, they may or may not be sold. With the person separated from their body parts, the question then arises of their legal and anthropological status[14] The body is no longer a unit of the subject, but a temporary conglomeration of substitutable elements. The status of the human body is nowadays often that of an object detached from the individual and often used practically in these terms by biotechnologies. It only corresponds minimally to the incarnation of the individual. Increasingly biologised and naturalised, *i.e.* detached from the singularity of the individual (excluding biological indicators), and broken up into a collection of elements for the purpose of analysis, it becomes incidental, uprooted, a mere commodity.

IV. – The law as an ultimate limit

In our pluralistic ethical societies, there are three conflicting lines of thought on the legal status of the individual and the body.

One conservative argument is strongly influenced by religious beliefs according to which any undermining of the traditional biological order (cultural but naturalised) is seen as a threat to the sovereignty of God or the principle of an intangible Nature, or even to a Symbolic Law, as some psychoanalysts have suggested during recent debates on marriage for all. In this context, if the body is an asset, it belongs not so much to the individual as to God or Nature. The individual is merely the custodian of his body.

A conflicting, liberal, line of argument puts forward the pre-eminence of the individual over the community. Autonomy is the supreme value, and the individual is always right about what he wants for himself if his decisions are based on his free consent. In this context, the individual is legally deemed to be the owner of his body and free to make use of it as he sees fit, within certain limits. However, this switching around of human bodily components introduces, in a legal context, a radical ontological difference between someone who sells part of his/her body (organs,

(14) D. Le Breton, *Anthropologie du corps et modernité*, *op. cit.*; C.M. Mazzoni, "Il corpo nascosto dei giuristi", *in* C.M. Mazzoni (*a cura di*), *Per une statuto del corpo*, Milano, Giuffré, 2008.

tissues, gametes, etc.) or "rents" it to others (surrogate mother). These are persons of modest circumstances, sometimes suffering from psychological problems, who have no other choice than to resign themselves to the worst for financial reasons by agreeing, for example, to carry a child for a couple, to donate their eggs or to sell a kidney. It is hard to imagine 'the lady of the house' donating or selling part of her person to help her maid have a child or receive a kidney transfer. In market terms, it is really a matter of "profiting" from the social condition of individuals who have been stripped of their independence in decision-making, although they may try hard to maintain their positions. As a property, the body, once it becomes an organism, is transformed into a financial asset. However, the freedom of some is also the restriction of others. This freedom to dispose of one's body is not the same for the poor and the wealthy, even though both may at some point have a use for it. Do some people own their bodies to a greater extent than others? While some refrain from impairing their physical integrity, others have to give up this privilege in order to temporarily preserve the financial conditions of a decent life (or even avoid starvation), in the absence of other options. Such an ethic gives rise to the principle that the interests of each guide the actions of the whole. With each individual having their own values, no other authority can make a judgment; everyone has to exercise a freedom of choice and action guaranteed by law. The liberal trend of thinking levels the balance between the values by according them the same significance. Such a position results in a sort of moral dissolution. What is best for me is what I decide for myself. However, can we imagine a society that is completely disinterested in the sum of all individual choices and leaves everyone to be responsible for themselves? By doing so, it emphasizes social inequalities and even profits from them. Is it not the responsibility of a State to protect the most vulnerable and ensure that the choices made by some do not threaten the freedom of others? What restrictions should be placed on this claim to have control over one's body when this freedom is distorted by social inequalities that prevent certain categories of the population from exercising their choice independently and benefiting from a *quid pro quo*, simply because they lack the financial resources to support it? Some will always be a source of organic raw material for others, without any possibility of reciprocity except in the form of money. What restrictions can avoid running the risk of "moral erosion in favour of a calculation of costs and profit"[(15)]? According to this line of thinking, the body is basically the property of the individual, who has the right to do what he wants with it.

A third line of thinking draws its inspiration from anthropology and underlines the necessary combination of individual demands with the symbolic configuration that underpins social bonds. According to this argument, the body remains united with the person from conception to death, and even beyond, when the possible uses of the corpse are taken into consideration. Such values as dignity and solidarity are fundamental to this, with autonomy also playing a crucial role, albeit offset by the other values. The rule of law rises above the individuals and, therefore, above religious diktats and the economic imperatives of the market, and guarantees the protection of the weakest against cynical exploitation of poverty or psychological vulnerability, creating equal dignity for individuals and equal access to medical resources, regardless of their social situation.

V. – The law is always a matter of opinion

The law is not morally neutral; it supports some values to the detriment of others. It is never completely technical either in its wording or in its application. Any legal decision affects the order of things, acting within the complexity and ambivalence of social bonds. The concepts of the person and the body are always to some degree value judgements historically woven into a culture or social class. They vary from one legal system to another. In the same way, the meaning of such concepts as dignity, consent, freedom, autonomy, etc. change according to the social context. Any concept is a moral choice. In anthropological or legal terms, the definitions of "person" and "body" are part of an unending and inconclusive debate that calls on the ethical pluralism of our societies out of the necessity, regardless, to reach a decision. In this regard, the law plays the role of arbitrator and is therefore, in some way, fittingly arbitrary. Today, it either validates scientific and technological advances in an endless race and accedes to the progress of the biotechnologies, thereby turning the body into an asset and leaving

(15) J. Habermas, *L'avenir de la nature humaine. Vers un eugénisme libéral*, Paris, Gallimard, 2002, p. 37.

each person with the subjective right to establish their own limits, or it creates compromises and plays an anthropological role by preserving the values of solidarity and concern for social bonds, making the individual dependent on a certain number of principles. This is not a matter of "commonplace conflicts of interest, (but) of questions of principle related to the status of scientific authority in a democracy and to the status of man and his fundamental rights, which it was never thought would come into conflict with science"[16]. The solution most faithful to the spirit of the law is to bring scientific and medical procedures under its jurisdiction by recalling the rule of law and refusing to allow research and technology, or economic power, to lead the law.

However, globalisation makes the legal and moral boundaries between States somewhat porous. It introduces a corruption in this regard that is exploited by some. Something that is prohibited in one place may be practised in another where the law is more accommodating. More so some individuals and businesses now circumvent the rule of law in their country to suit their own interests, disregarding the community they are part of, on which they nevertheless impact as a result of their legal situation that must be resolved: in France, for example: the purchase of organs, tissues or eggs, the use of surrogate mothers, etc.

Another ambiguity should be noted: a resident of Bangui or Tozeur does not live in the same world as a resident of New York or Brussels (and even in these latter cities, some citizens do not have the same rights with regard to health). It is not even quite the same human species any more with regard to the inequalities that are overwhelming the planet. In this sense, bioethics is often a western issue relating to research that is detached from tangible reality with regard to the experiences of billions of individuals. The latter have more chance of coming into contact with modern medicine by selling their kidneys or blood than by being treated themselves.

Final comment: individuals do not always enjoy the same protection in all countries. Some populations barely have access to healthcare resources, and yet they are the first to need to sell parts of their body (or person) in order to get by. Even in large countries such as the USA or in Europe, citizens do not always have the same

(16) C. Labrusse-Riou, *Écrits de bioéthique*, Paris, PUF, 2007, p. 131.

social protection[17]. Similarly, the status of women in some legal systems makes them dependent on their husbands or fathers by denying them any personal power or keeping them in a financially subordinate position[18]. These are the facts that undermine the principles of dignity, freedom, autonomy, justice, etc., often arising in principles crucial to the protection of the person or the body.

(17) D. Manaï, *Droits du patient et bioéthique*, Bern, Stämpfli Editions, 2013.

(18) B. Feuillet-Liger and A. Aouij-Mrad (eds.), *Corps de la femme et biomédecine. Approche internationale*, Brussels, Bruylant, 2013.

THE INDIVIDUAL SELF-DETERMINATION OVER ONE'S BODY A PHILOSOPHICAL AND ETHICAL PERSPECTIVE

Pierre LE COZ

Professor of Philosophy at the Faculty of Medicine, Marseille UMR 7268 ADES, Aix-Marseille University / EFS / CNRS (France)

The body alludes to the fragility of the human condition, referred to by philosophers as the "finitude". We declare that we "have" a body, but at the same time we feel that it does not belong to us. We cannot use it entirely as we wish. The evidence is universal: we have only a relative, uncertain and ephemeral power over our bodies. It can betray us at any moment. Acknowledging this fact, the Greeks used to refer to humans as "mortals" as opposed to the gods of Olympus, unconcerned by the future and mundane things.

From the Apollonian stature to the flesh sullied by original sin, representations of the body have considerably varied over the course of western history. The modern era is a significant cut-off point: for the first time an individual can contemplate changing his or her condition by modifying their body. Transformed into a machine by Descartes in the 17th century, the body is shying away from its sinful decline and moving across to the more productive category of objects subject to the control of human will(1).

At the end of the 18th century, when faith was relinquishing its authority to reason, the body found itself open to unprecedented ethical questioning. Kant formulated a "deontological" moral theory that highlighted the duty to respect dignity and ruled out the idea that the body could be treated as a mere instrument(2). Under the influence of utilitarian ideas originating from the Anglo-Saxon world, the western body pursued its emancipation from the theological and political tyranny. John Stuart Mill rejected

(1) R. Descartes, *Discours de la méthode*, coll. G.F., Paris, Flammarion, [1637], 2000.
(2) E. Kant, *Fondements de la métaphysique des mœurs*, trans. V. Delbos, Paris, Delagrave, [1785], 1957, p. 108.

the Kantian concept of "duty to oneself" and called for the scope of public power to be limited to acts detrimental to the physical integrity of others[(3)].

The contention between deontology and utilitarianism continues to this day. In the meantime, since the 1970s, the spectrum of moral theories has been enriched by the emergence of new ideas supplied by libertarianism[(4)]. It is currently developing under the influence of globalisation, technological progress and biomedical practices (surrogacy, the sale of organs, etc.).

I. – Different models for understanding the body in the West

A. – *The body as "Eros" in Platonism*

The history of philosophy includes several perspectives on the body that are not easy to classify chronologically. Thus, since ancient times, we find the hedonist ethics (which would today be called "libertarian") that highlight the pleasure of the senses. At the other end of the spectrum, we encounter the ascetic morality that regards the body as an impediment to the salvation of the soul. One writer can have varying views of the body, as we can see in the case of Plato[(5)]. *Phaedrus* is dominated by a notion of the body as a reality that is inferior to and separate from the mind to which it must be subordinated. In this work, Plato depicts the body as the "tomb of the soul", mired in the material world. Salvation consists in detaching oneself from the senses "to the greatest possible extent" to elevate one's soul to the contemplation of Ideas[(6)]. The body is discounted into a gnostic and dualistic vision with some Pythagorean overtone. It cannot be accepted as it is; it demands to be remodelled and domesticated in line with the ideal of excellence.

(3) J.S. Mill, *L'utilitarisme*, trans. G. Tanesse, coll. Champs, Paris, Flammarion, [1861], 1988.

(4) The first issue of the *Journal of Libertarian Studies* founded by M. Rothbard was published in the USA in 1977. It is an academic review currently published by the "Ludwig von Mises Institute", a privately funded research institute.

(5) Concerning the ambivalence of the status of the body in Plato, see L. Brisson and F. Fronterotta (eds.), *Lire Platon*, Paris, PUF, 2006.

(6) Platon, *Phédon*, presentation and translation by M. Dixsaut, coll. G.F., Paris, Flammarion, 1999.

At a political level, in his work *The Laws*, Plato encourages a discipline of the body from the earliest age so that children "grow to be as upright as possible with the greatest physical beauty"[(7)]. A child's body must be stimulated even before birth, while still in the mother's womb. Little time passes after the birth before the newborn child becomes subject to a regime of physical exercise to prove its strength. Control over the anarchical movements of the body is the condition required to achieve an "orderly discipline of pleasure and pain"[(8)]. The guardian must require the child to walk barefoot, including in the snow, and the physical exercises will channel the excess energy that leads a child to fidget and speak loudly and indiscriminately. A harsh and patient upbringing is therefore necessary for the noblest characteristics to overcome the basest[(9)]. It is, however, acknowledged that the body itself plays a part in the flourishing of our being (this was not the case in *Phaedrus*). Man can achieve happiness here on earth by establishing harmony within himself. It is the degree of control over our bodies that determines our social status. Insofar as women are capable of this domination of the self by the self, they can exercise public functions on an equal footing with men[(10)].

The Platonic picture of the body is completed in *The Banquet*, a work devoted to the love that sees the body from an energetic and dynamic perspective. The body becomes a vital power, the focal point of the emergence of a desire that inspires man to transcend himself. Plato reveals that there is, behind the production of these masterpieces, the desire for immortality through beauty. The mind is no longer a principle of thought separated from the body. Both now support each other with their mutual strength. The body is motivated by the mind, and no longer dominated by it. The sight of a beautiful body becomes a spiritual experience that communicates to the soul a Desire (*Eros*) to make itself worthy of this beauty. In his theory of sublimation, Freud was to recall the theoretical audacity of Plato, the first thinker in western history to

(7) PLATON, *Les lois*, trans. L. BRISSON and J.-F. PRADEAU, t. 2, livre VII, 788d, coll. G.F., Paris, Flammarion, 2006, (Books VII to XII).

(8) *Ibid.* 653b.

(9) It is described at length in PLATON, *La République*, trans. R. BACCOU, coll. G.F., Paris, Flammarion, 1966. We have written a commentary on this *in* P. LE COZ, "L'allégorie de la caverne : un paradigme pour appréhender l'adolescence", *in* B. FEUILLET-LIGER and R. IDA (eds.), *Adolescent et acte médical. Regards croisés. Approche internationale et interdisciplinaire*, coll. Droit, bioéthique et société, Brussels, Bruylant, 2011.

(10) PLATON, *La République*, *op. cit.*, pp. 451c-457b.

detect an erotic element in the sources of the most diverse human motivations (in poetry, science, politics, etc.). Sexual reproduction is valued in Plato's *The Banquet* as a modality of a shared desire to continue one's existence beyond death: "The purpose of love is also immortality[11]. With the person we love, we desire a child that will possess the characteristics of his or her beauty. As the fruit of a beautiful body, how could the child not be beautiful in its own right? This love that we feel for the body will be the prelude to more spiritual forms of attraction for beautiful souls, beautiful gestures, beautiful works, etc.

According to Gadamer, it is this notion of the body as a vital engine favoured by writers in the Hellenistic era. "Any expert on Antiquity knows that for the Greeks, the terms soul and life had essentially the same meaning"[12]. Reworked by Aristotle, this vitalist and finalist interpretation of the body was to exist throughout the Middle- Ages. However, the doctrine of original sin (unknown to the Greeks) was going to profoundly change its moral significance.

B. – *Cartesian dualism*

In assimilating it into a den of sin and iniquity, the theological dogmatism of the Middle- Ages was a serious blow to free philosophical reflection on the body[13]. The political corollary to this pessimistic anthropology is the criminalisation of the uses of the body by the government (suicide, perversion, homosexual relations, etc.). From this theocratic perspective, our flesh is sullied and the suffering it inflicts on us is seen as the legacy of the original sin. Man must work and woman must deliver children in pain; to prevent them from doing so would be to repeat the transgression of the divine interdiction.

The modern conscience has awakened and broken the chains that bound it to this Judeo-Christian dogma. It is identified with

(11) PLATON, *Le Banquet*, presentation by Luc BRISSON, 5th ed., coll. G.F., Paris, Flammarion, 2007.

(12) H. GADAMER, *Philosophie de la santé*, trans. M. DAUTREY, Paris, Grasset-Mollat, 1998, p. 150.

(13) J. DELUMEAU, *Le Péché et la peur : La culpabilisation en Occident (XIIIe-XVIIIe siècles)*, Paris, Fayard, 1983.

the phrase "I think therefore I am"[14] from Descartes, a key figure of the new times. The philosophy of Descartes symbolises the start of an era that was to highlight the value of autonomy, the capacity for self-determination, emancipation from tradition, the exploration of new territories and the conquest of new knowledge. In this way, Descartes intends to promote a more scientific understanding of the body and the passions. He suggests a dualistic approach to man that dissociates the soul from the body, giving to the former the title of "thinking substance" and incorporating the latter into so called "extended substances"[15]. In making a *machine* of the body, Descartes partially restores it by assigning an axiological neutrality to that body: there is no more "flesh", "sin" or "evil temptation". What is the body? Robotics, springs and pulleys... What happens inside our bodies is as morally irrelevant as what happens inside a watch.

Descartes throws the theological perception of the body into the vestiges of the past. He invites us to see in the manifestation of an emotion, a challenge that the power of the "body as machine" is making to the power of the "will"[16]. Wisdom must also divest itself of religion. It has no need for the support of grace; it is the autonomous work of self on self through which the soul avoids yielding to the bodily movements it naturally tends to make when in sadness, anger or fear: "The soul may easily overcome the smaller passions, but not the most violent and strongest [...]. The most the will can do, while this emotion is in its full strength, is not to consent to its effects and to restrain the different motions where unto emotion leads the body. For example, if wrath makes me lift up my hand to strike, the will can usually restrain it. If fear pushes my legs to fly, the will can stop them, and so of the rest"[17]. The body is capable of ill-using the will but, in absolute terms, it is possible to resist. We are "under the influence" of emotion, yet we are not entirely ruled by it. We *have* an emotion, but we *are* not our emotion. The will endows the soul with a certain power over the body. Descartes had no doubt that the science of tomorrow would

(14) R. Descartes, "Les principes de la philosophie", *in Œuvres philosophiques*, t. III, coll. Classiques Garnier, Paris, Bordas, 1989.

(15) R. Descartes, *Méditations métaphysiques*, t. 1, coll. Bibliothèque de La Pléiade, Paris, Gallimard, La Pléiade, 1979.

(16) R. Descartes, "Les passions de l'âme", in *Œuvres philosophiques*, t. III, *op. cit.*, p. 1038.

(17) *Ibid.*

consolidate this power by giving us a better understanding of the mechanism of emotions and of all bodily phenomena in general.

C. – *The advent of material monism*

Cartesian posterity was to follow up with the secularisation of the body by definitively sanctioning the end of the Christian era of sin. Spinoza would rush into the breach opened by Descartes while desperately trying to answer a metaphysical question that Descartes left unresolved: how does the soul come into contact with the body? How can an invisible substance act on a material substance? According to Spinoza, by making the soul and the body two heterogeneous entities, Descartes placed himself in the impossible position of having to explain the relationship between them. In Spinoza's opinion, the solution to the problem lay in a *monistic* concept that perceives the soul and the body as two attributes of a single substance. This substance is none other than nature, a life force that pushes us to "persevere in our being"(18). The soul is stripped of the ontological supremacy that it possessed with Descartes. It is no longer to be regarded as an entity outside the body. It is no longer endowed with a "free will" capable of resisting its passions(19). Our individuality (an indissoluble "soul-body" entity) is the manifestation of a natural appetite that drives every being to want to increase its power: the *conatus*. The amplification of our power to act is manifested by joy and, conversely, its restraint results in sadness. Spinoza replaces the soul/body distinction of Descartes with a division between joyful passions and sad passions. The wise man cultivates the intellectual joy born of understanding, the only power that provokes neither envy nor rivalry between men. He holds himself apart from ordinary mortals for whom happiness resides in glory, wealth and prestige. The ordinary man is not free, as he lives his life under the control of emotions related to bodily afflictions: anger, resentment, hatred, guilt, etc. He has a passive relationship with his body.

(18) B. SPINOZA, *Éthique*, V, proposition XXXIX, démonstration et scolie, coll. G.F., Paris, Flammarion, 1965, pp. 336-337.
(19) B. SPINOZA, *Lettre 58 à Schuller*, trans. Ch. APPUHN, t. 4, Paris, Garnier-Flammarion, 1955, pp. 303-304.

The monistic vision of Spinoza anticipates the Nietzschean interpretation of the body as the manifestation of the "will to power"[20]. In Spinoza, Nietzsche recognises a craftsman of the "twilight of the idols",[21], the discredit heaped on these "despisers of the body",[22], the priests and moralists. The rehabilitation of the body and the revenge of the "evil instincts" would not have been possible without the free thinkers who participated in "the death of God".[23]. In the eyes of Nietzsche, the development of atheism and the concurrent decline of religion in Europe from the 19th century constitute "an enormous event whose impact we have yet to fully understand"[24]. We entered the era of materialism that overturned the relationship between the spiritual self and the bodily self: "Body am I entirely, and nothing else!" proclaims Zarathustra, the mouthpiece of Nietzsche.

II. – Contemporary ethical debates

We can see from the above that the history of philosophy shows how a monistic notion of the body has gradually established itself in the West. The body has become an integral part of the self, an essential dimension of our being, sometimes even a cult figure in advertising. Philosophers have most contributed to the defence of physical integrity by working against the religious depreciation of the body and by asserting the "natural right" to freedom of thought. To do away with the religious punishments inflicted on the body (sorcery, blasphemy, heresy, etc.), several thinkers of the Enlightenment such as Beccaria, Montesquieu and Voltaire advocated the abolition of such "sins" as heresy, sacrilege, obscenity and blasphemy[25]. The liberation of the body found the condition for its achievement in the development of the freedom of expression.

(20) F. Nietzsche, *Par-delà le bien et le mal*, trans. H. Albert and J. Lacoste, coll. Bouquins, Paris, Robert Laffont, [1886], 1993.

(21) F. Nietzsche, *Le crépuscule des idoles*, trans. H. Albert (revised by J. Lacoste), coll. Bouquins, Paris, Robert Laffont, 1992 p. 957.

(22) F. Nietzsche, *Ainsi parlait Zarathoustra*, Paris, Le livre de poche, 1983.

(23) Concerning the influence of Spinoza in the development in the West of material monism, see A. Tosel, *Du matérialisme, de Spinoza*, coll. Philosophie, épistémologie, Paris, ed. Kimé, 1994.

(24) F. Nietzsche, *Par-delà le bien et le mal, op. cit.*

(25) Voltaire, *Prix de la justice et de l'humanité*, Paris, L'Arche, [1777], 1999.

However, although in intellectual circles liberal ideas were the subject of a political consensus, the argument remained alive with regard to the moral relationship of the person with the body. What must I do? What am I to do with this body that is now free of sin? These are the questions that would occupy moral philosophy from the 18th century to the present day.

A. – *Deontology*

As we have already seen, after Descartes, modern philosophy sought to move beyond the soul/body dualism in favour of an ontological union. However, for the moral theory to have any meaning, it appears necessary to suppose a divide within oneself. Do the key concepts of moral life, such as "obligation" or "duty" not imply a rift in the conscience, an internal division between the self as a *sentient being* and the self as a *moral being*? It is in any case the starting point for the ethics of Kant, according to whom acting morally consists of obeying one's conscience and not allowing oneself to be governed by one's feelings. Kant laid the foundations for a normative ethical theory that is today known as deontology (from the Greek "deon", "what must be done"). Acting morally consists of honouring the dignity for which we are ourselves responsible, which involves the absolute necessity of not yielding to the proclivities of the body. For my conduct to be moral, I must not only avoid causing harm to the bodies of others, but also take care of my own body. I must not give in to my basest instincts (gluttony, drunkenness, etc.). I must fight against idleness and, through my will, nurture the seeds that nature has planted in me. It is my duty to discipline my body to ensure my survival and my independence of mind: "If the mind does not overcome the weaknesses of the body, the body will come to dominate it"(26).

Deontology means one cannot treat one's body as a piece of merchandise or a resource to be exploited. To be a person means respecting yourself as an "end in itself", as beings who "do not have merely a relative value, that is a price, but an inner value, that is dignity"(27). This point brings to mind the well-known rule of the categorical imperative: "Act in such a way that you treat humanity, whether in your own person or in the person of any

(26) E. Kant, *Leçons d'Éthique*, trans. L. Langlois, Paris, Le Livre de Poche, 1997, p. 282.
(27) E. Kant, *Fondements de la métaphysique des mœurs*, *op. cit.*, p. 108.

other, never merely as a means to an end, but always at the same time as an end"[28]. It follows logically that a human being must not "sell one of his organs, not even one of his fingers, as otherwise all of his limbs might be sold off"[29]. If a man were to use his body as a source of marketable detached parts, he would be denying the essence of his being. One cannot be both a means and an end. In Kant's words, "it is impossible to be at the same time a person and a thing, an owner and a property"[30]. Unlike objects that can be reduced to their physical characteristics, a person cannot have a price, because the price is a value indexed to the rate of obsolescence; it varies according to the degree of change in the properties of the object. However, as a moral agent endowed with dignity, the person is intrinsically unavailable and must cause his dignity to exist through the respect he has for himself as well as for others. Furthermore, no one can "deprive himself of an integral part or organ (self-mutilation), for example, to give away or sell a tooth so that it can be planted in the jawbone of another person, or to submit oneself to castration in order to gain an easier livelihood as a singer, etc"[31]. All acts of mutilation that give rise to the use of one's body for commercial purposes amount to "partial self-murder"[32].

In the same way, prostituting oneself and agreeing to be sold, rented or exploited comprise a violation of the principle of the equal dignity of every person. A man does not have the right to dispose of his body as he wishes, because, in disposing of his body, he also disposes of his person. It is true that when the mutilation of a part of one's body is the price to be paid to preserve one's being, it is not a violation of our dignity. Kant cites the case of "the amputation of a dead organ, or one on the verge of mortification and thus harmful to life"[33]. We should be careful not to confuse the use of organs with the use of superficial parts of the body such as hair, "although selling one's hair for gain is not entirely free from blame"[34].

Many comments regarding Kant's position relates to whether his school of thought would approve of organ donations. For the

(28) *Ibid.*
(29) E. Kant, *Leçons d'Éthique*, *op. cit.*, p. 236.
(30) *Ibid.*
(31) *Ibid.* p. 97.
(32) *Ibid.*
(33) *Ibid.*
(34) *Ibid.*

most part, post mortem donations are in no way contrary to his ethic, provided that the choices made by those concerned during their lifetimes are respected. "In certain circumstances, it is even a duty of virtue [toward others] to authorise such transplantations in advance, as they do not in any way violate the dignity of a person and can save lives; it is a duty to allow them, just as helping someone who is drowning is a virtue"(35). The dearth of organs and its consequences cause some upholders of Kant's philosophy to defend the authorisation of the removal of vital organs from the living, such as the kidney, on condition that the decision is not coerced or paid for. However, it is reasonable to wonder if this interpretation does not contravene the principle of self-preservation to which Kant remained steadfastly committed(36).

The deontological position with regard to dignity is therefore a subject of debate. It is true that Kant himself was undecided on the subject. In some works of the Kantian corpus, dignity is an intrinsic and inalienable attribute of man, regardless of his circumstances or state of health. In other cases, however, dignity is dependent on man's capacity for self-determination. In this second perspective, man is inclined to lose his dignity as he loses his free will. Liberty becomes his most essential characteristic. It is this theory that was to serve as a model for moral liberalism, initially in a moderate way (the utilitarianism of the 19th century), then in a more radical version (the libertarianism of the 20th century).

B. – *Utilitarianism*

The utilitarianists' intention is to loosen the stranglehold in which they believe the body to have been held by Kantian rigorism. J.S. Mill, according to some commentators, was the first philosopher to maintain that we have no moral duty with regard to ourselves(37). Utilitarianism is a naturalism that wants to respond to the demands of the body regarding happiness and fulfilment. Through his body, man is a being of nature as much as culture.

(35) J.-C. Merle, "A Kantian Argument for a Duty to Donate one's Own Organs. A reply to Nicole Guerrand", *J. Appl. Philos.*, vol. 17, n° 1, 2000, pp. 93-109.

(36) C. Sambuc and P. Le Coz, "La dignité humaine kantienne : une justification des transplantations d'organes ?", *in* L. Barthélémy (ed.), *Imagination(s) environnementale(s)*, *Raison publique*, n° 17, Rennes, PUR, 2013, p. 190.

(37) R. Ogien, *L'éthique aujourd'hui. Maximalistes et minimalistes*, coll. Essais, Paris, Folio, 2007, p. 20.

Respecting his body means accepting and even accentuating what his nature inevitably encourages him to seek: the maximisation of pleasure and the minimisation of pain. It is necessary to build an ethic based on a realist anthropology that reconciles man with his body. It will be possible to offset the egotism against the calculation of his clearly understood interest. In addition, no longer will the majority of men have to deal with duties that run counter to nature. According to Hume for example, if we manage to make parents aware of their duty to love their children, it is because they are already naturally inclined to do so(38). Likewise, the duty of beneficence that commands us to work for the benefit of others is a virtue deeply rooted in a natural disposition that inclines us spontaneously to sympathy and compassion.

From the utilitarian perspective, we are therefore justified in believing that all acts caused by our natural predisposition to seek pleasure and avoid pain are a result of "autonomy". For a Kantian, the same definition of autonomy as the possibility to choose what gives us pleasure or spares us displeasure is a rudimentary and an animal like behaviour that could be more accurately qualified as heteronomous. Effectively, it is not reason, but something other than myself (*hetero-*), in the case of bodily instincts, that rules (*-nomos*) me. Yet utilitarianism is not an unrestrained form of hedonism. The quest for pleasures is subject to a system of regulatory standards. The search for personal satisfaction gains moral significance when it contributes to *the happiness of the greatest possible number of people*. To put it negatively, an action is ethical when the freedom to choose one's pleasures (to have personal preferences) clearly results in "reducing the amount of suffering in the world"(39). Utilitarianism therefore invalidates the desire for greediness and gives a meaning to community life. "According to the greatest happiness principle, the ultimate end with reference to and for the sake of which all other things are desirable, is an existence as exempt as possible from pain, and as rich as possible in enjoyments both in quantity and quality"(40). In other words, a behaviour will be considered more ethical according to the intensity of the suffering it enables to avoid and the number

(38) D. Hume, *Traité de la nature humaine. Essai pour introduire la méthode expérimentale dans les sujets moraux*, trans. A. Leroy, Paris, Aubier, 1946.
(39) J.S. Mill, *L'utilitarisme*, *op. cit.*, pp. 68-69.
(40) *Ibid.*

of people who are spared. We will therefore do "whatever, for all future generations, achieves the greatest possible differential between happiness and suffering"(41).

This model of reasoning can lead to tolerance with regard to prostitution as a means of reducing sexual frustration in the world. It can also lead to the justification of biomedical practices that contribute to increasing the collective happiness (until proven otherwise), as is the case with surrogacy. In view of the fact that few surrogate mothers share their painful experiences once they have given birth, and that we cannot actually show that children suffer from this type of assisted reproduction, this practice might be considered as complying with the norm of "the greatest happiness to the greatest number". Surely there will be here and there a few failures. However, in the words of J.S. Mill, "the utilitarian ideal is not the agent's own greatest happiness, but the greatest amount of happiness altogether"(42). Every time our decisions have a dual effect, that their repercussions are sources of both well-being and frustration, we will opt for those whose consequences are favourable to the majority and unfavourable to the minority(43).

It should also be noted that the utilitarian argumentative model does not necessarily provide different conclusions than the deontological model. On certain ethical problems, while starting out from a different line of argument, the two frames of reference can end up by reconnecting. In our commonplace moral reasoning, they are sometimes mixed together or mutually balanced. The example of severely disabled newborns can serve as an illustration. The French "*Comité consultatif national d'éthique*" (National Consultative Ethics Committee – CCNE) considered in the past that we could accept neonatal euthanasia in exceptional circumstances(44). The active termination of the life of newborns is approved in this opinion of the CCNE as a "transgression". The concept of "exceptions for euthanasia" put forward by the Ethics Committee is evidence of its concern that such lethal practices should not be normalised. According to the Committee, the notion

(41) D. Birnbacher, *La responsabilité envers les générations futures*, Paris, PUF, 1994.

(42) J.S. Mill, *L'utilitarisme*, *op. cit.*, p. 69.

(43) This idea begins to take hold in the 18th century with Francis Hutcheson (see on this point C. Audard, *Anthologie historique et critique de l'utilitarisme*, vol. I., Paris, PUF, 1999, p. 8).

(44) CCNE, Opinion n° 65, "Réflexions éthiques autour de la réanimation néonatale", 2000, available at: www.ccne-ethique.fr.

of a dignity that varies according to the state of health of the individual is unacceptable. That is the deontological aspect of its opinion: dignity is not relative to the judgment made on it. The termination of the life of a newborn child is not a denial of its *dignity*, but the result of an unfavourable evaluation of its *quality of life*. If an exception for euthanasia is allowed, it is because, on account of an extremely altered quality of relationships, the newborn child's life appears worse than death.

As a result, in terms of future well-being, this approach gives the CCNE's opinion a utilitarian component that combines with its deontology. A strictly utilitarian line of argument would have led to the approval of neonatal euthanasia by relying on its collective impact: the mental anguish caused within the child's family circle by its survival. This is the perspective seen in the writing of Peter Singer, a contemporary Australian author according to whom the arrival in the world of a deformed baby results in an overall decrease in the pleasure/pain differential (suffering of the parents, siblings, family circle, etc.), which is enough to give it its moral legitimacy[(45)].

The cut-off point set by utilitarians for the justification of a decision to terminate life by its consequences in terms of the suffering endured by the group is the respect for the interested party's consent. Even when it is considered that such a decision will clearly help lessen the suffering of numerous third parties (in terms of quantity but also intensity), a procedure cannot be performed on a person's body unless that person has first given their consent. It is true that in the above example, there is no free and informed consent for the euthanasia of a newborn baby. According to Singer, this planned death can only be considered if the basic presupposition of the newborn child's status of "person" has been contested[(46)]. This is the part that the public opinion contested regarding the Australian philosopher's views: he does not attribute to a mentally handicapped newborn baby any different ontological status than a foetus. The newborn is merely a 'future' human person, which means that the question of its presumed

(45) P. SINGER and H. KUHSE, *Should the Baby Live?*, Oxford, University Press Oxford, 1994.

(46) P. SINGER, *Questions d'éthique pratique*, trans. M. MARCUZZI, Paris, Bayard, 1997.

consent to its own termination is no more relevant than in the case of an animal(47).

Utilitarianism therefore leaves itself open to being a sacrificial doctrine. John Harris deliberately referred to this derogatory characteristic in a book entitled *The Survival Lottery*, in which he wants to show that an extreme utilitarian line of thinking, when applied to organ transplantation, would lead to the justification for people being killed in order to save their fellows from danger. By accepting one death, can we not avoid several? By cutting up the sacrificed body, a number of precious vital organs can be obtained, such as the kidneys, the liver, the lungs and the heart (not to mention the grafts that can be accomplished today: larynx, cornea, face, etc.). Doctors would use a central computer to designate an organ donor whose sacrifice would enable a number of lives to be saved and would increase the happiness of the greatest possible number of people. In place of the verb "kill", a more appealing term would be used, such as "giving one's life for others"(48).

The thought of such experiment sparks a repugnance that revives our commitment to the deontological values of respect for the autonomy and equal dignity of human beings. However, utilitarianism would defend itself from being 'sacrificial' by underlining that when the person is autonomous, he is not permitted to make his individual interest dependent on the the collective interest (except when it could be shown to be deliberately harmful to others)(49). No one may be sacrificed on the altar of societal or family happiness without being consulted. Jeremy Bentham, the founder of utilitarianism, had already warned us on this point: "collective happiness must be guaranteed while respecting the freedoms of all"(50). This safeguard is intended to forestall the objections of opponents of utilitarianism who believe that such a theory compromises individual freedoms(51). He was unable to

(47) See also on this point: A. Giubilini and F. Minerva, "After-birth abortion: why should the baby live?", *J. Med. Ethics*, vol. 39, n° 5, 2013, pp. 261-263.

(48) J. Harris, "The survival lottery", *Philosophy*, The Royal Institute of Philosophy, vol. 50, 1975, pp. 81-87.

(49) See J.S. Mill, *De la liberté*, trans. L. Lenglet: "The only legitimate reason a community can have for using force against one of its members is to prevent that person from harming others. Over himself, his body and his mind, the individual is sovereign", (chap. 1), Paris, Gallimard, [1859], 1990.

(50) J. Bentham, *Garanties contre l'abus de pouvoir et autres écrits sur la liberté politique*, coll. Versions françaises, Paris, Éditions Rue d'Ulm, 2001.

(51) J.-P. Dupuy, *Éthique et philosophie de l'action*, Paris, Ellipses, 1999.

convince the libertarians, who see no other way of avoiding the sacrificial danger than by refraining from pronouncing a standard external to the individual.

C. – *Libertarianism*

Advances in bioethics combined with the growth of the globalisation of individual exchanges by electronic means have challenged the moral regulatory systems established by the deontologists and utilitarians concerning the use of the body. Our era is contemporary to the rise of a school of thought that began to spread throughout the USA in the 1970s under the name of "libertarianism". Abandoning such external and universalist criteria as "respect for the dignity of the person" (deontology) and "the greatest happiness for the greatest number" (utilitarianism), libertarians believe in the duty to do no harm to others and assert the free ownership of oneself[(52)]. This school of thought helped to encourage the move from freedom as "autonomy" to freedom as "independence" that some authors have described as the move from a "modern" culture to a "post-modern" culture[(53)], from the age of the *person* to the era of the *individual.* [(54)] Libertarianism is related to the anarcho-capitalist movement that developed in the wake of the works of Hayek[(55)] and Nozick[(56)], its principal precursors. The libertarian joins the "anarchist" in challenging the exorbitant power that the State grants itself, but distances himself from the latter's anti-capitalist left-wing views. Conversely, the anarchists do not identify with the philosophy of the libertarians, whom they consider as ultraliberals. In fact, a libertarian is not in favour of collective self-management (like the anarchists), but in favour of a society where the interactions between individuals result only from freely agreed contracts[(57)].

According to Nozick[(58)], we have John Locke to thank for seeing that, in order to be the owner of something, one must first be the

(52) R. NOZICK, *Anarchie, État et utopie*, Paris, PUF, 1974.

(53) G. LIPOVETSKY, *Le crépuscule du devoir. L'éthique indolore des nouveaux temps démocratique*, coll. NRF Essais, Paris, Gallimard, 1992.

(54) A. RENAUT, *L'ère de l'individu*, Paris, Gallimard, 1989.

(55) F.A. HAYEK, *Droit, législation et liberté*, coll. Quadrige, Paris, PUF, 2007.

(56) R. NOZICK, *Anarchie, État et utopie*, *op. cit.*

(57) A. RAND, *La Vertu d'égoïsme*, coll. Bibliothèque classique de la liberté, Paris, Les Belles Lettres, 1993.

(58) R. NOZICK, *Anarchie, État et utopie*, *op. cit.*

owner of one's self and one's body. Indeed, Locke maintains that "every man has a property in his own person. This, nobody has a right to but himself [...]"[(59)]. Some commentators considered that this was a broad interpretation of Locke's school of thought, whose objective was limited to protecting the body against being used without consent such as in slavery[(60)]. For Locke, the concept of "self-ownership" had a critical and essential function. However, Nozick goes further by giving to the concept of "self-ownership" the meaning of a potential use of one's body in contractual relations, possibly for commercial purposes[(61)]. From this standpoint, the use that a prostitute makes of her body depends on her lifestyle choices and we have no valid reason to qualify it as dishonourable and thus meriting prohibition. The libertarians refuse to qualify the uses everyone can make of their own bodies in moral terms. We have the duty to respect the bodies of others, but we have no such duty with regard to our own bodies. Ruwen Ogien shares the arguments used by the libertarians in favour of recognising prostitution as a physical service[(62)]. Why should access to such physical intimacy be classified as indecent when the ground has already been broken by health professionals such as gynaecologists, nurses, dental surgeons and midwives? There will be objections on the grounds that prostitutes use their sexual or sexualised parts (chest, mouth). Supporters of the "minimalist" ethic[(63)] will reply that there are a number of professions and activities where these parts of the body make a contribution (wet nurse, gymnast, kinesitherapist or the osteopath who is often pressed against the patient, etc.). To which must be added actors and actresses in pornographic films, whose activity is largely tolerated in liberal countries. A deontologist will highlight the affective indifference of the prostitute with regard to her customers to denounce the commodification of her body. However, above and beyond the fact that there is nothing to prevent a prostitute having

(59) J. Locke, *Deuxième traité du gouvernement civil*, Paris, PUF, [1690], 1993, § 22 (cited by M. Marzano, *Penser le corps*, coll. Questions d'éthique, Paris, PUF, 2002, p. 130).

(60) M. Marzano, *Penser le corps*, *op. cit.*

(61) S.B. Drury, "Locke and Nozick on property" in *Political studies*, vol. 30, n° 1, pp. 28-41, M. Festenstein and M. Smith (eds), 2006.

(62) R. Ogien, *Le corps et l'argent*, coll. L'attrape corps, Paris, La Musardine, 2010, pp. 85-88. The author denies an affiliation to the libertarian school of thought, of whose central concept of "self-ownership" he is critical (considered by him to be impractically costly in intellectual terms). We will not go into the details here of the divergences between liberal and libertarian trends.

(63) D. Norton, "Moral minimalism and the Development of Moral Character", *Midwest Studies in Philosophy*, vol. XIII, 1988, pp. 180-195 (cited by R. Ogien, *op. cit.*, p. 211).

friendly and affectionate relationships with her customers, there are a number of professions that use the bodily faculties without being subjectively invested, in spite of being oriented toward the well-being of their customers or patients (masseurs, etc.).

It is true that one could also denounce the socio-economic conditions, lack of opportunities and emotional problems that cause some people to turn to prostitution. The libertarian would counter this with numerous testimonies from prostitutes describing working conditions that are not repressive. In the libertarian's eyes, for a form of prostitution to be ethically acceptable it is necessary only to be sure that there is no hierarchical domination (pimps, criminal organisations, etc.), that the prostitute always has the option of changing profession[(64)]. The same should apply to emotional and sexual support for the disabled[(65)].

On the grounds that an action that does not violate the rights of others should be allowed, libertarianism calls for the authorisation of practices made possible by biotechnological advances, such as surrogacy or the sale of one's organs. Any prohibition in this area is said to be a paternalist by-product of the principle of beneficence. It would speak to the dedication of the religious belief according to which the human body is sacred. The State would assume an illegitimate right by having a sort of implicit right of ownership over our organs. In a secular society, each individual's control and use of his or her body should be protected by the State. Those opposed to the sale of organs are not consistent as they have no alternative to offer to society, to those they prohibit from selling body parts. If they were consistent, they would offer them money or, at the very least, take steps to gather the sum needed by the claimants to avoid having to sell elements of their bodies. The lives of the poor cannot be improved by denying them their freedom of choice.

It should also be noted that in financial terms, the free trade of organs would have the benefit of adjusting supply and demand, while putting an end to parallel markets. In this regard, Ruwen Ogien believes that "the markets for anonymously purchased organs, if they were regulated, could have a certain moral value, inasmuch as they would enable the wrongs caused by existing

(64) S. Moller Okin, *Justice, genre et famille*, Paris, Flammarion, 2008, p. 2016.
(65) P. Sanchez, *Justice pour les personnes handicapées*, Grenoble, PUG, 2013, pp. 248-249.

unregulated markets to be eliminated"[66]. Of course, such a trade would have to be circumscribed by procedures clearly defined in advance. The agreement of the parties involved should be able to be withdrawn at any time, including after the express consent (right to remorse before the operation to extract the organ).

Conclusion

At the end, should the notion that every individual is the owner of his or her body be the final argument? Does the affirmation of individual freedom for all – and its correlate of doing "no harm to others" – offer the most effective guarantee for the protection of the body? For most present-day philosophers[67], such moral minimalism is inadequate, if not indefensible. It would lead to the idea that all forms of life are equal, whatever use or misuse could be made of their bodies or minds. Working the streets or pursuing one's studies would become morally irrelevant choices, and we would be unable to see why we should be so uncompromising on this issue with our children.

We are entitled to wonder if, in a desire to go beyond the dignity principle established by Kant, we will not end up falling into some kind of subordination even more insidious as it will claim to be operating under the umbrella of the principle of individual freedom. One point of consensus today emerges on the basis of Kantian ethics: dignity and freedom are inseparable. To be free is to respect dignity in oneself and in others. This does not imply that we must remain faithful to Kant on all points in order to consolidate the legal principles of protection of the human body. Kantian ethics are marked by a history that is now largely irrelevant, as we can see from his moral condemnation of suicide. We are now evolving in a post-moralist context in which happiness is recognised as a legitimate aspiration. The best safeguard against the misuse of the body probably lies in the cultural promotion of the critical exercise of reason against the emotional manipulation strategies[68].

(66) R. Ogien, "La 'marchandisation du corps humain' : les incohérences et les usages réactionnaires d'une dénonciation", *raison-publique.fr*, 2012, available at: www.raison-publique.fr/article534.

(67) As R. Ogien himself recognises (*cf.* R. Ogien, *L'éthique aujourd'hui. Maximalistes et minimalistes*, *op. cit.*, p. 13: "All recent moral philosophy gives the impression of being limited to a fight against minimalism").

(68) P. Le Coz, *Le gouvernement des émotions*, Paris, Albin Michel, 2014.

DIGNITY: THE CORNERSTONE OF THE BASIC GERMAN LAW IN PROTECTING THE HUMAN BODY WITH REGARD TO BIOMEDICINE[*]

Françoise FURKEL

Emeritus Professor at the Franco-German Legal Centre Saarland University (Germany)

"If anything is sacred, the human body is sacred." We would have liked the author of this beautiful quotation, the American writer and poet Walt Whitman[1], to clarify what he meant. What does he mean by the idea of "sacred", and why should this be applied to the human body?

Long associated with religion, this notion is today understood in a broader sense: certain values, certain principles are considered to be sacred, intangible. Yet it is in modern Germany that this concept of intangibility appears for the first time, in line with the notion of "sacred". In fact, in the Basic Law of 1949 – the Constitution of modern Germany[2] – the dignity of the human being is declared to

(*) We would like to dedicate this article to Claire Neirinck, eminent specialist in family law. Fascinated by the comparison of legal systems, she recently published an article on the new confidential birth system in Germany that has opened up new horizons for all, but particularly German legal experts!

Main German abbreviations used: AG = Amtsgericht / District Court; BGB = Bürgerliches Gesetzbuch / Civil Code; BGBl. = Bundesgesetzblatt / Federal Official Journal; BVerfG = Bundesverfassungsgericht / Federal Constitutional Court; BVerfGE = Entscheidungen des Bundesverfassungsgerichts / Decisions of the Federal Constitutional Court; BVerwG = Bundesverwaltungsgericht / Federal Administrative Court; BVerwGE = Entscheidungen des Bundesverwaltungsgerichts/ Decisions of the Federal Administrative Court; JUS = Juristische Schulung (periocal); JZ = Juristenzeitung (periodical); LG = Landgericht / Regional Court; NJW = Neue Juristische Wochenschrift (periodical); OLG = Oberlandesgericht / Superior Regional Court; RGSt = Reichsgericht in Strafsachen / Supreme Criminal Court; RGZ = Reichsgericht in Zivilsachen / Supreme Civil Court; StGB = Strafgesetzbuch / Criminal Code; VG = Verwaltungsgericht / Administrative Court; ZPO = Zivilprozeßordnung / Civil Procedure Code.

(1) W. Whitman, *Leaves of Grass*, Penguin Classics, 1990.

(2) The Basic Law has been the Constitution of Germany since May 23, 1949, initially of West Germany, and then, since reunification on 3 October 1990, of the entire country.

be intangible, therefore sacred. That the human body can also be considered sacred, like the dignity that protects it, is a matter for philosophers to consider rather than lawyers.

Yet, when we reflect on the protection given to the body by German law, we should not forget that Germany is the motherland of Kant. Kant now has an indisputable place among those who have drawn the world's attention to dignity, the very essence of the human condition and the source of other fundamental rights responsible for ensuring the protection of the person and the body. One observation immediately comes to mind. Although the essential question that German philosophers try to answer is more related to the dignity of the person than that of the body?[(3)] It is quite difficult to separate these two concepts in legal terms, with man being hard to dissociate from the body in which he exists. How can we effectively isolate the body of the subject who inhabits it when every being is flesh and blood? At the start of the 20th century, however, didn't the physicians, through an anatomical perspective separate the body from the person? In the 1960s, did we not begin to ask questions about the female body, at a time when the supremacy of the male body was becoming less obvious? In spite of these questions and numerous others concerning the union of the body and the person, it appears difficult to deny that respect for the dignity of the person does not go hand in hand with respect for the person's body[(4)].

While Kant's influence on the concept of dignity with regard to the protection of the body must not be forgotten, it is also important to bear in mind the memories that German people have of the National Socialism era and the extreme violations of the human body perpetrated by the Nazis. In Germany, we now see ourselves as an example to others in terms of respect for human rights.

For obvious reasons, and undoubtedly to a greater degree than other countries, Germany was extremely keen to make a catalogue of fundamental rights, a key element of its 1949 Constitution, some of which were intended to protect the human body. Before considering these, however, a brief reminder is required regarding

(3) See in particular I. Kant, *Fondements de la métaphysique des mœurs*, trans. V. Delbos, Vrin, 2004.

(4) Concerning the possible gap between the body and the person, see, in French, D. Le Breton, "Médecine, corps et anthropologie", *in* E. Hirsch (ed.), *Traité de bioéthique*, Éres, 2010, pp. 74 et seq.

the role of international law in the protection of the person and the body.

In a far from exhaustive list, we will refer only to the Nuremberg Code adopted in 1947, after the Nazi criminal proceedings, an instrument that stipulates the absolute necessity for doctors to obtain the patient's consent for biomedical experiments, as do the 1964 Helsinki Declaration and the 1981 Manila Declaration that also establish the principle of the free and informed consent of the patient. We will also refer to the 1948 Universal Declaration of Human Rights which, based on the concept of dignity(5), guarantees every individual the right to life and security of person(6), as do the European Convention on Human Rights of 1950(7), the United Nations International Covenant on Civil and Political Rights of 1966(8) and the Charter of Fundamental Rights of the European Union adopted in 2000(9).

Other instruments related to bioethics, such as the 2005 UNESCO Declaration on Bioethics and Human Rights(10) and, at a European level, the Council of Europe Convention on Human Rights and Biomedicine of 1997(11), also highlight the dignity of the human being and, therefore, the dignity of the body(12).

We should, however, explain that unlike other countries, Germany does not consider international treaties as an authority above that of the national law. Treaties are usually the subject of an 'approval act' allowing them to be applied within the German legal order(13), and are subject to the "*lex posterior priori derogat*" principle. It is always a dualistic notion of the relationship between

(5) In the Preamble to the Universal Declaration of Human Rights, the recognition of dignity is considered to be the foundation of freedom, justice and peace in the world.

(6) Art. 3 UDHR.

(7) Art. 2 ECHR.

(8) Art. 6.

(9) Chap. 1, art. 2.

(10) The article 3, paragraph 1, of this Declaration proclaims that "human dignity [...] is to be fully respected".

(11) Note the exact title of this Convention, called the "Oviedo Convention" on human rights and biomedicine: "Convention for the Protection of Human Rights and the Dignity of the Human Being with regard to the Application of Biology and Medicine". We know that this Convention was supplemented by a number of protocols, particularly on the prohibition of the cloning of human beings in 1997, the transplantation of organs and human tissues in 2001 and on biomedical research in 2004.

(12) Concerning the differences between the dignity of the human being and the dignity of the body, see *supra*.

(13) Art. 59, § 2, Basic Law (hereinafter referred to as "BL").

international law and domestic law that triumphs in Germany(14). Nevertheless, due to an interpretation of certain articles of the Basic Law(15) that would take too long to go into here, the judiciary endeavours to reconcile new laws with the existing international treaties. Only the European community law is recognised as having a value above German legislation(16).

Let us also not forget how vague and susceptible to different interpretations are the principles proclaimed by all the international instruments protecting human dignity and sometimes, more specifically, the human body.

For all the aformentioned reasons, the role of international law in the protection of the person and the human body is therefore relatively insignificant in Germany, even though the German Federal Constitutional Court tries to ensure compliance with Community law, in spite of its infra-constitutional value, as it does with the case law of the European Court of Human Rights(17). It is the fundamental rights, proclaimed by the 1949 Constitution, that indisputably fulfil this essential protective role.

These rights, now an essential part of the German legal order, were not created by the 1949 Constitution, but appear intermittently throughout the history of this country. Present in most German States before the 1848 revolution, the fundamental rights were not then considered to be human rights, but rules of positive law limiting the power of the Prince. At the time of the creation of the German Reich in 1871, no fundamental rights were to be included in the Constitution, and the fundamental rights recognised by the German states (Länder), considered to be inferior to the laws, had no relevance. Although in1919 the Weimar Republic established a new list of fundamental rights, they gave way to the legislature and could not be directly invoked by the citizens(18). After the National

(14) According to this notion, international law and domestic law are considered as independent legal orders. On the other hand, countries that support a single concept, such as France, the Netherlands and Luxembourg, defend the principle according to which international law and domestic law constitute a single system.

(15) Art. 24 and 25 BL in particular.

(16) However, Community law must respect the Constitution. For explanations of the place of the European Convention on Human Rights in German domestic law, Cl. Witz, *Le droit allemand*, coll. Connaissance du droit, Dalloz, 2013, pp. 36 et seq.

(17) BVerfG, 14 October 2004, BVerfGE 111, 307; see also Cl. Witz, *Le droit allemand*, *op. cit*, pp. 60 et seq.

(18) D. Grimm, "Die Entwicklung der Grundrechtstheorie in der deutschen Staatsrechtslehre des 19. Jahrhunderts", *in* D. Grimm, *Recht und Staat der bürgerlichen Gesellschaft*, Francfort,

Socialist party disposed of any rules likely to limit its power, it was only after World War II that the fundamental rights reappeared in the 1949 Constitution. Endowed with a legal value they had never had before, they are expressly recognised as directly applicable rights(19) and now link the three powers(20).

Although the current protection of the person and their body is principally provided in Germany by the fundamental rights, other protective principles, proclaimed by ordinary law and other non-legislative bodies, support these rights (I).

Extremely protective of the person and the body, which have long since been considered to be a unit(21), Germany now successfully provides more specific protection of the human body in the context of biomedicine, an essential duty of any legal system since medical law has dissociated the two concepts (II).

I. – The principles of protection of the human body and their sources

There are three fundamental rights in Germany that protect the human body: the rights to dignity, to life and to bodily integrity. While the last two provide this protection more directly than the right to dignity, it is however the right to dignity that inspires all the other norms, whether they are contained in the Basic Law or in other instruments. "The radiating effect" of the right to dignity is often referred to in Germany(22).

A. – *The fundamental rights*

In the first article of the Basic law, the dignity of the human being is declared to be "intangible", a strong qualifier, used just once

1987, pp. 308 et seq.; in French, D. Grimm, "L'interprétation constitutionnelle. L'exemple du développement des droits fondamentaux par la Cour constitutionnelle fédérale", *RID pol.*, n° 6, 2011, available at: www.juspoliticum.com/L-interprétation-constitutionnelle.html.

(19) Art. 1, § 3, BL.

(20) The article 1, paragraph 3, of the Basic Law states that the fundamental rights are directly applicable, and this rule is imposed upon the legislative, executive and judicial authorities. It should be noted that Germany recognises a judicial authority that is considered to be the equal of the other two authorities (art. 20, § 2, BL).

(21) In many ways at least. See *supra*, prev. page.

(22) In French, M. Fromont, "L'autonomie de la volonté et les droits fondamentaux en droit privé allemand", in *Études à la mémoire du Professeur Alfred Rieg*, Brussels, Bruylant, 2000, p. 339.

in this vital text. The Basic Law thus echoes the Preamble to the 1948 Universal Declaration of Human Rights(23). The inviolability of dignity is both an objective principle of German law and a subjective right that every individual can invoke. Although it is a value, this principle, which touches on the essence of Mankind, is legally binding and must be translated into the rules of substantive law. There are numerous debates about the concept of dignity, among both philosophers and legal experts(24) who often, following the example of a growing doctrine in neighbouring countries(25), emphasize the ambiguity of the idea, sometimes even evoking a "concept void of any substance"(26). Reporting the details of these debates and all the proposed interpretations of this concept would exceed the scope of this study. We will restrict ourselves to stating that any hopes of seeing the German Federal Constitutional Court provide a definition of the notion of dignity have always been dashed. At the time of the enactment of the Basic Law(27), German constitutionalists simply, but negatively, sought to clarify the notion by defining the potential violations likely to harm human dignity(28). Today, the concept of human dignity is presented in Germany as having to meet the existential need of people to protect the rights that are theirs by virtue of their humanity. For this reason, alongside the right of protection of one's body, a number of other rights take their place, in particular those related to protection against inequality or poverty.

Since 1949, writers have raised the question of knowing if this concept inherent to the human person also had to protect the "future" person – the embryo – and the deceased. The answer is 'yes', the German Federal Constitutional Court having had the

(23) Note the statement in this Preamble: "Whereas recognition of the inherent dignity and of the equal and inalienable rights of all members of the human family is the foundation of freedom, justice and peace in the world".

(24) Among others, E. Benda, "Verständigungsversuche über die Würde des Menschen", *NJW*, 2001, pp. 2147 et seq.; E.W. Böckenförde, "Bleibt die Menschenwürde unantasbar?", *Blätter für die deutsche und internationale Politik*, 2004, n° 10, pp. 1216 et seq.

(25) Especially in France, see A.-M. Le Pourhiet, "Touche pas à mon préambule", *Le Figaro*, 24 May 2008.

(26) See among others H.J. Sandkühler, "La dignité humaine et la transformation des droits moraux en droit positif" *in* J. Poulain and H.J. Sandkühler (eds.), *La dignité humaine, Perspectives transculturelles*, Peter Lang, 2009, p. 9.

(27) 23 May 1949 (see *supra*, note 2).

(28) G. Dürig, "Der Grundrechtssatz von der Menschenwürde" in *Archiv des Öffentlichen Rechts*, vol. 81, 1956, pp. 118 et seq.

opportunity on a number of occasions to refer to the right to dignity of the embryo, as well as that of the corpse(29).

The binding principle of "the inviolability of human dignity" has resulted in two other fundamental rights protecting the human body: the right to life and the right to bodily integrity. As stated in article 2, para. 2 of the Basic Law, the right to life means the right of every individual not to be deprived of their life; killing is criminally punishable(30) and the death penalty abolished(31). Transformed at the present time by advances in biomedicine and by the interventions that can be carried out on the living person, this right to life is no absolute, as a woman can, within a certain time limit, decide to end the life of the embryo she carries(32). The right to life parallels today a right to death which is now being debated in Germany with considerable intensity(33).

Included in the same article, the right to bodily integrity was defined by doctrine and German case law. Any physical assault, and indeed any psychological assault likely to lead to the subject being violated "to the same degree as physical damage", constitutes an infringement of bodily integrity(34). On the other hand, the right to bodily integrity, which includes a right of access to healthcare, does not imply a right to be kept in good health(35).

Not every infringement of bodily integrity is necessarily considered to be a violation under German Constitutional law. For example, performing a medical act on a subject who has freely consented is perfectly legal(36).

In addition, the absence of an infringement of integrity has frequently been proclaimed by case law when the infringement in question was considered minimal and tolerable(37).

---

(29) Among others, BVerfG, 28 May 1993 (BVerfGE 88, 203) for the embryo; on dignity post mortem, see *infra*, p. 69.

(30) Art. 211 StGB.

(31) Art. 102 BL.

(32) *Infra*, p. 68.

(33) *Infra*, p. 62.

(34) U. Di Fabio, *in* Th. Maunz and G. Dürig, Grundgesetz-Kommentar, 2013, art. 2, § 2, BL, note 56. The role of the European Court of Human Rights should be noted in passing in this regard. The ECHR did not hesitate to censure Germany for having harmed the bodily integrity of a drug trafficker who, after swallowing some bags of cocaine, was administered vomit-inducing substances (ECHR, 11 July 2006, *Jalloh v. Germany*, n° 54810/00).

(35) U. Di Fabio, *in* Th. Maunz and G. Dürig, *op. cit.*, art. 2, § 2, BL, note 57.

(36) *Infra*, p. 67.

(37) Such was the case with army haircuts, which caused a lot writings in Germany! (BVerwG, 25 July 1972, BVerwGE 46, 1).

Unlike the right to dignity, the right to bodily integrity, like the right to life, is therefore not absolute but relative[38]. For that matter, on the subject of these two rights, the Basic Law states that "they can only be breached by virtue of a law".

These three fundamental rights initially appeared to be interpreted in an exclusively negative way by the State. That is the why, in the name of these rights, the death penalty, euthanasia and experiments on people were prohibited. Following a quite remarkable development by the Federal Constitutional Court, a positive obligation to protect the fundamental rights was subsequently imposed on the State. It is therefore in the name of the right to life that the State must, in particular, protect the embryo[39]. This positive obligation will require the courts to interpret the existing legislation in such a way as to ensure as much as possible that the fundamental rights can be enacted particularly with regard to the protection of the human body.

The fundamental rights have a considerable scope. Since they link the three powers "as directly applicable rights", the laws adopted by the Federation, as by the Länder, the administrative regulations and judicial decisions must conform to them.

In addition, under the terms of the Basic Law itself[40], any Constitutional revision concerning the principle of dignity set down in article 1 of the Basic Law is prohibited.

Furthermore, while the fundamental rights may be infringed by virtue of a law, [41] the very substance of these rights must never be affected[42].

However, it is above all the protection of the fundamental rights by the Federal Constitutional Court that must, in this case, be the focus of our attention. Created in 1951, the mission of this High Court is, among others, to ensure compliance with these rights. It is responsible both for verifying the conformity of the legislation to the Basic Law (*Normenkontrollverfahren*) and for a robust control

(38) L. Michael and M. Morlok, *Grundrechte*, ed. Nomos, Nomos Lehrbuch, 2008, p. 106.

(39) It was, in fact, on the subject of the right to life that the Federal Constitutional Court first ruled. Thus, in a decision of 25 February 1975, (BVerfGE 39, I), the Court invalidated a law that decriminalised abortion carried out before the end of the twelfth week, on the grounds that it violated "the right to life of the unborn human being" (see above).

(40) Art. 79, § 3, BL.

(41) Art. 19, § 1, BL.

(42) Art. 19, § 2, BL.

of standards. This means that any court considering that a law (on whose validity its decision depends) is unconstitutional must delay its ruling and refer the question of constitutionality to the judgement of the Federal Constitutional Court.

Finally, let us emphasize that Germany gives litigants the possibility of appealing directly to the Federal Constitutional Court for protection of their fundamental rights(43). Let us refer, for example, to a recent decision by which the higher judiciary invalidated the provision requiring transsexuals to undergo certain interventions before they could legally change gender on the grounds that it was a violation of their right to bodily integrity(44).

Thanks to this possibility of appeal, each individual in Germany therefore has a truly effective weapon to ensure the protection of his body. The fundamental rights to dignity, life and bodily integrity will certainly justify decisions made by the Federal Constitutional Court, "the cornerstone of the German political system", for the purpose of guaranteeing this protection.

The fundamental rights, however, do not have a monopoly on the protection of the human body.

B. – *Some other principles of protection of the body*

One observation must be made straight away. Although protected so effectively by the fundamental rights, the human body is also protected by other instruments. For example, the Criminal Code punishes murder(45), the violation of bodily integrity by negligence(46) as well as assisted suicide (*Tötung auf Verlangen*)(47). The German Civil Code (BGB), for its part, considers any medical act without the patient's consent to be an infringement of bodily integrity in the same category as intentional assault and battery(48). It also sets out the compensation that the victim can obtain in such cases.

(43) For a detailed analysis of these questions of constitutional law, see. Ch. Autexier, *Introduction au droit public allemand*, coll. Droit fondamental, Paris, PUF, 1997, pp. 78 et seq.
(44) BVerfG, 11 January 2011, BVerfGE 128, 109.
(45) See *supra*, p. 57.
(46) Art. 229 StGB.
(47) Art. 216 StGB.
(48) Art. 823 BGB.

Alongside the rights to dignity, life and bodily integrity, an extensive right to self-determination (*Selbstimmungsrecht*) is another front-line safe-guard of the protection of the human body. Although this right stems indirectly from the Basic Law, and more specifically from the rights of all individuals to freedom and to the free fulfilment of their personality[49], it is the legislature and particularly case law[50] that shape its boundaries, at least in medical law. The BGB, it should be noted, implicitly establishes the right of self-determination in the form of contractual freedom[51]. This is a dual freedom, as it includes the freedom to agree to a contract and the freedom to decide on its content. Some limitations are imposed, however, stemming particularly from the invalidation of illegal or immoral contracts[52]. Inspired at least in part, by Kantian philosophy, this respect for individual free will is also a reaction to the mystique of National Socialism and its negation of the individual. With regard to biomedicine, perhaps more so than in other countries in which the collective will, represented by the State, sometimes takes precedence over the individual's will the virtually absolute respect for the wishes of the patient are here practically elevated to the status of dogma[53].

This right to self-determination, as broad as it is, does not, however, mean complete freedom to control one's body. Two principles must be distinguished: that of bodily integrity, definitely relative, and the principle that the human body may not be subjected to a property right. In the absence of any general law, it is case law that has given substance to these two principles, considered to be unwritten rules for the protection of human dignity.

In cases where the body is identified with the person, there can be no property rights of the body or its parts. Surprisingly this theory has not always been absolute in Germany in that, until the law on the protection of the embryo (*Embryonenschutzgesetz*)

(49) Art. 2, § 1, combined with art. 2, § 2, BL. See U. Di Fabio, *in* Th. Maunz and G. Dürig, Grundgesetz-Kommentar, *op. cit.*, art. 2, § 1, BL, notes 204 et seq.

(50) *Infra*, p. 67.

(51) Art. 305 BGB.

(52) Art. 134 and 138 BGB.

(53) *Infra*, p. 72.

of 1990[54], surrogacy was viewed in a more positive way[55]. Furthermore, it might be surprising to know that prostitution is legal in Germany, with prostitutes viewed in the eyes of the law as workers like any other. Apart from these rare cases, the body as the corporeal envelope of the person cannot be disposed of.

It is, however, a different matter with regard to human body parts and products which, as an exception and within the limitations set by law can be the subject of contracts. Thus, under certain conditions, donations of organs and bodily products have been gradually approved[56]. Thus it is possible to reconcile the therapeutic interests of others with the protection of human dignity, by preventing any commodification of the human body in the name of a quite relative principle of bodily integrity. It can also be noted that according to this principle, when an individual is on hunger strike, Germany has occasionally allowed force-feeding when that person's life was endangered[57].

However, bodily integrity (total or partial) should not be confused with the principle that the human body may not form the subject of a property right and that there can be no commercialisation of the human body.

While the limited availability of human body parts and products is recognized in certain cases, contracts that attach a monetary value to these are considered null and void. It is essentially §138 BGB, under the terms of which "any legal act causing an infringement of moral standards is null and void", which forms the basis for the prohibition of any commercialisation of the human body[58]. Although this concept of "moral standards" (*gute Sitten*) remains undefined, the Supreme Court (*Reichsgericht*) ruled in 1928 that it is based on the "sense of decency of all those who think justly and fairly"[59]. "This notion is considered as an instrumental and powerful mean of the ethical and moral standards of the

(54) Law on the protection of the embryo (Embryonenschutzgesetz), 13 December 1990, *BGBl.* 1990, I, pp. 2746 et seq. See the French translation in the *Revue Éthique, la vie en question*, n° 1, Paris, 1991, pp. 101 et seq.

(55) D. Coester-Waltjen, "Rechtliche Probleme der für andere übernommenen Mutterschaft", *NJW*, 1982, pp. 2528 et seq.

(56) *Infra*, p. 67.

(57) However, prison doctors can refuse to implement this.

(58) On this prohibition, see, among others, J. Taupitz (ed.), *Kommerzialisierung des menschlichen Körpers*, Springer, 2007.

(59) Reichsgericht, 9 February 1928, RGZ 120, p. 148. On this concept of moral standards, in French, F. Ferrand, *Droit privé allemand*, coll. Précis Dalloz, Paris, *D.*, 1997, p. 249.

contractual life"[60], limiting the most flagrant abuses of contractual freedom.

Autonomy, the limited disposition of the body, the non-commercialisation... these principles stemming from the fundamental rights, from specific legal texts, and shaped by case law are complemented by the other extra legal standards that also guarantee the protection of the human body.

An important source of such standards, the German Medical Association (*Bundesärztekammer*) regularly issues guidelines (*Richtlinien*). Once they are adopted by the Regional Chamber of Physicians of a State, these guidelines become mandatory directives that must be followed by the doctors in that State. That is the case among others, of cost-free and anonymous principles governing donation in most guidelines. It was also in this way that, to the contrary, the fact that anonymity could not be guaranteed to a sperm donor was established by a 2006 directive[61]. Finally, the Principles of the Federal Chamber of Physicians concerning end-of-life assistance[62] are the ones to set up the difficult conditions in which treatment required to keep the patient alive can be withdrawn. The quotation "*in dubio pro vita*", "when in doubt favour life", tends to be the guideline currently applied when the dying person has not expressed any wishes with regard to the end of life[63].

In addition, the Annual Medical Assembly (*Ärztetag*), which establishes the mandatory ethical and deontological rules, regularly deals with problems inherent to the protection of the human body. In the name of dignity, there is an absolute priority given to individual rights in human subject research[64].

It should also be noted that there are a number of committees responsible for making recommendations in those fields not

(60) Cl. WITZ, *Droit privé allemand*, t. 1, Actes juridiques, droits subjectifs, Paris, Litec, 1992, n° 247; see also, *ID.*, *Le droit allemand*, *op. cit.*, pp. 113 et seq.

(61) "(Muster-)Richtlinie zur Durchführung der assistierten Reproduktion", *Deutsches Ärzteblatt*, 17 February, 2006, cahier n° 20, pp. A 1392 et seq.

(62) "Grundsätze der Bundesärztekammer zur ärztlichen Sterbebegleitung", *Deutsches Ärzteblatt*, 2011, 108, cahier n° 7, pp. A 346 et seq.

(63) For further details, F. FURKEL, "Le rôle majeur des proches au service d'une réelle autonomie du patient en fin de vie", *in* B. FEUILLET-LIGER (ed.), *Les proches et la fin de vie médicalisée - Panorama international*, coll. Droit, Bioéthique et Société, Brussels, Bruylant, 2013, pp. 83 et seq.

(64) A. ROGERS and D. DURAND DE BOUSINGEN, *Une bioéthique pour l'Europe*, Conseil de l'Europe 1995, p. 203.

regulated by legislators. For example, it was the working group established by the Federal Ministry of Research and the Federal Ministry of Justice that rejected surrogacy in the famous "Benda Report" of 1985[65].

The role of numerous ethics committees must also be noted. The goal of the newly created German Ethics Committee (*deutscher Ethikrat*), with jurists, academics and theologians, is to give opinions on the new questions raised by biomedical advances. It was referred to, among others, after the Cologne Regional Court ruled that circumcision violated the child's fundamental right to bodily integrity[66]. The regional ethics committees are, for their part, an essential instrument of protection of the human body in that they exist mostly in institutions that carry out clinical trials. The doctors who conduct these trials are now required by the guidelines of the German Medical Associations to refer to an ethics committee before starting their work in order to receive an ethical recommendation.

Aside the legislature, various courts and traditional bodies of all kinds – an important source of 'extra-legal' standards concerning the protection of the human body – the doctors also, individually, play a significant role, often managing to make their conceptions take precedence, sometimes against the existing principles[67].

However, even if they finally boil down to just a few major principles, the judicial and extra-legal standards intended to protect the human body are exceptionally effective in Germany, both through their rarely controversial existence and through a strict compliance mostly ensured by the Federal Constitutional Court, whose influence can no longer be denied.

The surprisingly faithful translation into the field of biomedicine of the principles laid down deserves particular attention in Germany.

(65) "Fécondation *in vitro*. Analyse du génome et thérapie génique", 1985, La Documentation française, 1987.

(66) *Infra*, p. 65.

(67) Some gynaecologists opposed to reproduction using a donor tell their potential patients that such a procedure is prohibited by law!

II. – The application of the principles of protection of the human body in the field of biomedicine

Before we continue, one pivotal observation must be made. A defining principle of the German constitutional framework[68], the respect for human dignity is at the heart of every provision, whatever the source, adopted to ensure that the principles of protection of the human body match reality in regard to biomedicine. Some of these provisions undoubtedly stem more directly from the right to bodily integrity, while others seem more related to the (related) principle that the human body may not form the subject of a property right or of non-commercialisation. Regardless of the content of the rule in question, the right to dignity nevertheless always remains implicit[69].

A. – *Some provisions resulting directly from the right to life and the right to bodily integrity*

The legal texts prohibit both female sterilisation[70] and male vasectomies without the subject's consent. In the same way, although castration can be performed at the request of the individual on medical grounds or to reduce sex drive, it cannot be imposed under any circumstances[71]. Any forced castration would be considered to be in breach of the fundamental right to dignity and the right to bodily integrity[72].

The law of 2012 on the circumcision of children on religious grounds[73] is significant in more than one way with regard to the right to bodily integrity. Adopted to resolve an issue that recently divided German opinion almost as violently as the Dreyfus case brought the French people into conflict at the beginning of

(68) *Supra*, p. 55.

(69) With regard to the "radiant effect" of the right to dignity in Germany, see *supra*, note 22.

(70) R. Ratzel and B. Luxenburger, *Handbuch Medizinrecht*, Deutscher Anwalt Verlag, 2011, p. 680. For more details of the turbulent history of sterilisation in Germany, A. Laufs, Ch. Katzenmeier and V. Lipp, *Arztrecht*, Beck, 2009, pp. 225 et seq.

(71) Gesetz über die freiwillige Kastration und andere Behandlungsmethoden (KastrG), 15 August 1969, modified on November 23, 1973, § 3. See also U. Di Fabio, *in* Th. Maunz and G. Dürig, Grundgesetz-Kommentar, *op. cit.*, art. 2, § 2, BL, note 71.

(72) A. Laufs and B.-R. Kern, *Handbuch des Arztrechts*, Beck, 2010, p. 1385.

(73) Gesetz über den Umfang der Personensorge bei einer Beschneidung des männlichen Kindes, 20 December 2012 (*BGBl.* 2012, I, pp. 2749 et seq.).

the last century, the new provision is a perfect example of the implementation of the famous principle of proportionality enabling the settlement of a conflict likely to happen between several fundamental rights[74]. In this case, the various courts and then the lawmaker had to evaluate the competing interests to try to strike a balance between them. In June 2012, the Cologne Regional Court made circumcision performed on religious grounds a criminal offence, on the basis that such an intervention irreversibly changes the child's body without any medical justification[75]. In the opinion of the Court, "the fundamental right of a child to its bodily integrity takes precedence over the right of the parents to freely practise their religion". The conflict of fundamental rights that needed to be resolved here was between the parents' right to educate their child[76] and religious freedom[77] on the one hand, and the child's fundamental right to physical integrity protected by the State on the other[78]. In order to end the storm of reactions provoked by this decision, legislators intervened at the end of 2012[79], authorising the circumcision of children on religious grounds if the operation was performed by a qualified person and if an effective form of pain management was provided[80]. This contentious argument, which has not taken place in all countries, shows the degree of importance given to the fundamental right to bodily integrity in Germany. It should be noted that, based on the decision of the Cologne Regional Court[81], a Berlin judge even maintained that the act of piercing the ears of a 3-year-old girl to attach earrings amounted to a violation of her bodily integrity liable to criminal sanctions[82] !

---

(74) Concerning this principle, see in French, M. Fromont, "Le principe de proportionnalité", *AJDA* 1995, pp. 156 et seq.

(75) LG Köln, 7 May 2012, *NJW*, 2012, pp. 2128 et seq.

(76) The article 6, paragraph 2, of the Basic Law in fact states: "The care and upbringing of children is the natural right of parents and a duty primarily incumbent upon them."

(77) Art. 4, § 1, BL.

(78) Art. 2, § 2, BL.

(79) Gesetz über den Umfang der Personensorge bei einer Beschneidung des männlichen Kindes, 20 December 2012, cited above.

(80) For more details of the conditions imposed by this instrument, S. Rixen, "Das Gesetz über den Umfang der Personensorge bei einer Beschneidung des männlichen Kindes", *NJW*, 2013, pp. 257 et seq.

(81) LG Köln, May 7, 2012, cited above.

(82) Amstgericht (Court of first instance) Berlin-Lichtenberg, 31 August 2012. These civil proceedings brought by the parents against the practitioner responsible for the procedure, on the grounds that the ears had not been pierced at the same height, finally reached a settlement (14C58/12); see also *die Frankfurter Allgemeine Zeitung*, 1 November 2012, p. 8.

It should be added that since 24 September 2013, a new paragraph of the Criminal Code has considered female genital mutilation, traditionally prohibited in Germany, to be a crime liable to severe sanctions(83).

In addition, since the 1976 law on medications (*Arzneimittelgesetz-AMG*)(84), experimentation has been partially regulated by the legislature. However, although biomedical experiments create a conflict of principles between the freedom of research guaranteed by the Basic Law(85) and the constitutional guarantee of the dignity of the human being, no experimentation in modern Germany – so very sensitive on this subject – has ever been justified without the subject's consent.

Again in accordance with the protection of bodily integrity, on the subject of corporal punishment, Germany forms part of the group of abolitionist countries. Indeed, since a law enacted in 2000(86), children have had the right to an education without violence, which means the prohibition of corporal punishment, psychological abuse and other humiliating behaviour(87). Germany has a zero tolerance policy on this issue, as not only physical blows, but also the act of "violently pushing or pulling a child, twisting its ear or pulling the hair" is illegal(88). "Smacking teachers", beware!

The field of DNA testing must also be mentioned, with two texts protecting the dignity of the person and, more specifically, the right to bodily integrity have just been adopted.

In the first place, illicit paternity tests are prohibited by a 2008 law(89). Without the authorisation of a judge, and subject to

---

(83) Art. 226 a StGB.

(84) Law on medications (*Arzneimittelgesetz*), 24 August 1976, *BGBl.* 1976, I, pp. 2445 et seq., law subsequently amended numerous times.

(85) Art. 5, § 3, BL.

(86) Law that established the article 1631, paragraph 2, in the BGB.

(87) This article 1631, paragraph 2, introduced in the BGB, perfectly translates article 19 of the Convention relating to the rights of the child which, since 1989, has stated that the States must "protect the child against all forms of physical or mental violence, harm or brutality".

(88) See LG Berlin, 18 December 2009, *JUS*, 2010, pp. 458 et seq. See also the article 340 StGB which, more broadly, prohibits and sanctions any form of violence in exercising a public function.

(89) Das Gesetz zur Klärung der Vaterschaft unabhängig vom Anfechtungsverfahren, 26 March 2008, *BGBl.* 2008, I, pp. 441 et seq. On this law, M. Wellenhofer, "Das neue Gesetz zur Klärung der Vaterschaft unabhängig vom Anfechtungsverfahren", *NJW*, 2008, pp. 1185 et seq.

sanctions, no one may now take samples of skin or hair for the purpose of establishing parentage.

Secondly, and once again in the name of the dignity of the person and the protection of the body, a 2009 law on genetic diagnosis[(90)] prohibits geneticists from informing a family of a predisposition to a disease discovered in one of the family members[(91)].

Finally, to illustrate the applications of the fundamental right to bodily integrity, a recent piece of case law needs to be mentioned. Since a law enacted in 1980[(92)], in order to legally change gender, transsexuals have been required to undergo several surgical interventions intended to give them an appearance resembling that of the other sex. In addition, they must be permanently incapable of reproduction. Subsequently, in a ruling on 11 January 2011[(93)], the German Federal Constitutional Court declared the two requirements to be unconstitutional on the grounds that they violated the rights to bodily integrity universally guaranteed by the Basic Law.

Some violations of the body are, however, justified. That is the case in medical law, when the subject consents to the violation. The absolute requirement for free and informed consent to any medical intervention, a consent deemed to be 'justification', expresses the right to self-determination guaranteed to everyone. With regard to consent to a medical act, it was undoubtedly Germany that led the way in the 19th century[(94)]. Then in the "Directives concerning the new treatments and scientific experimentation on human beings" published in 1931, it declared the need for the patient's consent prior to treatment[(95)]. After a dark period during which this rule was

(90) Das Gendiagnostikgesetz (GenDG), 31 July 2009, *BGBl.* 2009, I, 2529 et seq., art. 11, § 3.

(91) For further details, F. Furkel, "Le corps féminin et la biomédecine en République fédérale d'Allemagne", *in* B. Feuillet-Liger and A. Aouij-Mrad (eds.), *Corps de la femme et biomédecine – Approche internationale*, coll. Droit, Bioéthique et Société, Brussels, Bruylant, 2013, p. 30.

(92) Law on transsexuals (Transsexuellengesetz – TSG), *BGBl.* 1980, I, 1654 et seq., amended on 17 July 2009, *BGBl.* 2009, I, 1978 et seq.

(93) BVerfG, 11 January 2011, BVerfGE 128, 43.

(94) See in particular, Reichsgericht, 31 May 1894, *RGSt*, 25, pp. 375 et seq.

(95) To illustrate the emerging requirement for consent to medical treatment, the example of Bismarck is often cited, imposing in 1887 as a condition for the larynx operation that had to be performed on Crown Prince Frederick III, that he give his consent (O. von Bismarck, *Gedanken und Erinnerungen*, vol. II, Propyläen, 1898, p. 497).

abandoned[96], Germany rediscovered its role as a pioneer in this area, giving the patient a particularly wide-ranging right of self-determination, confirmed by case law on numerous occasions[97]. In order to further clarify the relationship between doctor and patient, then an exclusively judicial affair, legislators recently intervened[98], defining, among others, the content of information requirements intended to assist the patient in consenting and, therefore, to justify the violation of their physical integrity.

Such a violation can also be legitimised by a legal text, requiring for example individuals to have certain vaccinations or to have samples taken to discover the biological truth. One original aspect of German law must be referred to here. Unlike most other European countries[99], when a judge orders a blood or saliva sample to be taken for parentage tests, Germany applies a principle that requires the persons directly concerned and third parties to submit to any tests likely to lead to the discovery of the biological truth, the principle of "*Duldungspflicht*"[100]. In case of a refusal to comply, as well as fines and imprisonment, force may be used! While such a system may be surprising in a modern country so attached to the principle of the integrity of the body, it can be explained by the absolute priority given in Germany to the quest for the biological truth[101].

The rights to life and to the bodily integrity of the body are aimed equally at the beginning and the end of life.

With regard to the embryo, there is a certain ambiguity in the use of the concept of dignity, which is applied in Germany to justify both the right of the woman to an abortion under certain conditions and the refusal to legalise abortion, which is nevertheless decriminalised in certain situations[102]!

---

(96) In 1937, the Professional Code of German doctors abandoned the requirement for prior consent.

(97) *Münchener-Kommentar zum BGB*, Beck, 6th ed., 2012, § 241, n°s 197 et seq.

(98) See the law on improving the rights of patients, 20 February 2013 (*Gesetz zur Verbesserung der Rechte von Patientinnen und Patienten*, *BGBl.* 2013, I, pp. 282 et seq.).

(99) Countries which, like France, prohibit the use of force and even the ordering of a test, subject to sanctions (See in particular Paris, 24 November 1981, *D.*, 1982, p. 355).

(100) Art. 372 a, § 1, ZPO.

(101) On this principle, see in French F. FURKEL, "L'incidence de la biomédecine sur la parenté ou le triomphe de l'amour de la vérité biologique", *in* B. FEUILLET-LIGER and M.-C. CRESPO-BRAUNER (eds.), *Les incidences de la biomédecine sur la parenté*, coll. Droit, Bioéthique et Société, Brussels, Bruylant, 2014, pp. 27 et seq.

(102) On this ambiguïty, E. DEUTSCH and A. SPICKHOFF, *Medizinrecht*, Springer, 2014, pp. 465 et seq.

The legal situation concerning the deceased person is quite clear. While the protection of the deceased's image and memory is guaranteed, the protection of the dead body is also assured in the name of dignity. The corpse is regarded as the clothing of the deceased person, which must never be treated as a common object. Accordingly, autopsies are prohibited other than for criminal or medical reasons. Germany is currently undoubtedly one of the countries in which funerals are most strictly regulated. That is why, in the name of the dignity of the body after death (*die postmortale Würdeschutz*), numerous prohibitions are in place, including the disposal of the ashes in a natural environment, the preservation of the urn in a private place and cryopreservation(103). It was in accordance with this same dignity that the anatomical exhibition "Body Worlds" ("*Körperwelte*") was the talk of Germany for several months, as it had been in France, for that matter. In this unusual exhibition, human bodies with visible organs(104) were displayed to the public with a scientific and artistic goal. However, in the interest of post mortem dignity and in spite of the prior consent of the deceased, a number of court rulings banned the display of the bodies for purely artistic purposes(105). Yet through the application of the principle of proportionality already referred to(106), the freedom of research, guaranteed by the Basic Law, allows the exposure of bodies if there is a scientific interest.

Once again in the name of post mortem dignity, according to the law on transplantation(107), anyone removing an organ from a corpse without the consent of the subject before death or of the immediate family is liable to sanctions(108). It is therefore an authorisation regime that is prevalent in Germany, once more expressing the very broad right of self-determination of each individual.

(103) On post mortem dignity, see the comprehensive article of B. SCHMIDT and A.M. BUSCH, "Postmortaler Würdeschutz und gesetzgeberische Gestaltungsfreiheit", *Der Staat*, 2010, Band 49, n° 2, pp. 211 et seq.

(104) These bodies were preserved using the plastination technique developed by Professor Gunther Von Hagens.

(105) Among others, VG Augsburg (adm. Court), 4 September 2009, Az. Au 7 S 09.1266; VG Berlin (adm. Court), 26 May 2010, Az. 21 K 48.10.

(106) *Supra*, note 74.

(107) Law on donations, samples and organ transplantation (Transplantationsgesetz – TPG), 5 November 1997, *BGBl.* 1997, I, p. 2631, modified 4 September 2007, *BGBl.* 2007, I, pp. 2206 et seq.; concerning the system established by the law of 1997, E. DEUTSCH, "Das Transplantationsgesetz vom 5. Nov.1997", *NJW*, 1998, pp. 777 et seq.

(108) Art. 3 and 4 TPG.

Finally, it should be noted that due undoubtedly to the principle of "*Duldungspflicht*" referred to above; the exhumation of the body of a deceased person for the purpose of identification by genetic fingerprinting to establish or rule out a parentage connection is not prohibited. However, due to a fairly broad consensus based on post mortem dignity, it does not appear as if this type of action will ever be carried out.

B. – *Some other measures stemming from the (relative) principles of the non-property rights and non-commercialisation of the body*

Mostly prohibitive, the majority of these measures appear to be corollaries of these two principles.

Crucial to this subject is the law on the protection of embryos(109), one of the first legislative instruments adopted in Europe in the fields of genetics and assisted reproductive technology (ART). It is a criminal text that sanctions, among others, gestational surrogacy and oocyte donations(110), declaring both that the body cannot be disposed of and cannot be commercialised. In addition, the principle that the human body may not be disposed of justifies the prohibition of the fertilisation of an egg by the sperm of a deceased man. The law also prohibits cloning, for reproductive as well as therapeutic purposes, considered to be detrimental to the human condition. In the same way, stem cell therapy is also prohibited, because of the risk of altering the human genetic heritage(111).

The law on transplantation(112), for its part, clarified the legal regime concerning the removal of organs from a living person. Intended to guarantee the exercise of the three fundamental rights that ensure the protection of the human body, this text highlights the principle that the human body may not form the subject of a property right, protecting the individual against him/herself. The removal of segments of organs that do not regenerate is restricted to transfers for the benefit of persons very closely related to the

(109) Embryonenschutzgesetz, 13 December 1990, see above, note 54.

(110) Art. 1, § 1, n°s 2 and 7 Embryonenschutzgesetz. One original aspect of the instrument must be noted. In fact, although heavy penalties are imposed against practitioners responsible for such operations, neither the surrogate mother nor the oocyte donors incurs any sanction.

(111) Art. 5 and 6 Embryonenschutzgesetzt. The creation of chimeras and hybrids is also prohibited (Art. 7 Embryonenschutzgesetz).

(112) Transplantationsgesetz (TPG), 5 November 1997, modified on 4 September 2007, see above.

donor[113]. The donor is therefore not free to dispose of his body as he sees fit. However, the law on transplantation, under the terms of which trading in organs and tissues is prohibited and punishable by five years in prison[114], also establishes the principle of non-commercialisation of the body.

With regard to the principle of non-commercialisation of the body and cost-free donations established in numerous texts we should take note of the criticisms applied to an indisputably excessive "compensation" for blood and sperm donors[115], a misleading compensation that now seems to cast doubt on the cost-free and profit-free principle. This practice is often compared to the possibility of buying breast milk on the Internet and sometimes even to the flourishing trade in hair. However, this comparison can be unwarranted as breast milk after it has been expressed and hair that has already been cut become commodities so there is no violation of the bodily integrity of the subject. The complaint of commercialisation of the body is therefore, in this case, unfounded.

Still in the name of the principle, not explicitly referred to, that the human body may not be disposed of the freedom guaranteed to the human subjects of experimentation is extremely limited, as is that in the case of samples and grafts. Two types of experimentation are covered: experiments in the form of "therapeutic trial", which use a drug likely to heal the subject of the experiment, and experiments with no direct therapeutic benefit. With regard to this second category, the conditions in which an individual can agree to undergo experimentation and thus dispose, or have control, of his body are extremely strict[116]. Here, once again, limits are imposed on the freedom of choice.

There can be no doubt that when one addresses the issue of a right relating to decisions about one's own death, the principle that the human body may not be disposed of seems the most

(113) Art. 8, § 1, TPG. The recipient can be a relative up the second degree, the spouse, the fiancé or a third party with especially close links to the donor.

(114) Art. 17 and 18 TPG. The 2007 law on tissues extends the scope of the original law on transplantation to bone marrow as well as foetal and embryo organs and tissues. See H. Jung, "Organtransplantation im Licht der ethischen Herausforderungen", *JZ*, 2004, pp. 559 et seq.

(115) Approximately 30 euros for blood donations and 100 for sperm (some students are therefore encouraged to make numerous donations!).

(116) On this subject, see in French, R. Grote, "Aspects juridiques de la bioéthique dans la législation allemande", *RID comp.*, 1999, pp. 85 et seq.

relative. The right to self-determination guaranteed to every individual with regard to his own body is expressed in Germany by an exceptional autonomy in decision-making granted to the patient. The binding force of the advance directives, or living will (*Patientenverfügung*), is a perfect illustration of this principle. These written documents, which have steadily increased in number in Germany, enable those who wish to do so to decide in advance, in case they subsequently become incapable of doing so, the limits and even the withdrawal of certain forms of medical treatment(117). It is therefore increasingly the patient who, by means of these directives, controls the disposition of his body, refusing a medical treatment and thereby accelerating his/her end of life.

Although suicide and attempted suicide are not subject to any criminal proceedings, the right to euthanasia is not recognised in Germany. Homicide at the request of the victim is punishable by a prison sentence of six months to five years(118). We should notice here the ill-defined line between homicide by request, which is punishable, and assisted suicide, allowed and not punishable provided that the "assistant" takes no active part in the act!

Conclusion

The list of the provisions referred to, which is evidence in Germany of the reality of the principles of protection of the human body with regard to biomedicine, is far from exhaustive. Numerous directives, i.e. recommendations adopted by the German Medical Association as well as various ethics committees, should also have been included. At a time when violations of the human body can take alarming proportions, the number of all kinds of texts and decisions intended to oppose these violations is growing, which is reassuring.

The fact that these various provisions sometimes appear to be excessively fragmented is due to the absence, in Germany, of a set of general regulations concerning problems related to the development of biomedicine, although the need for very strict

(117) There are currently estimated to be 15 million "*Patientenverfügungen*" in Germany; see F. Furkel, "Le rôle majeur des proches au service d'une réelle autonomie du patient en fin de vie", *in* B. Feuillet-Liger (ed.), *Les proches et la fin de vie médicalisée – Panorama international*, coll. Droit, Bioéthique et Société, Brussels, Bruylant, 2013, pp. 101 et seq.

(118) Art. 216 StGB.

control of medical research and practices is felt particularly keenly in Germany. The federal structure of the country, which largely explains the restraint of legislators with regard to the biomedical sciences, certainly limits those who would like more comprehensive legislation in this area.

Be that as it may, whenever a question arises concerning the protection of the human body within biomedicine, even in the absence of specific provisions, it is the absolute need to guarantee the fundamental rights established by the Constitution which prevails. With the rights to life and bodily integrity being no more than a manifestation of the principle of dignity, it is this principle, a true cornerstone of the German constitutional system that makes the law. However, the reader will have noticed that the right of self-determination given to every individual in Germany is crucial. This right explains, in particular, the continued necessity, subject to exceptions, for the consent of the subject before his death to donate an organ. It also explains why Germany has still not signed the 1997 European Convention on Human Rights and Biomedicine[119] on the grounds that this text sometimes allows experimentation without direct individual benefit on persons incapable of giving their consent. In the face of the very broad right of self-determination of every individual, one question is raised. More so than other countries, is Germany not going to find itself frequently compelled to make a choice between two fundamental values which, at first sight, can appear to contradict each other? On one hand, human dignity which sometimes encroaches upon individual freedom, and on the other, the right to self-determination which leads to respect each individual's will. However, to the extent that, like all other rights that protect the human body, the right of self-determination also stems from the principle of dignity, there is no reason for any such contradiction to exist. Although, in the name of the principle of dignity, protecting the human body with regard to third parties asserts itself on a daily basis in Germany with increasing vigour, it is logical that, again in the name of this same principle and in spite of a right of self-determination that has become almost legendary in Germany, protecting the body against the person that inhabits it should be asserted on equal basis.

(119) *Supra*, note 11.

AN INDIVIDUAL'S AUTONOMY OVER THEIR BODY: EXTENT AND BOUNDARIES IN BELGIAN LAW

Geneviève SCHAMPS

Full Professor at the Faculty of Law and Criminology[1]

Director of the Centre of Medical and Biomedical Law
Catholic University of Louvain (Belgium)

In Belgian law, there is no legal instrument establishing a general regime of protection of the human body as such. Some pertinent provisions principally aimed at the protection of the person are enshrined in international or European instruments[2], the Constitution, the Criminal Code, the Civil Code and specific laws, as well as the implications of the decisions of the European Court of Human Rights[3]. They also appear in the Code of Medical Ethics, although that is not legally binding, and they are taken into consideration in the opinions given by, in particular, the Belgian Advisory Committee on Bioethics and the Federal Commission on Patient Rights[4].

The phrase "principles of protection of the human body" does not appear expressly in the provisions of domestic law. There are references in legal doctrine and case law to the personality rights,

(1) The author is the Vice-President of the Belgian Advisory Committee on Bioethics. The arguments put forward in this essay are the personal opinions of the author.

(2) See in particular the Universal Declaration on Human Rights of 10 December 1948, the European Convention for the Protection of Human Rights and Fundamental Freedoms of 4 November 1950, the Charter of Fundamental Rights of the European Union, the International Covenant on Civil and Political Rights of 19 December 1966, the Convention on the Rights of the Child of 20 November 1989, the Convention on the Rights of Persons with Disabilities of 13 December 2006, ... A distinction must also be made between those treaty provisions that are directly applicable and those that are not.

(3) For an analysis of the decisions of the European Court of Human Rights, see G. WILLEMS, "L'appréhension par la Cour de Strasbourg du droit de la personne et de la famille : respect des singularités nationales et commune garantie des droits de l'homme", *in* D. FRIES (ed.), *Les droits de l'homme. Une réalité quotidienne*, Limal, Anthemis, 2014, pp. 167-204.

(4) Available at: www.patientrights.be.

concepts of dignity, of the "unavailability"[(5)] of the human body, of self-determination, cost-free (non-payment), anonymity, public order, etc. Violations of the legal provisions are punishable under criminal law or may be subject to contractual or non-contractual civil liability[(6)].

Different ideas are put forward in legal doctrine to characterise the personality rights it has developed and which are protected by case law or the law: these are sometimes considered to be freedoms[(7)] or, on the contrary, subjective rights[(8)] granted to the person[(9)], or even as private fundamental rights, with the characterisation of personality rights developing between these two extremes of freedoms and rights[(10)]. They protect "the attributes which constitute the person's individuality against infringements"[(11)] by the authorities as well as by third parties. In particular, they concern the physical, psychological, mental and social aspects of the personality: life, integrity, name, honour, image, etc.[(12)] They include protection through prevention, particularly by means of criminal sanctions[(13)], from attacks on the component parts of the personality, and through self-determination, *i.e.* with regard to the use of some of these attributes, subject to certain limits. They are generally considered to be non-commercial and they cannot

(5) This word is understood in the meaning that the human body cannot be disposed of (in French: "l'*indisponibilité du corps humain*").

(6) See also the law of 31 March 2010 on compensation for damages resulting from healthcare; G. SCHAMPS, "Le Fonds des accidents médicaux et l'indemnisation des dommages résultant de soins de santé", *RGAR*, 2014, n° 15.035/1-15.

(7) See, F. RIGAUX, *La vie privée. Une liberté parmi les autres ?*, Brussels, Larcier, 1992, pp. 134 et seq.; ID., *La protection de la vie privée et des autres biens de la personnalité*, Brussels, Bruylant, Paris, LGDJ, 1990, pp. 734 et seq.

(8) Y.-H. LELEU, *Droit des personnes et des familles*, coll. Faculté de droit de l'Université de Liège, Brussels, Larcier, 2010, pp. 112 et seq.

(9) E. LANGENAKEN, "L'indemnisation des atteintes aux droits de la personnalité et son implication quant à la nature de ces droits", *TBBR/RGDC.*, 2011, pp. 422-444.

(10) F. SWENNEN, *Het personen- en familierecht. Identiteit en verwantschap vanuit juridisch perspectief*, 4th ed., Antwerpen, Cambridge, Intersentia, 2015, pp. 52-53.

(11) Y.-H. LELEU, *Droit des personnes et des familles, op. cit.*, p. 111.

(12) *Ibid.*, p. 111; F. SWENNEN, *op. cit.*, pp. 56-62; N. GALLUS, "Les droits de la personnalité", *in* A.-C. VAN GYSEL (ed.), *Traité de droit civil belge*, t. I, coll. De Page, Brussels, Bruylant, 2015, pp. 138 et seq. On personality rights, see also the contributions to the work J.-L. RENCHON (ed.), *Les droits de la personnalité. Actes du Xe Colloque de l'Association "Famille & Droit", Louvain-la-Neuve, 30 November 2007*, coll. Famille et Droit, Brussels, Bruylant, 2009; M. ISGOUR, F. OMRANI and J.-M. VAN GYSEGHEM, *Droits de la personnalité*, Limal, Antemis, 2013, 151 p.

(13) See also E. LANGENAKEN, *op. cit.*, pp. 422-444, on compensation for violations of the personality rights.

be disposed of(14), which means that they do not form part of the person's property and that they have no monetary value(15).

In Belgian law, while the fundamental rights of the person are subject to legal rules intended for their protection, an increasingly extensive autonomy is granted to the individual, perhaps even a right of self-determination with regard to one's body and parts of it, or even to one's life, through specific pieces of legislation. The legislator combines the exercise of this autonomy of limits, which translate into strict conditions in terms of both the content and the procedure, with the protection of the person as a priority. He sometimes provides for a formalisation, to contractualise certain acts on the body, provided that the boundaries imposed are respected, as with assisted reproductive technologies.

After exploring ideas emphasising, at the present time, the increasingly engaged self-determination of the individual with regard to privacy and family life (I), this paper examines the scope of the autonomy of the person regarding acts performed on their body, which is recognised in Belgian law (II). The right to protection against violations of the body goes hand in hand with a right to an element of self-determination with regard to the body, albeit subject to legal limits. Interventions on the body with the person's consent will be examined – whether at the beginning, during or at the end of life – along with the existing boundaries, whether the procedures in question are autologous or altruistic. We will also look closely at some violations of physical integrity that are permitted by law and at procedures that may be performed on the body of a deceased person.

I. – Moving towards a much broader concept of autonomy of the individual: some contemporary ideas

Over time, a more extensive autonomy has gradually been granted the individual with regard to his privacy and family life. J.-L. Renchon emphasises that it is with regard to the human body that the general principle of the "unavailability" of the person has been most used: from this principle, a general principle of the

(14) For a different perspective, see F. Rigaux, *La protection de la vie privée et des autres biens de la personnalité*, *op. cit.*, p. 761.

(15) F. Swennen, *op. cit.*, p. 54; Y.-H. Leleu, *Droit des personnes et des familles*, *op. cit*, p. 116.

"unavailability" of the human body has been developed, to which a variety of legal effects have been attached since the enactment of the Napoleonic Code[16].

The advances in science and medicine since the 1960s[17] led to a relationship with the human body "which became a form of 'control'", with repercussions for the status of the human being and family ties, particularly with regard to human reproduction[18].

This author states that over thirty years, the supremacy of the interests of society over the protection of individual interests and the "unavailable" status of the person and personal family relationships – and therefore their removal from the autonomy of individual wills – were fundamentally called into question. He notes the existence of a "new cultural model of the self-realisation of the individual" and states that the principles underlying the new concepts of the legislator or of case law are those of freedom and equality, *i.e.* the autonomy of individual wills, to the point where the old considerations concerning the nature of public order or collective interest in the subject have gradually been eliminated[19]. He goes on to say, however, that an individual is also an integral part of different human communities and cannot "withdraw from the need to understand the collective interest of the different entities that also make up its identity and, in the longer term, although it appears to be urgent, of the collective interest of the entire human population"[20].

(16) J.-L. Renchon, "Le droit belge de la personne et de la famille : de l'indisponibilité à l'autodétermination ?", *ERPL*, 2007-3, pp. 349 et 362. On this subject, see also the contributions to the following works: *Le corps humain et le droit*, Journées belges 1975, Travaux de l'Association Henri Capitant, t. XXVI, Paris, *D.*, 1977, p. 536; *Over zichzelf beschikken ? Juridische en ethische bijdragen over het leven, het lichaam en de dood,* Antwerpen, Maklu, 1996, p. 628; C. Trouet, *Van lichaam naar lichaamsmateriaal. Recht en het nader gebruik van cellen en weefsels*, Antwerpen, Intersentia, 2003, p. 590.

(17) As well as these advance improving our understanding and the quest for control of the functioning of the human body, the author cites two other convergent and decisive factors for the new perception of things. One is the sudden and dramatic increase in the standard of living in western societies during the same period, and the growing surplus in the economic production of goods and services, going hand in hand with the boost to purchasing and consumption needs. The other factor put forward is the collapse in eastern societies of collective ideologies and the consequent demand for individualist values (J.-L. Renchon, *op. cit.*, pp. 369 and 371).

(18) J.-L. Renchon, *op. cit.*, p. 369.

(19) *Id.*, pp. 349-350.

(20) *Id.*, p. 372.

In this regard, X. Dijon[21] states that the subject is not at liberty to make decisions about his body in the same way as with an external piece of property. To the question of whether an individual has a right on his body, he responds that it is "in accordance with the dual theory of the subjective right (both power and interest) that, with regard to the human body, traditional doctrine granted a right of protection to the subject *in* his body, without according him the power to have full control *over* his body". However, he points out that theories have been developed which challenge the non-commercialisation of the body or the principle of the "unavailability" of the body[22]. At the same time, he believes that dignity, which is part of what makes us members of the human race, must sometimes infringe upon the right to autonomy[23]. According to him, the question of personal development, which is central to ethics, must not be confused with the fulfilment of all desires.

Believing that self-determination contributes to personal fulfilment, Y.-H. Leleu and G. Genicot consider that the human body must be differentiated from the individual, without becoming a "mere object" that may be subject to a right *in rem*, and that it is controlled by the person. According to them, the right to control the body should be regarded as a personality right, stemming from the right to life and the right to respect for physical integrity, although more extensive as it includes all procedures performed on the body[24]. From their perspective, the uses for the body and the procedures to which it may be subject are dominated by the subject's right to self-determination, which is exercised freely and "within the general framework of open, tolerant and non-interventionist ethics". They place the emphasis on the autonomy of the person and the protection to which it is entitled, stating that

(21) X. Dijon, "Vers un commerce du corps humain", *J.T.*, 2006, pp. 501-504; see also *id.*, *La raison du corps*, Brussels, Bruylant, 2012, pp. 29-30; *id.*, *Le sujet de droit en son corps, une mise à l'épreuve du droit subjectif*, Brussels, Larcier, 1982, pp. 60-142.

(22) He responds to this by pointing out that "Is it not true that reducing dignity to autonomy is to fall into the liberal temptation of wanting to think of the subject without a body and without a link (without the body that characterises the dependency on the link)? Does this not mean wanting the subject to define himself by himself?"

(23) On this subject, see also M. Verdussen, S. Depré and Th. Bombois, "Les devoirs fondamentaux en droit constitutionnel compare", *in* H. Dumont, F. Ost and S. van Drooghenbroeck, *La responsabilité, face cachée des droits de l'homme*, Brussels, Bruylant, 2005, pp. 282-283.

(24) However, see F. Rigaux, *La vie privée. Une liberté parmi les autres ?*, *op. cit.*, p. 137.

a number of pieces of legislation[25] have embodied the scope and limits of a right to control of the body, going beyond the "traditional debate between the 'patrimonialist' and 'personalistic' theories" and "broadly placed under the banner of human dignity". In their opinion, it is up to the individual to consider the implications of his own idea on the integrity of his body[26]. The ability to dispose freely of one's body, via free and informed consent, would be limited by standards drawn from the law and ethics: public order, human dignity and the protection of the species[27].

N. Gallus also believes we should be considering the current merit and relevance of the rule on the "unavailability" of the human body, as it is not included, as such, in any legal instrument and does not, in her opinion, demonstrate the general nature required to qualify as a general principle of law, given the numerous exceptions made in recent legislation. Nevertheless, she emphasises that the rule on human dignity constitutes a general principle of law and ethics that imposes limits on contractual freedom. It is with regard to this concept of dignity that the subjects of autonomy and "unavailability" must be analysed and understood. The most important recognition by the law of the control of one's body and the products and parts removed from it, as a personality right, does not imply an absolute individual freedom. In this way, while providing autonomy, the law sets limitations on it[28].

The Advisory Committee on Bioethics had already highlighted, specifically in its opinion of 8 March 2004 on sperm and ovum donations[29], and in that of 5 July 2004 on surrogacy[30], the existence of a growing tension between the "unavailability" of the personality rights – these rights being considered as non-commercial or 'not for

(25) See the legislations explained in this paper, in particular with regard to abortion, assisted reproductive technologies, patient's rights, research on embryos *in vitro,* experiments on human subjects, the removal or transplantation of organs, activities related to human body parts, transsexualism, etc. On these legislations, see the contributions to *Handboek Gezondheidsrecht*, TH. VANSWEEVELT and F. DEWALLENS (eds.), Antwerpen, Intersentia, 2014.

(26) Y.-H. LELEU and G. GENICOT, "Le statut juridique du corps humain en Belgique", in *Le droit de la santé : aspects nouveaux*, Journées suisses 2009, Travaux de l'Association Henri Capitant, t. LIX, Brussels, Bruylant, 2012, pp. 68-71; see also Y.-H. LELEU and G. GENICOT, "La maîtrise de son corps par la personne", *J.T.*, 1999, pp. 589-600.

(27) Y.-H. LELEU, *Droit des personnes et des familles, op. cit.*, pp. 131-132.

(28) N. GALLUS, "La validité de la convention de gestation pour autrui en droit belge actuel", *in* G. SCHAMPS and J. SOSSON (eds.), *La gestation pour autrui : vers un encadrement ?*, Brussels, Bruylant, 2013, pp. 185 et seq.

(29) Opinion n° 27 of 8 March 2004 on sperm and ovum donations, p. 46.

(30) Opinion of 5 July 2004 on surrogacy, p. 13.

sale' and therefore unable to be involved in any transaction (art. 1128 of the Civil Code) – and a clear development in the direction of the increasing "availability" of the human body, due to the growing number of decision-making options open to an individual with regard to his own body, for the purpose of treatment, research, donation, or in a prenatal (contraception, termination) or end-of-life (the right to request euthanasia) context.

Finally, J.-L. Renchon emphasises that the number of restrictions gradually imposed on the traditional principle of the "unavailability" of the human body became so high that recent doctrine has effectively reversed this principle and supported or affirmed a person's right to decide what happens to his body(31).

This author goes on to say that taking this concept a step further would mean allowing or granting the option to place personal prerogatives "on the market", such as body parts or products, the rights and obligations associated with one's family situation and family (or emotional) relationships. He notes, however, that the principle of the "availability", in the sense of a transferability (by contract), of the person and his personal rights has not (yet) been achieved in Belgian law, although some initial opinions in this direction have already been heard. In addition, there is still no general theory, as with the law of obligations or contract law, which would be applicable to personal or extra-patrimonial rights. It is therefore unclear at the present time if the provisions of the Civil Code relating to the law of obligations or contract law should be transposed into rules or agreements covering these rights(32). This question is also now raised with regard to surrogacy, as stated later in this document.

The case can now be made that there are different "levels of availability" – determined by the extent of the legal constraints governing the exercise of autonomy or its translation into a written agreement(33) – rather than a clear demarcation between "unavailability" and "availability"(34). As well as the ethical considerations, the law marks out the autonomy of the individual,

(31) J.-L. Renchon, *op. cit.*, p. 380.
(32) J.-L. Renchon, *op. cit.*, pp. 359, 374 and 377.
(33) With regard to assisted reproductive technologies.
(34) G. Schamps and G. Willems, "La convention de gestation pour autrui entre autonomie, ordre public et droits fondamentaux : quelles garanties formelles et substantielles ?", in *La gestation pour autrui : vers un encadrement ?*, *op. cit.*, p. 329.

particularly with regard to the legislator's view of the concept of dignity or public order. It negates the effectiveness of, and even introduces sanctions for, the arrangements or commitments made by the individual beyond certain limits placed on his freedom, all in the interests of protecting the general interest or competing individual interests. It also seeks a balance between the general interest, individual interest and the protection of legitimate competing interests, with regard in particular to the fundamental rights included in numerous instruments of domestic or supranational law.

II. – The right to protection of the body and the autonomy over one's body: scope and boundaries

A. – *The rights guaranteed by the Constitution and other provisions*

The Belgian Constitution[35] affirms the equality of Belgian citizens before the law and equality between men and women (art. 10 and 11*bis*), the fact that the enjoyment of the rights and freedoms accorded to Belgians must be provided without discrimination (art. 11), the guarantee of individual freedom (art. 12), the freedom to express one's opinions on all matters (art. 19) and the right to respect for one's private and family life[36] (art. 22).

The Constitution pays special attention to the child. It states that every child has the right to respect for its moral, physical, mental and sexual integrity. Children have the right to express themselves on any subject concerning them, and their opinions must be taken into consideration, with due regard to their age and faculties of understanding. They have the right to benefit from the measures and services designed to further their development. In any decision concerning them, the child's interests must be given priority (art. 22*bis*). These elements, and sometimes a right to autonomy, also feature in specific pieces of legislation, as

(35) On the constitutional rights, see the contributions to M. Verdussen and N. Bonbled (eds.), *Les droits constitutionnels en Belgique*, vol. 1 and 2, Brussels, Bruylant, 2011, 1898 p.; M. Verdussen, "La protection des droits de l'homme par la Cour constitutionnelle", in *Les droits de l'homme. Une réalité quotidienne*, *op. cit.*, pp. 135-149.

(36) See the developments on the subject and the analysis of Belgian case law by M. van Overstraeten, "Le droit au respect de la vie privée et le corps humain", *op. cit.*, pp. 933-970.

indicated later in this document. Belgium is also a signatory of the Convention of 20 November 1989 on the Rights of the Child.

The right to lead a life in keeping with human dignity is also included in the Constitution, with a guarantee to this end of economic, social and cultural rights, taking into account the corresponding obligations. These rights include, among others, the right to social security, health care and social, medical and legal aid (art. 23).

The concept of dignity is not defined in the Constitution or in any specific law, where it is rarely mentioned. The Law of 22 August 2002 on patient's rights – which is a *lex generalis* for health care provided by a professional practitioner – can be cited in this regard. It states that "the patient has the right to receive quality services from the professional practitioner that meet his needs, with due respect for his human dignity and autonomy and without any form of distinction being made"(37). As well as dignity, this provision places the emphasis on the autonomy of the patient and respect for equality.

The right to life is not specifically included in the Constitution. It is nevertheless covered by the penalties for offences against the person(38). Particular attention is paid to the protection of a person in a vulnerable situation, especially if this due to age, pregnancy, illness, disability or a physical or mental deficiency, whether or not this is evident or known to the offender(39). Furthermore, the European Convention for the Protection of Human Rights and Fundamental Freedoms specifically states that everyone's right to life shall protected by law (art. 2)(40). The right to physical integrity prohibits torture or inhuman or degrading treatment (art. 3).

Offences are also provided for breaches of the legal provisions concerning medicine or cosmetic surgery, assisted reproductive

(37) Art. 5 L. of 22 August 2002.

(38) See art. 392 et seq. of the Criminal Code (assault and battery or homicide, torture, inhumane or degrading treatment, human trafficking, the prohibition on female genital mutilation, etc.).

(39) See the amendments introduced by the law of 26 November 2011 amending and supplementing the Criminal Code in order to criminalise the abuse of those in positions of vulnerability and to extend criminal protection to persons vulnerable to maltreatment. On the opinions of the Advisory Committee on Bioethics, see G. Genicot, "Les recommandations du Comité consultatif de Bioéthique relatives aux personnes vulnérables", *T. Gez./Rev. dr. santé,* 2011-2012, pp. 267-290.

(40) See also, in article 2, situations where death was not considered to be in breach of this provision.

technologies, research on embryos *in vitro*, experimentation, the removal and transplant of organs, activities related to parts of the human body, and euthanasia. In addition, the offence of human trafficking includes that undertaken for the purposes of the removal of organs or human body material(41). There is also a self-defence provision for homicide or assault, but only for the protection of the person, not property(42).

The fact that the victim consents does not make it legal. It can sometimes be used in "mitigation" – removing the penalty but not the culpability – as stated in the Court of Cassation in a case relating to private sadomasochistic practices(43). In a judgment involving Belgium, the European Court of Human Rights(44) stated that the expression "private life" has a broad scope and that aspects such as sex, sexual orientation and sex life are important components of the personal sphere protected by article 8 of the Convention.

While highlighting the fact that this provision guarantees the right to personal fulfilment, whether in the sense of personal growth or personal autonomy, the Court considered that this right involves the right to establish and maintain relationships with other humans and the outside world, including in terms of sexual relationships, which are the most intimate of relationships. According to the Court, the right to engage in sexual relations derived from the right of control over one's own body, an integral part of the notion of personal autonomy(45).

---

(41) Art. 433 *quinquies*, § 1, of the Criminal Code, which also covers the purposes of the exploitation of prostitution or other forms of sexual exploitation. In addition, Belgium signed the Council of Europe Convention against Trafficking in Human Organs, adopted by the Committee of Ministers on 9 July 2014 and intended to prevent and combat such trafficking by having Member States establish offences for certain acts. It also covers the protection of victims' rights and cooperation at national and international level to prosecute such offenders more effectively.

(42) Art. 416 and 417 Crim. C.

(43) Cass., 6 January 1998, *R.D.P.C.*, 1999, p. 562, note A. DE NAUW.

(44) ECHR, February 17, 2005, *K.A. and A.D. v. Belgium*, more specifically, n°s 79 to 88; See J.-L. RENCHON, "La liberté sexuelle n'a-t-elle plus d'autre limite que la liberté sexuelle ? À propos de l'arrêt K.A. et A.D. c/ Belgique du 17 février 2005 de la CEDH", in *Hommage à Francis Delpérée. Itinéraires d'un constitutionnaliste*, Brussels, Bruylant, 2007, pp. 1309-1320; Y.-H. LELEU, *Droit des personnes et de la famille, op. cit.*, pp. 152-154 and the decisions of the European Court of Human Rights and fundamental freedoms referred to.

(45) It also stated that "the ability for each individual to live his life as he wishes can also include the possibility of devoting oneself to activities seen as physically or morally harmful or dangerous to the person. In other words, the concept of personal autonomy can be understood as the right to make decisions concerning one's own body", (n° 83). In this case, the intrusion comprising the criminal sentences imposed on the perpetrators of these practices was not deemed to be disproportionate: the right to engage in sexual practices

Although it can sometimes be subject to limitations, the right to respect for privacy is specifically included in the Convention for the Protection of Human Rights and Fundamental Freedoms (art. 8), the Constitution, the Criminal Code and the law of 22 August 2002 on patient's rights. The protection of privacy with regard to the processing of personal data is governed by the law of 8 December 1992. However, there is no 'right to privacy' theory that applies to the body[(46)].

Finally, in the interests of the protection of the person in particular, the legislator has prohibited the transmission of genetic data in certain situations. Accordingly, genetic testing is not permitted in the context of employment[(47)]. In addition, even if the person gives consent on the grounds that it would be beneficial, genetic data may not be disclosed for the purposes of an insurance policy[(48)]. What is more, a medical examination required for the conclusion or execution of a policy may only be based on medical history determining the current state of health of the person applying for insurance, and not on genetic analysis techniques intended to determine his future state of health[(49)].

B. – *The right to free and informed consent and other legal parameters for procedures performed on the body*

The rights to respect for life and physical integrity go hand in hand with the prohibition on any unlawful violations, which are subject to sanctions under criminal law. These also involve the right to control over one's physical integrity, and even one's life, within certain legal limits. Individual autonomy requires in principle that free and informed consent is obtained for procedures performed on the body. If the person is unable to give consent, for

with as much freedom as possible was limited by respect for the will of the victim of such practices, which was not the case on this occasion. See also the comments on this decision of G. Willems, "L'appréhension par la Cour de Strasbourg du droit de la personne et de la famille : respect des singularités nationales et commune garantie des droits de l'homme", *op. cit.*, pp. 179-108 and ECHR, 12 April 2012, *Stübing v. Germany*.

(46) M. van Overstraeten, "Le droit au respect de la vie privée et le corps humain", *op. cit.*, p. 970.

(47) Subject to those cases that can be determined by Royal Decree discussed in the Council of Ministers (art. 3, § 1, subpara. 2, and art. 5 L. of 28 January 2003 on medical examinations in the context of employment).

(48) Art. 58 L. of 4 April 2014 on insurance contract.

(49) Art. 61 *id.*

example due to his mental state, consent must be given by his representative.

In some cases, the legislator imposes specific requirements, principally with the aim of protecting the person, such as the requirement for consent to be given in writing or in the form of a written agreement, as indicated below. Although the personality rights are 'not for sale', the legislator has effectively authorised some parts of the body to be subject to a contract, as is the case with activities related to assisted reproductive technologies. It is sometimes considered that this relates "less to one-off exceptions to the principle of the 'unavailability' of personality rights than to examples of their being exercised by those who hold them"(50).

1. – *During life and end of life*

a. *Health care and palliative care*

An individual's right to autonomy is referred to in general terms for health care in the law of 22 August 2002 on patient's rights. This legislation concerns all stages of human life(51). It also confers such a right on a minor, if he is considered to have a reasonable understanding of his own interests(52); there are no age criteria for granting this autonomy or for determining the level of understanding. The doctor is also bound by medical secrecy, even with regard to the parents(53).

---

(50) Y.-H. Leleu, *Droit des personnes et des familles, op. cit.*, p. 115.

(51) See G. Schamps, "L'autonomie du patient dans le cadre des soins de santé et les interventions possibles de proches en droit belge", in *Mélanges en l'honneur de Gérard Mémeteau. Droit médical et éthique médicale : regards contemporains*, Bordeaux, Les études hospitalières, 2015, pp. 1-15; id., "L'autonomie de la personne en matière médicale : du début à la fin de la vie", in *Le temps et le droit. Hommage au Professeur Closset-Marchal*, Bruxelles, Bruylant, 2013, pp. 543-573; id., "Les missions légales des proches pour une autonomie effective du patient en fin de vie", *in* B. Feuillet-Liger (ed.), *Les proches et la fin de vie médicalisée*, Brussels, Bruylant, 2013, pp. 139-173 and the authors quoted.

(52) Art. 12, § 2, L. of 22 August 2002 on patient's rights. On this subject, see G. Schamps, "Le degré d'autonomie du mineur dans le domaine des soins médicaux en droit belge", *in* B. Feuillet-Liger and R. Ida (eds.), *Adolescent et acte médical, regards croisés. Approche internationale et pluridisciplinaire*, Brussels, Bruylant, 2011, pp. 83-141 and the authors quoted; J. Fierens and G. Mathieu, "Les droits de la personnalité des personnes mineures ou vulnérables", *in* J.-L. Renchon (ed.), *Les droits de la personnalité. Actes du Xe Colloque de l'Association "Famille & Droit", Louvain-la-Neuve, 30 November* 2007, Brussels, Bruylant, 2009, pp. 253-279; A. Nottet, "Mineurs et droits personnels", *Rev. trim. dr. fam.*, 2010, pp. 15-43; F. Reusens, "La débition de factures de soins de santé prodigués pendant la minorité de l'enfant", note under Civ. Gand, 18 February 2010, *J.J.P.*, 2011, pp. 209-216.

(53) Art. 12, § 2, L. of 22 August 2002.

The law on patient's rights sets out the rights to information and free and informed consent, which already exist under ordinary law, particularly with regard to the right to respect for life and physical integrity. The law states that the patient has the right to obtain all information that concerns him and that may be necessary to understand his state of health and its likely evolution[(54)]. Respect for the patient's autonomy means that the fact that there is no available treatment does not justify a failure to provide information. The law goes on to specify the information that must be communicated to the patient so that he can give[(55)] or withhold[(56)] consent in full knowledge of the facts. The patient may refuse consent when a medical act is suggested or during the treatment. He may also state in advance and in writing, in an advance directive, his refusal of a particular act, in case he is not in a position to express his will[(57)].

The patient's autonomy with regard to health care is broad, as a refusal given freely and clearly must be respected by the doctor or by the patient's representative, even if it represents a threat to his physical integrity or places his life in danger[(58)]. In its opinion of 22 March 2003, the National Medical Council stated that "when it is established in the eyes of the doctor treating the patient that the refusal is consistent with the patient's firm convictions, the doctor must respect this, just as he must accept that patients in a position to exercise their rights sometimes refuse treatment that

(54) Art. 7, § 1, *id.*

(55) The law on patient's rights did not specifically mention the case of the advance directive in which the patient requests a specific intervention to be taken if he is no more able to give his consent at the appropriate time. This directive may be prepared by the patient verbally or in writing. The practitioner is free to decide on the requested intervention. In the case of a refusal, he should state his reasons in the medical file.

(56) Art. 8, § 1-4, L. of 22 August 2002 on patient's rights. The patient has to be clearly informed of the consequences of a refusal; on this subject, see P. Henry and B. Decoquéau, "L'information et le consentement du patient : les nouvelles balises", *in* G. Schamps (ed.), *Évolution des droits du patient, indemnisation des dommages liés aux soins de santé : le droit médical en mouvement*, Brussels, Bruylant, Paris, LGDJ, 2008, pp. 26-82.

(57) On this subject, see M. van Overstraeten, "Une manifestation particulière du droit du patient au consentement libre et éclairé : la faculté de rédiger une déclaration anticipée", in *Évolution des droits du patient, indemnisation des dommages liés aux soins de santé : le droit médical en mouvement*, *op. cit.*, pp. 83-153; I. Lutte, "L'expression de la volonté en période de fin de vie", in *Actualité de droit familial et de droit médical. Les droits des personnes les plus faibles*, Brussels, Bruylant, 2007, pp. 58-59; E. Thiry, "La représentation du patient incapable et le rôle du médecin", in *Actualité de droit familial et de droit médical*, *op. cit.*, p. 100.

(58) M. Aelvoet, Rapport du 18 juillet 2002 fait au nom de la Commission des affaires sociales par Remans and de Roeck, *Doc. parl.*, Sén., sess. 2001-2002, n° 2-1250/3, p. 54.

could be important for their health"[59]. The Council pointed out that withdrawing or failing to implement a course of treatment is ethically permissible if it has been scientifically established that there is no further hope of a reasonable improvement, at the risk of moving into the domain of futile medical care[60].

In addition, while the patient has the right to receive palliative care, as stipulated by the law of 14 June 2002, he may also refuse it. This legislation states that the patient has the right to obtain information concerning the option of palliative care. This must be communicated in an appropriate form and in appropriate terms, in accordance with the patient's situation, wishes and capacity to understand (art. 7).

The patient also exercises his autonomy by designating a trustworthy person with a responsibility to provide assistance to the extent determined by the patient. He may also appoint a representative, in a signed agreement, who will make decisions if the patient is no longer able to do so. Drawing up an advance directive can encourage a dialogue with the doctor and his team and help plan the care to be provided in collaboration with the patient. The patient's will expressed in advance in this way must be respected by his representative, whether he is an authorised representative or a legal representative[61], and by the care provider. Under this system, even when the patient is no longer able to exercise his patient's rights, the legislator has ensured that his will has to be respected. In addition, the law states that the patient must then be involved with the exercising of his rights as far as is possible, taking account of his faculties of understanding[62].

In a more general context that goes beyond health care, and in accordance with the new regime introduced by the law of 17 March 2013, a person may also exercise his autonomy by taking measures in readiness for the eventuality of one day becoming subject to a judicial protection order concerning property or the person. He may thus file a directive in which he states his preferences regarding the administrator of the property or the person[63] appointed by

(59) Opinion of July 26, 2003, "Loi relative aux droits du patient".

(60) Opinion of 22 March 2003 "relatif aux soins palliatifs, à l'euthanasie et à d'autres décisions médicales concernant la fin de vie"; see also the Opinion of the National Medical Council of 22 September 2009, "Validité des déclarations anticipées - Soins palliatifs".

(61) Art. 14 L. of 22 August 2002.

(62) Art. 14, § 3, L. of 22 August 2002.

(63) Or a person of trust [*personne de confiance*] (art. 496 Civ. C.).

the judge. The legislator also wanted to expressly uphold the right to autonomy, as the judge issuing a judicial protection order concerning the person needs to decide what actions the person under protection is incapable of accomplishing, taking account of his personal circumstances and state of health. In the absence of any indication to the contrary, the protected person remains capable with regard to all actions concerning his person. The judge must nevertheless make an express declaration on his capacity to, among other things, choose where he wants to live, exercise his patient's rights, consent to human research or to the removal of an organ or body material during his lifetime[(64)].

More specifically, in relation to patient's rights, if the protected person has not appointed a representative[(65)] or if the representative takes no action, the patient's rights are exercised by their "administrator of the person", subject to the judge's authorisation[(66)], for as long as the protected person is not in a position to exercise his rights himself. This administrator is in this way included in the legal hierarchy of representation, after the appointed representative and before the relatives specified by law. If there is no administrator authorised to represent the patient, the patient's rights are exercised by his close relatives, in the legal prescribed order[(67)].

The legislator has, however, adopted measures protecting the patient with respect to his representative, which are contained in the law of 22 August 2002. If the professional practitioner considers that the representative's decision poses a risk to the patient's life or may cause serious harm to his health, the practitioner must not, in the interests of the patient, comply with this decision, if necessary by means of a multidisciplinary consultation[(68)]. The law nevertheless accords particular importance to the appointed representative's decision, thus respecting the autonomy of the patient who appointed the person to act as his representative. The practitioner may only overrule the appointed representative's decision if the representative is unable to demonstrate that it is consistent with the patient's express will.

(64) Art. 492, § 1, Civ. C.
(65) When he was able to do so.
(66) In accordance with art. 499/7, § 1, Civ. C.
(67) Art. 14 L. of 22 August 2002.
(68) Art. 15, § 2, L. of 22 August 2002.

The patient's right to autonomy is also associated with a right to respect for his privacy, with regard to any health care intervention by a professional practitioner, particularly in relation to information concerning the patient's health. The patient also has a right to respect for his physical privacy. Unless otherwise agreed, only those whose presence is necessary as part of health care services dispensed by a professional practitioner may be present during the care, examination or treatment. No intrusion is authorised in the exercise of this right to privacy unless it is provided for by law and is necessary for the protection of public health or for the protection of the rights and freedoms of third parties[(69)]. The professional practitioner must also ensure that the patient's privacy is respected with regard to the representative. Protective measures have therefore been established governing access by the representative to the patient's records during his lifetime or after death[(70)].

b. *The right to request euthanasia*

The autonomy of the patient can be exercised up to the very final point, as the patient has the right to request that his life is ended[(71)] if he is affected by the medical conditions stipulated by the law of 28 May 2002 on euthanasia[(72)]. The doctor must consider with the patient the therapeutic options available and those offering palliative care, together with their consequences[(73)]. As well as the legal parameters concerning the conditions and the procedure to be followed, the patient's autonomy is limited by the doctor's right to refuse to agree to the patient's request.

During preliminary discussions for the law, arguments in favour of the introduction of a right to request euthanasia referred to the right to die with dignity as an example of exercising personal

(69) Art. 10 L. of 22 August 2002.

(70) Art. 15, §§ 1 and 9, § 4, L. of 22 August 2002.

(71) On the decisions of the European Court of Human Rights concerning end-of-life situations, see F. Swennen, *op. cit.*, pp. 57- 58; N. Gallus, "Les droits de la personnalité", *op. cit.*, pp. 147-151; see also ECHR, 5 June 2015, *Lambert and others v. France*, which considered that the domestic authorities complied with their positive obligations deriving from article 2 of the Convention, given their margin of appreciation (n° 181).

(72) On this subject, see E. Delbeke, "Juridische aspecten van zorgverlening aan het levenseinde", Antwerpen, Intersentia, 2012, 1249 p.; G. Schamps, "La fin de vie - soins palliatifs et euthanasie - en droit belge. Situation actuelle et perspectives", *Rev. gén. dr. méd.*, 2013, pp. 123-150 and the authors quoted.

(73) Art. 3, § 2, L. of 28 May 2002.

autonomy. It was claimed that dignity corresponded to protection of the quality of life and that only the person concerned could determine this quality[74]. Others, on the other hand, believed that human dignity is distinct from the right to self-determination, that it has an intrinsic value independent of the quality of life, and that it is bestowed on the individual by others[75].

These opinions were again expressed during the parliamentary discussions[76] held prior to extending the right to request euthanasia to minors in 2014[77]. Minors may now request euthanasia if they have the faculty of discernment and are "in an irresolvable medical situation of constant and unbearable suffering that cannot be alleviated, leading to imminent death and resulting from a serious and incurable accidental or pathological ailment". However, the consent of the child's legal representatives is required.

2. – *The beginning of life*

Individual autonomy likewise manifests with regard to those interventions relating to reproduction or the refusal of reproduction[78].

a. *Contraception and sterilisation*

A person can therefore decide to use a method of contraception or to be sterilised without their partner's knowledge. Free and

(74) "Discussion générale, Proposition de loi relative à l'euthanasie du 9 juillet 2001, Rapport fait au nom des Commissions réunies de la Justice et des Affaires sociales par Mmes LALOY and VAN RIET", *Doc. parl.* Sén., sess. 2000-2001, n° 2-244/22, p. 194.

(75) L. CASSIERS, "Auditions, Proposition de loi relative à l'euthanasie du 9 juillet 2001", Rapport, n° 2-244/22, p. 24: "Ainsi, pour les uns, c'est la personne atteinte elle-même qui seule peut juger de sa déchéance, alors que, pour les autres, la dignité humaine vient de ce qu'elle est conférée par les autres"; see "Discussion générale, Rapport fait au nom de la Commission de la Justice par M. TH. GIET, Mmes A. VAN DE CASTEELE, A. BARZIN et J. SCHAUVLIEGE", 23 April 2002, n° 50-1488/09, *Doc. parl.,* Ch. repr., sess. 2001-2002, pp. 16 et seq.; see also Opinion n° 59 of 27 January 2014 of the Advisory Committee on Bioethics concerning the ethical aspects of the application of the law of 28 May 2002 on euthanasia.

(76) See Discussion générale, Rapport fait au nom de la Commission de la Justice par Mme S. SMEYERS, *Doc. parl.*, Ch. repr., sess. 2013-2014, n° 53-3245/004, pp. 46-47.

(77) L. of 28 February 2014 modifying L. of 28 May 2002 on euthanasia to extend euthanasia to minors; E. DELBEKE, "Euthanasie bij minderjarigen", *T. Gez./Rev. dr. santé*, 2014-2015, pp. 163-171.

(78) On this subject see G. SCHAMPS, "L'autonomie de la femme et les interventions biomédicales sur son corps en droit belge", *in* B. FEUILLET-LIGER and A. AOUIJ-MRAD (eds.), *Corps de la femme et biomédecine. Approche internationale*, Brussels, Bruylant, 2013, pp. 39-68 and the authors quoted.

informed consent is the only requirement, with the doctor being bound by professional secrecy.

With regard to female or male sterilisation[79], there is no specific legislation governing a person's decision to request such a procedure. In a judgment of 14 December 2001[80], the Court of Cassation stated that there is no legal provision requiring a husband to consent to his wife's sterilisation, even if it is irreversible and not necessary for medical reasons. The Court stated that each individual enjoys personality rights, which include the right to life and physical integrity, and that only the consent of the person concerned is required to legalise a medical act affecting that person's physical integrity[81].

b. *Abortion*

The conditional decriminalisation in 1990 of abortion, when performed by a doctor in a health care establishment, was the first significant crack in the principle of the "unavailability" of the human body. It was introduced primarily for public health reasons, in view of the serious consequences of an illegal abortion. A woman's right to self-determination and the right to have control over her body (or a "product" of the body) were also referred to: it is effectively up to her alone, as a minor or an adult, to request an abortion, provided her situation satisfies the legal requirements. The information of the partner is not required. If the pregnant female is a minor, it is neither required to inform her parents or obtain their consent[82]. In addition, this procedure is almost entirely funded by health care insurance.

(79) On the issue of the sterilisation of mentally ill persons and case law, see in particular N. Colette-Basecqz, "Quelques réflexions autour des conditions légales qui encadrent la stérilisation médicale", *T. Gez./Rev. dr. santé*, 2006-2007, pp. 2-10; Opinion n° 8 of 14 September 1998 of the Advisory Committee on Bioethics on the issue of the sterilisation of mentally ill persons.

(80) Cass., 14 december 2011, *TBBR/RGDC*, 2002, p. 328, note C. Trouet, "De bewijslast van de geïnformeerde toestemming tot een medische ingreep"; J.-L. Fagnart, "Stérilisation et consentement éclairé", *T. Gez./Rev. dr. santé*, 2001-2002, pp. 242-245; Y.-H. Leleu and G. Genicot, "Autonomie corporelle de la personne et responsabilité médicale", *JLMBi*, 2002/13, p. 537.

(81) When a person is subject to a protection order, consent to sterilisation may not involve the assistance or representation of the administrator (art. 497 § 2 Civ. C.).

(82) This provision was introduced by the law of 3 April 1990. In a decision of 19 December 1991, the Court of Arbitration found that the principle of equality does not require a female minor planning an abortion to be obliged, subject to the risk of committing an offence, to consult her parents, and it gives the parents no recourse to the courts (C. Arb., 19 December 1991, judgment n° 39/91, n° 6.B.1.8.).

This means that no offence is committed, under the terms of article 350 of the Criminal Code[83], when a pregnant woman in distress requests an abortion, and this takes place before the end of the twelfth week of pregnancy. An abortion may nevertheless be performed after this period if continuing the pregnancy constitutes a serious risk to the woman's health, or if it is certain that the unborn child is suffering from a serious condition recognised as being incurable at the time of diagnosis. In this case, the opinion of a second doctor must be attached to the file.

The autonomy of the pregnant woman is far-reaching. While the doctor she has approached must be convinced of her determination to have this procedure, there is a complete discretion in assessing this determination and the level of distress.

c. *Assisted reproductive technologies*

An individual's autonomy with regard to the body or body parts of it – whether this relates to those wishing to become parents or to a person donating surplus gametes or embryos – is broad when it comes to activities concerning assisted reproductive technologies. The legislator also assigns importance to the fertility clinic, which has a duty to ensure that the legal conditions are complied with and benefits from a conscience clause allowing it to refuse to agree to a request on account of its ethical views, even if the legal requirements have been satisfied. No judicial body is involved in the process. The law of 6 July 2007[84] governing activities related to assisted reproductive technologies (ART) reflects previous practice.

(83) A doctor was convicted of failing to comply with the legal conditions, specifically the requirement for the free and informed consent of the pregnant woman, who was involved in prostitution. See Corr. Antwerpen, 23 February 2011, *T. Gez./Rev. dr. santé*, 2012-2013, p. 128; Antwerpen, 13 January 2012, *T. Gez./Rev. dr. santé*, 2012-2013, p. 132; Cass., 5 June 2012, *T. Gez./Rev. dr. santé*, 2012-2013, p. 141; Th. Vansweevelt, "Zwangerschapsafbreking onder morele dwang", *T. Gez./Rev. dr. santé*, 2012-2013, pp. 136-140.

(84) The law of 6 July 2007 concerning activities related to assisted reproductive technologies and the use of surplus embryos and gametes; on this subject, see G. Schamps and M.-N. Derèse, "L'anonymat et la procréation médicalement assistée en droit belge. Des pratiques à la loi du 6 juillet 2007", *in* B. Feuillet (ed.), *Procréation assistée et Anonymat. Panorama international*, Brussels, Bruylant, 2008, pp. 125-152; M.-N. Derèse and G. Willems, "La loi du 6 juillet 2007 relative à la procréation médicalement assistée et à la destination des embryons surnuméraires et des gametes", *Rev. trim. dr. fam.*, 2008/2, pp. 279-359; C. Herbrand, "La loi sur la procréation médicalement assistée en Belgique : reflet de la diversité familiale ?", *in* N. Gallus (ed.), *Droit des familles, genre et sexualité*, Limal, Anthemis, 2012, pp. 321-338.

For example, the legislator has not imposed any conditions related to the stability of a couple planning parenthood. The freedom of an adult woman is extensive as she may have access to assisted reproductive technologies whether she is single, married or in a partnership, heterosexual or homosexual. She may also receive a sperm or embryo donation, and surrogacy is not prohibited in Belgium.

As well as the legal stipulations concerning, in particular, the woman's age[(85)], the legislator's concern to protect the individual is manifested by an element of formality: the need to conclude a written agreement between the clinic and the prospective parents, or even between the clinic and the donor(s) of the gametes or embryos. Honest and comprehensive information must be provided in advance by the clinic, as well as psychological support for the people involved, before and during the assisted reproductive technology procedure.

The removal of gametes, surplus embryos, gonads or fragments of gonads for cryopreservation may be carried out on a minor if medically indicated. The minor, however, has no autonomy with regard to the conclusion of an agreement with the fertility clinic. The agreement must be signed by the clinic and the parents with parental authority or, if appropriate, the guardian[(86)].

Autonomy also applies with regard to the use of preimplantation genetic diagnosis (PGD), through the conclusion of a written agreement with the fertility clinic. PGD is not subject to any special conditions. It is not, however, permitted[(87)] to perform a PGD for eugenic purposes[(88)] or for gender selection, unless this is for the purpose of removing embryos afflicted by a gender-related illness[(89)]. A GDP may exceptionally be authorised for the purpose of treating a couple's sick child[(90)].

(85) Adult females aged under 45 may request the removal of gametes, the implantation of embryos or the insemination of gametes. The implantation of embryos or the insemination of gametes may not be performed on a woman aged over 47 (art. 4, subpara. 1 to 3, L. of 6 July 2007). There are no age limits imposed on male partners.

(86) Art. 4, subpara. 4, and art. 42, subpara. 3, L. of 6 July 2007.

(87) Art. 67 L. of 6 July 2007.

(88) In other words, focused on the selection or amplification of non-pathological genetic characteristics of the human race, within the meaning of article 5paragraph 4, of the law of 11 May 2003 on *in vitro* research on embryos.

(89) See also art. 5, § 5, L. of 11 May 2003.

(90) Art. 68 L. of 6 July 2007. The fertility clinic must, however, be of the opinion that the procedure does not have this concern as its sole aim. This opinion must be confirmed by the human genetics centre consulted, whose opinion will be attached to the file.

The autonomy of those who request an ART procedure is extensive as it is they who determine, in the agreement concluded with the fertility clinic, the fate of surplus embryos and gametes: the cryopreservation of surplus embryos or gametes for a future pregnancy, their destruction, their use in a research protocol or their allocation to a donation programme(91).

If surplus embryos are cryopreserved, the agreement must stipulate their use in the event of one of the following situations arising: separation, divorce, the permanent loss of the decision-making capacity of one of the intended parents, an irresolvable difference of opinion between them, the death of one of them, and the expiry of the preservation period(92). As for cryopreserved surplus gametes, the agreement must indicate what happens to them in the event of the permanent loss of the decision-making capacity or death of the person who requested the cryopreservation, or on expiry of the preservation period(93). Accordingly, if this is provided for in the agreement, a separated or divorced woman may, as appropriate,(94) give birth to a child as a result of the implantation of an embryo or of the insemination of the cryopreserved gametes(95) of her former partner.

Nevertheless, the autonomy of the prospective parents remains limited, in that they may not determine the parentage of the unborn child, something that remains within the jurisdiction of the legislator. It is, however, regrettable that the legislator has not

(91) Art. 10, 13, 20, 30, 37, 40, 42, 49 and 59 L. of 6 July 2007.

(92) Art. 13 *id.*

(93) Art. 42 *id.*

(94) However, the question arises of the consequences of a subsequent disagreement between the couple and of the reconciliation of articles 12 and 14 of the law of 6 July 2007. According to article 12, subpara. 2, the fertility clinic must ensure the effective consent of both potential parents to the implantation of the cryopreserved surplus embryos. Article 14, subpara. states that in the event of a disagreement between the prospective parents, after the agreement has been signed, concerning the use of the surplus embryos, the fertility clinic will take account of the most recent instruction mutually agreed by the couple; M.-N. Derèse and G. Willems, *op. cit.*, pp. 315-316, n° 52 and the preparatory works quoted ; see also, ECHR, 10 April 2007, *Evans v. United Kingdom* and the developments of N. Gallus, (*Bioéthique et droit,* Limal, Anthemis, 2013, pp. 73 et seq.; "Les droits de la personnalité", *op. cit.*, pp. 172-177) on this decision, and on ECHR, 4 December 2007, *Dickson v. United Kingdom* and ECHR, 28 August 2012, *Costa and Pavan v. Italy*.

(95) According to article 41, subpara. 2, of the law of 6 July 2007, in the event of a request for the insemination of gametes cryopreserved at the request of a couple now planning a subsequent pregnancy, the fertility clinic consulted must ensure, prior to any medical procedure, that the couple have consented fully to the new insemination.

adopted a legislative regime specifically for establishing parentage when the child is born as a result of an ART[(96)].

With regard to prenatal examinations or genetic tests during the person's lifetime, they are not subject to any specific legislation and are covered by the notion of health care within the meaning of the law of 22 August 2002 on patient's rights and the right of the free and informed consent of the patient.

d. *The freezing of eggs in anticipation of age-related infertility*

In 2013, the Advisory Committee on Bioethics gave an opinion on the ethical aspects of freezing eggs in anticipation of age-related infertility, with a view to a different autologous use[(97)]. The opinion states that none of the members considered this practice to be unacceptable in ethical terms. Some members emphasise the fact that this is a matter of the woman's right to make a choice in complete autonomy and without pressure. Others believe that it is an example of the excessive medicalisation of a natural process or of the use of medicine for the purpose of resolving a social problem which could be solved by other means, encouraging women to have children at a younger age.

Two orientations have emerged within the Committee with regard to the social security reimbursement of the costs of egg freezing. Some members believe that the freezing of eggs for social reasons should not be reimbursed. Others are of the opinion that there should be no distinction between medical and social indications, and would like an identical reimbursement to be made in both cases, while taking account of the "efficacy, effectiveness and efficiency" factors. The members consider that reimbursement of a removal beyond the age of 40 is very hard to justify from a social point of view.

(96) G. Schamps, "Les incidences de la biomédecine sur la parenté : le hiatus entre les actes liés à la procréation médicalement assistée et l'établissement de la filiation en droit belge", *in* M.-C. Crespo-Brauner and B. Feuillet-Liger (eds.), *Les incidences de la biomédecine sur la parenté. Approche internationale,* Brussels, Bruylant, 2014, pp. 55-82 and the authors quoted; see the law of 5 May 2014 on establishing parentage in shared parenting cases, which in particular establishes the presumption of co-maternity for the female spouse of the woman who gives birth (art. 325, § 2, Civ. C.); J.-E. Beernaert and N. Massager, "La loi du 5 mai 2014 instaurant le régime de la comaternité : Trois femmes, un homme et un couffin", *Act. dr. fam.*, 2015, liv. 4, pp. 74-84.

(97) Opinion n° 57 of 16 December 2013 on the ethical aspects of the freezing of eggs in anticipation of age-related infertility, pp. 32-34.

The Committee members also emphasise the need to carry out information campaigns to highlight the decline in fertility in line with the age of the woman, the possibilities and limitations related to IVF and the possibility of vitrifying eggs to reduce the risk of age-related infertility caused by delaying pregnancy for an extended period. Finally, they consider it necessary to introduce suitable social measures for both men and women to reduce the obstacles to carrying out parental projects at the time the intended parents decide to do so.

e. *Surrogacy*

Surrogacy is practised in Belgium, although it is not governed by any specific regulations[98]. It is not prohibited, provided that the activities related to assisted reproductive technologies comply with the aforementioned law of 6 July 2007.

On the other hand, surrogacy agreements are generally deemed to be void, on the basis of the "unavailability" of the human body and civil status[99]: the cause or the object of such a contract – essentially, to conceive the child and then hand it over to the intended parents – is often deemed to be unlawful, as it concerns the female body and the intimate function of carrying a child, as well as the child's parentage.

However, Y.-H. Leleu considers that a surrogacy agreement is valid, on the grounds that there is no legal rule making it null and void, if the subject of the agreement is the body of the surrogate mother, over which she has control, and if it makes no provision for payment, for arrangements for monitoring the pregnancy that are prejudicial to the dignity of the pregnant woman, or for the handover and status of the child. According to him, the legal modalities of such an agreement are likely to be executed: specific performance if the execution does not impinge upon the surrogate

(98) See the articles in G. Schamps and J. Sosson (eds.), *La gestation pour autrui : vers un encadrement ?*, Brussels, Bruylant, 2013, p. 458.

(99) N. Gallus, "La validité de la convention de gestation pour autrui en droit belge actuel", in *La gestation pour autrui : vers un encadrement ?*, *op. cit.*, pp. 182; for a different view, see G. Genicot, "Gestation pour autrui, autonomie personnelle et maîtrise corporelle. Plaidoyer pour un droit neutre et libéré", in *La gestation pour autrui : vers un encadrement ?*, *op. cit.*, p. 156.

mother's physical integrity or, if it does, by the payment of damages corresponding to any material or moral damage[100].

In Opinion n° 30 of 5 July 2004 on surrogacy, the Advisory Committee on Bioethics considered that surrogacy was ethically acceptable in principle, but that it should be managed with particular care. Among its recommendations, the Committee stated that it should be subject to strict medical conditions (lack of a uterus, strict contraindications to pregnancy and uterine infertility)[101]. Some members felt that the conclusion of an agreement should be permitted between those persons involved who are not in contact with each other. Others were opposed to this, fearing it would result in a move toward the commercialisation and commodification of those less advantaged. The positions of the Committee members varied between prohibiting and authorising such commercialisation[102].

Furthermore, a distinction is made in Belgian case law between the unlawful nature of the contract and establishing the parentage of a child born in this way in Belgium or abroad. The determination of parentage is based on the rules contained in the Civil Code and the provisions of the law of 6 July 2007, according to which the donors, the recipients of the child and the child itself have no legal recourse with regard to the parentage or its property consequences[103].

A large number of draft laws have been submitted to authorise, subject to certain conditions, and oversee the practice of surrogacy. Several of them are being reviewed by a parliamentary commission[104]. Some have the agreement as a central element of

(100) Y.-H. Leleu, *Droit des personnes et des familles*, *op. cit.*, pp. 143 and 144. According to G. Genicot, there should be no opportunity for the surrogate mother to make a profit, although a reasonable compensation payment should be allowed, as well as a remuneration of her expenses by the social security department and/or the prospective parents ("Gestation pour autrui, autonomie personnelle et maîtrise corporelle. Plaidoyer pour un droit neutre et libéré", *op. cit.*, p. 178).

(101) Opinion of 5 July 2004 on surrogacy, pp. 4, 23, 24, 34 and 35.

(102) For an analysis of the choice of using a contract and the "non-payment" nature of surrogacy, with regard to draft laws and comparative law, see G. Schamps and G. Willems, *op. cit.*, pp. 325-374.

(103) Art. 27 and 56 L. of 6 July 2007.

(104) Some draft laws include the text of previous drafts, see Draft law of 10 September 2014 supporting the Criminal Code with provisions relating to the commercialisation of the surrogacy arrangement and mediation for that purpose, *Doc. parl.*, Ch. repr., sess. 2014, n° 54-0242; Draft law of 7 October 2014 modifying the Criminal Code with regard to surrogacy for financial gain, *Doc. parl.*, Ch. repr, sess. 2014, n° 54-0423; Draft law of 7 October 2014 on

the proposed system. They contain provisions relating to conditions of access to surrogacy, to the modalities of the agreement with regard to fundamental rights, to establishing the unborn child's parentage and to possible relationships with the surrogate.

If the legislator were to introduce a legal framework for a surrogacy agreement, this decision would constitute an additional element in the withdrawal of the "unavailability" of the human body.

f. *Refusal of care by a pregnant woman*

The autonomy of the individual is also far-reaching, given that, in accordance with her right to free and informed consent, a pregnant woman has the right to refuse health care, even if this care is necessary to preserve the health or life of the foetus. The foetus is not a person under Belgian law. In criminal terms, the foetus is only considered to be a person when it is in the process of being born[105]. In civil law, on the other hand, a child only becomes a person when it has been born alive and viable.

In 2012, the Belgian Advisory Committee on Bioethics gave an opinion on the question of the pertinence of introducing an exception to the right of the pregnant woman to refuse care[106].

3. – *Changes made to the human body*

a. *Medical acts or cosmetic surgery, tattoos and piercings*

As a result of abuses in cosmetic surgery, sometimes performed illegally, the legislator introduced legislation concerning the qualifications required to perform non-surgical aesthetic medicine and cosmetic surgery[107]. Developed with the assistance of industry professionals, the law of 23 May 2013 introduced provisions relating to the competence of the practitioners and the protection of patients. It also includes specific provisions on the information

the organisation of surrogacy, *Doc. parl.*, Ch. repr, sess. 2014, n° 54-0425. For a comparative analysis of previous draft laws, see the contributions to *La gestation pour autrui : vers un encadrement ?*, *op. cit.*, pp. 287-450.

(105) Cass., 11 February 1987, *R.D.P.C.*, 1987, p. 812.

(106) Opinion n° 53 of 14 May 2012 on the refusal of medical care by a pregnant woman impacting on the foetus; see the conclusions and recommendations on pages 38 and 39 of this Opinion.

(107) L. of 23 May 2013 on the qualifications required to perform non-surgical cosmetic procedures and cosmetic surgery.

and consent of the patient and stipulates a cooling-off period of at least fifteen days between the signing of the information report and the proposed procedure.

The law also establishes a special regime for the protection of minors. It departs from the autonomy accorded to minors for health care by the law of 22 August 2002, if they are considered capable of having a reasonable understanding of their own interests. Cosmetic procedures or surgery may therefore only be performed on a minor with the written consent of their legal representative(s). Such procedures must also be the subject of a prior consultation between the minor, the legal representative(s) and a doctor specialising in psychiatry or a psychologist(108).

As regards tattoos and piercings, there is also legislation designed to protect the individual by, among other things, imposing the requirement to provide clear information about the effects, risks and hygiene conditions in which they must be carried out. Consent must be given in writing. The professional has an obligation to ensure that the customer is "mentally (particularly in terms of maturity) and physically capable of undergoing the procedure", and if this is not the case, he may not carry it out. The customer must be allowed a cooling-off period before the procedure is performed, with the option of returning later. Pregnant women "are requested" to consult a doctor in advance. Anyone who has undergone such a procedure must declare it when donating blood(109).

b. *Gender reassignment surgery*

When a person's body has undergone a sex change, a simple administrative procedure is all that is required to establish a record by the Civil Registrar of their new gender following gender reassignment surgery. This record does not affect the existing parentage relationships or the ensuing rights, powers and obligations.

Thus, any Belgian or foreign national entered in the population registers who has the permanent and irreversible inner conviction

(108) Art. 17 L. of 23 May 2013.

(109) Art. 6 to 8 Royal Decree of 25 November 2005 on tattoos and piercings; F. BOUCHAT, "Enfin une réglementation pour les piercings et les tatouages ! Oui mais... et les mineurs d'âge ?", *JDJ*, February 2006, n° 252, p. 29.

of belonging to the opposite sex to that stated in the birth certificate and whose body has been changed to this opposite sex may, to the extent that it is possible and justified from a medical perspective, declare this conviction to the civil registrar. This option is also open to a transsexual unemancipated minor, provided it is done in the presence of the minor's mother, father or legal representative(110).

Although the autonomy of the individual makes it possible to obtain a change in the civil status record without having to seek the authorisation of the courts, there are some who denounce the fact that it is necessary to have undergone surgery before being able to obtain a certificate containing a reference to the new gender.

4. – *Procedures allowed for altruistic purposes*

While encouraging people to exercise their autonomy over their bodies or parts of their bodies, the legislator has ensured that there are provisions in place to protect the individual.

a. *Donation of surplus embryos or gametes for research*

As well as donations for a parental project by third parties, as referred to above, the autonomy of the individual over elements of the body also makes it possible to donate surplus embryos or gametes for research, subject to the terms of the law of 11 May 2003(111). Egg stimulation, for example, is allowed, provided the woman is an adult, has given her consent in writing, and the stimulation is scientifically justified(112). The creation of embryos *in vitro* for research purposes is in principle prohibited. It is nevertheless allowed if the goal of the research project cannot be achieved by research on surplus embryos(113). This exception does not appear in the Convention on Human Rights and Biomedicine(114), which Belgium has not signed.

---

(110) See art. 62 *bis*, § 1, subpara. 1 and 2, Civ. C., introduced by art. 2 L. of 10 May 2007 on transsexualism. On this subject, see S. Cap, "La loi du 10 mai 2007 relative à la transsexualité", *Rev. trim. dr. fam.*, 2009/1, pp. 79-80; G. Hiernaux, "Approche de la transsexualité en droit belge", in *Droit des familles, genre et sexualité, op. cit.*, pp. 35-62.

(111) Art. 3 L.of 11 May 2003 on research on embryos *in vitro*.

(112) Art. 4, § 2, L. of 11 May 2003.

(113) Art. 4, § 1, L. of 11 May 2003.

(114) Art. 18 Convent.

Human reproductive cloning is prohibited[115]. The same applies to research or treatment for eugenic purposes or for gender selection, unless this is in order to remove embryos suffering from a gender-related illness[116].

b. *Taking part in research*

The autonomy of the individual also means the ability to decide to take part in research, a concept much broader than that of the clinical trials referred to in Directive 2001/20/EC[117]. The law of 7 May 2004 contains provisions for the protection of the participant, particularly if he is incapable[118]. In the future, it will also be necessary to take account of the European Union Regulation of 16 April 2014 concerning clinical trials, which will not, however, take effect until 28 May 2016[119].

The protective legal provisions apply to any individual participating in research, whether they are part of the experimental group or the control group[120]. An initial measure covers compliance with good clinical practice. In addition, an experiment may only be undertaken or continued if a number of conditions have been met, concerning in particular the scientific justification for the experiment and the requirement for the free and informed consent of the participant or his representative[121].

The information to be provided – in advance, in writing, and in a clear and comprehensible manner – must include at least the nature, scope, goals, consequences, anticipated benefits and risks

(115) Art. 6 L. of 11 May 2003.

(116) Art. 5, §§ 4 and 5, L. of 11 May 2003.

(117) Directive 2001/20/EC of 4 April 2001 of the European Parliament and of the Council on the approximation of the laws, regulations and administrative provisions of the Member States relating to implementation of good clinical practice in the conduct of clinical trials on medicinal products for human use.

(118) L. of 7 May 2004 on human research. For more developments, see G. Schamps, "Les réglementations belge et européenne relatives aux expérimentations sur la personne humaine et les mesures de protection des personnes vulnérables : les mineurs, les majeurs incapables et les personnes en situation d'urgence", *in* M.-L. Delfosse, M.-H. Parizeau and J.-P. Amann (eds.), *La recherche clinique avec les enfants : à la croisée de l'éthique et du droit. Belgique, France, Québec*, Québec, Presses de l'Université Laval, Louvain-la-Neuve, Anthémis, 2009, pp. 159-221.

(119) Regulation (EU) n° 536/2014 of the European Parliament and of the Council of 16 April 2014 on clinical trials on medicinal products for human use and repealing Directive 2001/20/EC.

(120) Art. 2, § 20, L. of 7 May 2004.

(121) Art. 4, 5 and 6 L. of 7 May 2004.

of the experiment, and the circumstances in which it will take place, as well as identifying and stating the opinion of the relevant ethics committee. The individual must also be informed of his right to be able, at any time, to revoke his consent or withdraw from the experiment, without incurring any prejudice or loss as a result.

The law also includes protective measures that are specific to minors, which consist in particular of requirements concerning the validation of previous data, the direct benefits and an understanding of the risks incurred within the framework of the experiment. The free and informed consent of the legal representative must also be obtained[122].

The influence of the legislation concerning patient's rights is nevertheless apparent, in that the law of 7 May 2004 states that the minor must be involved in exercising the right of informed consent, taking account of his age and level of maturity. The express will of the minor may even be considered to be essential in Belgian law, as they must be examined and respected by the clinical researcher, provided that the minor is capable of forming an opinion and evaluating the information relating to his participation in an experiment, his refusal to take part in it or his wish to withdraw. Furthermore, the consent of the minor's representative must express the presumed will of the minor. The directive sets out however the express wishes of the minor.

In an opinion dated 5 July 2004, the Belgian Advisory Committee on Bioethics issued recommendations for the protection of pregnant and breastfeeding women and of the unborn child. These recommendations concern, in particular, the potential direct benefit for the woman and child, the quality of the consent, particularly when the woman is from a disadvantaged background, and the importance, in the eyes of the Committee, of concertation with the father or partner[123].

(122) Art. 7 L. of 7 May 2004; see also art. 8 *id.*, on the protection of adults incapable of giving their consent to participation in research.

(123) Opinion n° 31 of 5 July 2004 on experiments involving pregnant and breastfeeding women.

c. *Donations of blood, organs or human body material by a living person*

i. *Blood donations*

Only an adult donor can consent to the taking of a sample of blood or blood derivatives. Nevertheless, in a case of extreme medical necessity, a sample may also be taken from a person under 18 years of age, with the written and signed consent of the parents (or legal representative) and if authorised by a doctor of the establishment where the sample is taken.

In addition, if the minor is capable of giving consent or expressing an opinion, the doctor is required to obtain it[(124)].

ii. *Organ donations*

An individual may also exercise his autonomy by donating, during his lifetime, an organ for transplant to another person. This does not require the authorisation of the courts. As well as the requirements concerning, in particular, quality and safety control, the traceability of organs and the reporting of incidents, the law of 13 June 1986 contains a number of provisions for the protection of the donor[(125)].

Any removal from a living person must consequently be the subject of a prior multidisciplinary consultation between the doctors and the other health care providers, with the exception of those treating the recipient or those performing the removal or transplant. They must make an independent assessment of the potential donor, particularly with regard to his capacity to consent to the removal of an organ[(126)].

In theory, only an adult may give his free and informed consent to the removal of an organ[(127)]. The doctor planning to perform such a removal is required to provide the donor with clear and comprehensive information about the physical, psychological, family and social consequences of the removal. He must confirm that the donor has made his decision exercising responsible

(124) Art. 5 and 9 L. of 5 July 1994 on blood and blood derivatives of human origin.
(125) See G. Schamps, "Le don d'organes ou de matériel corporel humain en droit belge", *Rev. gén. dr. méd.*, 2015, pp. 97-110 and the authors quoted.
(126) Art. 8 *bis* L. of 13 June 1986.
(127) Art. 5 and 8 *id.*

judgment and for unquestionably altruistic reasons(128). The revocable consent must be given in writing in the presence of an adult witness; the document must be dated and signed by the donor and the witness(129).

In addition, if the removal can have serious consequences for the donor or if it concerns non-regenerative organs, it may only be carried out if the life of the recipient is in danger and an organ transplant from a deceased person cannot produce an equally satisfactory result(130). For example, a relationship by blood or marriage between the donor and the recipient is not required.

Until a few years ago, if the donor was under 21 years of age, the removal was also dependent on the consent of the person(s) who would be required to consent to the marriage of a minor. If the donor was married, the spouse living with him or her was also required to give consent. These requirements were repealed by the law of 25 February 2007(131), which thus strengthened the autonomy of the donor, with the particular intention of increasing the number of donors.

A minor may also make an organ donation during his lifetime. However, this is only permitted if the removal would not normally have serious consequences for the minor and concerned regenerative organs. A new legal wording, introduced in 2001(132), states that these conditions are cumulative, in addition to the requirement originally included that the removal must be intended for transplant to a brother or sister. However, the age of consent for a minor – who alone may give consent – has been lowered from 15 to 12. The requirement to obtain the child's consent falls within the context of the autonomy of the minor, which is contained in broad terms within the framework of health care in the law of 22 August 2002 on patient's rights. In addition, the prohibition

(128) Art. 9 *id.* He must also ensure that the conditions of articles 5 to 8 of the law of 13 June 1986 have been satisfied.

(129) Art. 8 *id.*

(130) Art. 6, §1, *id.*

(131) L. of 25 February 2007 modifying L. of 13 June 1986 on the removal and transplantation of organs, which came into force on 23 April 2007.

(132) Art. 7, § 1, L. of 13 June 1986; L. of 7 December 2001 modifying art. 7 L. of 13 June 1986 on the removal and transplantation of organs.

on performing a removal on a child under 12 years of age was introduced by the law of 3 July 2012[133].

Furthermore, this same legislation, adopted when the directive of 7 July 2010[134] was transposed into Belgian law, removed the possibility of performing organ removal on a living person aged over 18 who is not capable of expressing his will.

The removal of organs from an incapable living person was not originally specifically covered by the law of 13 June 1986. With the need to encourage organ donations in mind, the legislator authorised it in the law of 25 February 2007, on the simple basis that this was a legislative loophole[135]. At that time, this extension of the law attracted little attention. It seems, however, that such a removal from an incapable person has never been carried out in Belgium. Voices were subsequently raised to denounce this possibility, emphasising that the legal protection for the removal of organs from such a person was more restricted than that provided to minors and for that covering the removal of human tissue. It was also pointed out that it was less extensive than that included in some international legal instruments[136].

In 2011, at the request of the Ministry of Public Health, the Advisory Committee on Bioethics also gave an opinion on the removal of organs from a living adult incapable of expressing his will due to his lack of mental capacity[137]. It rejected on ethical grounds the regulations existing at the time, considering that such a removal exposed an incapable donor to serious health risks. Some members of the Committee also supported the opinion according to which the only ethically acceptable position was a total and unconditional prohibition of removals on living persons who were incapable of expressing their will. They made the point

(133) Art. 7, § 2 L. of 13 June1986; L. of 3 July 2012 modifying L. of 13 June 1986 on the removal and transplantation of organs, and L. of 19 December 2008 on the procurement and use of human body material intended for human medical applications or scientific research.

(134) Directive 2010/53/EU of 7 July 2010 of the European Parliament and of the Council on standards of quality and safety for human organs intended for transplantation.

(135) Projet de loi modifiant la loi du 13 juin 1986 sur le prélèvement et la transplantation d'organes, Exposé des motifs, *Doc. parl.*, Ch. repr., sess. ord. 2005-2006, n° 51-2680/001, pp. 3 and 6.

(136) On this subject, see G. SCHAMPS and A.-C. SQUIFFLET, "Le prélèvement d'organes sur des donneurs vivants majeurs, incapables de manifester leur volonté en raison de leur état mental : quelles perspectives ?", *TBBR/RGDC*, 2011, pp. 318-331.

(137) Opinion n° 50 of 9 May 2011 concerning certain ethical aspects of the changes made by the law of 25 February 2007 to the law of 13 June 1986 on the removal and transplantation of organs, p. 104.

that the capacity to express one's will and the consent of the donor were essential conditions that must be met for such a removal to proceed. The legislator was of the same opinion, repealing in 2012 the possibility of a removal from a person incapable of expressing his will.

iii. *Donations of human body material*

An individual can also exercise his autonomy by donating human body material, for allogeneic purposes and for scientific research, in accordance with the law of 19 December 2008[(138)]. Organ donation for scientific purposes is also covered by this legislation. The requirements relating to the information that must be provided are extensive and the consent must normally be given formally in writing.

Thus, the removal of body material from a living person can in theory only be carried out on an adult donor, provided that his free and informed consent has been given in advance[(139)]. In addition, the donor has the right to be systematically informed of the purposes for which the body material will be preserved, and his prior consent to this use and purpose must be obtained. This consent may be withdrawn at any time, before the material has been used for the first time following its procurement[(140)].

For the protection of the donor, the law lays down the following conditions in particular: when the removal can have serious consequences for a living donor or when it concerns non-regenerative body material, it may only be carried out if the recipient's life is in danger or if the expected benefit to his health makes this risk acceptable, and a removal from a deceased person cannot produce an equally satisfactory result. The removal of human body material is prohibited if the expected consequences for the living donor are not proportionate to the aim pursued[(141)].

A minor may also give consent to a donation of human body material during his lifetime, provided that the removal would not normally have serious consequences for him and is related to regenerative cells and materials. Such a removal can also be carried

(138) L. of 19 December 2008 on the procurement and use of human body material destined for human medical applications or for scientific research purposes.

(139) Art. 10, § 1, L. of 19 December 2008.

(140) Art. 10, § 5, *id.*

(141) Art. 8, § 1 and art. 10, § 2, *id.*

out on an incapable adult[142] In this case, the representative must give his informed consent[143]. The individual must therefore be involved in the decision-making process[144].

The legislator has not imposed an age condition for the removal of human body material. The law of 19 December 2008 refers to the provisions of article 12 of the law of 22 August 2002 on patient's rights: if the minor is considered to be capable of reasonably assessing his best interests, he may exercise his rights autonomously[145]. If this is not the case, the parents or, if appropriate, the guardian have the authority to decide. The minor must always be involved in exercising his rights, in line with his age and maturity.

In the case of a secondary use of the human body material, *i.e.* any use other than that for which the donor or his representative gave their consent for the removal[146], it is the manager responsible for the human body material, not the doctor who carried out the removal, who must obtain the written, explicit, free and informed consent of the donor[147]. However, the legislator allows this requirement to be waived if it is impossible to request consent or if this request would, exceptionally, be inappropriate. In such cases, the ethics committee must have issued a positive opinion[148].

However, the consent required becomes 'opt-out' for residual human body material[149] used for scientific research. In this case, consent is considered to have been given, provided that the donor or a competent person providing it has not communicated, prior to any use of the residual human body material, his refusal to the

(142) This concerns an adult declared unable to exercise these rights under the terms of article 492/1, § 1, subpara. 3, 19, of the Civil Code, or who is unable to express his will to exercise his rights, within the meaning of article 14 of the law of 22 August 2002 on patient's rights.

(143) Art. 10, § 3, subpara. 1, L. of 19 December 2008.

(144) Art. 10 § 3, subpara. 2, *id.*. This provision refers to articles 12 and 14 of the law of 22 August 2002 on patient's rights.

(145) Art. 10 § 3, subpara. 2, L. of 19 December 2008.

(146) Art. 2, 30 and art. 20 et seq. *id.*.

(147) The provisions of article 10, paragraph 5, of the law of 19 December 2008 must be complied with.

(148) Art. 20, § 1, L. of 19 December 2008.

(149) Residual human body material is "that part of the body material removed to form a diagnosis or treatment of the donor, which, after an adequate and pertinent part has been preserved to establish, perfect or complete the diagnosis or treatment of the donor on the basis of new scientific data, is redundant with regard to these objectives and which may now be destroyed" (art. 2, 33, L. of 19 December 2008).

doctor performing the removal or the senior doctor of the hospital where the removal took place. The intended use of the material and the possibility for the donor or representative to refuse their consent are notified in advance in writing[(150)].

If, during a procedure carried out on the human body material or while it is being used, analyses produce information with significant consequences for the donor's health, the donor has the right to be provided with this information[(151)].

C. – *Anonymity and non-payment*

1. – *Anonymity*

a. *Secrecy with regard to conception and assisted reproductive technologies*

Maintaining or lifting anonymity, within the framework of assisted reproductive technologies (ART), involves a conflict of differing, and sometimes conflicting, interests: in particular, the interest of the child to know its origins[(152)], that of the donor with regard to privacy, that of the recipient parents benefiting from a donation, or to preserve their autonomy in raising their children, etc.

The issue of secrecy with regard to the method of conception consists in particular of considering the best time to inform the child that it was conceived through ART. The Belgian Advisory Committee on Bioethics examined this question in two opinions issued in 2004[(153)]. This was also the case with the Council of State, in the opinion it gave as part of the development of the law of 6 July 2007[(154)]. The legislator chose not to regulate this aspect. However, he regulated the issue of donor anonymity in the aforementioned law of 6 July 2007.

(150) Art. 20, § 2, *id.*

(151) Art. 11 *id.*, which provides for the application of articles 7, §§ 2 to 4 of the law of 22 August 2002 on patients' rights.

(152) On this subject, see G. Mathieu, *Le secret des origines en droit de la filiation*, Waterloo, Kluwer, 2014, p. 581.

(153) Opinion n° 27 of 8 March 2004 concerning sperm and egg donations, pp. 21-22; Opinion n° 29 of 21 June 2004 concerning embryo donations, p. 8.

(154) Opinion of the Council of State, 14 February 2006, *Doc. parl.,* Ch. repr., sess. 2005-2006, n° 3-417/3, pp. 40 et seq., n°s 54 et seq.

In this way, he imposed anonymity without exception with regard to the identity of donors in the case of surplus embryo donations. In the case of gametes donations, they must be anonymous in principle, unless the donor and the recipient(s) agree to lift the anonymity(155). This option corresponds to the previous practice of the fertility clinics and reflects the concern of the Belgian legislator to take account of the scarcity of egg donations. As indicated above, the legislator ruled out the possibility of legal action concerning the parentage relationship between the donor and the child born as a result of the donation. Anonymous childbirth is not permitted in Belgian law.

During the parliamentary debates, it was also proposed to authorise the non-anonymous donation of surplus embryos, provided that this was agreed between the donors and the recipients(156). However, this suggestion was rejected on account of the risk of making the donation of surplus embryos the subject of financial and other agreements.

With regard to information about other data, the fertility clinic must gather medical information concerning donors that is likely to have a significant bearing on the healthy development of the child(157). This information can be communicated to the receiving mother or couple requesting it when the time comes for them to make a choice. It may also be passed on to the doctor treating a child born as a result of the donation and to the doctor of the receiving mother or couple, provided the child's health requires it(158). The centre also collects information about the physical characteristics of both biological parents of surplus embryos and of the gametes donor(159). The law effectively authorises matching between donors and recipients(160).

b. *Donations of blood, organs and human body material*

Donor anonymity is imposed for the donation of blood and blood derivatives, except in the case of extreme medical necessity, and

(155) Art. 22, subpara. 2, and art. 57 L. of 6 July 2007.

(156) See amendment n° 169 of M. VANKRUNKELSVEN and co., *Doc. parl.,* Sén., sess. ord. 2005-2006, n° 1440/11, pp. 1-2.

(157) As well as the medical information enabling the doctor to ensure that the health of the donated embryos or gametes is assured (art. 30 and 59 of the law of 6 July 2007).

(158) Art. 35, 36 and 64, 65 L. of 6 July 2007.

(159) Art. 35 and 64 *id.*

(160) Art. 24 and 53 *id.*

the traceability of the products must be guaranteed. Nevertheless, the identity of the donors and recipients may be communicated, under the cover of medical secrecy, if the circumstances make this necessary[(161)].

With regard to organs, the donation is in principle anonymous: the identities of the donor and recipient cannot be communicated unless they already know their respective identities within the framework of a removal from a living person[(162)]. The identity of the donor or the recipient may not be communicated in the case of a removal of organs from a deceased person for transplant[(163)].

2. – *Non-payment*

The donation of surplus embryos or gametes is free of charge, whether it is done on behalf of the prospective parents or for use in a research programme. The commercialisation of embryos or gametes is prohibited[(164)].

For experiments, apart from compensation, no inducement or financial advantage can be granted to a minor or his representatives, or to an incapable person or a person whose consent cannot be obtained in an emergency situation[(165)].

Blood donors are volunteers and are therefore not paid. The price at which blood and blood derivatives are dispensed and delivered is set by the Minister for Public Health, so as to prevent any profit-making[(166)].

Organ donations are also not paid for, whether from a living or deceased donor. The donor or his immediate friends and family may not claim any entitlements from the recipient. However, compensation may be paid to a living donor, provided that it is limited to the direct and indirect expenses of the donation, and

(161) Art. 5, subpara. 2, L. of 5 July 1994.
(162) Art. 4 *bis* L. of 13 June 1986.
(163) Art. 14 L. *id.*
(164) Art. 19, 22, 48 and 51 L. of 6 July 2007. Nevertheless, with regard to gametes, a royal decree can set compensation that covers travel costs or loss of salary for the donor. This compensation can also cover hospitalisation costs associated with egg removal.
(165) Art. 7-7°, 8-6° and 9-5° L. of 7 May 2004.
(166) Art. 6 L. of 5 July 1994.

any loss of income associated with it. This must not be a financial inducement or constitute a profit or gain for a potential donor[167].

Procedures using human body material must be carried out on a non-profit basis[168]. No material benefit may be offered in exchange for a donation. The recipient, his right holders or any other person with a personal link to him may not make any claim with regard to the donor. The donor may, however, receive compensation for expenses or loss of income directly resulting from the donation. Human body material banks and those persons responsible for the removal may receive compensation covering no more than the costs arising from the removal or procedures carried out within the body material bank[169].

In addition, the donor may not choose to reserve human body material for an identified recipient, with two exceptions: either, at the time of the removal and/or procurement, the recipient presents an exceptionally high and scientifically proven risk of an illness for which the usefulness of the procedures has been scientifically proven; or the human body material remains available for therapeutic use for a third party and is recorded[170].

With regard to surrogacy, the Advisory Committee on Bioethics developed a number of lines of argument on the question of commercialisation in the aforementioned Opinion of 5 July 2004, in terms of both authorisation and, contrarily, prohibition. The aforementioned draft laws prohibit the remuneration of the surrogate and intermediaries. They allow, to differing degrees, the reimbursement by the prospective parents of costs related to the pregnancy.

In its Opinion of 10 December 2007[171], the Committee considered the question of whether or not it is acceptable for some body parts removed from a living person to be traded. The Committee issued one observation, an agreement in principle and three standpoints.

(167) Art. 4 L. of 13 June 1986. On the issue of the commercialisation of organs, see E. Nordin, "Een onderzoek naar de voor- en nadelen van de (gereglementeerde) markt in organen", *T.P.R.*, 2010, pp. 93-185.

(168) On biobanks, see art. 22 L. of 19 December 2008. They provide storage of and access to human body material for scientific research. This provision includes amendments that are not yet in force.

(169) Art. 6 L. of 19 December 2008.

(170) Art. 8, § 1-4°, *id.*

(171) Opinion n° 43 of 10 December 2007 on the problem of commercialisation of human body parts, pp. 43-44.

It observed that more measures to encourage organ donations – after death and from living donors – would go a long way to overcoming the shortage of organs. It underlines the importance of any initiatives such as "Beldonor" to sustain or strengthen social and individual access to organ donations. The Committee goes on to reject the full-scale liberalisation of the market in the human body, where only the laws of supply and demand regulate prices and transactions.

The three standpoints held are as follows. The members are of the opinion that the commercialisation of certain body parts – in particular, gametes, cells, tissues and organs – could be considered, to put an end to shortages and address illegal and clandestine practices in those countries where they exist. They recommend lifting the legal ban on such commercialisation in Belgian law(172). Other members are, on the contrary, opposed to any commercialisation of human body parts, on the grounds that it would be a violation of human dignity. According to them, a human being may not, and does not have the right to have a relationship of ownership with his own body. The freedom to control parts of the body can only be seen in the spirit of a donation and in a context of social cohesion. Other members recommend maintaining the legal ban on commercialisation on the grounds that liberalising the sale of body parts would benefit the strongest in society and lead to the exploitation of the weak. They emphasise that human society should protect its relations on the basis of reciprocal gifts and not only rely on what is saleable.

D. – *Legal restrictions to the right to respect for physical integrity and personal autonomy*

Some protective measures (observation, hospitalisation) can be taken with regard to a mentally ill person, if his condition makes this necessary, when he puts his health or safety at great risk or if he poses a serious risk to the life or integrity of other people(173). The law of 22 August 2002 on patient's rights is in theory applicable

(172) For a critical analysis of this view and the arguments put forward, see X. Dijon, "Vers un commerce du corps humain ?", *op. cit.*, pp. 501-504.

(173) L. of 26 June 1990 on the protection of the person of a mentally ill patient; see also, for the commission of an act defined as a crime or offence punishable by a prison sentence, L. of 5 May 2014 on the internment of persons, which will come into force no later than 1 January 2016.

to the health care to be provided to this individual[174]. In addition, as stated earlier, a new regime for the protection of the vulnerable person was established by the law of 17 March 2013[175]. Thus, a person can be placed under protection when, due to his state of health, he is completely or partially incapable of assuming on his own, without assistance or other protective measures, even on a temporary basis, the management of his patrimonial and non-patrimonial interests[176].

Some health or public safety measures, sometimes stated as being part of public order, can also be taken, by imposing certain vaccinations or tests for disease, within the working environment. In addition, the vaccination against poliomyelitis in newborns is compulsory in Belgium[177]. This legal requirement was considered to be lawful by the Court of Cassation[178]. According to the Court, article 8, §1 of the law of 22 August 2002 introducing the right to the free and informed consent of the patient protects the rights of this person in his individual relationship with the professional practitioner. It does not have the same aim as a provision such as article 1 of the health law[179] which, with a view to preventing or fighting a transmissible illness presenting a general danger, provides for the option of imposing a treatment based on the need to protect public health, which is part of public order. However, voices are regularly raised with regard to government interference in the exercise of the right to respect for a private and family life[180] and demanding the introduction of no-fault civil liability by the State[181].

Within the framework of the production of evidence, violations of physical integrity may lawfully be performed in criminal cases, for example a blood alcohol content test or identification by DNA,

(174) See also Opinion n° 21 of 10 March 2003 of the Advisory Committee on Bioethics concerning forced treatment in the case of enforced hospitalisation.

(175) L. of 17 March 2013 reforming the incapacity systems and introducing a new status of protection consistent with human dignity.

(176) Provided that this is necessary in order to protect his interests (art. 488, § 1, Civ. C.).

(177) Royal Decree 26 October 1966 making the polio vaccination compulsory.

(178) Cass., 18 December 2013, *T. Gez./Rev. dr. santé*, 2013-2014, p. 302.

(179) Health law of 1 September 1945.

(180) Art. 8 of the Convention for the Protection of Human Rights and Fundamental Freedoms; art. 16 of the Convention on the rights of the child.

(181) On this subject, see S. Dalessandro, "La vaccination obligatoire : l'analyse de l'exception de légalité au principe du consentement et l'examen du régime des restrictions aux droits et libertés individuelles", *T. Gez./Rev. dr. santé*, 2013-2014, pp. 306-316 and the decisions of the ECHR referred to.

by taking a sample of blood or body fluid[182]. In civil cases, the consent of the person is required, for example with regard to parentage. Although the courts can order a compulsory blood test, or any other type of test using established scientific methods[183], to establish the existence or absence of a parental relationship, the person may refuse to submit to a DNA test by invoking the right to respect for his physical integrity. The court then considers the reasons put forward to justify this refusal and can conclude a presumption from a refusal without legitimate grounds.

Case law[184] states that there should be a balance between the interests of each individual, with regard to the right to respect for private life, the right to physical integrity and the right of the child to establish its parentage, taking account of article 8 of the Convention for the Protection of Human Rights and Fundamental Freedoms. Some judges have already considered that the violation of physical integrity invoked by a person from whom a saliva sample is taken or a few drops of blood from a fingertip is insignificant when compared to the interest of the child in having its parentage established, in respect of both the mother and the father[185].

E. – *Procedures performed on the body of the deceased*

1. – *The right to respect for the body of the deceased*

The right to respect for the body of the deceased features in the regulations covering procedures that may be performed on it[186]. The body is something that deserves respect. Its physical

(182) See in particular art. 44 *bis* et seq., art. 90 *undecies* Crim. Proc. C., art. 63 L. of 16 March 1968 on the traffic police, L. of 22 March 1999 relating to the identification procedure via DNA analysis in law enforcement. See on this subject, C. Desmet, "Het menselijk lichaam als bewijsmiddel in strafzaken", *T. Gez./Rev. dr. santé*, 2006-2007, pp. 86-101.

(183) Art. 331 *octies* Civ. C.

(184) See G. Mathieu, "Le recours à l'expertise génétique comme mode de preuve de la filiation : le droit au respect de la vie privée et de l'intégrité physique face au droit de l'enfant de voir sa filiation établie", note under Brussels, 12 September 2011, *Rev. trim. dr. fam.*, 2012/3, p. 761, the Belgian case law and that of the ECHR referred to; see also G. Mathieu, "L'article 7 de la Convention relative aux droits de l'enfant dans la jurisprudence belge en matière de filiation", *Rev. trim. dr. fam.*, 2012/3, p. 802, note under Mons, 14 May 2012.

(185) See Brussels, 11 October 2010, *Rev. trim. dr. fam.*, 2011/2, p. 356; Liège, 13 October 2010, *Rev. trim. dr. fam.*, 2011/1, p. 167; Brussels, 12 September 2011, *Rev. trim. dr. fam.*, 2012/3, p. 749 and the aforementioned note of G. Mathieu; Mons, 21 May 2012, *Rev. trim. dr. fam.*, 2012/3, p. 808.

(186) See also the offences referred to in art. 315 (breaches of the laws on burials), 340 (possession of a corpse) and art. 453 (violation of tombs or graves) Crim. C.

protection is distinct from the protection of the memory of the deceased person. This memory is a matter for the close relatives, without that necessarily meaning the heirs in terms of law of succession(187).

An autopsy is sometimes legally permitted in criminal cases and in the event of a violent death or a death whose cause is unknown and suspicious(188). It could be ordered by a judge ruling in civil proceedings, for example, to establish parentage(189).

It is also possible to perform an autopsy, free of charge for the parents, on a child under 18 months old whose death is unexpected and medically unexplained, in order to identify the causes. The doctor who certifies the death must inform the parents of all aspects of the *post-mortem* report and of any questions arising from it. The parents have the right to challenge the autopsy and must be informed of this right(190).

The autonomy of the individual is also displayed with regard to the funeral arrangements, which can consist of burial or cremation (with the ashes dispersed or preserved)(191). In the Brussels-Capital Region, the parents can request that a stillborn foetus whose birth took place between the 106th and 180th day of pregnancy, is buried in a "*parcelle des étoiles*", a special burial plot created for this purpose in local or regional cemeteries, or that it is cremated(192).

2. – *Post-mortem reproduction*

The autonomy of the prospective parents is extensive, so that in the event of the death of her partner, a woman can request the performance of the agreement they jointly concluded with the fertility clinic, if it expressly provides for the possibility of implanting cryopreserved surplus embryos or performing an insemination of cryopreserved surplus gametes(193). A *post-mortem*

(187) Y.-H. Leleu, *Droit des personnes et des familles*, pp. 155-156, concerning autopsies in criminal and civil matters or for medical and scientific reasons.

(188) Art. 44 Crim. Proc C.

(189) Y.-H. Leleu, *Droit des personnes et des familles*, *op. cit.*, pp. 593 and 621.

(190) Art. 3, 4 and 8 L. of 26 March 2003 regulating the performance of an autopsy after the unexpected and medically unexplained death of a child under eighteen months old.

(191) Art. 15 *bis* L. of 20 July 1971 on funerals and graves; see also the Flemish Decree of 16 January 2004 on funerals and graves.

(192) Art. 15 *ter* L. of 20 July 1971 on funerals and graves; C. Rommelaere, "Article 80 *bis* du Code civil, deuil périnatal et droit", *Act. dr. fam.*, 2010, liv. 2, pp. 25-39.

(193) Art. 15, 16, 44, 45 and 67-69 L. of 6 July 2007.

implantation or insemination can only take place after a period of six months, from the time of the partner's death, and within no more than two years. Any provision to the contrary is deemed void. It is, however, regrettable that the legislator has made no provisions for establishing the parentage of a child born in this way.

3. – *The removal of organs or human body material*

The legislator has authorised the removal of organs or body material from a deceased person. In an effort to address the organ shortage, it has decided to introduce an opt-out system for consent. It is, however, possible to take a proactive approach by expressly declaring that one wishes to donate organs after death(194) or by stating one's objection to the removal of organs.

After death, organs may be removed for transplantation(195) from the body of any person entered in the population register or for more than six months in the aliens' register(196), unless it is established that an objection has been lodged. The doctor who plans to perform such a removal must make enquiries about the possible existence of an objection by the potential donor(197).

An adult who is capable of expressing his will is the only person who can lodge an objection to a removal after his death(198). This may be lifted at any point during the person's lifetime(199). If he is capable of expressing his will, a minor may lodge an objection himself. One of the parents exercising parental authority or the guardian(200)

(194) This relates to any person entered in the population register or for more than six months in the aliens' register, who is capable of expressing their will. Only the person concerned may do this (art. 10, § 2 *bis,* L. of 13 June 1986; art. 4 Royal Decree of 30 October 1986 regulating the mode of expression of the will of the donor or of the persons set out in article 10, § 2, L. of 13 June 1986 on organ removal and transplantation).

(195) And for the preparation, subject to the conditions determined by article 2, of therapeutic substances.

(196) The other persons must have specifically expressed their consent to the removal.

(197) Art. 10, § 1, L. of 13 June 1986.

(198) Art. 10, § 2, *id.*

(199) Art. 3 Royal Decree of 30 October 1986 referred to above.

(200) According to art. 10, § 3 *bis* L. of 13 June 1986 (modified by L. of 3 July 2012 and whose entry into force is yet to be confirmed by royal decree), an objection to removal registered at the request of one of the parents of a minor (or the guardian, if appropriate) will cease to be effective when he reaches the age of majority. A royal decree must set out the process for cancelling this objection, and the individual concerned will be duly notified. This cancellation will not apply in the case of a person who is not in a position to express his will due to his mental state. Individuals who will be adults when this provision comes into force will also be concerned by the aforementioned cancellation.

can also object to removal during the minor's lifetime. The same applies if the child is incapable of expressing their wishes(201). If a person is not in a position to express his will due to his mental state, an objection can be expressed by his legal representative, his administrator or, failing that, his closest relative(202).

As with a donation made during a person's lifetime, the aforementioned law of 25 February 2007 removes the ability of family members to object when the person is dead(203). A first-degree relative or the partner who lived with the deceased may no longer object to a removal after death. As before, such an objection cannot take precedence over the express will of the donor.

There are also some situations in which a person requesting euthanasia also wishes to donate his organs or body material. This case is not specifically covered by the law and is subject to the terms of the law on euthanasia, the law on the removal of organs and the law on human body material.

With regard to the removal of human body material after death, the law of 19 December 2008 provides for the application of certain provisions of the law of 13 June 1986 on the removal of organs(204), including those relating to the opt-out(205) consent system referred to above. The opt-out system therefore applies. However, although this perspective is perfectly understandable when the organ or human body material is intended for transplant, some people believe it is harder to justify when the organ or body material is to be used for scientific research.

Conclusion

In Belgian law, there is no legal instrument establishing a general regime of protection of the human body as such. A number of provisions principally aimed at the protection of the individual are enshrined in international conventions, the Constitution, the Criminal Code, the Civil Code and specific laws, as well as the implications of the decisions of the European Court of Human

(201) Art. 10, § 2, subpara. 2 to 3, L. of 13 June 1986.
(202) Art. 10, § 2, subpara. 4, *id.*
(203) See also N. Broeckx, "Artikel 8 EVRM en het verzetsrecht van de nabestaanden bij orgaanwegneming *post mortem*", *T. Gez./Rev. dr. santé,* 2014-2015, pp. 122-125.
(204) Art. 10, 11, 12, 13 and 14, L. of 13 June 1986 on organ removal and transplantation.
(205) Art. 10 *id.*

Rights. Legal doctrine and case law also refer to the personality rights, to the concepts of dignity, the "unavailability" of the human body, self-determination, non-payment, anonymity, public order, etc. They are taken into consideration in the opinions issued by the Belgian Advisory Committee on Bioethics and by the Federal Commission on Patients' Rights.

The personality rights – developed by legal doctrine and protected by case law or the law – include a component on protection from violations of the component parts of the personality and a component concerning the individual's control over their body, within certain limits. With the scientific and technological advances, an increasingly extensive autonomy has been gradually granted the individual with regard to their private and family life, to the point that some people consider that a right to ownership of one's body should be able to be developed as a personality right, derived from the right to life and the right to respect for physical integrity, but more extensive as it covers all procedures performed on the body. They also highlight the fact that the ability to own one's body or some of its parts or elements, via free and informed consent, is restricted by standards drawn from the law and ethics: public order, human dignity and the protection of the human race. Others make the point that a human being is an integral part of different human communities and that it is necessary to assess the collective interest of the different entities – which also constitute an individual's identity – as well as the interest of humanity as a whole. It is then emphasised that the imperative of dignity, which is part of what makes us members of the human race, must sometimes encroach upon the right to autonomy.

It is also believed that the rule of the "unavailability" of the human body would not constitute a general principle of law, in view of the numerous exceptions contained in recent legislation concerning procedures performed on the body. The emphasis is also placed on the fact that recognising the right to own one's body as a personality right does not imply an absolute individual freedom. In this way, while ensuring the autonomy of the individual, the law sets limitations on it.

As stated by the Advisory Committee on Bioethics, there is a growing tension in Belgian law between the "unavailability" of the personality rights and a clear trend towards the increasing availability of the human body, due to an individual's increased autonomy over their body, for personal or altruistic reasons (donation of organs or body material, research or experiments, etc.), whether this concerns the beginning of life (contraception, abortion, assisted reproductive technologies), during life (health care) or the end of life (palliative care, euthanasia, etc.).

The case can now be made that there are different levels of availability, which are determined in particular by the extent of the legal constraints governing the exercise of autonomy, rather than a clear demarcation between "unavailability" and availability. The right to protection of the body goes hand in hand with a right to some "disposal" of the body, albeit subject to legal limits. As well as the ethical considerations, Belgian law provides a framework for this autonomy of the individual, in particular in line with the idea the legislator has of the concept of dignity or public order, and taking account of the general interest and individual interests present, with regard to the protection of the individual and of the fundamental rights.

The question now being asked concerns the possible legal framework for surrogacy, which is not prohibited in Belgium, but for which a written agreement is considered void. A considerable number of draft laws have been submitted to regulate this practice. Some of them, which are being examined by a parliamentary commission, have the contract as a central element of the proposed system. They contain provisions relating to conditions of access to surrogacy, to the terms of the agreement with regard to fundamental rights, to establishing the unborn child's parentage and to possible relationships with the surrogate. Commercialisation and the use of intermediaries are, however, prohibited. If the legislator decides to provide a legal framework for surrogacy using the way of the agreement, this would represent further legal affirmation of the autonomy of the individual and would constitute a backwards step for the idea of the "unavailability" of the human body.

THE PRINCIPLES OF PROTECTION OF THE BODY AND THEIR INFLUENCE ON SPANISH HEALTH LEGISLATION

Verónica SAN JULIÁN PUIG

Professor of Civil Law Faculty of Law, University of Navarra (Spain)

What is the foundation on which the protection of the body and the person relies in Spanish legislation with regard to health and biomedicine? The Spanish legislature regulated this issue and what was deemed worthy of protection on the basis of a group of principles and rights related to various fields (ethics, bioethics, philosophy, law, etc.). Previously, this set of principles and rights was formulated in ethical terms so that it could subsequently be inserted into health legislation, where it is usually referred to in the "Statements of Reasons" or in the initial articles of the laws. It is therefore necessary to make a distinction between the bioethical principles and their impact on health legislation. In strictly legal terms, this underlying element is made of a central principle (human dignity) from which other secondary principles and certain fundamental rights and personality rights are derived. Furthermore, the Spanish legislature has not demonstrated any originality, as these principles and rights are referred to in the laws of many other countries. They are, in fact, the result of a common consensus adopted after World War II to defend individual rights and their application regarding the rights of the patient.

Two clarifications are necessary with regard to these principles of protection of the human body. Firstly, Spanish legislation makes no specific mention of the "body" and its protection, but refers to the person, the body being considered to be subsumed by the person, forming a single whole, and therefore does not benefit from a separate or a specific form of protection. The protection of the body is the protection of the person. Secondly, it should be noted that Spanish law not only protects the human body of a living person, but also after death. Although the personality and entitlement to subjective rights disappear after death[1], the dignity of the "person who was" remains in force after his death.

I. – Principles and rights stemming from international consensus

When selecting the principles and rights to be used as a basis for creating the defence and protection of the person and his body in such sensitive areas as health and biomedicine, the Spanish legislature was not innovative, using the principles arising from the predominant international ethical sensitiveness after World War II. At that time, a consensus on a variety of issues emerged between States that was translated into the "fundamental legal references" developed by international bodies. Despite being extremely varied in their format and legal scope, these references had a very real and undeniable impact in this regard.

A. – *International legal instruments*

1. *The Universal Declaration of Human Rights of 10 December 1948:* this declaration remains a key point of reference for all subsequent constitutional instruments. The Spanish Constitution of 29 December 1978 referred to the dignity of all human beings, as mentioned in the Declaration of Human Rights[2], as one of the fundamental pillars of the legal system[3]. Given the central position within the Constitution, directly influenced by the Universal Declaration of Human Rights, the principle of human dignity supplies all of the precepts of the Spanish legal system and, in particular, those concerning the fields of biomedicine and health.

2. *The Declaration on the Promotion of Patients' Rights in Europe of 28–30 March 1994* (put forward by the Regional Office for Europe of the World Health Organisation). This declaration is aimed at

(1) Art. 32 Civ. C.

(2) Art. 1 UDHR: "All human beings are born free and equal in dignity and in rights. They are endowed with reason and conscience and should act towards one another in a spirit of brotherhood."

(3) Art. 10.1 Spanish Constit. (the first article of Part I, devoted to the fundamental rights and duties of citizens): "The dignity of the person and the inviolable rights inherent to the person, free development of the personality, respect for the law and for the rights of others are the foundation of political order and social peace."

encouraging the implementation, in the field of health, of the rights stemming from those intergovernmental declarations made since 1948[4]. It contains the rights to be taken into consideration in the overall practice of medicine: the right to respect for the person as a human being, the patient's right to self-determination, the right to physical and mental integrity and personal security, respect for one's private life, respect for one's moral and cultural values and religious and philosophical beliefs and the right to the protection of one's health by appropriate measures. The content of some of these rights is developed by the recognition of other rights, such as the right to information, consent or confidentiality. This is the first declaration to make a specific reference to patients' rights. It is intended to implement human rights in the medical domain by aiming specifically at the sick individual.

3. *The Convention for the Protection of Human Rights with regard to Medicine and Biomedicine of 4 June 1997* (or *The Oviedo Convention*). It has been signed and ratified by Spain[5]. Put forward by the Council of Europe, this Convention has significant value, as it is the first legally binding international agreement on the subject. It constitutes a collection of legal and ethical principles intended to ensure, in the fields of medicine and biology, respect for human dignity and the rights and freedoms stemming from this. For all of the signatory countries, it establishes a common framework for the protection of human rights in these areas[6]. This Convention sets out a number of fundamental principles: human dignity, identity, non-discrimination, respect for integrity, respect for private life, the right to information and informed consent.

4. *Since the Oviedo Convention*, there have been a number of different declarations, recommendations and updates of instruments. Although these instruments, unlike the Oviedo Convention, are not legally binding, they constitute a frame of reference that must be taken into consideration. These include, among others, the Universal Declaration on Bioethics and Human Rights of 19 October 2005, the World Medical Association's Declaration of Helsinki on Ethical Principles for Medical Research Involving Human Subjects

(4) This is specifically stipulated in the introduction to the European Declaration of 1994.

(5) Signed on 4 April 1997 and ratified by the Spanish Parliament on 25 June 1999, it came into force on 1 January 2000.

(6) As indicated in the Preamble to the Convention.

(approved in June 1964[7]), the International Ethical Guidelines for Biomedical Research Involving Human Subjects by the Council of International Organisations of Medical Sciences (approved in 1982[8]) and the European Union Charter of Fundamental Rights of 12 December 2006. All of these instruments refer to respect for human dignity, human rights and fundamental freedoms, and to the priority given to the interest and well-being of the person in relation to science or society. They also relate to respect for the autonomy of the person with regard to his ability to make decisions, to the requirement for free, prior informed consent for any preventive, diagnostic or therapeutic medical intervention, and to the respect for integrity, confidentiality and privacy.

Principles of particular ethical significance and legal principles converge at this supranational level. Whether a principle is ethical or legal is not without significance, as it has repercussions on the protection actually afforded to the person, since the effectiveness of these principles and the consequences if they are violated are not identical.

B. – *Reception of these instruments by Spain*

In Spain, human dignity was from the outset at the heart of legislation concerning health and patients' rights stemming from this essential principle. Two points need to be made with regard to the protection of the patient. Firstly, patients are recognised as being independent adults capable of making their own decisions. The development of the reference to autonomy and self-determination over recent decades is undeniable and has led to the introduction of this principle into health legislation alongside the principles of dignity and equality. Secondly, patients' rights were gradually established as subjective rights imposed on doctors, healthcare staff and researchers. A significant number of the patients' rights currently recognised by the law were just a few years ago, basic ethical duties stated in the medical codes of ethics. However, once they were enshrined in the health laws, they became legal duties for healthcare staff (doctors in particular). This was a profoundly important change, as certain types of conduct formerly considered being moral duties now constitute the *lex artis ad hoc* and are

(7) And modified in 1975, 1983, 1989, 1996, 2000, 2008 and 2013.
(8) And modified in 1993 and 2002.

consequently legally binding. That being the case, the line between what is morally or ethically reprehensible and what is legally punishable is far from clear. As a result, the Spanish Supreme Court has to explain in some of its decisions that, although certain ethical duties had been incorporated as duties expected of doctors, they are not, however, legal obligations(9).

II. – Principles and rights of protection of the body

Before addressing the principles and rights of protection of the person pronounced in Spanish legislation in the fields of health and biomedicine, whether the person is alive or dead, a conceptual distinction will give us a better understanding of this issue.

A. – *Ethical and legal principles, fundamental rights and personality rights*

Medicine, as a profession that deals with life, health and death, has always had an ethical dimension and has consequently always been guided by principles and rules of a moral nature(10). The codes of ethics therefore expressed – and still do – all of the ethical principles that govern the practice of medicine, and any failure to comply with these rules results in a disciplinary liability of a "pseudo-legal" nature(11). However, although this medical morality has existed since the dawn of time, a "bioethics" movement, in other words "a sub-group of normative ethics"(12), has developed since the middle of the 19th century. Bioethics has given rise to a multidisciplinary reflection on medicine(13).

(9) This was the case in a Supreme Court judgment of 5 December 2006 (RJ 2007, 232) in which the Court had been petitioned by the family of a patient who had lodged a complaint against the doctor who had shown "a lack of humanity " on the death of the patient. The High Court considered that behaviour "intended solely to offer spiritual comfort or make the death more bearable in strictly humanitarian or spiritual terms" was a type of behaviour that "does not stem from the *lex artis ad hoc* and is not part of the professional duties and responsibility of this nature, but clearly falls within the moral sphere, and it is therefore in that context that it must be evaluated".

(10) P. de Lora and M. Gascon, *Bioética. Principios, desafíos, debates*, Madrid, Alianza Editorial, 2008, pp. 15-16.

(11) D. Gracia, *Procedimientos de decisión en ética clínica*, Madrid, Eudema, 1993, p. 22.

(12) P. de Lora and M. Gascon, *Bioética. Principios, desafíos, debates*, *op. cit.*, p. 26.

(13) Nature emphasised unanimously, M. Vidal, *Bioética. Estudios de bioética racional*, Madrid, Tecnos, 1989, p. 16.

In this context, a *prior* condition is necessary: respect for life and the promotion of health are the two major principles governing any medical act[14]. On this basis, autonomy, dignity and equality are considered as traditional ethical principles. Other principles have been developed from these traditional principles adopted in the field of bioethics, such as the principle of information (stemming from autonomy), the principles of non-maleficence, beneficence and non-commodification (stemming from dignity) and the principles of justice and fairness (stemming from equality)[15]. As principles, they are not intended to order, prohibit or even allow but, rather, they establish legal requirements and objectives to be achieved.

It is clear that the issues discussed in the context of bioethics, closely related to the right to life and to physical and moral integrity, are significant enough to call the law into question. An analysis of Spanish health law reveals such terms as human dignity, free development of the personality, self-determination, integrity, private life, health and well-being of the person, gratuity and non-discrimination. Used in the various health laws, these terms do not refer to the same legal concepts. Some of them (human dignity and the free development of the personality) form the basis of the law, while others constitute the fundamental rights enshrined in the Constitution (life, physical integrity, individual freedom, the right to individual privacy)[16] or personality rights (life, physical integrity, individual freedom, the right to privacy and the right to an identity)[17]. As a result, each of them has a different scope and affords different legal protection.

Considered by the Constitution to be "the pillars of the Spanish legal system", the principles of human dignity and of the free development of the personality[18] represent a reality that is difficult to understand in legal terms as it is designated in

(14) P. de Lora and M. Gascon, *Bioética. Principios, desafíos, debates*, *op. cit.*, p. 40.

(15) *Ibid.*, pp. 40 et seq.

(16) Based on the Constitution, the doctrine expresses a broad range of freedoms and fundamental rights: the right to life and integrity, to religious and ideological freedom, the right to privacy, the right to respect for one's self-image and honour, freedom of expression and information, political rights and the right to an education and a family life. Only those relating to the protection of the body will be presented here.

(17) The doctrine establishes different categories of rights that constitute or are considered to belong to the category of personality rights. Despite some differences in the classifications, all refer to the right to life, physical integrity, personal freedom, honour, privacy, image, copyright and the right to an identity. However, only those that relate to the subject of the study will be addressed here.

(18) Art. 10.1 Constit.

different ways by authors (general provisions, major principles, universal and indivisible values, etc.). Whatever the term used, the only certainty is that these are not fundamental rights, since they are far beyond that, at the root or even at the very foundation of the rights. It can be said that they are principles and, as such, that they serve the purposes of justice and fairness, that they meet moral needs, and that although they do not require any specific types of conducts, they do provide the opportunity to define these conducts(19). Their value is therefore interpretative: their content is defined in the interpretation and application of the rules. As a result, unlike in other countries, no claim can be based on them and they cannot be used in support of a claim if the behaviour reported qualifies as a violation of another right provided for in the instruments(20). Human dignity is considered to be the direct basis for the recognition by the legal system of a variety of rights and freedoms(21), and, in the case of the Spanish health system, it is a crucially important and central principle.

In Spain and other European Union countries (Germany, Italy, etc.), the expression "fundamental rights" refers to the rights guaranteed by the Constitution, whose purpose is to preserve certain values deemed to be essential(22). In this sense, the fundamental rights are key elements of natural law as constitutional standards forming the basis of the State's legal order(23); however, they also confer subjective rights on individuals and thus offer the possibility of taking legal action in the event of a violation of these rights. In this second meaning, the State and public authorities are passive subjects (they are obligated) and the individuals are active subjects, *i.e.* they are the holders of these rights. To say that public authorities are passive subjects means that they must guarantee these rights not only by refraining from any unlawful interference in the legal sphere of the individual, but

(19) A. Aparisi Miralles, "El significado del principio de dignidad humana: un análisis desde la Ley 41/2002 sobre derechos de los pacientes", *in* L. Sanz (ed.), *La implantación de los derechos del paciente*, Pamplona, Eunsa, 2004, p. 79, note 1.

(20) L.M. Díez-Picazo, *Sistema de Derechos Fundamentales*, 3th ed, Madrid, Thomson-Civitas, 2008, p. 71.

(21) A.M. García Cuadrado, *Principios de Derecho Constitucional*, Léon, Eolas Ediciones, 2011, p. 521.

(22) L.M. Díez-Picazo, *Sistema de Derechos Fundamentales*, *op. cit.*, p. 38. Human rights are rights that, referring to fundamental values, are recognised in international agreements, while fundamental rights are declared and protected by national legal systems. *Id.*, p. 40.

(23) A.M. García Cuadrado, *Principios de Derecho Constitucional*, *op. cit.*, pp. 534 and 581.

also by guaranteeing individuals a minimum of protection in the event of these rights being violated[24].

The personality rights[25] are subjective rights resulting from human nature and the inherent dignity of the person and are intended to protect the personal sphere of the human being, in both physical and spiritual terms[26]. This legal category, which appeared in the German legal system in the second half of the 19th century, was incorporated into Spanish law in the middle of the 20th century. In this way, Civil law joined Criminal law and Constitutional law in their mission to defend and protect the human being. Due to their importance and their relationship to the privacy of the person, these rights are absolute (of general effect and enforceable *erga omnes*), non-patrimonial, innate (attached to the person), non-transferable, inalienable and imprescriptible[27].

Although some of the rights identified in the Constitution as being fundamental coincide with the rights pronounced in the civil order (personality rights), this is a question of a single right (to integrity, to privacy, etc.) that can be qualified differently according to different, but complementary, perspectives (civil and constitutional). In fact, each qualification has consequences for the protection of these rights[28].

The regulations concerning patients' rights introduced into Spanish law consisted of a transposition of the fundamental and personality rights in the field of health. The situation therefore went from abstract and general to applied and specific[29].

(24) J. ALFARO AGUILA-REAL, "Autonomía privada y derechos fundamentales", *Anuario de Derecho Civil*, vol. 46-1, 1993, pp. 65 and 67.

(25) J. CORBELLÀ DUCH, "La relación jurídica sanitaria afecta especialmente los llamados derechos de la personalidad" in *Manual de derecho sanitario*, Barcelona, Atelier, 2006, p. 100.

(26) C. MARTINEZ DE AGUIRRE ALDAZ, *Curso de Derecho Civil I, Derecho Privado. Derecho de la Persona*, 4th ed., Madrid, Colex, 2011, p. 546.

(27) L. DÍEZ-PICAZO and A. GULLÓN BALLESTEROS, *Sistema de Derecho Civil*, vol. 1, 11th ed., Madrid, Tecnos, 2003, p. 329 et seq.

(28) See *infra*.

(29) J. CORBELLÁ DUCH, "La relación jurídica sanitaria afecta especialmente los llamados derechos de la personalidad", *op. cit.*, p. 105.

B. – *Principles and rights providing the protection of the body of a living person*

All of the principles and rights protecting the person, a basic framework of Spanish health legislation, are organised in a hierarchical structure. At the top of this pyramid is human dignity, a central principle from which the secondary principles are derived; the free development of the personality and autonomy, as well as an array of rights. These principles and rights are not defined by the legislature or in the codes of ethics governing the health professions. They are, however, defined and described by doctrine and formulated by case law.

1. – *Human dignity: central principle of the entire system*

The reference to human dignity constitutes the starting point of *all* existing laws in this field. This reference to dignity appears in the "Statements of Reasons", the Preambles and the initial articles relating to the fundamental principles. There is, however, nothing surprising about this as the Constitution enshrines human dignity as a principle and as a basic cornerstone of the Spanish legal system. The principle therefore constitutes the foundation or *humus* on which all protection of the person and health is built. From this foundation, the principle is sub-divided into secondary principles and a series of rights related to the protection of the person[(30)].

Although human dignity is a key concept, the legislature has not defined it. There is a comprehensive debate among legal experts on its content, its justification, its scope and its goals. The Constitutional Council had to define it in a series of decisions. According to the Constitutional Council, human dignity is "a moral and spiritual value inherent to the person"[(31)], which

(30) L. n° 14-198625 April 1986, on health: rules relating to the removal and transplantation of organs and tissues (L. n° 30-1979, 27 October 1979, on the removal and transplantation of organs, Royal Decree n° 1088-2005 on blood donation, Royal Decree n° 1723-2012 on the acquisition, use and territorial coordination of the transplantation of organs, Royal Decree n° 9-2014 on the tissue and cell donations); L. n° 41-2002, 14 November 2002, on the autonomy of the patient; Royal Decree n° 223-2004, 6 February 2004, on clinical trials of medications; L. 14-2006, 26 May 2006, on assisted reproduction; L. n° 14-2007, 3 July 2007, on the biomedical research; L. n° 3-2007, 15 March 2007, on the correction of civil status in cases of transsexualism; L. n° 2-2010, 3 March 2010, on sexual and reproductive health; and autonomous laws on death with dignity pronounced in 2010-2011.

(31) Constitutional Council judgment n° 53-1985, 11 April 1985.

"remains unchanged irrespective of the person's situation [...] and consequently constitutes an inviolable *minimum* that the law must guarantee. The limits imposed on the enjoy mant of individual rights can therefore never lead to the esteem merited by the individual being disregarded[32]. In view of these judgments, human dignity constitutes respect for the humanity in each person, hence its absolute character (it cannot be abolished or violated)[33]. This applies not only to relations between individuals, but also to relations between the individual and the State or public authorities[34].

It is unanimously accepted that human dignity is the source of all rights. It is even considered by many to be the foundation of the entire legal system[35]. As a result, no one should be surprised by the impact that this ethical and legal principle has – and must necessarily have – in the field of medicine, where life, health and death are at stake and where scientific advances have been particularly significant over the course of recent decades. It is precisely in this field that the principle of dignity highlights three essential ideas: every human being has an inherent value and is worthy of unconditional respect on that basis; every human being is a person and not merely an individual; every member of the human species, as a result of his ontological dignity, is an "end in himself". Dignity does not therefore rely on personal opinion or social consensus and it cannot be based only on certain manifestations of the person, like rationality and quality of life[36]. On this basis, the other rights and principles of protection acquire their true dimension.

(32) Constitutional Council judgment n° 120-1990, 27 June 1990.

(33) A.M. García Cuadrado, *Principios de Derecho Constitucional*, *op. cit.*, p. 526.

(34) From a constitutional perspective, the reference to the dignity of the person emphasises "the priority of the person – in other words, of each individual – over the State". The public authorities are therefore "an instrument in the service of human beings and not the other way round. Human beings must never be treated as means to be used with regard to the purposes and policies of the State". L. Díez Picazo, *Sistema de Derechos Fundamentales*, *op. cit.*, pp. 70-71.

(35) A. Aparisi Miralles, "El significado del principio de dignidad humana: un análisis desde la Ley 41/2002 sobre derechos de los pacientes", *op. cit.*, pp. 80-82.

(36) *Ibid.*, pp. 85, 89, 91 and 92.

2. – *The free development of the personality: a secondary principle*

The free development of the personality features in the Constitution as one of the fundamental cornerstones of the legal system[37]. Although the expression is used in the Constitution with regard to health, it is established as a principle issuing from human dignity, its foundation. It is therefore a secondary principle.

In accordance with this principle, each person must define his life plans by himself, without the intervention of anyone else, even the State (unless it is to protect similar rights). This is a way of avoiding the ever present paternalistic tendencies of State interferences[38].

This principle is present, in the background, in all health-related legislation, but it is only specifically mentioned twice with regard to subjects related to sexuality and female reproduction and to identity related to transsexualism. The law on sexual and reproductive health[39] refers to the free development of the personality with a view to providing, in particular, a right to freely decided motherhood. This is also the case with the 2007 law allowing the correction of civil status in cases of transsexualism[40], intended to protect those whose gender identity does not correspond to the sex previously entered in the Civil Status Register.

3. – *Autonomy*

In the field of bioethics, autonomy constitutes a principle involving a right and a duty: the right of the person to decide on issues that concern him (such as health) and the duty of others to respect these decisions. In the legal sphere, traditionally, freedom of choice was closely related to legal acts – particularly contracts – to anything concerning legal agreements made by a private individual. For a number of years, this autonomy has been highlighted in other areas, including health. The development of the idea of freedom of choice in numerous fields is due to the Constitution, which states that autonomy is a constitutionally

(37) Art. 10.1 Spanish Constit.

(38) L. Díez Picazo, *Sistema de Derechos Fundamentales*, *op. cit.*, p. 71.

(39) Organic L. n° 2-2010, 3 March 2010, on sexual and reproductive health.

(40) L. n° 3-2007, 15 March 2007, allowing the correction of civil status in cases of transsexualism.

protected legal right, stemming from freedom[41] and closely related to dignity and the free development of the personality[42]. This statement in general terms has had repercussions with regard to health.

Indeed, in recent decades autonomy has gained considerable significance, scope and a degree of implementation in the field of health, to the extent that it has become, *de facto*, an essential principle in health legislation. In fact, respect for freedom of choice is included in *all* of the laws relating to biomedicine and health, including the law on patient autonomy[43], which establishes it as a "Basic principle" alongside the dignity of the person and respect for one's privacy. In spite of the critics of the doctrine, who believe that this wording is inappropriate as it places the principles of freedom of choice, private life and human dignity on an equal footing[44], this wording used by the legislation is significant. Nevertheless, although autonomy can be thought of as an inspirational principle, it is, like the free development of the personality, a secondary principle derived from that of human dignity.

In general terms, with regard to health, autonomy means the right of the patient to be informed in an intelligible and clear manner adapted to the circumstances and the requirement for informed consent prior to any medical intervention However, depending on the regulated field, this principle of autonomy can have a number of different meanings[45]. This link between autonomy, information and consent is extremely important with regard to bioethics. The principle of information or publicity derives from the principle of autonomy[46]. The European Convention on Biomedicine of

(41) The Constitution states that freedom is one of "the higher values" of the legal system. Art. 1.1 Spanish Constit. "Spain is hereby established as a social and democratic State, subject to the rule of law, which advocates freedom, justice, equality and political pluralism".

(42) C. Martinez de Aguirre Aldaz, *Curso de Derecho Civil I, I, Derecho Privado. Derecho de la Persona*, *op. cit.*, p. 231; J. Corbellá Duch, "La relación jurídica sanitaria afecta especialmente los llamados derechos de la personalidad", *op. cit.*, p. 133.

(43) L. n° 41-2002, 14 November 2002, on the autonomy of the patient.

(44) A. Aparisi Miralles, "El significado del principio de dignidad humana : un análisis desde la Ley 41/2002 sobre derechos de los pacientes", *op. cit.*, p. 83.

(45) Thus, in Law n° 41/2002, 14 November 2002, on patient autonomy, respect for autonomy includes the right to freedom of choice, the right not to be informed and even the right to refuse treatment. With regard to the rules concerning the removal and transplantation of organs, they allow for the expression of 'no objection' by the deceased. With regard to the laws concerning death with dignity, respect for the patient's consent includes consent expressed in advance in the patient's "advance directives".

(46) P. de Lora and M. Gascon, *Bioética. Principios, desafíos, debates*, *op. cit.*, p. 43.

1997[47] and the Code of Medical Ethics[48] work along these lines. Information is an essential prerequisite for the person to be able to choose freely between different therapeutic options and, in this sense, it is presented as a prior condition for the exercise of the freedom to choose and the development of personality[49].

The courts do not try to define autonomy or self-determination, but limit themselves to emphasizing informed consent that makes autonomy and freedom of choice a reality[50]. The principle of informed consent provides protection for the physical and moral integrity of the person, to the extent that the Constitutional Council has mentionned it on a number of occasions[51]. In numerous judgments, the Supreme Court bases the need for the informed consent of the patient either on the constitutional principles of the dignity of the person, or on the right to life, physical integrity and freedom of conscience or on the personal freedom to make one's own decisions[52].

4. – *Respect for the integrity of the person*

The right to physical and mental integrity was traditionally expressed in the field of bioethics as the "principle of non-maleficence", which implies the moral obligation to do no unnecessary or disproportionate harm to the patient. Thus the constraints related to the medical intervention must be outweighed by the benefit to the patient[53]. Hence the close link between this ethical principle and those of "beneficence" (aimed at ensuring the welfare of the patient and planning the best possible alternatives for the patient, in both clinical practice and in research) and of "non-commodification" (the obligation to treat the person as an

(47) Art. 5 and 10.

(48) Art. 12-16 MEC.

(49) J. Corbellá Duch, "La relación jurídica sanitaria afecta especialmente los llamados derechos de la personalidad", *op. cit.*, p. 107.

(50) In some judgments, the Supreme Court qualifies it as "a fundamental human right". Supreme Court judgments of 12 January 2001 and 11 May 2001, among others.

(51) Informed consent provides protection for "bodily integrity" (STC 207/1996, of 16 September), "the inviolability of the person, not only against attacks intended to injure his body or mind, but also against any type of intervention on his property" (STC 120/1990, of 27 June; and STC 119/2001 of 24 May).

(52) Cass. (1st civ.), 24 May 1996, 2 October 1997, 16 October 1998; and Cass. (3rd ch.), [administrative litigation], 4 April 2000, 3 October 2000, 10 October 2000 and 7 June 2001, among others.

(53) P. de Lora and M. Gascon, *Bioética. Principios, desafíos, debates*, *op. cit.*, p. 44.

"end in himself" and not as a mean. The principle of human dignity is applied through these three principles.

In the legal domain, the right to physical and mental integrity is a right enshrined in the Constitution(54). The asset or legal good protected by this right is the inviolability of the human being: the person is worthy of respect, and neither his body nor his mind may be violated(55). This right includes not only the right not to be subjected to torture and inhuman or degrading treatment, but also the right not to be subjected to physical or psychological interventions without his consent(56). The Constitutional Council has specifically stated that the right to personal integrity carries an obligation not to cause harm or adversely affect the health of the person(57). As a result, any intervention that causes harm or constitutes a serious and certain threat to physical integrity must be agreed to by the patient after receiving information provided by the medical staff. Hence the link referred to above between informed consent and this right.

There is also a link between integrity and the free development of the personality as, by means of informed consent, the patient exercises his free will by deciding which treatment he accepts or not. That is why the unjustified failure to provide information is considered to be a limitation or a denial of this right(58).

The question that now arises is whether the right to dispose freely of one's own body exists. The answer seems to be no: there is no absolute right to dispose of one's body or elements of it. This is the result of the provisions of the Criminal Code, which stipulates that, in the case of unlawful medical interventions, the consent of the person affected does not exonerate the doctor from his criminal liability, although its existence can lead to lighter penalties(59).

(54) Art. 15 Spanish Const.: "Every citizen has the right to life and to physical and mental integrity, and under no circumstances may be subjected to torture or to inhuman or degrading punishment or treatment. The death penalty is hereby abolished, except as provided for by military criminal law in times of war."

(55) L. Díez Picazo, *Sistema de Derechos Fundamentales*, *op. cit.*, p. 235.

(56) Constitutional Court judgement of 27 June 1990.

(57) STC 35/1996 of 11 March. In addition, a specific reference to the right to integrity features in the Law on patient autonomy, the Law on biomedical research and the Law on sexual and reproductive health.

(58) N. Sanz Mulas (ed.) and M. Hernandez Ramos, *Relevancia jurídica del consentimiento informado en la práctica sanitaria: responsabilidades civiles y penales*, Granada, Comares, 2012, p. 4.

(59) Art. 155 Crim. C.

However, it is possible, to a degree, to dispose of one's body[60]. In the first instance, this is possible when it is in the person's own interest for therapeutic reasons (surgery intended to heal illnesses or eliminate defects or health risks) or aesthetic reasons (cosmetic surgery). In this context, sterilisation and surgery carried out on transsexuals are possible as they are related to the free development of the personality. Secondly, it is possible in the interests of third parties, in particular for therapeutic reasons (donations of organs or bodily elements: blood, bone marrow, and sperm).

The principal protection of the human body is provided by the Criminal Code, although it is also possible to bring civil liability into the equation in the case of reparation for damages resulting from a violation of this right with regard to physical integrity.

5. – *The right to privacy*

The right to *privacy* has an important position in the legal arsenal protecting the person. Privacy as well as human dignity and freedom of choice are references that appear in all existing laws concerning biomedicine and health, although privacy is always expressed as a right.

The right to privacy is a constitutional right[61], linked to respect for dignity[62]. It is provided for by law[63]. It is a fundamental right and, as such, it is enforceable against public authorities. In addition, it fis part of the personality rights, which is important as the most common violations of this right are usually committed by other individuals. The mechanisms of civil protection and criminal measures play a decisive role in guaranteeing and defending these rights. It is, however, also possible to apply to the Constitutional Court by using the indirect route referred to below.

Although this right is not defined in law, the abundant case law of both the Constitutional Court and the Supreme Court nevertheless provides us with a framework. It is a dual-component concept, both

(60) C. Martinez de Aguirre Aldaz, *Curso de Derecho Civil I, Derecho Privado. Derecho de la Persona*, *op. cit.*, pp. 558- 559.

(61) The Constitution, in article 18.1 states: "The right to honour, to personal and family privacy and to one's own image is guaranteed."

(62) This is reflected in certain judgments from the Constitutional Court: 144/1999, of 22 July 1999 and 196/2004 of 15 November 2004.

(63) Organic L. n° 1-1982, 5 May 1982, on the civil protection of the right to honour, to personal and family privacy and to one's own image.

positive and negative: negative, because it allows for the ability to exclude anything concerning the most intimate personal life of the individual from the knowledge of others; positive inasmuch as the holder of this right has control over the details and information concerning himself(64). This positive aspect endows the holder with the power of disposition over anything relating to his privacy(65).

The right to privacy encompasses what is known as physical intimacy and anything related to information about one's health. The Constitutional Council declares that physical intimacy is "protected by principle [...] against any unwanted interference on the individual's body whose modesty and decency are thus protected by the legal system acting according to the norms and criteria rooted in the culture of the community"(66). It is not, however, an absolute right as "it can be limited when there is reason to do so and when this limitation is implemented under the appropriate and proportionate circumstances of the intended purpose"(67). With regard to information related to health, it should be noted that the Constitution stipulates that "the use of information technologies shall be limited by the law in order to guarantee respect for the honour and personal and family privacy of citizens"(68); and that such personal information benefits from special protection(69).

The right to privacy is closely linked(70) to professional confidentiality(71). The patient communicates confidential information and opinions to the health professional (either directly or following any medical examination, or lab. tests); this information until that point was exclusive and private, and by doing

(64) J.L. Lacruz Berdejo (ed.) and F. Rivero Hernández, *Elementos de Derecho Civil*, t. I, vol. 2, Barcelona, Bosch, 1990, p. 74.

(65) C. Martinez de Aguirre Aldaz, *Curso de Derecho Civil I, Derecho Privado. Derecho de la Persona*, *op. cit.*, p. 563.

(66) Constitutional Council judgment 37/1989, 15 February.

(67) Constitutional Council judgment 57/1994, 28 February.

(68) Art. 18.4 Spanish Constit. Although its wording can be criticised, this precept means that it is necessary to "contain any abuse of the use of new technologies". L. Díez Picazo, *Sistema de Derechos Fundamentales*, *op. cit.*, p. 325.

(69) Art. 7 Organic L. n° 15-1999, 13 December 1999, on the protection of personal data.

(70) As the Constitutional Council warns in its decision of 11 December 1989.

(71) The content of paragraphs 1 and 2 of article 27 of the 2011 Code of Medical Ethics are worthy of being highlighted: "1. Medical secrecy is one of the pillars on which the doctor-patient relationship is built; it is based on mutual trust, irrespective of the method of its professional implementation. 2. For the doctor, secrecy means the obligation of discretion and confidentiality concerning everything revealed and confided to him by the patient, but also everything related to the patient's health and private life that the doctor sees and deduces in the exercise of his profession, including his medical records".

so this private or exclusive information becomes a confidential relation(72). It is in the context of this relationship of trust that the doctor's discretion is engaged, together with his obligation to keep the confidentiality of the information which cannot be divulged without the express authorisation of the patient or to achieve specific regulated objectives. It is essential to understand the importance that confidentiality has in this field, as it concerns privacy and "a healthcare activity which, without this guarantee of confidentiality would mean a threat to the patient's freedom thus to his self-determination(73). In spite of its importance, there is currently no legislation providing a unified legal approach to professional secrecy and, consequently, to medical confidentiality.

6. – *The health and well-being of the patient: the principle of beneficence*

The legal reference to "the health and well-being of the person" refers to the ethical principle of "beneficence". The content of this bioethical principle refers to the defence of the patient's best interest and to seeking the best possible alternatives for the patient, both in clinical practice and in research. In the legislation, the regulations relating to the removal and transplantation of organs and tissues(74), the Law on assisted reproduction(75), the Law on biomedical research(76) and the laws concerning death with dignity(77) refer specifically to this principle, stating: "The health,

(72) J. Such Martínez, "El secreto profesional médico y la ley de protección de datos. La responsabilidad médica en el ámbito administrativo", *in* Camas Jimena (ed.), *Responsabilidad médica*, Valencia, Tirant lo Blanch, 2013, p. 222.

(73) R. Altisent Trota, "Cuestiones éticas en el uso de la historia clínica", *in* P. Leon-Sanz (ed.), *La implantación de los derechos del paciente*, Pamplona, Eunsa, 2004, p. 316.

(74) L. n° 30-1979, 27 October 1979, on the removal and transplantation of organs and tissues, Royal Decree n° 1088-2005, 16 September 2005, on blood donations, Royal Decree n° 1723-2012, 28 December 2012, on the acquisition, use and territorial coordination of organ transplants, Royal Decree n° 9-2014 on tissue and cell donations all feature a number of basic rules already established in the Oviedo Convention of 1997, namely: the removal must be compatible with life and not risk the lives of the donor or recipient.

(75) L. n° 14-2006, 26 May 2006, on assisted reproduction.

(76) The instruments state that research involving humans can only be carried out if there is no alternative of comparable effectiveness and must not cause risk or discomfort that is disproportionate to the potential benefits (art. 14).

(77) L. n° 2-2010, 8 April 2010, on the right to and guarantee of death with dignity in Andalusia; L. n° 8-2011, 24 March 2011, on the rights to and guarantees of death with dignity in Navarre; and L. n° 10-2011, 24 March 2011, on the right to and guarantee of death with dignity in Aragon. The aim of this expression is to ensure the well-being of the person by providing full support for any physical, emotional, social and spiritual needs of the patient and his family that may arise during the patient's end-of-life experience.

interest and well-being of the individual must take precedence over the interest of society or science." Once more, human dignity and the value of the person puts the patient above other interests.

7. – *Respect for the identity of the person*

Respect for the identity of the person is mentioned in the laws on assisted reproduction and biomedical research which stipulate the prohibition of human cloning and the creation of human embryos for the sole purpose of research. The right to an identity is a personality right in Civil Law whose content covers not only the right to have a "name" that enables the State to identify its citizens, but also the right to have a personal identity, seen as a requirement of the dignity of being recognised as different from others[78]. In this sense, "the name does not only have a distinctive character, it evokes the person himself in his social and mental qualities [...]. As a result, his protection includes the protection of his personality, in terms of his physical, mental and social uniqueness"[79]. It is therefore possible to state that when the health laws refer to the identity, they refer specifically to this requirement to recognise the personal uniqueness inherent to human dignity. On account of this link with human dignity, the "right not to be genetically programmed, the right to be genetically unique and irreplaceable" is referred to[80].

8. – *The principle of free care*

Also derived from human dignity, the non-payment within healthcare is inarguably linked to the bioethical principle of the "non-commodification" of the person. It is referred to in all of the laws concerning donations (of organs, tissues, blood and genetic or biological material)[81]. However, all of these rules provide for a "justified remuneration", which can take the form of

(78) C. Martinez de Aguirre Aldaz, *Curso de Derecho Civil I, Derecho Privado. Derecho de la Persona, op. cit.*, p. 547.

(79) L. Díez-Picazo and A. Gullón Ballesteros, *Sistema de Derecho Civil, op. cit.*, p. 369.

(80) C. Lema Añon, "Dilemas ético-jurídicos de la reproducción humana", *in* M. Gascón Abellán (ed.), *Derecho sanitario y bioética: cuestiones actuales*, Valencia, Tirant lo Blanch, 2011, p. 860.

(81) This can be found in all of the laws concerning the removal or transplantation of organs; in the Law on assisted reproduction, in the law on biomedical research and in the Royal Decree on blood donations.

reimbursement of the donor's travel expenses[82] or compensation for any damages incurred by the donor, to ensure that the donation does not cause the donor undue expense[83]. Likewise, non- payment is not incompatible with what the donor is entitled to. All of the medical consequences arising from the donation or the donor's action on behalf of medicine must be paid for. In this sense, with regard to the removal of organs from a living donor, it is stipulated that "medical care will be provided to the living donor for his recovery"[84]; the law concerning medications expressly provides for the reimbursement of the patient's expenses[85] in the case of clinical trials that could affect the health of the person undergoing them, without, however, specifying which expenses it is referring to, while the law on biomedical research provides for the possibility of compensation for the damages incurred – which must at the same time be covered by insurance – particularly with regard to the costs for the person making himself available for research[86], although this compensation must not be of a profitable or commercial nature.

9. – *The principle of non-discrimination*

While the principle of equality is one of the main guidelines with regard to bioethics, in legal terms, the Constitution defines equality as a superior value of the legal system and non-discrimination as a fundamental right [87]. The principle of non-discrimination is implicit in all the health laws, but it only actually appears directly in four of them[88]. On the one hand, it is stated that the patient cannot be subject to discrimination "based on race, religion, convictions or opinion, gender, disability, sexual orientation, age, civil status or any other personal or social condition circumstance" in the context of his relations with the public health authorities,

(82) Art. 4.1. Royal Decree on blood donations, aforementioned.

(83) Art. 2 L. n° 30-1979, 27 October 1979, on the removal and transplantation of organs and art. 8 Royal Decree n° 1723-2012, regulating the activities of obtaining and using human organs for clinical purposes and art. 3 Royal Decree n° 9-2014 on the donation and use of human tissues.

(84) Art. 9 Royal Decree n° 1723-2012, aforementioned.

(85) Art. 60.9 L. on medications.

(86) Respectively, art. 18, 58.3 and 69 L. on biomedical research.

(87) Art. 1.1 and 14 Spanish Constit.

(88) L. n° 14-1986, 25 April 1986, General law on the health; L. n° 16-2003, 28 May 2003, on the consistency and quality of the National Health System; L. n° 2-2010, 3 March 2010, on sexual and reproductive health; and L. n° 14-2007, 3 July 2007, on biomedical research.

access to National Health services or services related to sexual and reproductive health(89). On the other hand, the Law on biomedical research mentions another type of non-discrimination, "the prohibition of any discrimination based on genetic grounds or on the refusal of the practice of genetic tests or participation in a research project"(90). A person who refuses a genetic test or to take part in research may not be subjected to discrimination by the doctor, who must provide the medical service to which the person is entitled.

A minority opinion refers to the health-related liability for negligence with regard to the health of women, pointing out that the Spanish government provides healthcare for all citizens, but in terms of equality makes no contribution to protecting women's health. This doctrine considers that the current state of science provides an understanding of the influence of gender in female health, but that these features are not covered by the law or by any occupational health measures. Therefore, in that perspective, there is a liability on account of this negligence(91).

C. – *Principles and rights providing protection of the body of a deceased person*

Reflecting on the protection of the body leads one to wonder about the protection provided after a person's death.

In Spain, "the civil personality ceases to exist at the death of a person"(92). This means that with death, the rights based on his or her personality – the most personal rights – cease to exist; they disappear along with the person concerned. However, those rights that are not personal remain momentarily without a holder and are passed on through inheritance.

What had until then been the body of the person becomes something else: a corpse. However, although it may then be considered an object, it is not just 'anything'. The dignity of

(89) Respectively, art. 3.4 L. n° 14-1986, aforementioned; art. 2, § a), L. n° 16-2003, aforementioned; art. 3.3 L. n° 2-2010, aforementioned.

(90) Art. 6 L. n° 14-2007, aforementioned.

(91) C. Ruiz-Rico Ruiz, "La desprotección del derecho constitucional a la salud desde una perspectiva de género como causa de responsabilidad sanitaria", *in* M.J. Gallardo Castillo (ed.), *La responsabilidad jurídico-sanitaria*, Madrid, La Ley, 2011, pp. 602-604.

(92) Art. 32 Civ. C.

the person it once was continues to have effects and becomes a matter for a specific legal framework[93]. Although death leads to the extinction of the personality, the disappeared personality continues to be protected by the law even after death. The law protects not only certain personality rights related to the personal and social esteem of the deceased, such as the right to honour, to respect privacy or to a self-image, but also the body, as the corpse benefits from a specific legal framework[94]. First of all, the dignity entitled to the human being must be respected beyond death even towards the corpse. It is stated, for example, that the corpse is an extra-patrimonial asset, that making the dead body or its parts available is ruled out and that the possibility of making legal agreements concerning the corpse is limited. Next, when the wishes of the deceased concerning the fate of his body after his death are known, they must be respected (burial or cremation, the place of burial, the destination of the ashes, the use of his organs or tissues for transplants or the use of his body for medical or scientific purposes, etc.).

In the special laws concerning biomedicine and health promulgate dover the last few years in Spain, some provisions relate to the fate of the corpse and the health information of the deceased person. In particular, the regulations concerning clinical autopsies guarantee "that there must be no obvious disfigurement of the corpse and no marketing of its parts" and that preservation of the body should be in "appropriately equipped premises"[95].

III. – The defence of the principles of protection of the body

In case of a violation of the principles and rights guaranteeing the protection of the body, the legal system reacts vigorously, as there are basic legal rights at stake. Such a violation can be referred to a number of different bodies.

(93) J. Delgado Echeverría, *Elementos de Derecho Civil, Parte General. Personas*, t. I, vol. 2, 5th ed., Madrid, Dykinson, 2008, p. 20.

(94) C. Martinez de Aguirre Aldaz, *Curso de Derecho Civil I, Derecho Privado. Derecho de la Persona*, *op. cit.*, p. 349.

(95) Art. 3.2 L. n° 29-1980, regulating clinical autopsies.

A. – *Constitutional protection*

When there is a violation of fundamental rights, constitutional protection is invoked. Those rights that are both fundamental rights and personality rights (integrity and private life) benefit from stronger protection and, it is possible to petition the Constitutional Council and the ordinary courts if they are violated by a public authority[(96)].

While it is true that recourse to a writ of *amparo* before the Constitutional Court only concerns violations of these rights by the public authorities, it is equally true that the Constitutional Council has also granted this protection, in an indirect manner, when violations have been committed by private individuals. This procedure does not allow a ruling on the violation of the right, but results in a judicial decision being challenged, which is an act by the public authorities (the judicial authority) that has failed to prevent the violation of the fundamental right suffered by the person[(97)]. This route is used, for example, to seek the protection of the Constitutional Council in the case of a violation of the privacy right.

Since human dignity constitutes one of the cornerstones of the Spanish legal system on which other principles and rights are based, it should be entitled to the strongest possible protection provided by our law, *i.e.* the protection of the Constitution, when it subject to a violation. Yet there is nothing of the sort. Indeed, as a key principle, dignity inspires all of the rights protecting the person, so a violation of this principle can only be cited as such before the courts. The only claims that can be brought before the courts are those based on a violation of the other legally recognised rights of protection of the body.

Finally, it should be noted that the Constitutional Council[(98)] pointed out that the absence of informed consent is considered

(96) Art. 53.2 Spanish Constit. This article states that any citizen may obtain respect for the freedom and rights recognised in article 14 and the first Section of Chapter 2 (referring to the integrity of the body and privacy) before the Constitutional Court and, by a special procedure, before the ordinary courts.

(97) L. López Guerra (ed.) and J. García Morillo, *Derecho Constitucional*, vol. 2, coll. Manuales de Derecho Constitucional, 9th ed.,Valencia, Tirant lo Blanch, 2013, p. 274.

(98) Constitutional Court judgement, 28 March 2011. This judgment concerned a person who, after a medical intervention, suffered the functional loss of his/her right hand. The

to be a violation of the fundamental right to physical and mental integrity and, as such, benefits from constitutional protection.

B. – *Criminal protection*

It is possible to request the intervention of the criminal courts if, in accordance with the Criminal Code, the conduct in question can be considered to be a criminal offence or misconduct. Criminal protection constitutes the strongest response the legal system can offer in the case of a violation of the principles of protection of the body. The Spanish Criminal Code provides for the following specific cases.

Bodily harm (or injuries): When dealing with a violation of the right to physical integrity, criminal protection constitutes the main form of protection, by means of the offence of grievous bodily harm(99), although the victim can also apply to the civil courts for compensation for any damages resulting from the violation of this personality right. In criminal terms, bodily harm is often the result of negligence(100). The Spanish Criminal Code provides for different types of bodily harm, depending on the seriousness of the behaviour and the end result. Female genital mutilation is a specific example(101) that is subject to protection in Spain because it is a practice that "is a violation of the dignity of women and of their rights"(102).

Euthanasia: In Spain, active euthanasia, also called assisted suicide, constitutes a homicide and is therefore punishable by law(103). Direct active euthanasia is forbidden, even when the person receiving it is the victim of a chronic and incurable illness, or when this action is in response to a request made "expressly, seriously and unambiguously by the victim". Nevertheless, while these circumstances cannot justify ignoring the responsibility of the person practising euthanasia, they reduce the degree of

---

medical act was carried out without the informed consent of the patient, who had not been informed of the risks.

(99) Art. 147-158 Crim. C.

(100) There are numerous judgments on bodily harm resulting from the negligence – gross or minor – of the doctor. Cass. (Crim. Ch.), 15 October 2002, RJ 2002/9907.

(101) Art. 149, § 2, Crim. C.

(102) Teruel District Court (Crim. Ch.), 15 November 2011, Judgment 26/2011.

(103) Art. 143, § 4, Crim. C.

responsibility, the applicable penalty being less severe than that given for a case of homicide.

Passive euthanasia and indirect euthanasia are dealt with differently and are even authorised, as they are not considered to be unlawful acts. Their moral legitimacy is even recognised by the Code of Medical Ethics and Deontology(104). The limit is active euthanasia, which is intended to cause a person's death, which is prohibited by the Spanish law concerning the fundamental unavailability of human life, constituting a restriction on patient autonomy.

Purchase and sale of organs: The section of the Criminal Code concerning the offence of assault is aimed *in fine* at the purchase and sale of organs(105). In Spain, trafficking organs, as well as the individual purchase and sale of organs, are punishable by law. This prohibition is based on the idea that with the sale of an organ there is no real freedom on the part of the donor, as opposed to the case when the donation is altruistic. There is a *juris and de jure* presumption which implies that, when a price or some form of recompense is involved, the donor's decision-making process is not free, it is dependent on his precarious financial situation(106).

Genetic manipulation: The Criminal Code also deals with offences related to genetic manipulation(107), offences which affect dignity with regard to personal identity. Legal experts point out that these offences are virtually non-existent "on account of the uniqueness of the situations in which they occur"(108). These offences include: genetic manipulation (manipulation resulting in the modification of the subject's genotype); the use of genetic engineering for the purpose of extermination (in other words, its use to produce biological or other weapons capable of exterminating the human species); the fertilisation of human eggs for purposes other than reproduction (research, experimentation and other non-reproductive purposes); cloning and other procedures intended to select race; the use of assisted reproductive technologies without the consent of the woman (including the transfer of a greater

(104) Art. 36 MEC.
(105) Art. 156 *bis* Crim. C.
(106) J.A. Xiol Rius and F.J. Bastida, *Autonomía del paciente, responsabilidad patrimonial y derechos fundamentales*, Madrid, Fundación Coloquio Jurídico Europeo, 2012, p. 272-274.
(107) Art. 159-161 Crim. C.
(108) M.C. Gómez Rivero, "La responsabilidad penal del médico", *in* M. Camas Jimena (ed.), *Responsabilidad médica*, Valencia, Tirant lo Blanch, 2013, p. 76.

number of embryos than agreed by the woman or permitted by law).

Disclosing confidential information: Finally, the Criminal Code categorises this case as an offence against "privacy, against the right to control one's image and against the inviolability of the home"[(109)]. A violation "of the duty of confidentiality or non-disclosure", in other words of the duty of discretion and confidentiality imposed on professionals, is sanctioned. Therefore, the protected legal right in question is privacy. However, another interest is also guaranteed, without being qualified as a protected legal right: the relationship of trust existing between doctor and patient. This category of offence is committed, for example, by a doctor who discloses medical information on a patient to a third party[(110)], or who uses confidential information inappropriately or acquires confidential data from patients in a hospital or in a private practice[(111)].

C. – *Civil protection*

A violation of these rights can also result in a civil liability that can be taken before the ordinary courts (civil or administrative litigation, depending on whether they were violated by a private practitioner or by the public administration). There are numerous civil liability actions in the health sector.

In the absence of the patient's informed consent, a doctor's civil liability can be engaged when all of the following conditions are combined[(112)]: the subject suffers damage following a medical intervention; the damage suffered constitutes a risk that is typical of the intervention carried out; there is no malpractice by the doctor (since, in this case, the doctor faces the consequences of the absence of information alone) and in the case of a failure to provide information about a risk that subsequently happened leading to a reduction of the patient's physical integrity or to his

(109) Art. 199 Crim. C. Offences against the private life are set out in articles 197 to 201.

(110) Cass. (Crim. Ch.), 4 April 2001: case of a doctor who disclosed to a third party that one of his patients had undergone two abortions.

(111) Cass. (Crim. Ch.), 4 December 2001.

(112) J.L. Seoane Spiegelberg, "Apuntes sobre la responsabilidad civil médica: su tratamiento ante los tribunales", *in* D. Bello Janeiro (ed.) *Régimen jurídico de la responsabilidad sanitaria*, Reus, 2013, p. 84-87.

death[113]. The lack of information – which is a legal obligation for the doctor – transforms the medical act into an unauthorised action, as it jeopardises the patient's right to autonomy, meaning that the damage resulting from the intervention becomes unlawful and eligible for compensation.

At the same time, however, it is important to note that the existence of patient's informed consent does not exclude the liability of the doctor if the medical act performed was not legally authorised. Informed consent must not be confused with a "right to irresponsibility"[114].

Cases of civil liability for a violation of privacy are also common[115].

We have already stated that a violation of the principle of human dignity cannot be cited in isolation. In some cases, however, the courts have ruled that the moral harm caused by such a violation can give rise to compensation. Indeed, the Higher Court of Justice of Catalonia (Administrative litigation Chamber), on February 2, 1999, ordered the Catalan Health Service to pay compensation for the moral harm caused to the family of a AIDS inpatient who had been placed on a mattress on the floor surrounded by dirt[116]. The ruling was based on the fact that "the care in question was not that to which each human being is entitled, particularly when sick [...] and which requires all appropriate measures to be taken to guarantee his personality and human dignity".

D. – *Administrative protection*

This protection comes into play in the event of a violation of a fundamental right (integrity and privacy) by a public administration[117].

(113) The information was not provided or it was inadequate.

(114) Cass. (Adm. Litigation Ch.), 10 October 2000.

(115) That was the case, for example, in the judgment of the Supreme Court, Civil Chamber, of 29 September 1999, which ordered a doctor, the editor of a publication and the publishers to pay compensation for the publication of photos of a patient before and after breast surgery, in which her face was shown, without the patient's prior consent.

(116) Superior Court of Justice of Catalonia (Administrative Litigation Ch.), 2 February 1999.

(117) Procedures established by L. n° 29-1998, 13 July 1998, governing the administrative litigation courts (art. 114 et seq.).

In addition, the laws governing special medical practices also provide for administrative sanctions in the case of a failure by an authorised establishment to comply with the duties or principles imposed on them This is the case, for example, with the Law on assisted reproductive technologies(118): a failure by the establishment to comply with the duty of confidentiality concerning information on gametes donors is punishable by a financial penalty. For more serious offences, the penalty may go as far as ordering the establishment to be shut down.

Conclusion

Discussing the ethical and bioethical principles relating to health and medicine, *i.e.* concerning life and the person, leads one to consider their universal nature.

In Spain, these principles have been incorporated into key principles with regard to their categorisation and protection (fundamental rights and personality rights). This is hardly surprising as medicine has a direct impact on the human being at a time when he is particularly vulnerable. We must not forget that these rights – fundamental and personality rights – are not "granted" by the legislature, but are naturally "recognised" by it, insofar as they derive from human dignity.

In both ethical and legal terms, human dignity is the cornerstone of the entire system of protection in Spain. The maximum respect for the person, a unique and very special subject regardless of his or her condition is the focal point on which all legal regulation is based. The subjective rights of health legislation are based from this general protection of the person and his dignity. They are, therefore, not the result of the State's will, but rather are imposed on the State.

As a result of this definition of the principles of protection in Spain, the body cannot be separated from the person. It is not possible to protect and defend the body without defending the person who is, at the end of the day, the holder of the rights. It leads in any case, to avoid at all cost thinking of the body – the person – as an object. The protection exists not only with regard to the living person, but also the dead body, which is the continuation

(118) L. n° 14-2006, 26 May 2006, on assisted reproduction, chap. VIII.

of the person it once was. The death of a person does not result in a void in terms of protection; the substance of the person continues to be effective after death, hence the protection afforded by the legal system.

Addressing the question of the protection of the body is crucial since this protection is institutionalised by means of the very appropriate legal mechanisms.

THE PRINCIPLES OF PROTECTION OF THE HUMAN BODY IN FRENCH LAW: THE DETERMINING INFLUENCE OF BIOMEDICINE

Francis KERNALEGUEN

Emeritus Professor at the University of Rennes 1, IODE-CRJO UMR CNRS 6262, (France)

Dean Jean Carbonnier, defended paradoxically that French law held a disembodied notion of marriage that was contrary to that of Canon law (1). Likewise, it must also be noted that the body is excluded from the major categories of civil law that distinguish "persons" from "things" – which it deems to be commodities – endowed with duties.

In reality, however, although it has been omitted for long from the Civil Code, the human body has never been denied protection; far from it. Accordingly, criminal law has always included a significant number of offences of all kinds intended to punish any type of harm to the body. Article 1128 of the Civil Code introduced the prohibition and invalidation of agreements concerning the body (2), and civil liability has produced an abundance of case law on compensation for physical harm. The simple truth is that the fact the word is missing from the codes, is closely related to the notion of a human being as an inseparable combination of body

(1) J. CARBONNIER, "Terre et ciel dans le droit français du mariage", in *Mélanges Ripert*, vol. 1, Paris, LGDJ, 1950, p. 325.

(2) Not entirely consistent, as the wording states: "Only things which may be the subject matter of legal transactions between private individuals may be the object of agreements", while it is specifically understood that the body is not a commodity. The same inconsistency can be found in the *Code noir* (the Black Code) in the edict of March 1685, which regulated slavery in the West Indies (you will note that the revocation of the Nantes edict marking the resumption of the persecution of Protestants occurred in the same year): article 43 (lightly) punishes a master who kills his slave, while article 44 qualifies the slave as personal property, thereby denying him the status of a person (see L. SALA-MOLINS, *le Code noir ou le calvaire de Canaan*, coll. Quadrige, Paris, PUF, 1987).

and mind: "the human body is not a thing, it is the very person"(3). Furthermore, is it not surprising that the protection of the body was included in a volume concerning "crimes and offences against the person"(4) or that the person is the subject of the first section of the Civil Code.

However, an explicit legislative foundation was missing from civil law regarding the treatment and protection of the body: for lack of a collection of specific articles in the Civil Code, it was left to case law to shape the principles and construct a legal system. The emergence and development of biomedicine gave rise to an even more urgent need to set standards. It appeared necessary, and even urgent, to clarify old principles, make explicit previously unexpressed principles and set down new principles. As so often legislators left it to the judges to contend with the issues raised, with the result that, once again, it was case law that gradually shaped a civil status for the body. It was only twenty years later that the laws of July 29th 1994, called the "bioethics laws"(5), codified the rules that the judges had patiently formulated: in particular law no. 94-653, which finally specifically included the body in the Civil Code by inserting a chapter entitled "Respect for the human body".

The principles of protection currently in effect are the result of a gradual, pragmatic and sometimes heterogeneous construction: in bioethics, case law has almost always preceded the law, which is divided among three codes: the Civil Code, the Public Health Code and the Criminal Code. Case law itself has benefited from the trial and error of contractual practices and deontological self-limitations. The influence of external authorities over the traditional public authorities, and even a growing openness towards civil society should, in particular, be mentioned(6). The *Cour de Cassation* itself

(3) G. Cornu, *Droit civil. Introduction, les personnes, les biens*, coll. Domat droit privé, 12th ed., Paris, Montchrestien, 2005, n° 479. The body is not subject to ownership (inc. the ambiguity in Art. 18 of the Declaration of Rights, Constitution Year I: "no man [...] can sell himself or be sold: his person is not a disposable property [...]"): According to an appropriate expression, *the person does not have a body, it is its body*.

(4) Section 2 of the Criminal Code provides a much broader protection that covers the entire human species.

(5) Subsequently amended or added to on several occasions: most recently L. n° 84-2011, 7 July 2011, itself amended on one point by L. n° 715-2011, 6 August 2013.

(6) As well as the role of the Ordre national des médecins (Medical Association), it should be noted that the National Consultative Ethics Committee (Conseil national consultatif d'éthique) has issued more than 120 notices since 1984. In addition, the law of 7 July 2011 was preceded by about one hundred public hearings by a Parliamentary Mission and by *États*

used a completely new *amicus curiae* procedure for the hearings of Jean Bernard, President of the National Consultative Ethics Committee, which led to the ruling of May 31st, 1991 making gestational surrogacy illegal[7].

The protection of the human body is ensured, ultimately, by a range of extremely variable standards: constitutional, legislative, case law and ethical criteria. However international law has a somewhat limited role in this system: not only does the "Conseil Constitutionnel" refer more naturally to the Declaration of Human Rights and the constitutional corpus, but the *Cour de Cassation* or the *Conseil d'État* most frequently turn to the European Convention on Human Rights and other international instruments simply to argue that the decisions they make are in full recognition of these texts[8]!

In conclusion, the principles of protection of the human body as they appear in the context of biomedicine constitute a complete system characterised by a variety of parts (I) organised and structured according to their contrasting value (II).

I. – The variety of principles of protection of the human body

The concern to protect the human body generated a set of principles whose variety is emphasized by the different terms used. This proliferation directly challenges the autonomy of the person: the protection of the body is not aimed solely at third parties, it can also affect the interested party him/herself, with the result that the person, in being physically protected against him/herself finds their own freedom constrained. Furthermore, determining the principles must require an effort to strike a balance between effectively protecting the human body and

généraux (general assemblies) for bioethics that gave rise, in particular, to "citizens" debates in the regional forums open to all.

(7) Cass., plen. Ass., 31 May 1991, *D.*, 1991, 417, rep. Y. Chartier, note D. Thouvenin, *JCP*, 1991, II, 21752, comm. J. Bernard, concl. Y. Dontenwille, note F. Terre.

(8) Concerning surrogacy carried out abroad, see Cass. (1st civ.), 6 April 2011, n° 09-17130: the reference to conformity with the ECHR and the ICRC has even been dropped, see Cass. (1st civ.), 13 September 2013, n° 12-18315, due to a change in the legal basis for the refusal to transcribe foreign laws (from international public order to fraud into French law). However, the judgments of 2011 resulted in the ECHR censuring France on 26 June 26 2014: ECHR, 5th sec., 26 June 2014, *Mennesson v. France*, n° 65192/11 and *Labassee v. France*, n° 65941/11.

preserving an individual's autonomy (A). The balance between these two principles isn't fixed: the relatively recent emergence and application of a cross-cutting principle that simultaneously embraces both protection and freedom has refocused a heated attention on this problematic issue. (B).

A. – *The quest for a balance between the autonomy of the person and the protection of the body*

Article 16-1 of the Civil Code proclaims the right of respect for one's body, which seems to impose an obligation on third parties that protects the autonomy of its beneficiary. The following two paragraphs set out two crucial elements of this protection: the principle of the inviolability of the human body and the principle that the human body may not be the subject of a property right.

1. *The principle of the inviolability of the human body* is, according to one author, "filled with an immemorial customary force"(9). It stipulates that everyone must respect the integrity of the bodies of others, as expressed by the prohibition in the phrase *noli me tangere*. This respect is imposed on others without any time limit, as set out in article 16-1-1 of the Civil Code arising from the law of December 19th, 2008, stating that "the respect due to the human body does not cease with death". Consequently, the law protects the corpse, the remains or the ashes of the deceased(10). On the other hand, this protection stands on less firm grounds before birth. The law of January 17th, 1975 on abortion introduced the principle of the guarantee of "respect of every human being from the commencement of *life*". This principle was modified with an editorial change by law 94-653 of July 29, 1994 with the result that the article 16 of the Civil Code states that "the law [...] guarantees the respect of the human being from the outset of life". For all that, the Constitutional Council believed that the legislature could decide "that the principle of the respect of every human being from the outset of life was not applicable to embryos fertilised *in vitro*"(11). The principle is only, consequently, fully effective in the case of an

(9) G. Cornu, *Droit civil. Introduction, les personnes, les biens, op. cit.*, n° 480.

(10) Art. 16-1-1, § 2, Civ. C.; art. L 2223-18-1, CGCT. See Cass. (1st civ.), 16 September 2010, *société Encore Events v. L'association Ensemble contre la peine de mort et autres*, (case called *Our body*), *D.*, 2010, 2750, note G. Loiseau and 2754, note B. Edelman prohibiting the display of corpses for commercial purposes.

(11) Const. C., 27 July 1994, *D.*, 1995, 237, note B. Mathieu.

embryo that has been implanted and is therefore involved in a process of *in utero* development.

Inviolability proscribes unlawful violations of the human body as well as unlawful acts relating to body parts or products. This implies, *a contrario*, that there is therefore the possibility of "legal" violations. The law indeed allows, quite naturally, invasions of the integrity of the body "in case of medical emergency for the person or exceptionally in the therapeutic interest of others"(12). However, the lawfulness does not depend only on a legitimate reason, it still requires the express prior consent of the person except, of course, when there is a need for a "therapeutic intervention to which he/she is not able to consent to"(13).

The sudden introduction of consent into this system emphasizes in an implicit but striking manner, the restatement of the principle of personal autonomy. That the person can decide for him/herself, body as well as mind, is at the heart of individual freedom and the ability of everyone to lead their lives as they see fit. In the words of William Henley, the individual can proclaim "I am the master of my fate, the captain of my soul"(14).

The question of the person's control over their body is often raised in critical terms from the perspective of the right over that body(15), with the conflict between holders of the right to "control their own bodies" and subscribers to a "principle of bodily integrity". Furthermore, it is this principle, together with that of the personal status being outside the scope of any transactions (legal personality), through which the *Cour de Cassation*, in the absence of any specific legislative provisions, intended to make surrogacy illegal, even if non-remunerated(16). The truth is that tackling the issue of a person's authority over his own body from a perspective of a right over that body does not come without a certain ambiguity: the capacity to have control of how one disposes

(12) Art. 16-3, § 1, Civ. C.

(13) Art. 16-3, § 2, Civ. C.

(14) W. Ernest Henley, "Invictus" (1875), *in* A. Quiller-Couch, *The Oxford Book of English Verse*, (1900). See, on the central importance of the wishes of the patient with regard to withdrawing care, CE Ass., 24 June 2014, case *Vincent Lambert*, n° 375081.

(15) See M. Gobert, "Réflexions sur les sources du droit et les 'principes' d'indisponibilité du corps humain et de l'état des personnes (à propos de la maternité de substitution)", *RTD civ.*, 1992, p. 489.

(16) Cass., plen. Ass., 31 May 1991, above note 7. The law has since prohibited this practice.

of something is one of the attributes of 'real' rights and therefore falls within the category of property[17]. Yet the law specifically claims to connect the human body to the person and not to consider it as a thing: proclaiming the bodily integrity paradoxically helps to commodify it! That is undoubtedly why the law of July 29th 1994 – and subsequently the *Cour de Cassation* – "no longer pronounces the principle of bodily integrity that was contradicted and belied by all the acts it allows"[18]. Article 16-1 of the Civil Code now states only, in the final paragraph, that "the human body, its elements and its products may not form the subject of a property right".

2. *The principle that the human body may not form the subject of a property right* "does not contradict the power of everyone over their own bodies"[19]. Intended to cover the human body, its parts and its products, this principle secures the body in the category of a being rather than a possession and removes it from the category of things and assets by declaring that anything taken from the body does not become an item of property: despite being separated from the body, an element of the body still belongs to humanity[20].

The recognition of this principle overshadowed the other ambiguous grounds used by doctrine or case law to rule out acts relating to the human body, in particular those agreements concerning assisted reproduction or surrogacy: in addition to the reference to a principle of bodily integrity, there was, traditionally, a further reference to article 1128 of the Civil Code, according to which "only material things which may be the subject matter of legal transactions between private individuals may be the object of agreements". It was, moreover, in endorsement of this article combined with article 6 of the same Code[21] that the Plenary

(17) We can also, it is true, talk of control over an action or a right. This is a question of control over the body or the right to which it is subject.

(18) G. CORNU, *op. cit.*, n° 481; *add.* the comments of M. GOBERT, *op. cit.* The *Cour de Cassation* no longer uses this principle to make surrogacy illegal: Cass. (1st civ.), 6 April 2011, *D.*, 2011, p. 1064, obs. X. LABBE and p. 1522, note D. BERTHIAU and L. BRUNET: as a result, only the principle of legal status being outside the scope of any transactions is categorised as an "essential principle of French law". (On the critique of this principle, see M. GOBERT, *op. cit.*, n° 31).

(19) G. CORNU, *ibid.*

(20) G. CORNU, *ibid.*: "the non-ownership of the elements and products of the human body is a radical affirmation of their non-animality and non-materiality; the memory of their humanity is indelibly imprinted on them".

For a reflection from a humorous work of fiction, see J.-P. BAUD, *L'affaire de la main volée, une histoire juridique du corps*, Paris, Seuil, 1993.

(21) Art. 6 Civ. C.: "Statutes relating to public policy and morals may not de derogated from by private agreements."

Assembly of the *Cour de Cassation* initially made all surrogacy operations illegal, considering that the subject of such agreements was outside the legal trading framework and therefore unlawful: these acts contravened to the public order principle of bodily integrity(22). The application of article 1128, which specifically and inevitably refers to the order of commodities, contributed to a sort of paradox: the commodification of the body for which protagonists of the unlawful procedure were blamed!

Law 94-653 of July 29th 1994 made these contortions futile by stating in the current article 16-7 of the Civil Code civil that "all agreements relating to procreation or gestation on account of a third party are void", this nullity being for reasons of public order in accordance with article 16-9. At the same time, the *Cour de Cassation* for its part stopped referring to the principle of bodily integrity(23). The principle of non-ownership more clearly ensures the primacy of the person proclaimed at the head of article 16 of the Civil Code by clearly stating that the body has no monetary value liable to be included among the assets of an estate.

Non-ownership therefore combines well with the principle of autonomy, which allows the individual control over his own body. It does not allow the exercise of this control to result in the "ownership" of the body or its parts and products, which is a risk amplified by biomedical advances. All of the laws relating to body parts and products not only require the consent of the person, but rule out any suggestion of payment: taking samples of bodily substances and collecting products must be cost-free and profit-free(24). Furthermore, this also applies to biomedical research(25). This requirement tries to avoid turning the body into a source of profit by linking the consent procedure to research with the request of a payment – the only compensation permitted – at a fixed rate if appropriate – is the reimbursements of the costs and of the losses imposed by the research(26). That is why these acts are

(22) Cass., plen. Ass., 31 May 1991, *D.*, 1991, 417; *JCP*, 1991, II, p. 21752, *supra* note 7.

(23) Cass. (1st civ.), 6 April 2011, *D.*, 2011, 1064 note X. Labbe; Cass. (1st civ.), 13 September 2013, *D.*, 2013, p. 2377, note C. Petit, p. 2382, obs. I. Gallmeister and p. 2384, note M. Fabre-Magnan; Cass. (1st civ.), 19 March 2014, n° 13-50005.

(24) Art. L 1211-4 Public Health C.: wording of principle used in various cases of collection and sampling.

(25) Art. L 1121-11 Public Health C.

(26) See Art. L 1121-11 and L 1221-3 Public Health C.; the cost-free nature of donations of gametes is currently under debate, following the observation that egg donations, unlike

referred to as "donations", in order to underline that they are, by their very nature, free and are purely an act of human kindness[27].

In French law, the altruism of acts relating to the body, and above all to body parts and substances, is not only guaranteed by the cost-free principle; it is also supported by another principle, that of anonymity. According to article 16-8 of the Civil Code, "No information enabling the identification of both the person that donates an element or a product of his body and the person who receives it may be disclosed. The donor may not be acquainted with the identity of the recipient and the recipient may not be acquainted with that of the donor"[28]. Only doctors can have access to such identifying information in cases of medical necessity. This principle protects both the donor, for example against legal action by the recipient[29], and the recipient against action by the donor[30]. Above all, it dashes any hope the donor might have of recognition or compensation and eliminates any feeling of obligation or indebtedness on the part of the recipient[31].

For all that, the principle of anonymity, at least with regard to parentage, is under debate. Some children, whether adopted or the result of a gametes donation, invoke the right to know their genetic origins, which calls into question, at least partially, the tradition of secrecy in French law[32]. The law of January 22, 2002 on the right to access one's personal origins has not challenged this tradition of secrecy. In spite of a stamp of Constitutional[33] and

sperm donations, are more restrictive and give rise to greater expenses due to the losses that require compensation.

(27) The unpaid nature of the donation for the person in question does not exclude payment to the practitioners and service providers who treat the donor and the receiver – *i.e.* a pricing mechanism (*e.g.* Decree of 22 March 2012 on pricing of blood products).

(28) This secrecy and anonymity principle is used with regard to parentage (Art. 311-20 Civ. C.) and Art. 1211-5, 1244-7 and 2141-5 Public Health C.

(29) *E.g.* Art. 311-19 Civ. C.

(30) Comp. Art. 311-20 Civ. C.

(31) In cases where there is, exceptionally, no anonymity, it is hoped that the relationship between donor and recipient will not be identified and that there will be no feeling of obligation. However, there is obviously some pressure, if only moral, on the donor: see art. L 1231-1 Public Health C., for live organ donations.

(32) Regarding this calling into question, see I. THERY, *Couple, filiation et parenté aujourd'hui. Le droit face aux mutations de la famille et de la vie privée*, coll. La Documentation française, Paris, Odile Jacob, 1998. For a European comparison (7 States), see the Senate summary note: *Le droit à la connaissance de ses origines génétiques*, 4 June 2014, available at: www.senat.fr.

(33) Const. C., 16 May 2012, decision n° 2012-248 QPC, *JORF*, 17 May 2012, p. 9154.

Conventional[34] approval, the survival of secrecy is not entirely sheltered from further questioning[35]. If this proves to be the case, it would have to be decided to what degree secrecy would be lifted, and how it would be achieved. Even if the principle of anonymity is preserved in a more limited form, it will be necessary to establish, in those cases with no further right to secrecy, the conditions of the disclosure of the identity of those persons concerned by acts relating to the body, in order in particular to preserve the ideal of solidarity against the temptation for profit.

It is indeed solidarity between humans that justifies biomedical practices implemented in the interests of others, just as it is medical necessity that legitimises their use in the best interests of the person him/herself; in both cases subject of course to informed consent. However, the authority of an individual will is not absolute: public order, as we have seen, sets limits to the ability to decide for oneself. Yet the emergence of a new principle, as ambitious as it is unspecific, offers public order, new intervention opportunities.

B. – *The emergence of a guiding principle*

After proclaiming the primacy of the person, article 16 of the Civil Code, resulting from the law of July 29, 1994, "[...] prohibits any infringement to the dignity of the person." Respect for human dignity was not mentioned in the initial draft: it was during the debates that this was proposed, as a foundation to the primacy of the person. In fact, dignity is inherent to the humanity of the person: all that is human is concerned by dignity, and dignity concerns only what is human. It is indeed this unfathomable link that requires the declaration of a primacy of the person, and

(34) ECHR, gde ch., 13 February 2003, *Odièvre v. France*, *JCP*, 2003, II, p. 10049, note A. Gouttenoire-Cornut.

(35) ECHR, 2nd Sect., 25 September 2012, *Godelli v. Italy* (censured for not improving access to origins). Comp. ECHR, 13 July 2006, *Jäggi v. Switzerland*, *RTD civ.*, 2006, 727, obs. J.-P. Marguenaud and 16 June 2011, *Pascaud v. France*, *D.*, 2012, p. 1433, obs. F. Granet Lambrechts on post-mortem genetic identification: the prohibition imposed by article 16-11 of the Civil Code is in breach of article 8 of the Convention. (The French Republic was ordered to pay the petitioner the sum of €2,750,000 by Order of 8 November 2012). However, for gametes donations, see EC Opinion, 13 June 2013, M. Molenat, *D.*, 2013, p. 1626, obs. R. Grand: the anonymity of the donation and the corresponding impossibility for the child to know the identity of the donor are not contrary to articles 8 and 14 of the European Convention on Human Rights.

therefore a hierarchisation between the community of mankind and the world of commodities.

The Constitutional Council, in its decision of July 27th 1994, based its declaration of conformity of the law to the Constitution by referring to the Preamble to the 1946 Constitution, which proclaimed constitutional rights, freedoms and principles, emphasizing that "in the wake of the victory of free people over the regimes that tried to enslave and degrade the human person, the French people affirms once again that all human beings, regardless of race, religion or belief, possess inalienable and sacred rights". For the Council, this means "that the protection of the dignity of the human person against any form of enslavement and degradation is a principle of constitutional value"(36). The introduction of the principle into French law is therefore not explicitly related to the international laws that had already sanctioned it; in particular the United Nations Charter(37), the Preamble to the Universal Declaration of Human Rights(38), the Oviedo Convention(39) and the Charter of Fundamental Rights of the European Union of 26 October 2012.

The principle of respect for human dignity can be found in case law in a wide variety of fields. It is particularly significant that the most important rulings concerned human remains, the specific subject of article 16-1-1 of the Civil Code arising from the law of December 19th 2008, under the terms of which "the respect due to the human body does not cease with death. The remains of deceased persons, including the ashes of those who were cremated, must be treated with respect, dignity and decency". In fact, the person disappears at the time of death: after death, there is no longer a person, there is no one(40), and thus the body-person becomes the dead corpse thing. This "corpse" is nevertheless to some degree "sacred", directly linked to the principle of respect for human dignity.

---

(36) Const. C., 27 July 1994, n° 94-343/344 DC, *D.*, 1995, p. 237, note B. Mathieu.

(37) San Francisco on 26 June 1945.

(38) Paris, 10 December 1948. Likewise the international law related to civil and political rights (16 December 1966) or the New York agreements of 1 March 1980 and 16 January 1990 concerning women and children respectively.

(39) Convention Oviedo, 4 April 1997, ratified 13 December 2011.

(40) See J. Carbonnier, *Droit civil. 1. Introduction, les personnes, la famille*, Paris, PUF, 2004, n° 210, citing the more radical, M. Planiol, *Traité élémentaire de droit civil*, t. 1, 12th ed., 1935, n° 371: "the dead are no longer persons; they are no longer anything".

This reasoning led the *Cour de Cassation* to condemn the publication, after his death, of a photograph taken by the torturers of a victim of acts of oppression and torture in order to make a ransom demand as "contrary to human dignity and constituting an infringement of the respect due to the dead"(41). In the same way, it deemed that the display of corpses for commercial purposes was in breach of article 16-1-1 para. 2, stipulating that human remains must be treated with respect, dignity and decency(42). However, while the commercial exploitation of a corpse is undoubtedly contrary to the requirement for dignity, its being displayed in a museum is a more delicate issue to assess(43).

The question was raised in particular with regard to the Maori heads displayed in the Rouen Museum, which the city intended to return to the New Zealand authorities who had made a claim to get them back. To comply with the claim from New Zealand, the city referred to the provisions of articles 16-1 and 16-5 of the Civil Code and, in particular, on the principles of dignity and non-ownership. The Administrative Court of Appeal in Douai reversed this decision on the basis of "the provisions of the Heritage Code that stipulates that the property of a public person belonging to a collection in the museums of France cannot be disposed of, placing these items under a specific regime of protection distinct from the property right pronounced in article 16-1 of the Civil Code"(44). Finally a special law was required, dated May 18th 2010, to authorise the declassification and then the return of the Maori heads.

The principle of respect for human dignity also challenges personal freedom and autonomy – the issue then becomes one of knowing if this principle can result in the prohibition or even punishment of behaviour or practices freely chosen by an individual. The *Conseil d'État* accordingly validated the decree

(41) Cass. (1st civ.), 1 July 2010, *D.*, 2010, 2044, note P.-J. Delage: case known as the "*gang des barbares*".

(42) Cass. (1st civ.), 16 September 2010, *D.*, 2010, 2750, note G. Loiseau: case of the exhibition "Our Body, the universe within", presented by its creators as being educational and scientific.

(43) See M. Cornu, "Le corps humain au musée, de la personne à la chose ?", *D.*, 2009, 1907.

(44) CAA Douai, 24 July 2008, *JCP*, II, 10181, note C. Saujot: it is symptomatic of the "specificity" of public law that the administrative judge referred to "the patrimonial right pronounced in article 16-1 of the Civil Code" while this law specifically repudiates such a right! As a result, the corpse and human remains can constitute public assets (inalienable according to the Moulins edict of 1566): in theory based on respect for dignity?

of the mayor who prohibited a "dwarf-tossing" event in his municipality, considering it to be an attraction that was damaging to the dignity of the human person, even though the individual in question was voluntarily participating to the event(45). The European Court of Human Rights is more focused on favouring freely expressed consent over an objective notion of dignity, so that personal autonomy can include the freedom to indulge in practices considered degrading, immoral or even dangerous for the person(46).

Respect for dignity nevertheless inspires numerous rules and principles: in addition to an entire chapter of the Criminal Code (articles 225-1 to 225-25), it is the direct foundation for the prohibition of harm to the integrity of mankind and, as a consequence, the prohibition of eugenic practices, of human cloning and of the modification of genetic characteristics in order to alter a person's descent(47). The fact is that dignity imposes itself on the individual as a mark of his belonging to humanity: he cannot renounce it for himself or for his descendants or, of course, for third parties. In some way, we are all custodians of the responsibility of belonging to mankind: no one should be able to escape that responsibility with their own free will alone.

This assortment of principles related to the protection of the human body can lead to a real risk of conflicts, occasionally intense between principles that can only be resolved by considering their respective value.

II. – The value of principles of protection of the human body

In order for the principles of protection of the body to fulfil their key function, it is necessary to ensure their coexistence through a

(45) EC Ass., 27 October 1995, *D.*, 1996, 177, note G. Lebreton: the individual concerned thus lost his livelihood and subsequently lived on benefits, as he stated 20 years later (the *Est républicain* journal, 16 February 2014)! Comp. for simulated killing games, ECJ 14 October 2004, *AJDA*, 2005, p. 152 (same solution).

(46) ECHR, 1st sect., 17 February 2005, *K.A. v. Belgium*, concerning sadomasochistic practices condemned only because one of the protagonists had stopped consenting! For a critical presentation of this judgment, see M. Fabre-Magnan, "Le sadisme n'est pas un droit de l'homme", *D.*, 2005, p. 2973. See the current debates on prostitution and the possible sanctioning of customers: a draft law adopted on 4 December 2013 at the Assembly is under discussion in the Senate.

(47) Art. 16-4 Civ. C.

hierarchy aimed at avoiding or resolving conflicts (A) and guarantee their effectiveness (B).

A. – *The hierarchy of principles*

Among the established principles, there is one that clearly stands out in French law: the principle of the protection of the dignity of the human person. In fact, in its decision of July 27th 1994 concerning "bioethical" laws, the Constitutional Council declared that "the protection of the dignity of the human person against any form of enslavement and degradation constitutes a principle of constitutional value" and this qualification was revisited and developed by the same Council in its decision of November 19th 2009 concerning the Prisons Regulation Act[(48)].

As a result, this principle is placed above all others inasmuch as it is the only one to have achieved this supreme value: although the 1994 decision certainly referred to other principles, it presents them as being intended to ultimately ensure the protection of dignity[(49)]. This is what led one author to qualify this principle as a "matrix principle", as it is the basis for all the others that seem to be placed to serve it[(50)]. In the field of bioethics, therefore, two categories of principles exist side by side; the first, the only one to have, directly and specifically, a constitutional value, serving as a basis to the others, which are necessary to ensure compliance with the first. However, it is necessary to take into account the impact of the individual freedom proclaimed by articles 1, 2 and 4 of the Declaration of the Rights of Man and of the Citizen of 26 August 1789 and, consequently, also incorporated into the constitutional corpus.

(48) Const. C., 19 November 2009, n° 2009-593 DC, *JORF*, 25 November 2009, p. 20222: to recall the constitutional value of the principle of protection of the dignity of the human person, the decision places it among the "inalienable and sacred" rights guaranteed to every human being by the Preamble to the Constitution of 1946.

(49) Const. C., 27 July 1994, aforementioned, recital n° 18: "The 'bioethics' laws pronounce a set of principles that include the primacy of the human person, respect of the human being from the outset of its life, inviolability, integrity, the lack of any patrimonial character of the human body and the integrity of mankind; the principles thus declared are intended to ensure compliance with the constitutional principle of the protection of human dignity."

(50) B. Mathieu, "Pour une reconnaissance de 'principes matriciels' en matière de protection constitutionnelle des droits de l'homme", *D.*, 1995, chron., p. 211. Similarly, we can also find the qualification of "cardinal principle".

The regulation of any tensions between these principles, rights or freedoms depends on this hierarchy. Using one proven method, notably practised by the European Court of Human Rights, case law seeks to maintain a "fair balance" between the conflicting values(51). The *Cour de Cassation* has been striving to do exactly this for more than a decade(52) by setting out the criteria to be taken into consideration to achieve it. For example, while the confrontation between freedom of expression and freedom of the press on the one hand, and the respect for one's privacy and the right of control over one's publicity on the other, results in the promotion of the right to information, the *Cour de Cassation* states that it is "under the sole condition of respect for the dignity of the human person"(53).

However, this unique position of the principle of dignity, the final refuge for the protection of the human body, raises serious problems: the power of the principle is equalled only by the arbitrary manner in which it is applied. In the first place, the implementation of this "exception of dignity" seems to be void of any rationality: in what way, for example, does the publication of the photograph of the dead body of an assassinated prefect do more harm to the dignity of the human person than that of a seriously injured woman lying on a stretcher following a bombing, or that of an adolescent in the same situation after an accident just before he dies(54)?

Secondly, the very idea of human dignity is subject to debate, particularly in terms of its possible conflict with the concept of personal autonomy. If we take an objective approach to dignity, the will of a person is limited even when nobody else is directly involved. If, on the other hand, we adopt a subjective approach, it is the individual will that determines the parameters of dignity:

(51) See ECHR, gde ch., 16 December 2010, *A., B. and C v. Ireland*, n° 25579/05, for a conflict, with regard to access to abortion, between a woman's right to respect for privacy and the rights of unborn children.

(52) See Cass. (1st civ.), 9 July 2003, *JCP*, 2003, p. 10139, note J. Ravanas for the necessary conciliation of the right to respect for one's privacy and freedom of expression having "an identical normative value" with regard to the provisions of articles 8 and 10 of the ECHR.

(53) *E.g.*, Cass. (1st civ.), 4 November 2004, *JCP*, 2004, II, 10186, note D. Bakouche; *D.*, 2005, 696, note I. Corpart: judgment given in accordance with art. 10 of the ECHR and 9 and 10 of the Civ. C.

(54) Respectively: Cass. (1st civ.), 20 December 2000, *JCP*, 2001, II, 10488, concl. J. Sainte Rose, note J. Ravanas; Cass. (1st civ.), 20 February 2001, *D.*, 2001, 119, note J.-P. Gridel; Cass. (1st civ.), 4 November 2004, aforementioned.

assuredly for the individual himself, and, as the case may be, for those persons who voluntarily take part in the same action[(55)]. This second approach appears to have, as we have seen, the approval of the European Court of Human Rights – at least for the time being – whereas the objective approach seems to be more appealing to French case law and legal doctrine[(56)]. Such uncertainty is harmful to the principle presented as fundamental to the protection of the human body, leading to challenge its effectiveness as well as that of the principles associated with it.

B. – *The effectiveness of the principles*

The principles of protection of the human body, like any principle, are expressed in general and often unconditional terms. Yet this does not make them effective to apply: their concise wording has to be supplemented by explanations, conditions, limits and even exceptions[(57)]. It is also necessary to ensure that they are enforced by imposing appropriate sanctions.

1. *The limitation of the principles* is relatively easy to implement with regard to those that have no particular constitutional value: the law can explain or limit what it has itself produced and proclaimed. For example, that is how the principle under the terms of which respect for the human being is guaranteed from the outset of life, expressly stated in article 1 of the law of January 17th 1975, becomes the subject of an exception under article 2, which legalises abortion: originally temporary, this exception was made permanent by the law of December 31st, 1979, while the deadline for abortion was changed to 12 weeks by the law of July 4th 2001. In the same way, the Constitutional Council gave the legislature the authority to judge that this principle should not be applied to

(55) For example, the debate on euthanasia, which sees dignity invoked both by those who oppose it (objective approach) and those who demand it (subjective approach): on this issue, see case of *Vincent Lambert*, EC Ass., 24 June 2014, cited above, and the seizure of jurisdiction of the ECHR, which on the same day urged the government to suspend the execution of the decree of the Council of State pending an order from the Court.

(56) See M. Fabre-Magnan, "Le domaine de l'autonomie personnelle", *D.*, 2008, p. 31; D. Roman, "À corps défendant, la protection de l'individu contre lui-même", *D.*, 2007, p. 1284; R. Desgorces, "Agir contre soi", *RRJ*, 2003, p. 37.

(57) For the expression of a principle in an absolute form and without restriction, with regard to the family name system, see Cass. (1st civ.), 15 March, 1988, *D.*, 1988, p. 549, note J. Massip, and on the same issue, the subsequent wording of limits and conditions, Cass. (1st civ.), 25 May 1992, *D.*, 1992, note F. Boulanger.

embryos fertilised *in vitro*, at least until they are reimplanted in the uterus[(58)]. That is how the principles of protection of the human body come to be allocated with conditions, limitations or exceptions that the law was able to legitimately provide them with, such as, for example, those relating to the inviolability of the human body set out in article 16-3 of the Civil Code or those concerning the principle of non-ownership.

However, the principle of respect for the dignity of the person, a principle with constitutional value, by its very nature escapes the authority of ordinary law: the legislature cannot limit it, only ensure that it is implemented. The fact remains that the judge, through his interpretation, has the quite powerful option of covertly transforming and redefining the scope of such a vague and imprecise principle.

The contrast between the forceful expression of a principle and the reality is not the only difficulty encountered with regard to its effectiveness: compliance with a principle implies sanctions in the event of a violation, and this point also has its share of pitfalls.

2. *Penalties related to the principles* of protection of the human body are an essential component of their effectiveness without which they would be worth no more than a mere moral precept. Given the importance of these principles, case law and legislators have associated strict civil and criminal penalties in case of violations.

According to liability laws, someone who causes any damages or infringes on these protected rights has to pay compensation to the victim... In case of situations created against the law, the judge will consider them as null. Surrogacy is a perfect example of this severity: any contract concerning assisted reproduction or surrogacy is not only null and void, but also the whole process including any resulting adoption[(59)]. The *Cour de Cassation* has even endorsed this solution (the invalidation of an adoption by the "intended" mother), even though the woman was the only adult involved in this illegal process who has continued to care for the

(58) Const. C., 27 July 1994, *D.*, 1995, p. 235, note B. Mathieu: "It is not the role of the Constitutional Council, which does not have the same discretionary power as Parliament, to question the provisions made in this way by the legislature." If, on the other hand, the principle had a constitutional value, the Council could legitimately have exercised its control.

(59) Art. 16-7 Civ. C.; Cass., plen. Ass., 31 May 1991, *D.*, 1991, 417 cited above.

child until age 9[60]! For the courts, the best interest of the child must not permit undermining or limiting the severe nature of the sanction, and the adoption must be invalidated, even at the risk of leaving the child without parentage!

As often, in the case of the French legal system, criminal law has been called on to play its part in complementing and supporting convictions handed down by civil law in this area. The second volume of the Criminal Code, devoted to crimes and offences against the person, contains a number of contraventions dedicated to sanctions on behalf of the principles of protection of the human body. However, the criminal system generally falls foul of the charade employed by those who are involved in illegal biomedical practices. The fact is that, rather than run the risk of a criminal prosecution by carrying out their operation in France, they take care to complete the entire project in a foreign country where this practice is legal, thus escaping the repression provided for under the terms of article L 113-6, para. 2 of the Criminal Code relating to offences committed outside of French territory: such acts are only punishable in France if they are committed by a French national. They can also be punishable according to the law of the country in which they are committed[61].

Indeed, in spite of the development of conventions, charters and other international instruments intended to determine common principles and practices on a European and even global level, there is still a significant variety of approaches in reality... At the same time, not all principles are common to all countries. This diversity, or perhaps these divergences tend to favour a form of avoidance of countries proven to be legally rigorous, and a preference for those known as more lax[62]. If criminal law has lost a significant portion of its efficiency in this case, can civil law still maintain such uncompromising positions?

The *Cour de Cassation* tries to maintain as much as possible the strict sanctions it traditionally applies to illegal practices regarding the principles of protection defended in French law, even

(60) Cass. (1st civ.), 29 June 1994, *D.*, 1994, 581, note Y. Chartier.

(61) See TGI Créteil (ord.), 30 September 2004, *D.*, 2005, p. 476: dismissal ruling in the Mennesson case (surrogacy in California), "as the acts were committed in their entirety in a country where they are not criminal offences".

(62) J.-J. Lemouland, "Le tourisme procréatif", *Petites Affiches*, n° 62, 2001: effect of globalization?

if this means changing the bases and grounds used. Accordingly, faced with outsourced surrogacy practices, the courts have stopped referring to the principle of bodily integrity as put forward in 1991, retaining only the principle that a human being's integrity cannot be violated and that this is an "essential principle of French law"(63). On this basis, the transcription of birth certificates issued abroad was refused on the grounds that they were contrary to French international public order.

However, this refusal is a problem regarding France's compliance with international treaties. Furthermore, the aforementioned decree of 2011 went to great lengths to maintain that "such an invalidation (of the transcribed birth certificates), which does not deprive the children of the maternal and paternal parentage that Californian law gave them or prevent them from living with Mr and Mrs X in France, inflicts no damage on the right to respect for the private and family life of the children or on (their) best interests"(64). More recently, further emphasising its severity, the Court considered that the birth of the child in question was the – fraudulent according to French law – outcome of an overall process including a surrogacy contract rendered null and void according to public order. The advantage of the reference to "fraudulent according to French law" is that, in this case, the Court was able to take it upon itself to broaden the scope of the conventional rules. It stated, "in view of this fraud, neither the best interests of the child guaranteed by article 3 of the International Convention on the Rights of the Child nor the respect for privacy and family life within the meaning of article 8 of the European Convention for the Protection of Human Rights could be usefully invoked"(65). There is therefore no need for specious arguments to try to convince us to comply with international agreements that are immediately invalidated!

The result was that the Supreme Judge seemed to have found an effective way to thwart the schemes of French nationals attempting to circumvent the prohibitions of their national laws. It was apparently a response that would guarantee compliance with

(63) Comp. Cass. (1st civ.), 6 April 2011, n° 10-19053, *D.*, 2011, p. 1522, note D. Berthiau and L. Brunet and Cass., plen. Ass., 31 May 1991, cited above.

(64) Art. 8 ECHR; Art 3, § 1, Int. CRC.

(65) Cass. (1st civ.), 13 September 2013, *D.*, 2013, p. 2384, note M. Fabre-Magnan; along the same lines, Cass. (1st civ.), 19 March 2014, *D.*, 2014, p. 901, obs. J.-P. Jean, and p. 905, note H. Fulchiron and C. Bidaud-Garon.

the fundamental principles and concepts of French law faced with more liberal – or laxer – legal systems. Even the international law that article 55 of the Constitution places above internal law does not seem able to prevail regarding these prohibited actions. This desire to ensure, whatever the cost, compliance with a few principles deemed to be essential is an echo of a piece of case law from the Constitutional Court which, in reference to the transposition of an EC Directive, clearly stipulated that it "could not be allowed to go against a rule or a principle inherent to the constitutional identity of France, unless the constituent authority in France has given its consent"(66).

In this particular case, however, compliance with the prohibition was ensured at the cost of the child's situation. The child paradoxically became the innocent victim of sanctions by suffering the consequences of the parents' conviction leading to his more uncertain status. Accordingly, in the judgment of March 19th 2014, the child (who had been the subject of a surrogacy agreement) had a local Indian civil status that connected him to the Indian woman (the surrogate mother) and the French man (the father who had provided his gametes). He therefore found himself deprived of a French civil status, which considerably compromised his quality of life(67). The real question is whether it is necessary to sacrifice the child in order to protect the principles developed by French law? The European Court of Human Rights did not believe so when France was condemned for violating the right of children to the respect of their privacy(68). The law is made for man, not man for the law(69)!

(66) Const. C., 27 July 2006, n° 2006-540 DC, *JORF*, 3 August 2006, p. 11541, See D. Rousseau, "L'identité constitutionnelle, bouclier de l'intérêt national ou branche de l'étoile européenne", in *L'identité constitutionnelle saisie par les juges en Europe*, Paris, Pédone, 2011, p. 89.

(67) H. Fulchiron and C. Bidaud-Garon, "L'enfant de la fraude", *D.*, 2014, p. 906. Comp. TGI Versailles, 30 April 2014, *D.*, 2014, p. 1041. H. Fulchiron, "*Fraus omnia corrumpit ?* À propos de la filiation des enfants nés par insémination avec don de sperme dans un couple de femmes", *D.*, 2014, p. 1162. *Add.* by the same author on surrogacy, *D.*, 2013, p. 2349.

(68) ECHR, 5th sect., 26 June 2014, *Mennesson v. France*, n° 65192/11, and *Labassee v. France*, n° 65941/11, *JCP*, 2014, note A. Gouttenoire. Finally, the Supreme Court gave up its severity: Cass., plen. Ass., 3 July 2015, n° 14-21323.

(69) Comp. Marc 2, 27.

BASIC PILLARS OF LEGAL THINKING ON THE HUMAN BODY IN THE HUNGARIAN MEDICAL LAW: DIGNITY, SELF-DETERMINATION AND THE PRINCIPLE OF NON-COMMODIFICATION

Judit SÁNDOR

Professor, Director of the Center for Ethics and Law in Biomedicine (CELAB), Central European University (Hungary)

Does the law protect the human body as such? Or should one argue that the law protects persons, first and foremost, and that this form of legal protection includes also the physical aspects of personality: the human body, as well? With the possibility of organ transplantation between humans (cadaver or living organ donation) and with the creation of human biobanks, including embryo, gamete, and ovarian tissue cryopreservation, the cases in which human specimens, tissues, organs, and cells become subjects of the law have significantly increased. However, by examining these developing legal norms more closely, one may realize that the basis of most of the emerging legal provisions is still about general personality rights – such as protection of *human dignity*, the *right to self-determination*, the *right to privacy*, and the *right not to be discriminated against*. Among the emerging legal provisions, only a few aims solely to protect the human body, as a material and as a form of property. Consequently, in Hungary the human body is predominantly defended by general legal instruments, within the protection of *personality rights*[1] (in Hungarian: *személyiségi jogok*). The legal prohibition of discrimination based on genetic traits, or on the privacy and data protection laws of human tissues and DNA in biobanks, show all that the basic rights are applied in the context of the body, as well. Even the principle of non-commodification can

(1) Title XI Hungarian Civ. C.

be interpreted as a principle that aims to protect persons, and therefore their organs and cells should not be harvested with the aim of financial gain. Protection of solely material aspects of the human body can be observed only in lower level legal norms, such as in material transfer agreements and in biobank policies when, for example, biological samples are exchanged between scientists. In this chapter I will describe the legal protection of the human body mainly through two domains which are extreme as they deal mostly (at least in transplantation) with *post mortem* bodies; one on organ transplantation, and one in the special case of a brain dead pregnant patient in Hungary.

I. – Fundamental norms on the human body in Europe

Although *human dignity* is often described as a genuinely European legal principle, surprisingly, at the regional European level, the European Convention for the Protection of Human Rights and Fundamental Freedoms of 1950 does not *expressis verbis* recognize human dignity. Nevertheless, its Article 3 protecting everyone from inhumane or degrading treatment has been interpreted as implicitly safeguarding human dignity. In contrast, in the Oviedo Convention or in the UNESCO Declaration on Human Rights and Bioethics human dignity is one of the core principles that provides a basis for numerous rights.

In 1997 the Council of Europe developed very influential bioethical norms incorporated in the so called *Oviedo Convention*(2). This Convention imposes a categorical ban on the commercialization of the human body in Article 21 by saying "The human body and its parts shall not, as such, give rise to financial gain"(3). The convention is based on broad consensus as already 29 countries have ratified it and 6 other countries have signed it without ratification. Interestingly no country submitted reservation concerning the categorical ban on financial gain. However, almost all reservations were related to transplantation itself and not to the financial gain possibly involved. Croatia(4), Denmark and Norway made a

(2) Convention for the Protection of Human Rights and Dignity of the Human Being with regard to the Application of Biology and Medicine: Convention on Human Rights and Biomedicine, Oviedo, 4.IV.1997.

(3) Art. 21.

(4) The Republic of Croatia excludes the limitation within Article 20, paragraph 2, sub-paragraph ii, of the Convention, which exceptionally allows the removal of regenerative

reservation on the restriction of regenerative tissue donation by minors. Organ trafficking constitutes also a growing concern as the need for organ transplantation has been significantly increased[(5)].

In the *Explanatory Note of the Convention* it is clarified that under this provision organs and tissues, including blood, *should not* be bought or sold or *give rise to financial gain* for the person from whom they have been removed or for a third party, whether an individual or a corporate entity such as, for example, a hospital. However, technical acts (sampling, testing, pasteurization, fractionation, purification, storage, culture, transport, etc.) which are performed on the basis of these items may legitimately give rise to reasonable payment. For instance, this Article does not prohibit the sale of a medical device incorporating human tissue which has been subjected to a manufacturing process as long as the tissue is not sold as such. Further, this Article does not prevent a person from whom an organ or tissue has been taken from receiving compensation which, while not constituting remuneration, compensates that person equitably for expenses incurred or loss of income (for example as a result of hospitalization). The provision does not refer to such products as hair and nails, which are discarded tissues, and the sale of which is not regarded as a violation of human dignity.

The *Additional Protocol to the Convention on Human Rights and Biomedicine, concerning Transplantation of Organs and Tissues of Human Origin* was adopted in 2002[(6)]. The Additional Protocol has much more detailed provisions on the legal safeguard of transplantation, including the removal of organs from the living donors. Article 10 requires that "Organ removal from a living

tissue from a person who is not able to consent solely when no compatible donor with the ability to consent is available, and the recipient is a brother or a sister of the donor. The limitation does not allow the removal of regenerative tissue (bone marrow) from a minor for the benefit of his/her parent. Such a limitation is not compatible with the Law of the Republic of Croatia in force (The Removal and Transplantation of Human Body Parts Act, published in *Official Gazette* n° 53 of 1991), which allows the transplantation of regenerative tissue from a minor for the benefit of his/her parent. The Republic of Croatia hereby protects the vital interests of an underage donor, thereby saving the life of the donor's parent who is of the utmost importance (for the minor).

The Republic of Croatia will apply Article 20, paragraph 2, sub-paragraph ii, of the Convention, to the effect that the receiver is a parent, a brother or a sister of the donor.

(5) The Council of Europe Convention against Trafficking in Human Organs was opened for signature on 25 March 2015.

(6) Additional Protocol to the Convention on Human Rights and Biomedicine concerning Transplantation of Organs and Tissues of Human Origin, Strasbourg, 24 January 2002.

donor may be carried out for the benefit of a recipient with whom the donor has a close personal relationship as defined by law, or, in the absence of such relationship, only under the conditions defined by law and with the approval of an appropriate independent body".

Regarding the protection of the human body, two other Articles are highly relevant: one is Article 21 – Prohibition of financial gain and the other is Article 22 on the organ and tissue trafficking(7). The latter one is extremely laconic. Without any specific definition it simply says: "Organ and tissue trafficking shall be prohibited". Article 21 seems to give more room for interpretation. It states that the human body and its parts shall not, as such, give rise to financial gain or comparable advantage. Under this Article the following payments do not constitute a financial gain or a comparable advantage, in particular: compensation of living donors for loss of earnings and any other justifiable expenses (caused by the removal or by the related medical examinations;) payment of a justifiable fee for legitimate medical or related technical services rendered in connection with transplantation; and compensation in case of undue damage resulting from the removal of organs or tissues from living persons. All these forms of payment, however, are consistent with previous laws and consequently they do not offer more exceptions to the general ban on the financial gain. Further restriction can be found in paragraph 2 which provides that "advertising the need for, or availability of, organs or tissues, with a view to offering or seeking financial gain or comparable advantage, shall be prohibited."

Directive 2004/23/EC of the European Parliament and of the Council, dated 31 March 2004, on setting standards of quality and safety for the donation, procurement, testing, processing, preservation, storage and distribution of human tissues and cells deals with general matters of safety and quality of the use of human tissues, however Article 12 clearly states that donations and procurement should be made without financial incentives.

Article 13 of the Directive reinforces the *principle of non-commodification* stated already in the Oviedo Convention:

(7) J. Sándor, *e.a.*, "Organ Trafficking, Organ Trade. Recommendations for a More Nuanced Legal Policy", *in* F. Ambagtsheer and W. Weimar (eds.), *The EULOD Project Living Organ Donation in Europe Results and Recommendations*, Lengerich, Pabst Science Publisher, 2013, pp. 147-175.

"(1) Member States shall ensure that donations of organs from deceased and living donors are *voluntary* and *unpaid*.

(2) Member States shall *prohibit advertising* the *need for*, or *availability* of, organs where such advertising is with a view to offering or seeking financial gain or comparable advantage."

Lots of expectation preceded the adoption of the Directive 2010/45/EU of the European parliament and of the Council of 7 July, 2010 on standards of quality and safety of human organs intended for transplantation. This Directive recognizes the need "for common quality and safety standards for the procurement, transport and use of organs at Union level"[8]. Paragraph 7 continues that "unacceptable practices in organ donation and transplantation include trafficking in organs, sometimes linked to trafficking in persons for the purpose of the removal of organs, which constitutes a serious violation of fundamental rights and, in particular, of human dignity and physical integrity"[9].

II. – Hungarian constitutional framework

In the Hungarian law legal protection of a person and the protection of the human body are closely connected concepts which cannot be separated from each other except in some extreme cases, such as the protection of the corpse[10] or the protection of parts of human body in the context of transplantation[11], reproduction and research. In other contexts the principle of self-determination stemming from the constitutional notion of dignity provides the basis for legal thinking. But even in the rare cases when the human body requires some special protection, the concept of human dignity is the starting point. The Hungarian Fundamental Law in Article I states that "Article I (1) The inviolable nature of human rights which cannot be disposed of shall be respected. It shall be the primary obligation of the State to protect these rights"[12].

(8) Directive 2010/45/EU of the European Parliament and of the Council of 7 July 2010 on standards of quality and safety of human organs for transplantation, *OJ*, n° L 207.14 of 6 August 2010, § 6.

(9) *Ibid.*, § 7.

(10) See *infra*.

(11) See *infra*.

(12) Adopted on 25 April 2011.

One of the basic and core rights in relation to the protection of human body can be found in Article II. It states that "Human dignity shall be inviolable. Everyone shall have the right to life and human dignity; the life of the foetus shall be protected from the moment of conception"(13). Human dignity is emphasized here as the core right; however, one cannot find a further indication for the hierarchy between right to life and human dignity in the text of the Fundamental Law. In the field of biomedicine inter-rights conflicts occur frequently between the right to life and the right to human dignity, for instance when a patient would like to defend his/her dignity by refusing life sustaining treatments.

The other basic principle in protecting the human body can be found in Article III that provides constitutional provision in cases of inhuman and degrading treatment. "(1) Nobody may be subjected to torture, inhuman or degrading treatment or punishment, or be held in servitude. Trafficking of human beings shall be prohibited."

Paragraph (2) of Article III is perhaps the most relevant in the context of biomedical interventions and in the field of health care. "It shall be prohibited to perform a medical or scientific experiment on human beings without their informed consent." And in paragraph (3) "Practices aimed at eugenics, the use of the human body or its parts for financial gain, or human cloning shall be prohibited". One may argue that not only medical experiment (it would be better to say "research") but all medical treatment should be based on informed consent unless a Parliamentary Act provides exception, such as in the case of medical emergency. Protecting human beings against eugenic practices aims to avoid illegal birth control and sterilization of minorities but as the term *eugenic* has been used in many different contexts it is hard to find a clear scope of this provision.

III. – Protection of the human body in the medical law: medical research, and transplantation

Informed consent is the main legal principle governing therapy and research conducted on the human body in the Hungarian

(13) This phrase indicates a stronger protection of the human foetus than the previous Constitution.

Health Care Act[14]. In case of medical treatment it goes without saying that in the lack of the patient' s consent no medical treatment can be performed except in specific cases[15]. It is more problematic to ensure that adequate information is given prior to medical research[16] but informed consent is always requested. In even in those research protocols in which research is conducted not on humans but on human specimens. The notion of research on human beings has been significantly expanded since 1997 when the Hungarian Health Care Act formulated the basic rules on medical research on humans. Since then[17], medical research on the human body was understood much more broadly[18] by encompassing the research not only on persons but on the human genetic materials, human gametes, cells from the alive and dead human body, human tissues etc.[19] Irrespective whether cells, gametes or DNA are harvested from the human body for the purposes of research or therapy, consent of the person is an essential criteria in the law. A specific law has been adopted in 2008[20] regarding research on genetic material and data. New forms of medical research, such as research on human genetic data and research on human embryo follow all the legal norms on human dignity and self-determination.

Protection of the human body often appears in the debates on the status of the corpse and in cases using the body of brain dead patients. Today the concept of death has become a more complex and more contested notion than ever before. First of all, the possibility of organ transplantation, moving an organ from a cadaveric source, has changed the medical approach to death. Although organ transplantation is a unique case, based on the declaration of brain death following special criteria; the body of the deceased donor is kept (for a short time) alive for the purposes of organ removal, to save the life of another patient. The patient may refuse post-mortem transplantation during his/or her life. Maybe this is

(14) Art. 15 Hungarian Health Care Act. on the patient's right to self-determination and Art. 20 on the right to refuse medical treatment.

(15) *Ibid.* Art. 17-18 in cases of medical emergency for instance.

(16) *Ibid.* Art. 159, § (1) e.

(17) Decree n° 23/2002 (V. 9.) of the Minister of Health.

(18) J. SÁNDOR, "Body Immortal", *in* J. GUNNING and S. HOLM (eds.), *Ethics, Law and Society*, Aldershot, Ashgate, 2007, pp. 123-135.

(19) Art. 1. Decree n° 23/2002.9 (V.9.) EüM r., aforementioned, relating to the medical research on human beings.

(20) The Parliamentary Act n° XXI. of 2008, relating to the protection of human genetic data, to the genetic research and testing and to the rules of biobanks.

the reason why medical terminology and colloquial language are also very inconsistent and vague when e.g. an organ donor is either referred to as a "patient" or as a "deceased person". A "cadaver" is used in the context of medical research, organ transplantation, and in certain cases for education but e.g. a brain-dead woman's pregnancy can also be maintained for a certain period of time due to the available medical technology. In these cases, difficult issues arise also from ethical and legal points of view. The field in which one can clearly see that the law protects the human body is the field of *post mortem respect* to the human body. A dead body cannot be treated and disposed as a mere object because it has belonged to a human person. Research conducted on cadavers requires the approval of ethics committees and based on the consent either by the deceased's statement during his/her lifetime or consent by his/her relatives.

Organ transplantation went through a remarkable development everywhere since the middle of twentieth century. The first transplant surgery in Hungary, a kidney transplantation, was performed in 1962 but it was unsuccessful(21). The first successful kidney transplantation was carried out only eleven years later, in 1973. The first successful liver transplantation, occurred 22 years later in 1995. In Hungary, nearly 300 transplantations are performed each year. Hungarian legal regulations follow the approach of *opting out* and are based on the principle of presumed consent(22). Any objections should be reported to the family doctor. Such regulations are problematic for two reasons. On the one hand, it is assumed that the public is not aware that objections will be considered only if expressed in that manner. On the other hand, such regulations are also problematic in terms of practical implementation, as it may not be possible to find the statement of objection in the urgent conditions in which the use of the organs is taking place.

Hungary ratified both the Oviedo Convention and the *Additional Protocol to the Convention on Human Rights and Biomedicine, on Transplantation of Organs and Tissues of Human Origin*. This latter

(21) R.M. Langer and F. Perner, "Transplantation in Hungary – Preface on the Occasion of Transplantation Proceedings Becoming the Official Journal of the Hungarian Transplantation Society", *Transplant Proc.*, July-August 2010, vol. 42, n° 6, pp. 2279-2280.

(22) Art. 211, (1), Hungarian Health Care Act (amended by the Parliamentary Act n° CCLII of 2013).

one was ratified by the Parliamentary Act No LXXX of 2006[(23)]. The European Parliament resolution of 22 April 2008 asked Member States "to remove, before January 2010, legislation that reserves donor organs for use solely within that Member State." For Hungary, joining Eurotransplant, the largest international donor exchange organization (currently representing a population of 125 million), may present an extraordinary opportunity to increase the limited number of available donor organs, and in particular, to find donor organs that better match recipients' profiles. Membership would, for example, multiply the chances of being allocated an organ for patients on the waiting list. In turn, organs for which no matching recipient is found in Hungary would not be lost, as they could be offered to patients in another member country.

Pursuant to Section 211(1) of the Hungarian Health Care Act, organs and tissues may only be removed from the deceased if the deceased had not expressed any objections, prior to their death. (If the deceased was underage and no statement of objection is found, organ or tissue removal may only take place with the written approval of the legal representative of the deceased.) Experience in Hungary is that although relatives' consent is not required by law, donation in many cases is prevented by objections raised by the family of the deceased.

The safety of the organ donor is protected by numerous restrictions on organ donation, for example, only the following organs or tissue parts may be removed: one half of a paired organ, if its removal does not cause severe and permanent deficiency; the segment of an organ, if after its removal, the organ does not suffer significant functional loss; a tissue part that regenerates itself[(24)].

Autonomy is secured by prescribing that only legally competent persons may donate organs or tissue parts. In exceptional cases where the recipient is related to the donor, bone marrow, haemopoetic parent cell, or any self-regenerating tissue part may be donated[(25)]. In these cases the consent of the legal representative of the minor becomes valid with the approval of the ethics committee of the hospital.

(23) Additional Protocol to the Convention on Human Rights and Biomedicine concerning Transplantation of Organs and Tissues of Human Origin (CETS n° 186).

(24) Art. 205, (1), Health Care Act.

(25) *Ibid.*, art. 206, (5).

A person with restricted legal capacity may make this donation only if the donor is related to the recipient as direct descendant; a sibling of a direct descendant; a sibling; a direct descendant of the recipient's sibling[26].

The donation of organs and tissue parts must be made *without any monetary* compensation[27]. The donor has the right to claim reimbursement of his/her costs, such as lost income as a result of the donation and any costs that are related to making the donation statement and travelling, but are not covered according to the contract with the health care system. These costs are paid by the state[28].

Principle of non-maleficence can be observed by the further condition that before transplanting an organ or tissue part, the doctor who performs the transplantation must ensure that the condition of the donor is favorable enough to removing the organ or tissue part; that the transplantation is not contraindicated; that it is justified for the recipient; that the conditions for the recipient are favorable for the implantation, and that the organ is suitable for transplantation.

Before transplanting an organ or tissue part, the donor must be informed in detail, verbally and in writing about all significant conditions related to the intervention/operation, with a special attention to the long and short term consequences of the removal and lack of the organ or tissue part, and to the rule that in case of the death of the donor, he or she shall be subject to mandatory autopsy. The donor must be informed by a doctor not directly involved in the transplantation[29].

The donor may withdraw his or her decision, without any form, before the organ or tissue part is removed. Even in case of valid agreement on the donor's part, the physician cannot continue the intervention involving the removal of an organ or tissue part, if new circumstances arise, which threaten the life of the donor or may lead to health impairment[30].

---

(26) *Ibid.,* art. 206, (2).
(27) *Ibid.*, art. 207, (1).
(28) *Ibid.*, art. 207, (2).
(29) *Ibid.*, art. 209, (1).
(30) *Ibid.,* art. 209, (4).

The agreement of the recipient concerning the transplantation must be a written consent. If the donor' health is compromised – beyond the immediate impairment that directly follows from the removal of any organ or tissue part – the donor becomes disabled or dies, and the physician and health worker conducting the intervention cannot be made liable, then the state will compensate the donor or his or her relatives for all damages that are not covered on the basis of the legal relations with the social security system.

IV. – Legal use of the human body in the Hungarian criminal law

Perhaps the most specific protection of the human body can be found in the Hungarian Criminal Code[31]. In 1998 several new criminal law provisions were enacted subsequent to the adoption of the new Health Care Act. A new Title was inserted in the Criminal Code: Title II that deals with Medical Procedures, the Order of Medical Research and Criminal Acts against the Right of Autonomy Concerning Medical Procedures.

Several new types of crimes were defined and sanctioned; e.g. "illegal use of the human body, violation of the rules of research conducted on the human embryo and gametes, illegal use of the gametes". In Hungary, human trafficking was defined as a crime in 1998[32].

Section 175/B has been in force since March 1, 1999. This Article defines human trafficking when someone sells, buys, transfers, exchanges or acquires someone else. This can be punished for up to three years in prison. The punishment increases from one to eight years if the victim of trafficking is under the age of 18 or if he or she has been deprived of their freedom, or if the purpose of trafficking is labor, sexual services, perversion or the illegal use of human organs or if it is done in an organized manner and for profit[33].

---

(31) Parliamentary Act n° C. of 2012 relating to the Criminal Code Chapter XVI, dealing with the Crimes against the Rules of Medical Interventions and Research; see Sect. 168-175.

(32) Act IV of 1978 relating to the Criminal Code Title III, entitled "Crimes against freedom and human dignity".

(33) The referring Article 175/B § 5 of the Penal Code has been amended. The amendment, which came into force on 9 August 2009, aiming at aggravating the punishment of those, who commit trafficking in human beings on a child under 12 for the purpose of sexual intercourse,

Based on simple grammatical analysis of the *actus reus* of Section 173/I. it becomes clear that this Section goes much beyond the classical cases of organ trafficking and any acquisition or simple placing human specimens, including organs, as well as gametes in the market would constitute the crime of "illegal use of a human body". In addition selling human body and its parts in a business-like manner(34) constitutes an even more serious form of crime(35). Furthermore even preparation for the illegal use of the human also constitutes a misdemeanor(36).

Under the Hungarian criminal law since 1998 certain medical procedures that are conducted without the consent of the person shall also be punishable(37).

V. – CONCEPT OF HUMAN DIGNITY IN SPECIFIC CASES: VIABLE, NON-VIABLE FOETUS AND BRAIN DEAD PREGNANT WOMAN

Sometime in the summer of 2013 the fight for the life of a pregnant woman was lost in Hungary. The case was revealed only months later in November 2013(38). What the public knows from newspaper articles, is that a few months earlier, a 32-year-old woman was in coma and could not be saved after a couple of days, and was declared brain-dead. At that time she was in the 15th week of her pregnancy. In the summer of 2013 the brain-dead mother's life functions were sustained for 92 days in Debrecen, and then the doctors delivered an apparently healthy foetus by performing a Caesarean-section. The C-section could be performed because of the successful cooperation of several specialists: among others, anaesthesiologists, endocrinologists, gynaecologists, neonatologists, intensive care experts participated in maintaining the pregnancy. The C-section was performed in the 27th week of the pregnancy. This case is also the result of a heroic technological effort from the medical team.

forced labor, or to produce forbidden pornographic material. The maximum penalty was raised from 15 years to 20 years of imprisonment.

(34) Art. 459, § 28, Crim. C. defines business-like manner when the source of income comes from repeatedly committed crimes.

(35) Art. 175, § 3, b), Crim. C.

(36) Art.175, § 4, Crim. C.

(37) This provision is also kept in the new 2012 Criminal Code. C. "Egészségügyi önrendelkezési jog megsértése", art. 218.

(38) See: http://figyelo.hu/cikkek/92-nappal-az-agyhalal-utan-adott-eletet-gyerekenek-egy-debreceni-anya.

Based on what we know about the Debrecen case it can be supposed that the members of the family shared the same view, and all of them wished to save the life of the foetus. So the outstanding and successful attempt of keeping the patient alive took place perhaps not at their explicit request but by all means with their approval. The case was announced to the public months after the C-section had taken place, for the sake of protecting the family and avoiding the identification of the child. The hospital team therefore basically took over the role of the parent and caretaker of the foetus, and dozens of medical professions contributed to maintaining the pregnancy despite the fact that the mother was considered deceased.

There has also been cases, in which shortly after the death of a pregnant woman it has still been possible to deliver a mature foetus developed in the womb. But new methods of intensive care have recently resulted in the increase of such special situations when the life functions of a brain-dead patient, even including her hormonal function, can be artificially sustained, which enables prolonging pregnancy even of a brain-dead woman for a certain period of time, even until the delivery of the foetus with Cesarian-section. While in case of the terminally ill patients the life-sustaining treatments raise ethical questions, nowadays the possibility of an *artificially maintained pregnancy* is also an issue. Such an outstanding medical intervention significantly depends on the available medical technologies, on professional expertise and substantial financial resources. In these cases, difficult issues arise also from ethical and legal points of view concerning the dignity and the rights of private life and reproduction of the late pregnant patient and the family. In these rare situations the issues are very different from those of euthanasia.

First of all it is important to distinguish between the artificial sustainment of the pregnancy of a brain-dead woman and the case when the pregnant mother is in a severe, terminal status but is still able to make decisions, and she has an advanced pregnancy. We know a lot of similar cases from the medical literature[39], and in situations when the mother is able to make decisions, she decides, but if she is no longer competent her relatives, acting as substitute decision-makers, make the decision representing *her will*. It means

(39) Such as in the Angela Carder case in US (In re A.C., 533 A.2d 611, 612 [D.C. 1987]).

that in these cases the *personal autonomy rights of the patient* govern. If she cannot express her will, the closest relatives may express her wishes. It is even a much more complex situation when the patient should be declared dead and the pregnancy is still in an early stage. In this case, if the efforts for the prolongation of life failed, declaration of death means the death of the foetus, as well. If the pregnancy is already in an advanced stage, the mature foetus may have been delivered with C-section and sustained in an incubator; but in such cases when there are several months left of the pregnancy and the pregnant mother dies, generally there is nothing to do but accept that the patient has deceased.

Finding a legal solution is made even more difficult by the fact that we have to consider the status of the body as different in a man versus a woman in the case of reproduction. While a woman can carry to term the foetus even after the death of her husband (and it is legal according to Hungarian law), it is generally not possible after the death of a woman. Only in extreme cases can artificial support of a woman's bodily functions be maintained to save the life of the foetus but this may also infringe on the dignity of this woman.

Due to the improvement of reproductive technologies nowadays a lot of posthumous pregnancies and births take place *after the death of the father*, but in case of the prolonged coma or terminal status of a pregnant woman who is no longer able to carry the burden of pregnancy, there are much more difficult medical and ethical questions which have to be answered. Should the medical team allow keeping the body functioning as an incubator, which is only possible in exceptional cases, in agreement with the presumed will of the woman either declared by her during her life or being represented by her relatives? Otherwise the world of *The Matrix*[40] would come to life and it could inevitably result in the woman's body being considered as a human incubator that is kept alive like a machine.

In most countries, if we would like to use the current legal regulations as points of reference, we can only build on distant analogies regarding the pregnancy of a brain-dead mother. It is because regulations of abortion or prenatal care do not apply to

(40) In the science fiction movie, *Matrix* the machines "grow" humans to provide a source of power.

a brain-dead woman. Law deals with these issues in terms that the woman is still alive or perhaps as a terminal patient. In case of a deceased person, law deals with regulations concerning organ transplantation or autopsy at most.

Although at the moment the number of such cases seems to be very low, however, as intensive care develops, the number of potential conflicts between the wish of family members and the medical team may significantly grow in the future. Therefore – in my opinion – the artificial prolongation and sustainment of life and pregnancy of a brain-dead mother will soon require a regulation that is based on the declarations made by the dead person during her lifetime[(41)]. In the absence of such statement a careful ethical assessment may become necessary. In my view the general right of refusing medical treatment cannot be applied in these cases, as we are not talking about a patient who faces life-threatening danger or terminal status but about the cadaver of a brain-dead person. Neither can the restriction of the personal autonomy right of a pregnant woman come into question (which I believe has become quite broadly applied in the healthcare law of Hungary), because this is a profoundly different situation. Besides the personal autonomy and mourning rights, the stage of the pregnancy must also be taken into consideration. The case of a viable foetus can be judged differently than that of an unviable foetus in the case of an early pregnancy, when the body of the mother is used only as a biological machine operated as an incubator. There are definitely such women who in their wills request that the life of their foetus be sustained at any cost given their family background or to ensure the survival of descendants. But there can be cases when the proper family background does not exist, and the mother would like to pass away with dignity without further intervention on her body. This must also be respected. Of course, there are such cases when the request of the mother during her life or of the family after her death is vain, since the survival chances of the foetus are slim and the likelihood of birth defects very high, and therefore their request related to the sustainment of the pregnancy is unfeasible from a medical aspect. A *brain-dead pregnant woman* represents such a

(41) B. GYÖRGY and F. BÉLA, "Eletem legszebb töténete" (The Most Beautiful Story in my Life), *Magyar Narancs*, available at: http://magyarnarancs.hu/tudomany/prof-dr-balla-gyorgy-ujszulottgyogyasz-prof-dr-fulesdi-bela-intenziv-terapias-szakember-a-de-oec-elnoke-es-dr-torok-olga-szulesz-egyetemi-docens-89731.

complex legal case that has been created by the latest technological possibilities of intensive care, and in which the rules of abortion or the right to refuse medical treatment cannot be applied. The regulations concerning the removal of organs from a cadaver are the ones that may be the closest legal situation to apply, though in a legal sense the foetus is not considered a cadaver organ. Based upon the known international cases we can conclude that serious legal debates arise mainly when the family, in particular the husband (life partner), makes a decision that is different from that of the medical team. I believe that the body of a pregnant woman cannot be considered as a mere object either in her lifetime or after her death, since if it were so, the principle of equal respect of women and their dignity would be damaged. New medical imaging technologies now contributed to the perception that the human foetus is seen as more 'living', it is more personalized. We should be glad to be able to save the lives of more and more foetuses and new-born babies nowadays, but dying should also be respected.

Conclusions

As we have seen in Hungary the protection of the human body and personhood are closely intertwined concepts in the law. We protect the person, not just the human body, when the law expresses respect for the origin of the cell, tissues and organs. *Principle of non-commodification* is perhaps the only body-bound and particularly European concept, based on the notion of human dignity but further elaborated in the Oviedo Convention in the context of biomedicine. Still the core element in this principle can be found in the concept of human dignity. One may assume that the protection of the human body can be examined in isolated cases of cadaver donation and in the case of brain dead pregnant women. But in those cases when the person is no longer capable of expressing his/her wish, the law takes into account either the previously expressed wish alone or its interpretation by close relatives. As it follows, even in these extreme cases there is a constant search and respect for human dignity, as the protection of the human body refers to the broader notion of personality rights.

THE PROTECTION OF THE HUMAN BODY IN ITALY ETHICAL AND LEGAL PRINCIPLES

Cosimo Marco MAZZONI

Professor of Law and Director of the Department of Law and Economics
University of Sienna, Florence (Italy)

I. – The human body and the person

The Italian legal system is an integral part of the tradition of Roman law, as is the case in most European countries. The Italian Civil Code of 1942 is inspired by both the *Napoleonic Code* (1804) and the German Civil Code (*BGB*, 1900). The key principles underlying the protection of the person and the human body are therefore common to all legal systems in Continental Europe deriving from these two civil codes. As a general principle, the issue of the protection of the person is quite close to the Romano-Germanic legal tradition. The German Pandectist school of the 19th century, in particular, brought the principles of Roman law from the Justinian compilation into the rights of the person: non-commercial subjective rights. Non-commercialisation is the element that characterises all rights relating to the human person. We traditionally use the expression "personality rights" to qualify subjective rights of protection.

The human body has never been part of legal discourse: it has only recently begun to be included in legal analysis, with the emergence of biotechnology, as we will see later. The jurist's reasoning uses representative symbols, models passed down for over two thousand years. These are (legal) forms that symbolise the material reality. Rather than referring to the human body, the jurist uses concepts such as "the person" or "the subject of law". The legal world is like a mirror that reflects the image of a man without a body. The legal element he relies on is not the body, but its likeness. The legal element is a formal element, expressed by the archetypal legal term "natural person". This is a conceptual unity, a syntagma, where an abstract element and a material element are nevertheless juxtaposed. Likewise, the other expression, "subject of law", is constructed like an artefact of the legal order. Hence the emergence of the distinction between the human and his "person".

The distinction between the man made of flesh, bones and muscles, with his weaknesses and strengths, both physical and moral, who is confronted with and opposed to his metamorphosis into a formal and abstract entity. The (legal) personality reveals almost nothing of the physical reality of the person, as it is reduced to a function consisting *only* in its capacity to hold and exercise rights[1].

The body has only recently entered the legal system. Similarly to what happened in France, where a chapter dedicated to the body was introduced to the Civil Code in 1994, Italy passed, during the same period, a series of specific laws on *bioethics*. The Italian legislature was thus led to recognise that the advances in biotechnology and medical and surgical practices obliged legal experts to perceive *the body as being separate from the person.*

II. – The Italian system of protection of the human body

Having put forward these general and theoretical reflections on the protection of the body, let us now analyse the legislative and ethical principles that govern compensation for any damage done to the human body.

However, I believe it is important to point out the blatant contradiction in the terms *body of the person* and *body of the man.* The return to the naturalist ontological principle of the concept of the body is foreign to the idea of the person, in all its possible meanings. "The person" effectively remains an abstract concept that the jurist uses for all the legal subjectivities (man, legal person, foundation) and is therefore not a synonym of "man".

(1) J.-P. Baud, *L'Affaire de la main volée. Une histoire juridique du corps*, Paris, Seuil, 1993; id., *Le droit de vie et de mort. Archéologie de la bioéthique*, Paris, Aubier, 2001; O. Cayla and Y. Thomas, *Du droit de ne pas naître. À propos de l'affaire Perruche*, Paris, Gallimard, 2002; P. Catalano, *Diritto e persone*, Torino, Giappichelli, 1990; C.M. Mazzoni, *Psiche o la forma del corpo*, Milano, Giuffrè, 2013; Y. Thomas, *Les opérations du droit*, M.-A. Hermitte and P. Napoli (eds.), coll. Hautes Études, Paris, EHESS – Gallimard – Seuil, 2011.

There is no uniform and general legislation in the Italian legal system concerning the protection of the body with regard to biomedicine. The general principles can be interpreted from a series of legal provisions relating to various levels in the hierarchy of standards and rules specific to certain biomedical practices.

The standards for the protection of the body included in the *Charter of Fundamental Rights of the European Union of 7 December 2000*[(2)], the *European Convention of Human Rights* of 4 November 1950 and the *European Convention on Biomedicine* signed in Oviedo on 4 April 1997 (not ratified by Italy, but quoted and applied by case law) form part of the general system of protection of the person in Italian law.

The *Italian Constitution,* which came into force on 1st January 1948, does not contain any provisions specific to the protection of the human body. However, the interpretation of some constitutional standards enables us to identify the founding principles of the protection of the body: art. 2 "[...] The Republic recognises and guarantees the inviolable rights of the person [...]"; art. 3 "[...] It is the duty of the Republic to remove those obstacles of an economic or social nature which constrain the freedom and equality of citizens, thereby impeding the full development of the human person"; art. 13 "Personal liberty is inviolable. No one may be detained, inspected or searched, nor otherwise subjected to any restriction of personal liberty except by order of the Judiciary, stating a reason and only in those cases provided for by the law"; art. 32 "The Republic safeguards health as a fundamental right of the individual and as a collective interest, and guarantees free medical care to the indigent. No one may be obliged to undergo any health treatment except in accordance with the provisions of the law. The law may not under any circumstances violate the limits imposed by respect for the human person."

In the *Civil Code* (1942), the body only appears in article 5 (Acts of disposal of one's own body). In view of this instrument, acts of disposal of the body are prohibited if they cause "permanent damage to physical integrity or are in violation of the law, public order or decency".

(2) Charter of Fundamental Rights of the European Union 2007/C 303/01, approved in Nice on 7 December 2000 and amended in Strasbourg on 12 December 2007.

While there are no general standards, some instruments have covered specific medical practices. These include compulsory health treatment[(3)], the institution of the National Health Service[(4)] abortion[(5)] assisted reproductive technologies[(6)] sex changes[(7)], live organ and tissue transplants (donations?)[(8)], organ and tissue transplants originating from a corpse[(9)] and clinical drug testing on humans[(10)].

In Italian law, the protection of the body embraces aspects of constitutional law, civil law, criminal law and administrative law. In addition, the Code of Medical Ethics (2006) and the Code of Ethics for Nurses (2009) complement the protection system.

III. – The principles of protection

A. – *Statement of principles*

As a general rule, the principles of protection of the body are not defined by the legal instruments, but rather by doctrine and case law. From the list of standards mentioned above and their application in case law, we can infer the following principles of protection: dignity, autonomy, inviolability of the human body, the cost-free principle and anonymity.

1. – *Dignity*

The specific reference to dignity can be found in article 33 of the law on compulsory health care treatments[(11)] and in the law instituting the National Health Service[(12)]. The Code of Medical Ethics[(13)] and the Code of Ethics for Nurses[(14)] also refer to it.

(3) Art. 33 L. n° 833-1978.

(4) L. n° 833-1978.

(5) L. n° 194-1978.

(6) L. n° 40-2004.

(7) *id.*

(8) L. n° 458-1967 on kidney transplants; L. n° 483-1999 on partial liver transplants; L. n° 219-2005 on blood donation and stem cell harvesting; L. n° 52-2001 on bone marrow donations.

(9) L. n° 91-1999 on organ and tissue transplants and grafts; L. n° 301-1993 on corneal transplants and grafts.

(10) Legisl. Decree n° 211-2003, implementing Directive 2001/20/EC.

(11) L. n° 833-1978 on compulsory health care treatments.

(12) Art. 1 *id.*, instituting the National Health Service: "The protection of public and mental health must involve respect for the dignity and liberty of the human being."

(13) Code of 16 December 2006, modified 18 May 2014.

(14) Code of 10 January 2009.

This is a principle that has no unanimously agreed definition, as legal instruments and authors are divided on the subject. It should be noted that the reference to dignity is rarely used, unless it is combined with other principles (liberty, equality, solidarity). It is non-specific and abstract concept that is difficult to apply in concrete terms to a particular case. The courts avoid referring to dignity due to its generic nature and because it is not a normative concept.

Two meanings are proposed: dignity as being synonymous with respect for the person(15), and dignity synonymous with the inviolability of human life(16).

Legal doctrine and case law favour the expression as a synonym of "respect for the person"(17). Recently, however, the term dignity has been used by Italian doctrine and, in certain rare but significant cases, case law: *Case of Englaro*(18); *Case of Welby-Riccio*(19).

2. – *Autonomy*

In the Italian system, the principle of autonomy is best known and most frequently used in the biomedical context, both by the legal doctrine and by case law (constitutional and ordinary). Other expressions are preferred to the word "autonomy":

– *self-determination*, the freedom to dispose of one's own body during one's lifetime(20) or after death(21); the freedom to decide for oneself(22).
– *informed consent*(23)
– *information and consent* (mentioned in the Code of Medical Ethics).

(15) *E.g.*,. Cass., n° 21748/2007.
(16) *E.g.*, Lecco Court, Decree 2 March 1999.
(17) See also. art. 32, § 2, Const.
(18) Lecco Court, Decree 2 March 1999; Cass., n° 21748/2007.
(19) Rome Court, order 16 December 2006.
(20) Laws on live organ and tissue transplants, sex changes, clinical drug trials on humans: see *supra*.
(21) Laws on the transplant of organs and tissues originating from a corpse.
(22) Art. 32 and 13 Const. on consent for medical treatment.
(23) L. n° 219-2005 on the donation of blood and blood derivatives; legisl. Decree n° 211-2003 applying Directive 2001/20/EC on clinical trials on medicinal products for human use; in case law: Const. Court, n° 438/2008; Cass., n° 21748/2007, aforementioned.

This principle is generally defined in Italian legislation as the "principle of consent". Other examples are as follows: "informed consent" is a "fundamental principle of protection with regard to the protection of health" as a "combination of two fundamental rights of the person: the right to self-determination and the right to health"(24); it "represents a value choice in the way we perceive the relationship between doctor and patient, in the sense that this relationship is primarily based on the rights of the patient and the freedom of self-determination with regard to treatment, rather than on the duties of the doctor"(25).

The only normative definition relating to the principle of autonomy concerns "informed consent" within the framework of clinical drug trials on human beings: "The decision is expressed by a subject capable of giving his consent, or, in those cases where a person is not in a condition to do so, by his legal representative or by an authority, person or body in respect of the legal provisions in force on the matter. If the subject is not in a condition to write, he may, exceptionally, give verbal consent in the presence of at least one witness, in accordance with the standards in force" (26). This definition simply reproduces that given by EC standards, which itself derives from the best clinical practice standards developed by the *European Medicines Agency*(27).

3. – *The inviolability of the human body*

The principle of the inviolability of the body is best expressed by the terms "intangibility of the body" and "integrity". In Italian doctrine and case law, this principle is taken from the Constitution(28).

It is a principle that has been defined by developments in case law, as can be seen from the example provided by the reasoning of

(24) Const. Court, n° 438/2008.

(25) *Id.*

(26) The legislative Decree of 24 June 2003 implementing European Directive 2001/20/EC defines "informed consent". The decision of a candidate to be included in a clinical drug trial, written, dated and signed, made spontaneously, after exhaustive information on the nature, significance, consequences and risks of the experiment and after receiving the appropriate related documentation.

(27) Art. 1, § 1, l), legisl. Decree. n° 211-2003 24 June 2003.

(28) Art. 13 and 32. See for example the following decisions: Const. Court n° 471/1990; Const. Court, n° 282/2002; Const. Court, n° 438/2008; Crim. Cass., 13 May 1993; Rome Court, ord. 16 December 2006.

the Court of Rome: "Any invasive physical act, whether therapeutic or non-therapeutic, may not be carried out without or against the consent of the person concerned, as physical inviolability constitutes the core of personal freedom itself"[(29)]. The notion of the "inviolability" of the human body is related to the concept of *Habeas Corpus* according to which no one may be arbitrarily arrested, and has become, along with the Universal Declaration of Human Rights of 10 December 1948, an expression of individual freedom and a fundamental right of the individual.

4. – *The cost-free principle*

This concept, referred to in numerous instruments, usually relates to assets – even those of considerable economic value – that are legally considered to be "non-commercial". With regard to Italian case law and doctrine, this term means that the asset is dissociated from its economic valuation. The sale of a kidney has a huge asset value on the illegal market; it has none at all under the cost-free transfer provided for by law. In the latter case, the asset is stripped of any notional monetary value. This relates to items to which an agreement between the parties, the law or the intended use attribute an "ethical" character; they cannot therefore have any monetary value. The assets, the property of the State, are by definition "non-commercial". Applied to the body, the transfer of a kidney or blood generally goes hand in hand with a prohibition on their sale.

Another meaning of cost-free consists in prohibiting any form of remuneration: it refers to something received without payment or consideration in return. In this sense, "cost-free" requires no compensation: it is the opposite of "subject to payment". Something given without remuneration can also have a considerable asset value, but the transfer takes place without compensation. The cost-free principle is therefore synonymous with a unilateral obligation (only the giver is obligated). Jurists understand the difference in interpretation between the two terms. The contract may be subject to payment or free of charge. Civil law experts speak of an exchange for pecuniary interest in the case of a reciprocal services agreement, or a synallagmatic contract; in other words, when a consideration is expected and requested from the other party. In

(29) Rome Court, ord. 16 December 2006.

general, an exchange is by definition for pecuniary interest, while the unilateral act is usually free of charge. However, this assertion must be qualified in view of certain legislative definitions. For example, the French *Civil Code* defines a contract of *beneficence* as one "in which one of the parties provides the other with a benefit completely free of charge"(30). It is unclear whether the term "free of charge" ("*la gratuité*" in French) refers to the benefit received for nothing in return, or to a benefit that has no economic value.

When applied to the human body, the cost-free service principle becomes tinged with moral overtones of great significance. It can even be said that under the terms of these public order and morality rules, any act directly or indirectly involving the use of the body or elements of the body must be free of charge.

The interpretation of the cost-free principle as a prohibition on making a profit from the use of one's own body or parts of it is drawn from article 5 of the Civil Code and instruments relating to organ and tissue donations(31). Article 3 of the Charter of Fundamental Rights of the European Union follows the same lines.

In fact, there are no normative or case law definitions of the cost-free principle. The principle stems, by analogy, from a reasoning of contract law and, more specifically, of the distinction between acts for pecuniary interest and those that are free of charge.

5. – *Anonymity*

In today's world there are numerous examples of anonymity in relation to donations. Anonymity is often used as an appropriate donation method, a discreet donation in which the donor's identity is concealed or restricted. Anonymity is possibly the most fitting tool for making the gesture of a donation, as it does not require payment or recognition in return. The strongest guarantee of the spontaneity of such a gesture and of a lack of personal interest (hidden or underlying) for the donor is provided by anonymity. Behind the anonymous donor, there can only be a person motivated by well-meaning and altruistic intentions.

Organ and blood donations are intended for unknown people. According to law, a sperm donor, providing the seed that gives life,

(30) Art. 1105 Civ. C.
(31) See *supra*.

must be anonymous. Legislative policies on the subject are based on the idea that it is the anonymity involved that causes donations to be based on community relations; it is due to anonymity that donations presuppose social proximity, basic sociality, solidarism. The transfer of an organ, inaccurately called a donation, takes place without any contract between the donor and the recipient. The latter receives the organ for transplantation from the health care facility and the medical team, just like any other form of medical service, and he has the right to receive it.

The blood and organs are received by the recipient via a system of intermediaries. In fact, the role of these intermediaries is to stop at source any link that might be formed between the donor and the recipient. These intermediaries (doctor, health care team, hospital structure) have therefore transformed the donation into merchandise. They have integrated the donation of blood or organs with a healthcare product, with other medications the patient is entitled to claim and receive. For the recipient, an organ is part of an anonymous circulation system. In this context, it is not received as a donation, but accepted as an item of merchandise, as a medication, or rather as an "artificial organ", like any other medical treatment. Therefore, and as Richard Titmuss very aptly remarked, the recipient claims it, when all is said and done, as a service he has the right to receive as a citizen[32]. Nevertheless, and this is a fundamental and original point, the recipient knows that the element was removed from the body by means of a free act. It was given, not sold. Has a social contract been established? Some people have put forward the idea that this development creates a sort of social bond between the – anonymous – donor and the recipient, and that this ideal closeness could be related to the constitutional principle of social solidarity.

The principle of anonymity is usually expressed to protect the principle of *privacy*; this principle does not apply when the requirements of biomedicine and solidarity take precedence (*e.g.* live organ transplant).

(32) R. Titmuss, *The Gift Relationship. From Human Blood to Social Policy*, London, Allen & Unvin, 1970.

B. – *The hierarchy of the principles*

In the Italian legal system, neither the Constitution nor the legislation organises a hierarchy of principles. In the case of a genuine incompatibility between the principles, it is necessary to seek a balance between the conflicting values on a case by case basis[(33)].

C. – *The protection of these principles*

The judges (ordinary and administrative courts) are the authorities responsible for ensuring the protection of the human body. The protection itself is based on the subjective rights accorded to the person. Failure to observe these rights can result in legal action.

The victim can, firstly, obtain protection and activate the protective measures[(34)], including the application of indirect coercion measures[(35)].

The patient can therefore apply to the ordinary or administrative courts to obtain the protection of health law and respect for his right to therapeutic self-determination. In practice, there are numerous possible courses of action[(36)]. In the case of treatments that are unwanted (or no longer wanted) by the patient, the issue is more controversial[(37)].

The victim of a violation can then seek reparation for the damage (patrimonial and non-patrimonial) suffered, not only for the violation of health law, but also for the violation of the right to self-determination[(38)].

---

(33) Const. Court , n° 471/1990.

(34) Including the application of art. 700 of the Code of Civil Procedure.

(35) Including art. 714 *bis* of the Code of Civil Procedure on the failure to observe obligations to act.

(36) With regard to assisted reproductive technologies but also in the context of traditional medical acts. See the cases of *Di Bella* et *Stamina* on innovative treatments.

(37) See Rome Court, ord. 16 December 2006 and Rome Court, G.u.p., 17 October 2007 on the *Welby* case.

(38) Cass. (1st civ.), n° 26972-26975/2008; and among numerous others: Cass. (3rd civ.), 9 February 2010, n° 2847/2010.

THE PRINCIPLES OF PROTECTION OF THE HUMAN BODY IN THE CONTEXT OF BIOMEDICINE IN GREEK LAW

Penelope AGALLOPOULOU

Emeritus Professor at the University of Piraeus (Greece)

A decent and civilised life must allow each individual to enjoy the respect and protection due to his person. Human rights are inherent to the status of being human and, as a result, are imposed on the legislator. Indeed, the study of human rights shows that the objective of these prerogatives is to protect the individual against arbitrary action by the State. However, the purpose of the personality rights is to defend the person from others. These rights protect both the physical and moral integrity of the person.

As the human body is a component of the person, its protection is provided by the rights to life, physical integrity and health. However, to protect the individual, it is not sufficient merely to protect the body. At the same time, the personality rights guarantee the protection of the personality through respect for freedoms, the individual's rights to honour and reputation, the right to privacy and the right to one's image.

In Greece, the protection of the human body is provided by a number of instruments (I) that enshrine the principles (II), contravention of which is punishable by law (III).

I. – The sources of protection of individuals

Alongside Greece's internal legislation (B), international instruments have a role to play (A).

A. – *International instruments concerning the protection of the person*

A number of international instruments ensure the protection of the person in Greece.

1. *The Universal Declaration of Human Rights*, adopted on 10 December 1948, was signed by Greece. This Declaration, which was hailed as one of the greatest achievements of the United Nations, entrusts the international community as a whole with the mission of including in its legislation the human rights and the fundamental freedoms contained in the Declaration.

It considers the individual not only as a citizen of a State, but as a human being and a citizen of the world. Since 1948, the Declaration has become a benchmark for all nations and all people. Unfortunately, this instrument has no binding force and there is no sanction for failing to respect its provisions.

2. *The European Convention on Human Rights*, signed in Rome on 4 November 1950 between the Member States of the Council of Europe, was ratified by Greece(1). Article 8 of the ECHR pronounces the right of every individual to respect for his private and family life, home and correspondence.

3. *The International Convention on Civil and Political Rights*, adopted by the General Assembly of the United Nations on 16 December 1966 and ratified by Greece(2), also proclaims, in its article 17, the right of every individual to respect for his private life.

4. *The Council of Europe's Convention on Human Rights and Biomedicine*, signed in Oviedo on 4 April 1997, has also been ratified by Greece. Conscious of both the rapid advances in biology and medicine and the need to respect human beings and recognise their dignity, Greece was, in fact, one of the first countries to ratify this Convention(3). The aim of the Convention is the protection of humans by protecting their dignity and identity, and it guarantees every individual, without discrimination, the respect for his integrity and for a number of fundamental rights and freedoms concerning the application of biology and medicine.

---

(1) L. n° 2329/1953.
(2) L. n° 2462/1997.
(3) 6 October 1998 ratified by L. n° 2619/1998.

5. *The Charter of Fundamental Rights of the European Union*, of December 2000, which represents a synthesis of the common values of the Member States of the European Union, has brought together for the first time in a single instrument the traditional civil and political rights, alongside economic and social rights, including references to biomedicine. Its goal is explained in its preamble: "It is necessary to strengthen the protection of fundamental rights in the light of changes in society, social progress and scientific and technological developments by making those rights more visible in a Charter." As a member of the European Union, Greece therefore applies this Charter.

B. – *Greek Law*

With regard to domestic law, a number of instruments ensure the protection of the person.

1. A number of provisions of the Constitution concern the protection of the person and relate to respect for and the protection of human dignity[4], the free development of the personality[5], the inviolability of private and family life[6], the prohibition of torture, bodily maltreatment, impairment of health, psychological violence and any other violation of human dignity[7], as well as freedom of expression and the free dissemination of ideas[8].

2. In civil law, the Civil Code concerns the personality rights in general, of which the protection of physical integrity is an element. According to this text[9], a person who has suffered an unlawful infringement on his personality has the right to claim the cessation of such infringement and also the non-recurrence thereof in the future. This protection applies to both the living person and the deceased person.

Any violation of these rights can give rise to the awarding of compensation[10].

(4) Art. 2 Constit.
(5) Art. 5 Constit.
(6) Art. 9 Constit.
(7) Art. 7, § 2, Constit.
(8) Art. 14 Constit.
(9) Art. 57 Civ. C.
(10) According to articles 57-59 of the Civil Code, together with articles 928-932 of the Civil Code, claims may be made for compensation, even for moral damage.

3. Criminal law punishes crimes against life[11], crimes causing personal injury[12], crimes against genetic freedom and financial exploitation of genetic life[13] and crimes against a person's honour[14].

4. The Code of Medical Ethics (CME) has legal force[15], as the legislative procedure followed for its promulgation, sets out in detail the issues of information and consent of the patient as well as the protection of physical integrity.

5. Likewise, there are specific laws on ART[16] and transplants[17] that provide some protection of the body.

II. – The principles of protection of the human body

Respect for the human body relies on the principles of the dignity of the person, the interdiction to dispose of the human body, the inviolability of the integrity of the human body, the informed consent of the subject, the non-commercialisation of the body and, in some cases, the anonymity.

Greek law does not include any hierarchy concerning the priority of these principles of protection of the body. From a legal perspective, they all have the same value. Nevertheless, it should be noted that the principle of human dignity is the only one with a constitutional value and forms the basis for all the other principles. Some principles, however, have a particular significance. For example, in the event of a conflict between the principle of the inalienability of the human body and the principle of non-commercialisation of the body, the latter will take precedence. The principle of the inviolability of the human body can lead to dismiss the principle of consent by prohibiting a person to dispose of his body.

(11) Art. 299 et seq. Crim. C.
(12) Art. 308 et seq.
(13) Art. 336 et seq.
(14) Art. 361 et seq.
(15) The Code of Medical Ethics was adopted by law n° 3418/2005, coming into force on 28 November 2005.
(16) L. n° 3089/2002 and n° 3305/2005.
(17) L. n° 3984/2011.

A. – *The principle of dignity*

This principle is constitutionally guaranteed and takes precedence over all other principles of protection from the beginning of life. Human dignity is inviolable. It must be respected and protected.

B. – *The principle of interdiction to dispose of the human body*

This principle was adopted to meet a need to protect people in the face of biomedical advances, but its content is not clear. In general terms, it means that the human body is not a "thing" (in the legal sense of the term) that can be the subject of a contract or agreement, whether it is free of charge or involves payment. However, the interdiction to dispose of the human body is only relative as, in Greek law, the person may sometimes have control over the disposition of the whole of the body (surrogacy and human research are permitted under certain conditions provided for by the law) or of parts of the body, provided this is free of charge and with the consent of the person concerned (organ donations[18], gametes, fertilised eggs and blood are authorised). On the other hand, Greek law continues to apply the principle that it cannot be disposed of the human body by prohibiting assisted suicide[19] and euthanasia[20].

(18) Art. 8 L. n° 3984/2011. With regard to organ removal, live donations are only allowed if the donor is a close relative of the recipient. The removal of an organ from a deceased person can only be performed under certain conditions and free of charge.

(19) art. 301 Crim. C. Assisting the suicide of a person is a punishable offence.

(20) The doctor may not, at the request of the patient, supply him with drugs likely to cause death. In such a case, it is an intentional homicide punishable under the Criminal Code (art. 299 Crim. C.). Even in the case where a doctor, following a serious and persistent request by the patient and through pity for a patient suffering from an incurable illness, causes the patient's death, this is homicide with the consent of the patient, punishable under the Criminal Code, but with lighter penalties (art. 300 Crim. C.). See P. Agallopoulou, "Patient rights at the end of life and the role of family and loved ones in Greek law", *in* T. Callus, B. Feuillet, K. Orfali (eds.), *Families and End-of-Life Treatment Decisions. An International Perspective*, coll. Droit, Bioéthique et Société, Brussels, Bruylant, 2013, pp. 199 et seq., esp. p. 202.

C. – *The principle of the inviolability of the integrity of the human body*

This is a public order rule meaning that no violation of the body of a person is possible. Inviolability is stipulated by law in order to protect the individual, but also the human species.

By virtue of this principle, all acts are prohibited that harm the body of the person when they are carried out without the person's consent. This means that if the person agrees, the violation is lawful. Medical procedures, abortion, the use of Assisted Reproductive Technologies and the removal or sampling of body elements and tissues with to the aim to transplantation are therefore lawful if the person concerned has provided his free and informed consent according to the legal procedures. Only in the case of medical error will the civil and/or criminal and/or disciplinary liability of the doctor or the hospital be invoked.

There are, however, lawful violations of the integrity of the human body, such as mandatory vaccinations.

D. – *The principle of the informed consent of the person*

This is based on the principle of autonomy of the person.

Before the patient gives his consent for a medical procedure, he must be fully and clearly informed(21). This right is guaranteed by the Greek Constitution within the context of the free development of the personality of each person and the protection of his human dignity(22). The requirement for the prior consent of the person is also provided for in the Council of Europe's Convention on Human Rights and Biomedicine, which has been ratified by Greece(23). With regard to patients being treated in a hospital, the law 2071/1992 on "the modernisation and organisation of the healthcare system" already included the right of patients to be fully informed(24).

(21) See I. Androulidaki-Dimitriadi, *Η υποχρέωση ενημέρωσης του ασθενούς* (The obligation to inform the patient), Ant. N. Sakkoulas, 1993, pp. 83 et seq.; K. Foudedaki, *Αστική ιατρική ευθύνη* (Medical civil liability), Sakkoula, 2003, pp. 174 et seq.; I. Karakostas, *Ιατρική ευθύνη* (Medical liability), Nomiki Vivliothiki, 2008, pp. 17 et seq.

(22) Art. 5, §§ 1 and 2 of the Greek Constit.

(23) Art. 5, §§ 1-2 and art. 10, §§ 1-2 of the Council of Europe's Convention on Human Rights and Biomedicine.

(24) Art. 47 L. n° 2071/1992.

In the same way, the Greek Code of Medical Ethics requires that the patient be provided with detailed information and that his consent is obtained. This consent can only, indeed, be free and informed if it is given following the delivery of detailed information from a healthcare professional on the nature and potential consequences of the planned procedure (or its alternatives) and without any pressure from third parties. In addition, the information must be provided in terms and language that can be understood by the person who is to undergo the procedure. Such information is a right of the patient, but any wishes expressed by the patient not to be informed must also be respected(25).

On the other hand, the law does not impose any formalism with regard to informing the patient and obtaining consent. However, a "carte blanche consent" given by the patient by signing a statement in which he declares that he has been informed and consents to any diagnostic or treatment procedure implemented by any means (surgical, pharmaceutical or radiological) would not be valid(26).

According to the CME(27), the patient must have the capacity to consent in order to provide consent to the medical act; the capacity to consent means that the person is capable of accomplishing legal acts(28). In the case of a minor, the CME states that the consent must be given by those persons exercising parental authority or acting as guardian(29).

The consent of the person is not required in a case of emergency, when the situation requires the provision of extremely urgent medical services(30).

With regard to organ donations, the principle of presumed consent is enshrined in legislation. According to law n° 3984/2011

(25) Art. 11-12, MEC. See K. FOUDEDAKI, "Η συναίνεση του ενημερωμένου ασθενούς σύμφωνα με το νέο Κώδικα Ιατρικής Δεοντολογίας" (The informed consent of the patient according to the new Code of Medical Ethics) in M. KAIAFA-GBANTI, *e.a* (eds), *Ο νέος Κώδικας Ιατρικής δεοντολογίας* (The new Medical Ethics Code), coll. Medical Law and Bioethics, Sakkoula, 2006, pp. 13 et seq.; V. SAKÉLLAROPOULOU, *Η ποινική αντιμετώπιση του ιατρικού σφάλματος* (Medical malpractice from the standpoint of criminal law), Sakkoula, 2007, pp. 16 et seq.; P. TSANTILAS, *Ευρωπαϊκό και εθνικό δίκαιο της υγείας* (European and national health law), Ant. N. Sakkoulas, 2008, pp. 56 et seq.; KARAKOSTAS, *op. cit.*, pp. 17 et seq.

(26) See Report n° 13218/26.11.2001 of the Mediator of the Republic, available at: www.synigoros.gr/reports/Porisma_Noemvrios_2001.pdf. See also the report on the grounds for law 3418/2004, concerning art. 11 and 12.

(27) Art. 12, § 2a, CME.

(28) Art. 12, § 2b, CME.

(29) Art. 12, § 2b, aa, CME.

(30) Art 12, § 3, CME.

on transplants, the removal of one or more organs from a deceased adult can be carried out when the person concerned has not, during his lifetime, informed the National Transplantations Organisation in writing of his refusal to such a removal[31] and after obtaining the consent of his family[32].

E. – *The principle of non-commercialisation of the body (or the cost- and profit-free principle) of the human body and its parts*

This principle means that any payment in return for a donation of parts of the human body (organs, gametes, fertilised eggs) is prohibited. Likewise, any financial reward granted to a surrogate mother is prohibited. These prohibitions constitute a powerful obstacle to the development of organ or egg trafficking and the commercialisation of surrogacy.

F. – *The principle of anonymity*

This principle concerns donations of organs and blood. In the case of organ transplants after the death of the donor, the donor's name must not be communicated to the recipient and his family, and vice versa. The family of the donor may, however, be informed only that the transplant was a success[33].

In the case of donations of gametes and fertilised eggs, the donors' anonymity is also guaranteed[34]. The identity of the child and that of its parents are not divulged to third-party donors of gametes or fertilised eggs[35]. This anonymity was provided to protect both parties: the "biological" family and the "social" family.

(31) If the deceased person is a minor, the consent of the parents (in the case of both parents exercising parental authority) or of one of them (if one parent has sole custody) is required. In the absence of parents or if they have been stripped of parental authority, it is the guardian who must consent (see art. 9, § 1, L. n° 3984-2011 and art. 12 CME).

(32) See article 9, § 3, L. n° 3984/2011, as amended by art. 55, § 4, L. n° 4075-2012.

(33) Art. 10 L. n° 3984/2011.

(34) Art. 1460, § 1, Civ. C.

(35) Art. 1460, § 2, Civ. C.

III. – Violation of the principles of protection of the human body

A. – *Violation of the principle of interdiction to dispose of the human body, of the principle of inviolability of the human body, and of the principle of the person's consent*

In the event of a violation of these principles, the civil and/or criminal and/or disciplinary liability of the doctor or the hospital may be invoked.

1. – *Civil liability*

Cases where the limits to the control of the free disposition of the human body or its parts are not observed or when the conditions laid down by the law are not complied with constitute an unlawful violation of the personality rights. According to the predominant doctrine in Greece, a medical intervention on the person, even for treatment purposes, constitutes such a violation. For the illegal nature of these interventions to be invalidated, the patient's informed consent must be obtained(36).

While the authors seem divided on the legal nature of the consent, the provisions concerning legal acts apply(37).

a. *Failure on the part of a doctor or hospital to meet their obligation to obtain the free and informed consent of the patient*

In this case, the provisions of the Civil Code concerning the protection of the personality apply, and the person has the right to

(36) See A. Litzeropoulos, *Στοιχεία Ενοχικού Δικαίου* (Elements of obligation law), Athens 1960, pp. 358 et seq.; P. Agallopoulou, "Η σημασία της συναινέσεως του τραυματισμένου σε χειρουργική επέμβαση κατά το Αστικό Δίκαιο" (Signifying the consent of an injured person with a view to a surgical operation), in *Essays in Honour of Professor A. Litzéropoulos*, t. I, Athens, 1985, pp. 36 et seq.; A. Georgiadis, *Ενοχικό Δίκαιο - Γενικό μέρος* (Obligations Law - General Section), Dikaio kai Oikonomia, P.N. Sakkoulas and Sakkoula, 2nd ed., 2015, § 60, n° 36, p. 664; P. Kornilakis, *Ειδικό ενοχικό δίκαιο* (Special obligations law), Sakkoula, 2002, p. 505. According to other authors, a therapeutic intervention does not constitute an illegal violation of the personality but, if it has been practised without consent, it constitutes a violation of the personality. In the case of non-therapeutic interventions, the consent negates the illegality, see K. Foudedaki, *Φυσικό πρόσωπο και προσωπικότητα* (Natural person and personality according to the Civil Code), Sakkoula, 2012, pp. 168, 174-176, 319-321.

(37) See Androulidaki-Dimitriadi, *op. cit.*, pp. 204 et seq.; P. Kornilakis, *op. cit.*, p. 505; M. Stathopoulos, *Γενικό Ενοχικό Δίκαιο*, (General Obligations Law), Athens, Sakkoulas, 4th ed., § 15, n° 60, 2004, p. 819.

demand the termination of the violation and the prevention of any recurrence in the future, although it is up to the patient to prove the absence of information and consent[38]. The burden of proof is on the patient.

A medical intervention without consent is wrongful, regardless of whether the doctor failing to obtain the consent has acted wilfully or negligently; this harm to the person constitutes an unlawful act entitling the patient to seek compensation[39], even for moral damage[40][41].

b. *Medical fault*

In the case of a medical fault, a distinction must be made between two possible scenarios. If a contract has been concluded between the doctor and the patient, the doctor's contractual and extra-contractual liability will be incurred; there are combined liabilities. If no contract has been concluded, or if it is void, the doctor's liability is only extra contractual.

i) With regard to contractual liability and in the case of a service contract, the doctor's liability is based on his obligation to execute the service with care. Failing that, he will have to compensate the harm caused by the defective execution of the service[42]. It is incumbent on the patient to prove the bad execution of the service[43].

(38) See K. Foudedaki, *Αστική ιατρική ευθύνη* (Medical civil liability), *op. cit.*, p. 229.

(39) Art. 57, § 2 Civ. C. together with art. 914 Civ. C. See K. Foudedaki, *Αστική ιατρική ευθύνη* (Medical civil liability), *op. cit.*, pp. 228 et seq.

(40) Art. 59 Civ. C.

(41) In the event of the medical intervention being arbitrary (*i.e.* it was carried out without the patient's consent) without also being wrongful, it is not possible to seek the termination of the violation and the prevention of any recurrence (art. 57, § 1, Civ. C.). In this case, doctrine nevertheless maintains that compensation can at least be sought for moral damage (art. 59 Civ. C.). This conception is based on the idea that the compensation for moral damage is not dependent on the intervention being wrongful. (A. Gazis, *Γενικαί αρχαί Αστικού Δικαίου* (General concepts of civil law), t. b', 1978, pp. 46 et seq.; N. Papantoniou, *Γενικές Αρχές Αστικού Δικαίου* (General concepts of civil law) Sakkoula, 3rd ed., 1983, p. 135; C. Simantiras, *Γενικές Αρχές Αστικού Δικαίου* (General concepts of civil law), Ant. N. Sakkoulas, 4th ed., 2008, n° 546, p. 387; I. Karakatsanis, in *Αστικός Κώδιξ* (Civil Code), A. Georgiadis, M. Stathopoulos, Sakkoula, 1978, art. 59, n° 6; A. Georgiadis, *Γενικές Αρχές Αστικού Δικαίου* (General concepts of civil law), Dikaio kai Oikonomia, 4th ed., 2012, p. 182. Against the case law: See Cass., n° 1987/2007, Cass., n° 8/2008 Cass., n° 17/2009, Cass., n° 488/2010, Cass., n° 660/2010, Cass., n° 846/2010 in *ΤΝΠ* "Νόμος"; CA Thessalonica, n° 682/2012 in "Αρμενόπουλος" 2012, 367.

(42) See art. 652 Civ. C. See K. Foudedaki, *Αστική ιατρική ευθύνη* (Medical civil liability), *op. cit.*, pp. 324 et seq.

(43) See K. Foudedaki, in *Δίκαιο προστασίας του καταναλωτή* (Consumer protection law), E. Aléxandridou (ed.), Nomiki Vivliothiki, 2008, p. 454.

ii) In the case of extra contractual liability, the doctor is liable for the damage caused by the unlawful and faulty medical act under the terms of articles 914 (and following) of the Civil Code. In such cases, the legal instruments relating to the death of the person, bodily injury and damage to health apply[(44)]. As well as compensation for any material damage caused by the unlawful act, the courts can award the person reasonable financial compensation for any moral damage[(45)]. It is incumbent on the patient to prove the existence of a medical fault, in other words the causal link between the damage and the wrongful behaviour of the doctor.

If the extra contractual liability of the doctor is invoked, in addition to the provisions of the Civil Code, other rules concerning unlawful acts apply in order to provide better protection with regard to life or bodily injury[(46)]. Regardless of whether the extra contractual liability of the doctor is invoked alone or is combined with a contractual liability[(47)], article 8 of law n° 2251/1994 on consumer protection applies. Although this instrument is based on the same conditions contained in the provisions of the Civil Code[(48)], it contains more favourable rules of evidence. Indeed, the burden of proof now falls upon the doctor (who must prove that his conduct was not wrongful or unlawful) and not on the patient[(49)].

(44) Art. 928, 929 and 931 Civ. C.

(45) Art. 932 Civ. C.

(46) See A. GEORGIADIS, *Ενοχικό Δίκαιο - Γενικό μέρος* (Obligations Law - General Section), *op. cit.*, § 63, p. 721 et seq.; I. KARAKOSTAS, *Δίκαιο Προστασίας του Καταναλωτή* (Consumer protection law), Nomiki Vivliothiki, 2004; K. FOUDEDAKI, in *Δίκαιο προστασίας του καταναλωτή* (Consumer protection law), *op. cit.*, pp. 444 et seq.; concerning case law, see: Cass., n° 1227/2007, in *ΤΝΠ* "Νόμος"; Court of 1st Inst. Thessalonica, 24582, in "Χρονικά ιδιωτικού δικαίου", 2009, p. 431; Court of 1st Inst Athens, 189/2010, in *ΤΝΠ* "Νόμος"; Court of 1st Inst. Thessalonica, 24772/2010, in "Χρονικά ιδιωτικού δικαίου", 2010, p. 772; Court of Appeal of Piraeus, 589/2011, in "Εφαρμογές αστικού δικαίου" 2012, p. 137; Cass., n° 687/2013, in *ΤΝΠ* "Νόμος".

(47) See K. FOUDEDAKI, in *Δίκαιο προστασίας του καταναλωτή* (Consumer protection law), *op. cit.*, p. 447. On the case law, see: Cass., n° 589/2001, in "Ελληνική δικαιοσύνη", 2002, p. 422; Piraeus CA, n° 862/2005, in *ΤΝΠ* "Νόμος"; Court of 1st Inst. Thessalonica, 11397/2007, in "Αρμενόπουλος", 2008, p. 1375; Court of 1st Inst. Athens, 189/2010, in *ΤΝΠ* "Νόμος"; Piraeus CA, n° 589/2011, in "Εφαρμογές αστικού δικαίου" 2012, p. 137; Court of 1st Inst. Larissa, 191/2012, in "Εφαρμογές αστικού δικαίου" 2012, p. 723.

(48) Art. 914 Civ. C.

(49) See K. FOUDEDAKI, in *Δίκαιο προστασίας του καταναλωτή* (Consumer protection law), *op. cit.*, pp. 451 *et seq.*

2. – *Criminal liability*

The criminal liability of the doctor or the hospital is invoked in the case of a violation of the conditions imposed by specific laws, such as the law on transplantations or the law on Assisted Reproductive Technologies[50], or of the provisions of the Criminal Code[51].

3. – *Disciplinary liability*

Disciplinary liability is also covered by specific laws and invoked in the case of violations of the conditions laid down, such as those for transplantations or Assisted Reproductive Technologies[52]; some provisions of the Code of Medical Ethics (CME)[53] also set out situations in which the disciplinary liability of doctors can be incurred.

B. – *Violation of the principle of non-commercialisation of the body or the cost- and profit-free principle, and of the principle of anonymity*

In the case of a violation of these principles, the criminal and/or disciplinary liability of those responsible may be invoked. The sanctions are fixed by specific laws (e.g. on transplantations, Assisted Reproductive Technologies[54]), as well as in the Criminal Code and the Code of Medical Ethics[55].

(50) Criminal sanctions imposed by articles 35-36 and 59-60 of law n° 3984/2011 on transplantations of elements and products of the human body and article 26 of law n° 3305/2005 on ART.

(51) Criminal sanctions imposed against doctors who cause the death of a person through negligence (art. 302 Crim. C.) or bodily injury (art. 308-315 Crim. C.). Abortion practised in violation of the conditions imposed by the law constitutes an offence punishable in accordance with article 304 of the Criminal Code.

(52) Art. 27 L. n° 3305/2005 on ART sets out disciplinary sanctions for those cases in which criminal sanctions also apply.

(53) Art. 36 CME.

(54) Art. 27 L. n° 3305/2005 on ART sets out disciplinary sanctions for those cases in which criminal sanctions also apply.

(55) Criminal sanctions are defined by articles 35-36 and 59-60 of law 3984/2011 on transplantations of elements and products of the human body and by article 323A of the Criminal Code (criminal sanctions against persons who trade in human beings for the purposes of the removal of organs and tissues). Articles 26, § 2 and 27, § 2, of law 3305/2005 on ART sanctions specialists (doctors or ART Centres) that buy or sell gametes or fertilised eggs. Article 26, § 11, of law 3305/2005 punishes any breach of the anonymity between donors and recipients of gametes.

Conclusion

The recent significant advances in biomedicine require a rapprochement between the development of scientific progress and the protection of the dignity of the human person. The development of biomedicine must be in the service of humanity. The Council of Europe's Convention for the Protection of the Dignity of the Human Being with regard to the Application of Biology and Medicine of 1997 was an essential instrument in the construction of biomedical law in Greece and thus contributed to Greek law's efforts to provide adequate guarantees with regard to reconciling biomedical advances with respect for the human being.

A PRAGMATIC APPROACH TO PROTECTING THE HUMAN BODY IN ENGLISH LAW

Thérèse CALLUS

Associate Professor of Law, University of Reading (United Kingdom)

The human body is at the centre of all biomedical practices and the very *raison d'être* of the latter is often the quest to improve the human condition. However, we need to guard against the human body becoming the mere object of biomedicine and it is necessary to ensure a certain level of protection for it. Although we talk about principles which 'protect', we nevertheless need to identify what we actually mean by protection? What exactly are we trying to protect? From whom? Or from what? Most importantly, how and why?

Literary interpretations of the world such as those in Adolph Huxley's *Brave New World*(1) or Mary Shelley's *Frankenstein*(2) reveal man's fear of the power of science. Consequently, it has become axiomatic to talk of protecting individuals and their bodies against the excesses of biomedicine. Such protection ranges from the macro level where we seek to protect the human race – for example by the almost world-wide prohibition on reproductive cloning(3) – to the micro individual level where we believe that each person has the right to respect for her physical integrity, translated by the principle of the inviolability of the human body. This chapter focuses on the latter – the individual and the protection of her body.

The vulnerability of each human person is at the heart of our concern. This chapter explores how English law can ensure a balance between protecting this vulnerability while at the

(1) A. HUXLEY, *Brave New World*, London, Flamingo Modern Classics, 1977.
(2) M. SHELLEY, *Frankenstein*, Penguin Classics, 1823.
(3) In the UK, the Human Reproductive Cloning Act 2001 prohibits reproductive cloning; available at: www.legislation.gov.uk/ukpga/2001/23/contents. See also, art. 11 of the Universal Declaration on the Human Genome and Human Rights, UNESCO 1997 and the Declaration on Cloning by the United Nations 2005.

same time allowing, and encouraging, beneficial progress in biomedicine. This question is posed in the context of a country where subjective rights are at the heart of society. Not only do we need to provide a framework for scientific progress, but we also need to guard against an explosion of individual claims of a 'right' to profit from every scientific advance. Indeed, the law is invoked to recognise individual rights which are bolstered by international instruments, notably by the European Convention on Human Rights. The State's protection of the human body thus includes protecting an individual's subjective rights.

In the light of the unwritten constitution[(4)], there is likewise no written declaration or list of principles which aim to protect the human body. Indeed, the common law favours the dynamic development of principles based upon all the concrete facts of individual cases[(5)]. It is a long process which evolves over time, but which has the advantage of enabling appropriate interpretations and applications of principles depending upon the circumstances of the case.

At the heart of protection is the respect for physical integrity. This implies the need to protect each individual against exploitation, commercialisation, discrimination, and to ensure respect for their physical body, both living and dead. The risk of violating this principle is increased with rapid scientific developments. Nevertheless, at the same time, we do not want to stifle beneficial progress which provides choices for us to fulfil our potential and enjoyment of life. We are thus faced with the challenge of ensuring that the human body and each individual are sufficiently protected, while at the same time allowing us to profit from scientific advances. Such advances allow us to treat more and more illnesses, as well as improving our quality of life and our perception of it.

In England, the pragmatic Anglo-Saxon approach results in a patchwork of sources of law accompanied by either criminal or tortious liability to promote a balance between precaution,

(4) For an introduction to the British Constitution, see amongst others, M. LOUGHLIN, *The British Constitution – a Very Short Introduction*, Oxford University Press, 2013.

(5) For a discussion on the different approaches between common and civil law jurisdictions, see for example: T.M. COOPER, "The Common Law and the Civil Law – a Scot's View", *Harvard Law Review*, 63/468, 1950; E. STEINER, *French Law – A comparative approach*, Oxford, Oxford University Press, 2010.

protection and promotion of biomedical progress. Our role is therefore to identify which principles will permit such a balance between protection of the individual and an individual's right to make use of scientific knowledge and its application. The first part of this Chapter will look at how the common law articulates such principles of protection. We will reveal a diversity of sources (A) before identifying a number of key principles (B). We can then explore in Part II how the principles can be applied by looking at some concrete examples (II A) and how the law deals with the violation of such principles (II B).

I. – Articulating principles through the common law

The elaboration of principles through the case law is both the strength and weakness of the common law. It allows principles to evolve over time in order to respond to contemporary dilemmas, but at the same time it permeates a level of uncertainty. Although legislation may provide some certainty, the legislator's role in the biomedical context is often limited. Principles relating to the human body have therefore evolved through a mix of case law, specific legislation and deontological rules.

A. – *A plurality of sources*

One of the first pronouncements of a principle relating to the protection of the human body can be found in the Hypocratic Oath: that of *prima non nocere* – first do no harm. But the scope of this obligation is far from clear. Its content can only be clarified through the elaboration of other more defined principles. Consequently, we see the development of deontological norms from professional bodies[6] which are then sometimes codified in legislation. In the same way, international instruments and declarations also play an important role. Although the English dualist system requires that in order to have force of law, any international text must be incorporated into national law, many deontological norms are an echo of those found in international instruments. For example, the Universal Declaration of Human Rights, or the Declaration

(6) See for example, the Professional Codes published by the British Medical Association (available at:www.bma.org.uk) and the General Medical Council (available at:www.gmc-uk.org).

of Helsinki from the World Health Organisation(7). However, it is interesting to note that the UK has not signed one of the more recent Conventions which is specific to biomedicine – the Orviedo Convention on Biomedicine(8). Despite its clear vocation, it is of limited port in English law.

On the other hand, the incorporation of the European Convention on Human Rights into English law by the Human Rights Act 1998, means that the Convention principles are directly applicable in English law. Although this Convention does not specify biomedicine, it allows us to concentrate on individual subjective rights which can be invoked within the context of biomedicine(9). Consequently, we see reference to the right to life (article 2), right to a private life (article 8), the principle of non-discrimination in the application of rights (article 13) and the prohibition on inhuman and degrading treatment (article 3)(10). In the same way, we should also note the potential scope of the EU Charter of Fundamental Rights. Its Preamble explicitly recognises the need to 'strengthen the protection of fundamental rights in the light of changes in society, social progress and scientific and technological developments'(11). However, the Charter has to be seen first and foremost as a declaration of aspirations and generic concepts as the Court of Justice of the EU noted in the case of *Omega*(12).

Alongside deontological and international norms, general principles of common law are invoked to ensure the protection of individuals against physical and mental violation. Indeed, in the

(7) More generally, see article 12 of the International Covenant on Economic, Social and Cultural Rights 1966 which provides "The States Parties to the present Covenant recognize the right of everyone to the enjoyment of the highest attainable standard of physical and mental health"; Likewise, the *Alma Mater* Declaration of the World Health Organisation 1978 which identifies health as a "fundamental human right".

(8) Available at: http://conventions.coe.int/treaty/en/treaties/html/164.htm.

(9) For an interesting analysis on the link between health and human rights, see T. Murphy, *Health and Human Rights*, Hart, Oxford, 2013.

(10) These rights were invoked in the well-publicised case of *Pretty* where a woman who wished to end her life, but who because of her illness was unable to do so without assistance, sought clarification of the policy on when legal action would be taken against the person (in this case, her husband) for the criminal offence of assisted suicide. The Court found that the right to life enshrined in article 2, did not comprise of a right to die. Likewise, there could not be said to be any violation of articles 3, 8 or 14: *Pretty v. Royaume-Uni*, n° 2346/02, available at: http://hudoc.echr.coe.int/sites/eng/pages/search.aspx?i=001-65003.

(11) Preamble of the EU Charter on Fundamental Rights, available at: http://ec.europa.eu/justice/fundamental-rights/charter/index_en.htm.

(12) ECJ, (1st ch.), 14 October 2004, *Omega Spielhallen und Automatenaufstellungs-GmbH v. Oberburgermeisterin der Bundesstadt Bonn*, n° C 36/02.

absence of a specific law or regulation, any conflict must be resolved by the court. Protection is thus assured through a patchwork of sources.

B. – *Identifying relevant principles*

Two main categories of principle can be identified. On the one hand, those which we can term generic; and on the other hand, those which translate the application of a generic principle to a given context, and which are often (but not exclusively) the result of a specific legislative provision. Such fundamental principles are therefore a tool to protect the vulnerability of each person from the excesses, even the abuse, of scientific expertise.

The following principles may be said to be generic: respect for human dignity, respect for the human body – living and dead, justice, non-discrimination, non-commercialisation, right to life, promotion of patient interests and even, a right to health. This latter has been expressly recognised by a number of international instruments such as the International Covenant on Economic, Social and Civil Rights 1946 or the Universal Declaration of Human Rights. Most principles come from the common law, often influenced by international norms. Interestingly, English law does not tend to refer to them as principles, but rather translates them into subjective rights. The incorporation of the ECHR into English law is at the heart of this tendency to link the promotion and protection of rights with the promotion and protection of health(13). Nevertheless, we are mainly concerned with abstract concepts whose scope is defined by reference to other, more tangible rights.

For the most part, these generic rights have a potentially wide ambit and do not directly refer to biomedicine. Further, they could all be said to derive from the principle of respect for human dignity. Indeed, as the International Covenant on Economic, Social and Civil Rights 1946 states, all rights come from the inherent dignity of the human being(14). The generic nature of the principles therefore implies a reliance upon the judicial interpretation or application within the context of biomedicine. The content and

(13) For an analysis on the emergence of this idea, see J.M. Mann, "Health and Human Rights – if not now, then when?", *Health and Human Rights*, vol. 2, n° 3, 1997, pp. 113-120.

(14) See B. Feuillet-Liger and K. Orfali (eds.), *La réalité du principe de dignité. Approche internationale*, Brussels, Bruylant, 2016.

scope of the principles vary not only according to their source, but also the context in which they are applied. We can thus identify more tangible principles which flow therefrom: personal autonomy, altruistic donation, access to medical techniques, professional confidentiality and public health. These principles are explicitly linked to biomedicine and some flow from professional obligations. For example, the principle of confidentiality which can be found in the guidelines of the General Medical Council[15]. Other principles may be questions of the State's public policy. Such principles may require application either by a professional regulator or by the Court. Some principles will result from specific legislation, for example the principle of altruistic donation of bodily parts and organs, provided by the Human Tissue Act 2004, or in the case of gametes, by the Human Fertilisation & Embryology Act 2008.

We turn now to our second part which will reveal how these general principles are applied in the context of biomedicine. It must be noted that the content of any principle is interpreted within a given context or, where relevant, under specific legislation. It is this predominantly case by case approach which typifies the pragmatic English response.

II. – A pragmatic application of fundamental principles

English law adopts a pragmatic approach to ensuring respect for the general principles which protect the human body. Where the principles are violated, both the common law and specific legislative texts impose either criminal responsibility or tortious liability. English law differs from continental European jurisdictions insofar as there is no general declaration of principles, but rather the use of judicial interpretation through the common law to deal with individual situations on a case by case basis. Consequently, if there is no legislative definition of a principle, the court may have recourse to professional, ethical or customary norms in elaborating the content and scope of the principle in question. It is thus (perhaps counter-intuitively) a concrete problem which gives the general principle its real meaning and relevance. It is a pragmatic approach to giving practical effect to generic principles. Autonomy

(15) *Confidentiality* – guidelines du *General Medical Council*, London, 2009, available at: www.gmc-uk.org/static/documents/content/Confidentiality_-_English_0414.pdf.

is a good example of how this works in the biomedical context (A). But this approach also reveals the relativity of the principles between themselves as the court is often called upon to decide between two fundamental, yet conflicting principles. Where any principle has been found to be violated, a mix of tortious liability and criminal responsibility is imposed (B).

A. – *The application of the principle of autonomy*

The principle of an individual's autonomy is translated by the requirement of a person's consent to any biomedical act carried out on her body. It is the corner stone of protection of bodily integrity. The principle evolved from the very early deontological texts and has since been confirmed by the common law[(16)]. Furthermore, it is sometimes enshrined in legislation when dealing with specific issues. However, where an individual is no longer capable of giving her free and informed consent, the principle gives way to another principle, that of the person's welfare. In such circumstances, the person's welfare or best interests will be decided either by the medical authorities or, if there is a conflict, by a court of law[(17)].

Autonomy then, is central in biomedicine. Quite clearly, it is engaged whenever a biomedical act is physically carried out on an individual's body. The law adopts the concept of consent to allow the practical application of the principle. However, mere consent alone may not be enough to ensure respect for bodily integrity. Indeed, consent must be free and informed, and it must also respect general principles of public policy. Consequently, a person cannot consent to a violation of her bodily integrity where the act in question is held to be contrary to public policy. Such was the case in *R v Brown* where on the basis of the human dignity of each individual and society as a whole, an individual was deemed not to be able to consent to acts of sadomasochism[(18)]. An individual's autonomy therefore is constrained by the greater good necessary

(16) See one of the many cases which expressly recognises the central component of consent required for all medical intervention on a competent adult: *Re T (Adult: refusal of treatment)* [1993] Fam 95.

(17) Numerous cases analyse what an individual's best interests may contain and proceed with a balancing checklist of the advantages and disadvantages of any proposed treatment for the best interests of the individual concerned. See for example, *Aintree University Hospital NHS Foundation Trust v David James* [2013] EWCA Civ 65.

(18) *R v Brown* (1994) 1 AC 212; the famous 'dwarf-throwing' cases in France raise the same issue of whether an individual can consent to an act which may be deemed by the

to respect the general principle of the integrity of the human body, not only for the individual, but also for humankind[19].

Consent is a very practical mechanism in order to promote, if not to fully ensure, individual autonomy and should not be seen as a mere formality, but rather as a process and communication over time. Indeed, the General Medical Council highlights the importance of discussion and communication between doctor and patient[20]. However, it is interesting that whenever a legislative provision requires consent to be obtained, it really only involves the procedural aspect of obtaining a signature on a consent form. Such provisions exist for example in the case of gamete or organ donation. But the process is not the true reflection of consent. Consequently, it is often the court which has to decide if the intervention in question satisfied the consent requirement thereby ensuring respect for the patient's autonomy, or if, on the contrary, whether true consent was lacking making the intervention an attack on the individual's bodily integrity. The court must be satisfied that the patient received all the necessary information to make an informed decision. But the case law is ambiguous as to how this condition is satisfied. Should the court ask what a reasonable or 'prudent' patient would understand, or should it be sufficient for the medical profession to decide what information is necessary, according to what a reasonable doctor would do? Although the answer may be the same in some cases, this is not always going to be the case[21]. However, a decision of the Supreme Court in February 2014 confirmed that the reasonable patient position should guide the assessment of the reality of consent, to promote patient autonomy[22].

As for those individuals incapable of making a decision for themselves, autonomy is inevitably compromised. In such a case,

State to be against the general interest or dignity of each human being as a member of the human race.

(19) Among many analyses on human dignity, see notably D. Feldman, "Human Dignity as a Legal value – Part I", *Public Law*, 1999, p. 682; D. Beyleveld, R. Brownsword, *Human Dignity in Bioethics and Biolaw*, Oxford, Oxford University Press, 2001.

(20) General Medical Council, Consent – doctors and patients making decisions together, London, 2008.

(21) A case which distinguishes clearly between these two approaches (in the majority and dissenting judgments) is *Sidaway v. Board of Governors of the Bethlem Royal Hospital* (1985) AC 871. Amongst a plethora of commentary, see in particular, M. Jones, "Informed Consent and other fairy stories", *Med. L. Rev.*, 1999, p. 103.

(22) *Montgomery v. Lanarkshire Health Board* (2015) UKSC 11. It's the minority judgment of *Sidaway* (*ibid.*) case that was preferred by the Supreme Court.

they are to be protected through the concept of their best interests or welfare. But the concept of best interests is particularly nebulous and depends on the opinion either of the medical team, or in case of conflict, of the court. Section 4 Mental Capacity Act 2005 provides a checklist of elements inherent in the best interest analysis, including, where possible to ascertain, the wishes and feelings of the patient herself. It is clearly a concept which must be applied on a case-by-case basis, but it remains ambiguous insofar as depending on the severity of the illness or incapacity of the patient, it may be difficult to actually identify any interests at all. For example, in the case of a patient in a permanent vegetative state, it is possible to suggest that her situation is so hopeless that she has no interest at all to be protected. This was suggested in the case of *Anthony Bland*, a victim of the Hillsborough disaster(23). However, in the context of research trials, the law on mental incapacity provides that clinical trials may be carried out on a patient who is unable to consent for herself, where the trial is simply shown not to be *against* the interests of the patient. The burden of proof is therefore much lower in this second case(24).

A further consideration in the invocation of the principle of autonomy is the apparent conflict between this principle and another, equally fundamental principle. For example, the right to life enshrined in article 2 of the European Convention on Human Rights may come into conflict with an individual's exercise of their autonomy. One such case is *Burke*(25). Here, the patient wished to adopt an advance directive which stated that should he become incompetent later on in life, he did not want artificial food and hydration to be withdrawn from him, even if a judge were to decide such a course of action would be in his best interests as his prognosis was nil. However, it was held that such an autonomous advance declaration could not bind the doctors if they believed that such treatment was not in his interests. The conflict between the two principles – autonomy and right to life was ultimately resolved by prioritising the principle of the best interests of the patient, as defined by the medical team, or indeed, the judge. The right to

(23) *Airedale NHS Trust v. Bland* (1993) AC 789.

(24) It is interesting to note that a recent Bill (*Medical Innovation Bill 2014*) proposed allowing doctors to use innovative treatments which have not yet been subject to sufficient trials to confirm their suitability, in cases where there is no other known treatment. However, this Bill was defeated in the Parliament in February 2015.

(25) *Burke v. UK*, n°19807/06.

life was thus circumscribed by other imperatives, notably the best interests of the patient, which are assessed at a time when the patient no longer has capacity.

Whereas autonomy is a principle enshrined through the case law, other principles are explicitly recognised in legislative provisions. For example, the principle of non-commercialisation of the human body and its parts is expressly stated in a number of texts which apply to specific practices. For example, concerning surrogacy (Surrogacy Arrangements Act 1985), gamete donation (Human Fertilisation & Embryology Act 2008) and organ donation (Human Tissue Act 2004). Where legislation provides for respect of general principles, liability is often also provided for in the event of their violation. However, even where a principle is purely deontological or recognised by case law alone, the common law also imposes sanctions where the principles have been violated.

B. – *Consequences of violation of general principles*

If there are no specific legislative principles, the common law imposes either criminal responsibility or tortious liability for violation of the general principle of respect for bodily integrity. Criminal law will sanction an act which is defined as a crime, whereas tortious liability aims to compensate the person whose bodily integrity has been violated.

Most often, liability is imposed for the particular act and is not dependent upon the biomedical context. However, some biomedical practices are expressly targeted to ensure certain limits and even prohibitions are respected. For these, it is the democratic expression in Parliament which has chosen to identify specific biomedical acts which must be regulated.

Criminal law is invoked to deal with crimes which may be identified by the common law. Such is the case for example, where no consent has been given to an intervention on the person's body or where the act itself is categorised as a physical or sexual assault[26]. Such cases are rare because in most situations there is not a complete lack of consent by the patient, nor the intent by the doctor to mislead or deceive the patient as to the quality of the act in question. Nevertheless, the option is there for the

(26) For example, a sexual assault in *R v. Healy* (2003) Cr App R (S) 87.

judge to so find[27]. On a procedural level, many laws explicitly provide criminal sanctions for violations of certain principles. For example, where public health measures are not respected; or where specific provisions concerning respect for the body and its parts have been violated in the context of the use of human tissue specifically provided for in the Human Tissue Act 2004. Likewise, in gamete donation, conservation and use, the Human Fertilisation & Embryology Act 2008 imposes criminal responsibility where the principles laid down in the Act are not respected[28].

Tortious liability on the other hand reinforces the importance of real and effective respect of the principles of protection of each individual's body. Consequently, if a patient consents to an intervention, the consent must be free and informed. If it can be shown that the Doctor has not satisfied her duty to inform, she can be pursued in negligence in the exercise of her profession, which, if proven, will give rise to compensation for the patient. It is an *ex post facto* protection which recognises where biomedical principles have been violated. The duty is therefore imposed on every doctor to act as any reasonable doctor would be expected to act, according to the general medical opinion and practice of the day[29]. This duty obliges the doctor to give all relevant information to the patient including possible risks and their consequences[30]. However, the assessment of the information given remains essentially a medical decision, and the duty does not prevent the violation of bodily integrity in the first place because its violation can only be shown once the act has taken place. Further, the patient must show a clearly identified loss. So if the intervention has brought a benefit for the patient despite a lack of full consent, the amount of damages awarded will be nominal. For example, in the case where a woman has a life-saving intervention despite her previously expressed wishes to the contrary, she was only awarded £100 in damages as the effects of the intervention could not be classed as a loss given

(27) *Appleton v. Garrett (1997)* 8 Med LR 75; *R v. Tabassum* (2000) 2 Cr App R 328.

(28) S 41 Human Fertilisation & Embryology Act 1990 (modified by the law of 2008).

(29) A principle laid down in the case law from *Bolam v. Friern HMC* (1957) 2 All ER 118.

(30) It is interesting to note the Directive 2001/83/CE of the European Parliament and Council relating to a code on the use of medicines. This directive requires the risks associated with each medicine to be listed. However, a study has shown that patients do not really understand how probable the risks really are, even when given this information: D.C. Berry, P. Knapp and D.K. Raynor, "Provision of information about drug side-effects to patients", *Lancet*, n° 359, 2002, pp. 853-854.

that it had saved her life[31]. It is therefore questionable whether allowing damages is enough to dissuade medics from violating the principle of bodily integrity and respect for the personal autonomy of the patient (whose wishes may sometimes have been expressed in the past, or in a form which is ambiguous)[32].

This study shows that the approach of English law remains rooted in domestic mechanisms despite the apparent universality of these general principles as declared in a number of international agreements. The interpretation and application of fundamental principles is a mix of legal, cultural, professional and social elements which dictate the scope of the protection of the human body in England and Wales. Moreover, it is often through the lens of individual rights that the principles are invoked, reinforced by the weight of the European Convention on Human Rights in English law. We can thus identify two levels of protection: first, a regulatory framework built upon principles of common law, or those explicitly identified in legislation; and second, an *ex post facto* protection ensured by the imposition of either criminal or tortious liability where the principles have been violated.

(31) *Ms B v. An NHS Trust* (2002) 2 FCR 1.

(32) In Canada, unlike in England, the damages awarded for a breach of an individual's wishes can be substantial, as in the case of *Mallette v. Schulman* (1990), 72 O.R. (2d) 417 (ON CA) where a previous declaration as to the woman's refusal of a blood transfusion was ignored by the medics who proceeded to treat her.

THE BODY, BETWEEN THE DYNAMIC OF SELF-DETERMINATION OF THE SUBJECT AND THE OBSTACLE OF RESPECT FOR HUMAN DIGNITY

Dominique MANAÏ

Emeritus Professor at the Faculty of Law University of Geneva (Switzerland)

The human body is not designated as such in Swiss law. It is only referred to in law through the person and his/her bodily integrity. Throughout the 20th century, jurists have identified the human body and the person. The body is an asset of personality. Both autonomy and bodily integrity are protected. The Federal Court declare thus that personal freedom seeks to guarantee the freedom to control one's own body and confers on the individual the right to respect for his/her bodily integrity(1). The human body is therefore protected by the general provisions of civil law(2) and criminal law(3).

Since the second half of the 20th century, advances in medicine and biology have obliged jurists to recognise that the human body is likely to be divided up and that its parts or substances can be dissociated from the person. As a result, at the end of the 20th century, the legislator defined a set of principles protecting the human body in specific laws dedicated to certain biomedical practices, thereby making medico-ethical standards dependent on the law(4). What is more, the Swiss legislator observes the international and European standards, whether they are legally binding or simply 'soft law'.

(1) Federal Court Judgment (ATF), 20 March 1963, ATF 89 I 92; and Federal Court Judgement, 26 October 1988, ATF, 114 Ia 357.

(2) Arts. 27 et seq. Civ. C., (CC, RS 210).

(3) Arts. 27 et seq. Civ. C., (CC, RS 311).

(4) In particular, the Code of Ethics of the FMH (Federation of Swiss Doctors) and the Directives of the ASSM (Swiss Academy of Medical Sciences).

I. – Protecting the body through the general principles of protection of the person

Until 1998, the principles of protection of the human body were formulated exclusively by case law and derived from the protection of the personality[(5)]. The right to bodily integrity is a prerogative accorded to every individual throughout their lifetime and continuing after death. The body is not a thing, it is an asset of personality. As such, it is inviolable and extra-patrimonial.

A. – *The body of the living person*

The body is firstly protected against excessive commitments that the person might make[(6)]. Assessing the excessive nature depends on the specific case and the overall assessment of the various factors in question[(7)]. This means that personal freedom is not unlimited. A commitment depriving a person of their decision-making freedom or that would offer her body or a bodily part to a third party in exchange for a significant sum of money would be deemed to be excessive and rendered void[(8)]. The *non-ownership*[(9)] of the human body arises from this general standard.

Furthermore, any intervention on the human body is deemed to be a violation, presumed to be unlawful. Such a violation becomes lawful if it is committed with the patient's consent[(10)]. This line of reasoning expresses the dual idea of the *intangibility* of the human body by third parties, and of a person's *control* over his/her own body. Without consent, the violation remains unlawful. The person therefore has various legal means of having their right to bodily integrity recognised in civil, criminal and administrative law. There are two forms of civil legal action: defensive actions to protect the person against unlawful violation, and remedial actions in the event of harm suffered. The first enables the victim

(5) Federal Court, 3 June 1987, ATF 113 Ia 257, 262, rec. 4b.

(6) Art. 27, § 2 Civ. C.: "No person may surrender his or her freedom or restrict the use of it to a degree which violates the law or public morals."

(7) A. Thevenaz, *La protection contre soi-même*, Study of article 27, paragraph. 2 of the Civil Code, Berne, Stämpfli, 1997.

(8) Art. 20, § 1 Code of Obligations (CO, RS 220).

(9) In French: "*non-patrimonialité*".

(10) Art. 28, §§ 1 and 2 Civ. C.: the justifying grounds are, in turn, consent, an overriding public or private interest, or the law.

to request the court to substantiate the unlawful nature of the violation suffered in the absence of any damage and any fault by the perpetrator(11). The second enables the victim to apply to the court for compensation for the material damage suffered, or moral damage in the case of serious violation(12). Criminal action is intended to punish the perpetrator of an act carried out without the person's consent, a violation constituting an offence (personal injury)(13). Disciplinary measures can be taken to sanction the perpetrator for the violation of his/her professional obligations by performing an intervention without the consent of the individual (or his/her representative), where this could and should have been obtained. Such measures include a warning, an official reprimand, a fine of up to CHF 20,000 and a temporary or permanent ban from practising(14).

This traditional system for protection of the body stems from personal freedom and is intended to ensure the self-determination of the individual. It enshrines the inviolability and intangibility of the human body. In addition, as an asset of personality, the body is extra-patrimonial.

B. – *The body of the deceased person*

The deceased is no longer a person(15). However, a dead body is not an thing, and Swiss law is very protective. The respect due to the dead stems from *human dignity*(16), and *personal freedom* continues to apply after death(17). Swiss civil law has rejected the idea of a representation of the person after death(18). The corpse is protected through the sense of devotion of the *family members*(19). It is therefore the close relatives who can take legal action on

(11) Art. 28a, § 1, ch. 3, Civ. C.: of course, this action only comes into play when the violation has already taken place; in other words, when action to prevent a violation (art. 28a, § 1, ch. 1) or an injunction to stop a violation in progress (art. 28a, § 1 ch. 2) are not possible. However, in medical matters, this action is the most frequently used.

(12) Art. 28a, § 3, *cum* 41 CO / 47 CO.

(13) Art. 122 et seq. Pen. C. (CP, RS 311).

(14) Art. 40c and 43 Federal Law on university medical professions of 23 June 2006 (RS 811.11); as well as the various cantonal health laws.

(15) Art. 31, § 1, Civ. C.

(16) Federal Court, 18 June 2001, ATF 127 I 115 c. 4a.

(17) Federal Court, 4 February 2010, 1C 430/2009 c. 2.1.11.

(18) Federal Court, 7 July 2003, *Journal des Tribunaux* (*JdT*) 2005 I 214.

(19) Federal Court, 18 June 2001, ATF 127 I 115 c. 6a and b.

their own moral damage caused by a violation of the body of the deceased[20].

However, criminal law accepts that the deceased continues to hold personality rights protecting the corpse; this is something of a "taboo subject" until the funeral[21]. Once a person has died, except for an autopsy, which can be ordered by the competent authority even against the wishes of the family if there is an overriding public interest[22], no removal from the body may be carried out unless the person consented to it during their lifetime or, failing that, the close relatives give their consent[23]. A violation of this principle constitutes an offence[24].

The European Court of Human Rights ruled on a Swiss case concerning the exhumation of a body in order to rule on a parentage relationship. On 22 December 1999, the Federal Court had rejected the legal action of Andreas Jäggi, aged 60, for a DNA analysis of the body of his putative biological father, deceased in 1976, in order to establish the latter's paternity. The European Court ruled that the petitioner's right to know his ancestry was preponderant and that Swiss law was in breach of Article 8 of the ECHR[25].

II. – Explanation of the principles of protection of the body by specific laws

Since the 1990s, Swiss legislators have been preoccupied with developing laws specific to the field of biomedicine in harmony with the principles adopted by international law[26] and European law[27]. Below, we examine the principles of protection of the body that apply to both the living person and the deceased. Alongside respect

(20) Art. 28a, § 3, Civ. C., *cum* art. 47 CO.
(21) Federal Court, 10 July 1992, ATF 118 IV 319 c. 2.
(22) Art. 70, § 3, Geneva law on health of 7 April 2006.
(23) Art. 8 Federal Transplantation Act of 8 October 2004 (RS 810.21); art. 36 Federal Act on research involving human beings dated 30 September 2011 (RS 810.3).
(24) Art. 69, § 1c, , Transplantation Act; art. 62, § 1b, Research Act.
(25) ECHR, 13 July 2006, *Jäggi v. Switzerland*, petition n° 58757/00, §§ 89-90.
(26) E.g., the UNESCO Declarations of 11 November 1997, 16 October 2003 and 19 October 2005.
(27) E.g., the Convention on Human Rights and Biomedicine of the Council of Europe, which has been in force for Switzerland since 1 November 2008; or the Charter of Fundamental Rights of the European Union; Art. 5, § 4, Federal Constitution of the Swiss Confederation of 18 April 1999 (Cst, RS 101).

for human dignity (A), we have the cost-free principle (B), the right to self-determination (C) and the principle of proportionality (D).

A. – *Respect for human dignity*

Although it remains undefined by the law, respect for human dignity is a very important principle in Swiss law, featuring at several levels of the hierarchy of standards.

Respect for human dignity is first and foremost a *constitutional principle*. The demand for this principle to be respected is related to the biomedical context, although its application extends well beyond this field. In fact, as a general principle, it tops the list of fundamental rights[(28)] and is relevant to the following specific contexts: assisted reproductive technologies[(29)], organ transplants[(30)] and research on human beings[(31)].

The Swiss legislator incorporated this constitutional principle in the laws on assisted reproductive technologies[(32)], organ transplants[(33)], genetic testing[(34)] and research involving human beings[(35)]. At cantonal level, legislators formulated a right to care with respect for dignity. This justifies the refusal of futile medical treatment and legitimises, in certain circumstances, the withdrawal of treatment at end-of-life.

However, its incorporation into the laws does not make it a subjective right or give it any special prerogative. It is more accurately a "guiding principle for all state activity"[(36)]. It is an objective principle that interprets and realizes fundamental rights[(37)], which means "recognition of the intrinsic value of the individual"[(38)].

---

(28) Art. 7 Cst.
(29) Art. 119, § 2, Cst.
(30) Art. 119a, § 1 Cst; the paragraph 2 requires the fair allocation of organs.
(31) Art. 118a, § 1, Cst.
(32) Art. 1, § 2, Federal law on assisted reproductive technologies of 18 December 1998 (RS810.11).
(33) Art. 1, § 3, Transplantation Act.
(34) Art. 2a, Act on human genetic testing of 8 December 2004 (RS 810.12).
(35) Art. 1, § 1, Act on research involving human beings.
(36) A. Auer, G. Malinverni and M. Hottelier, *Droit constitutionnel suisse*, t. 2, *Les droits fondamentaux*, Berne, Stämpfli, 2006, § 314.
(37) Federal Council, *Federal Gazette*, 1997, I, p. 142.
(38) *Ibid.*, p. 143.

Thus, for a living person, respect for human dignity consists of respecting his/her freedom and right to self-determination. The Federal Court ruled that a treatment administered against the will of the patient constitutes a serious violation of his physical and mental integrity and strikes at the essence of human dignity[39].

In the field of biomedical science, the affirmation of the *primacy of individual interests* over the interests of science[40] is an expression of respect for human dignity.

The *principle of non-discrimination* constitutes one of the principal aspects of respect for human dignity. This is a constitutional principle[41] that prohibits a person being treated differently due to his/her belonging to a particular group, when such treatment would put the person at a disadvantage. The principle of non-discrimination is stated alongside respect for human dignity in the laws relating to research on humans[42], human genetic testing[43] and transplantation. The latter law complements the prohibition on discrimination through the principle of equal treatment in the allocation of organs[44]. Discriminating against a person in the allocation of organs is an offence[45].

Respect for human dignity also applies to a deceased person and prevents acts of desecration of the body[46].

B. – *The cost-free principle and the prohibition of all commercialisation*

The human body or parts thereof may only be gifted, based on non-payment and on human dignity. 'Cost-free' excludes the provision of payment or other non-pecuniary advantage in return for body parts; a commitment that would then be excessive[47].

(39) Federal Court, 7 January 2004, ATF, 130, I, 16, 18.
(40) Art. 4 Act on research involving human beings of 30 September 2011.
(41) Art. 8, § 2, Cst.
(42) Art. 6 Act of 30 September 2011 on research involving human beings.
(43) Art. 4A, Act of 8 December 2004 on human genetic testing.
(44) Art. 17, Act of 8 October 2004 on transplantation.
(45) Art. 69, § 1g, Transplantation Act.
(46) The respect due to the dead stems from human dignity: Federal Court, 18 June 2001, *ATF* 127 I p.115.
(47) See *supra,* I. A.

This principle falls within the constitutional category with regard to organ donations[48].

The legislature extended the cost-free requirement to the donation of tissues or cells of human origin[49], sperm donation[50] and the transfer of elements of the human body for research purposes[51]. Failure to comply with this principle is subject to criminal sanctions (imprisonment or fine)[52].

The law on transplantation stipulates that the cost-free principle does not exclude payment for expenses related to the donation, compensation paid to the donor for loss of earnings or damages suffered by the removal, a symbolic gesture of gratitude after the transplant, or a crossover living donation[53].

However the cost-free principle excludes the patentability of the human body and its elements in their natural environment[54]. However, this principle does not prevent the patenting of an isolated and technically prepared element of the human body, in other words after its use and transformation.

The cost-free principle is complemented by a *prohibition on commercialisation*[55]. This prohibition is intended to prevent the trafficking of human reproductive material. It is explained in the law on research in these terms: "The human body or parts thereof may not be disposed of or acquired as such for research purposes in return for payment or other material benefit"[56]. Violation of this prohibition is subject to criminal sanctions (a term of imprisonment of up to three years or a fine)[57].

These two principles, cost-free and non-commercialisation, are closely related, but not always clearly defined by the legislator. Although the law on transplantation and the law on research define

(48) Art. 119a, § 3, Cst.

(49) Art. 6 and 69, § 1a, Transplantation Act.

(50) Art. 21 Federal L. on assisted reproductive technologies.

(51) Art. 9 Federal Act on research involving human beings.

(52) Art. 32, § 2, Federal L. on assisted reproductive technologies; art. 69, § 1a, Transplantation Act.

(53) Art. 6, § 2, Transplantation Act.

(54) Art. 1a and 1b Patents Act.

(55) Art. 119, §2e, Cst which prohibits trade in human germinal material; art. 119a, § 3, Cst, which only prohibits the commercialisation of organs, not that of tissues or cells; art. 7 Transplantation Act; art. 9 Act on research involving human beings.

(56) Art. 9 Act on research involving human beings.

(57) Art. 182 Pen. C.; art. 69, § 1b,, Transplantation Act; art. 119, § 2e, Cst; art. 62, §. 1c, Act on research involving human beings.

them clearly[58], the law on assisted reproductive technologies only refers to cost-free sperm donation[59] and punishes the disposal or acquisition of human germinal material for financial gain[60]. Furthermore, it is interesting to note the difference between the various sanctions. With regard to research, a violation of the prohibition on commercialisation is an offence punishable by a custodial sentence of up to three years or a fine[61], while a violation of the cost-free principle constitutes a minor offence resulting in a fine[62]. For organ transplants, a violation of the cost-free principle or of the interdiction of trade constitutes an offence punishable by a term of imprisonment or a fine[63]. In the context of assisted reproductive technologies, the disposal or acquisition of human genetic material for financial gain is punishable by a term of imprisonment or a fine[64].

C. – *The right to self-determination and its relaxation within the framework of research*

The right to decide stems from the constitutional right to personal freedom[65]. It expresses the idea of *the intangibility of the human body* and is based on respect for dignity. The free and informed consent of a person capable of judgement[66] or the authorisation given by the representative of a person incapable of judgement legitimises an intervention on the human body[67]. This legal principle has been confirmed by case law since 1973[68]. All cantonal health legislations require respect for the will of the patient and, since 2006, seeking the consent of the person concerned or his/her representative before undertaking a medical procedure is one of the duties of the medical team[69]. The same

(58) Art. 6 and 7 Transplantation Act; art. 9 and14 Act on research involving human beings.

(59) Art. 21 Federal L. on assisted reproductive technologies.

(60) Art. 32, § 2, Federal L. on assisted reproductive technologies.

(61) Art. 62, § 1c, Act on research involving human beings.

(62) Art. 63, § 1b, Act on research involving human beings.

(63) Art. 69, §§ 1a and 1b, Transplantation Act.

(64) Art. 32, § 2, Federal L. on assisted reproductive technologies.

(65) Art. 10, § 2, Constit.

(66) Art. 16 Civ. C.

(67) Art. 28, §§ 1 and 2, Civ. C.

(68) Federal Court judgment, 14 September 1973, ATF 99 IV 208, published in the *JdT*, 1974, I, p. 132.

(69) Art. 7a and art. 40 Federal L. on university medical professions of 23 June 2006 (LPMed, RS 811.11).

applies to genetic testing[(70)] for inclusion in a research project[(71)]; for live organ donation[(72)]; for donations of gametes for the purposes of assisted reproductive technologies[(73)]. Failure to respect the patient's will is an offence[(74)]. In addition, the victim of a violation of his/her bodily integrity – for which consent has not been given – can have his/her rights recognised by civil actions[(75)] and claim compensation in case of damage or moral harm[(76)].

The right to *biomaterial self-determination* refers to the will of the person with regard to the use of an element of his/her body taken in a care or research context. The individual has the right of control over his/her body and this extends to "biological material". This term refers to "bodily substances derived from living persons"[(77)].

It is in relation to this biological material in the context of research that Swiss law has revisited the principles of protection of the human body. In fact, biomaterial self-determination has indeed been relaxed. When the re-use of biological material is already envisaged by the researchers at the time the sample is taken, the consent of these individuals is obtained, where possible, and they must be informed of their of *opposition*[(78)]. If this is not the case, the biological material can only be re-used in a specific project in an uncoded form with the informed consent of the persons concerned for each research project[(79)]. However, a *general consent* for research or for any future project is sufficient for the re-use of biological material in a coded form[(80)]. The code allows the biological material to be used for research purposes under a pseudonym, and the identification of the person concerned requires the access key[(81)].

(70) Art. 18 Act on human genetic testing. For genetical analyses, the consent must be in writing for a presymptomatic genetical analysis or a prenatal genetical analysis or for a family planning analysis (art. 18, § 3, LAGH).

(71) Art. 16 and 62, § 1b, Act on research involving human beings; art., 22, 23 and 24 Act on research involving human beings.

(72) Art. 12 and 13 Transplantation Act.

(73) Art. 18 Federal L. on assisted reproductive technologies.

(74) Art. 122 et seq. Pen. C.; art. 34, § 1, L. on assisted medical technologies; art. 36, L. on human genetical analysis; art. 13, §§ 2 and 3, Transplantation Act; art. 62, § 1b, Act on research involving human beings.

(75) Art. 28a Civ. C.

(76) Art. 28a, § 3, Civ. C. *cum* art. 41 or 49 Obligations C.

(77) Art. 3e Act on research involving human beings.

(78) Art. 17 Act on research involving human beings.

(79) Art. 32, § 1, Act on research involving human beings.

(80) Art. 32, § 2, Act on research involving human beings.

(81) Art. 3h Act on research involving human beings.

In addition to this, the biological material can be *anonymised* for research purposes and re-used if the person concerned or the legal representative or the close relatives have been informed in advance and have not expressed their opposition(82). The anonymization rules out any link with the person; a link which could only be re-established by disproportionate effort(83) in terms of time, expense and labour.

Furthermore, notwithstanding the aforementioned principles, the biological material can, *exceptionally*, be re-used in other, later research projects without the informed consent of the persons concerned if the following three conditions are met(84): in case of impossibility or excessive difficulty to obtain consent or provide information to the persons concerned (e.g. extreme difficulty finding the persons in question); if there is no documented refusal of the person concerned; and if the interests of research outweigh the self-determination of the person.

It goes without saying that this exception must be interpreted most restrictively. It is up to a local ethics committee to decide, in a particular case, if these conditions have been met. However, the re-use of biological material without obtaining the prior consent required by law constitutes a minor offence (fine)(85).

In addition, the bodily substances removed within the context of a post-mortem examination may be used in a "very small quantity" for research purposes *without* requiring the *consent* of either the person during his/her lifetime or of his/her close relatives, in the absence of a documented refusal of the deceased(86).

In summary, we are therefore able to state that Swiss law has a graduated system for the protection of the human body: firstly, a right to self-determination in the disposal of the human body as a whole and a right to biomaterial self-determination with regard to the availability of body parts and uncoded biological material; next, there is a general right to self-determination in the case of non-specific research projects, to make a donation of coded biological material; then a right to object to the provision of anonymised biological material; finally, when it is impossible

(82) Art. 32, § 3, Act on research involving human beings.
(83) Art. 3i Act on research involving human beings.
(84) Art. 34 Act on research involving human beings.
(85) Art. 63, § 1c, Act on research involving human beings.
(86) Art. 38 Act on research involving human beings.

or very difficult to obtain the consent, the re-use of the biological material can be authorised on an exceptional basis. Doctrine[(87)] criticises this relaxation of the right to self-determination, which it believes to be incompatible with the law.

D. – *The primacy of the interests of the person*

The ethical principles of beneficence and non-maleficence require the interests of the patient to be given precedence. In law, the doctor must act diligently according to the rules of the medical profession, subject to being held liable. When there is a conflict between the patient's will and the patient's therapeutic interest, the former takes precedence. The doctor is therefore authorised to make care-related decisions and intervene in the patient's interests in only one situation: that where the patient is incapable of self-determination and is in an emergency medical situation[(88)].

With regard to research on human beings, the legal principle of proportionality is a reminder of the ethical principles of beneficence and non-maleficence, according to which the interests of the person must take precedence over the public interest of science. The principle of proportionality is a general principle of law[(89)]. It "means that the method selected to achieve the intended purpose is that which carries the least threat to private interests, bearing in mind the expected results from a public interest standpoint"[(90)]. In accordance with case law, doctrine has developed components of this principle[(91)]. Called on to protect the human body when the public interest is at stake, it is established as a constitutional principle in the context of research[(92)]. For it to be respected, there must be an evaluation at two levels: firstly, the risks and burdens must be reduced to a strict minimum[(93)]; secondly, the foreseeable risks and stress must be in proportion to the anticipated benefits of the

(87) A. Büchler and B. Dörr, "Medizinische Forschung an und mit menschlichen Körpersubstanzen – Verfügungsrechte über den Körper im Spannungsfeld von Persönlichkeitsrechten und Forschungsinteressen", *Swiss Law Review*, 2008, I, pp. 381-406.

(88) Art. 370 Civ. C.

(89) Art. 5, § 2, Federal Constit.

(90) Federal Court judgment, 30 August 2002, 2P.38/2001, c. 3.3.

(91) A. Auer, G. Malinverni and M. Hottelier, *Droit constitutionnel suisse*, vol. II, *Les droits fondamentaux*, 2nd ed., Berne, Stämpfli, 2006, §§ 229-237.

(92) Art. 118b, § 2b, Act on research involving human beings. "The risks and stress for the participants must not be disproportionate to the benefits of the research project".

(93) Art. 12, § 1, Act on research involving human beings.

project[94]. The risk is a "brief and insignificant deterioration in the state of health"; the stress relates to short-term, negligible symptoms or unpleasantness[95]. This evaluation enables a determination of whether or not a research project involving the human body is acceptable. For a person capable of judgement who participates in a research project without direct benefit, the acceptable level of risk is higher than for a vulnerable person, whether or not he/she is capable of judgement. Vulnerable persons, within the meaning of the law on research, are children under 14, adolescents over 14, adults incapable of judgement, pregnant women and persons deprived of their liberty. These persons can only participate in a research project without direct benefit if, in particular, the risks and stress are minimal[96], for example interviews, observations, samples of blood or biological liquids without invasive procedures (urine, saliva), smear tests, ultrasound, electrocardiograms or radiography. A failure to respect the principle of proportionality is not, in itself, punishable by law.

Conclusion

Although the Swiss legal system does not a have a specific law relating to the human body, its protection is extensive: this stems from the general principles of the law and from specific laws. Our analysis of Swiss law has enabled us to identify four principles.

The first is the principle of inviolability of the body. Any intervention on the body is unlawful if the person has not given prior consent. The right of control over one's body, including biomaterial self-determination, stems from the fundamental right to personal freedom, a freedom which is not unlimited.

The cost-free and non-commercialisation principles, the second principles of protection, enable the commodification of the human body to be avoided, regardless of the consent of the person concerned, by punishing excessive commitments. The principle of beneficence, the third principle of protection, is expressed in law by respect for

(94) Art. 12, § 2, *ibid.*

(95) Federal Council, Message of 12 September 2007 concerning art. 118b Constit., FF 2007, p. 6370; for deontological standards: Académie suisse des sciences médicales, *Recherche avec des êtres humain, Guide pratique*, Berne, 2009, p. 51.

(96) Art. 22, §§ 2a, and 4, art. 23, § 3a, art. 24, § 2a, Act on research involving human beings.

the interest of the patient. This interest is the cornerstone of a medical act carried out diligently. It is coupled with the principle of proportionality within the context of research when the public interest is at stake. Finally, human dignity, the fourth principle, is a principle to which there can be no exceptions, which underpins the other principles of protection of the human body.

THE PRINCIPLES OF PROTECTION OF THE HUMAN BODY IN TUNISIA: BETWEEN INADEQUACY AND INTERPRETATION

Amel AOUIJ-MRAD

Professor at Tunis El Manar University (Tunisia)

Although there are several principles in Tunisia aimed at protecting the human body, there is no overall and considered "system of protection" providing clear goals and guidelines. The existing principles, such as those of consent to a medical act, protection of physical integrity or the dignity of the patient, are more indicative of an authoritarian vision of health-related public order than of a desire to support the individual. This cannot help but raise the question of the efforts of the States to seek conformity with an international society considered to be the forerunner in terms of human rights.

An analysis of the principles of protection of the human body supports an impression of dispersion and a lack of structure. They are not assembled in a single legal instrument, code or law specific to biomedicine: they are to be found at different levels in the Tunisian legal order.

At the forefront of these instruments are the ratified international conventions, which attest to the will of the State to demonstrate its respect for human rights.

The international instruments[1] referred to are, therefore, mediate legal sources in Tunisia, in that their main purpose is not to protect the body or the person, although they can nevertheless

(1) We only refer in this presentation to international instruments with a universal scope. For regional international instruments, however, we should also refer to the African Charter on Human and Peoples' Rights of 26 June 1981, which proclaims that "[...] freedom, equality, justice and dignity are essential objectives for the achievement of the legitimate aspirations of the African peoples" (art. 3), and that "the right to respect for dignity is inherent to the human being [...]" (art. 5 and 19). Likewise, the Protocol of the African Charter on Human

provide this protection. The main documents referred to are the Helsinki Declaration[2] and the Protocol to the International Covenant on Civil and Political Rights[3]. It should, however, be noted that there has been a substantial movement in defence of human rights since the Revolution of January 2011[4].

The internal legal instruments are more indicative of the willingness of the State to provide this protection of the person. However, this legal framework appears, in Tunisia, to be somewhat sparse and inadequate, and usually quite difficult to interpret.

For some time now, action to affirm the worth of every human being, the citizen and the person has been evident, particularly with the Revolution of 14 January 2011, which was partially based on the leitmotiv of “dignity”, which gave this principle a certain political force[5].

The internal sources stating principles of protection are scattered. At legislative level, some laws are old and non-specific, but they nevertheless remain reference instruments, despite being open to interpretation. This is the case with the 1906 Code of Obligations and Contracts[6] and the Criminal Code of 1913, which do not specifically recognise principles of protection, but which confer subjective rights that can serve as a basis for protection or that sanction acts that can be considered violations of principles of protection of the person[7]. Furthermore, the law on organization

and Peoples' Rights concerning women's' rights states “all women have the right to respect for the dignity inherent to the human being”.

(2) Adopted by the 18th General Assembly of the World Medical Association in Helsinki (Finland) in June 1964 and amended several times.

(3) General Assembly of the United Nations, 16 December 1966.

(4) On 29 June 2011, the Tunisian Government declared that it recognised the competence of the Committee Against Torture established by article 17 of the Convention against Torture and Other Cruel, Inhuman or Degrading Treatment or Punishment (General Assembly of the United Nations, 10 December 1984) to receive the communications set out in articles 21 and 22 and thus to lift any reservations on the Convention. This recognition took the form of its accession to the Optional Protocol of the 1984 Convention. In the first days following the Ben Ali era, a Commission was established to hold an inquiry on these crimes and acts of torture during the 23 years of his regime.

(5) See *infra*, first part, 1.

(6) Art. 243 Obligations and Contracts C.: “Any commitment must be executed in good faith and be binding, not only with regard to what is expressed in it, but also to any changes that the law, usage or fairness give to the obligation according to its nature.”

(7) See part two.

of the health system uses the expression "fundamental human rights"[8].

Other laws specific to the field of medicine (drugs[9], mental patients[10], etc.) or biomedicine (blood[11], organ transplants[12], reproductive medicine[13], etc.) or related to other fields, but concerning incidentally one of the principles of protection of physical integrity (protection of personal data[14], assignment of a patronymic family name[15], the disabled[16], the elderly[17], social protection[18], etc.), undoubtedly constitute primary references with regard to the protection of the human body in Tunisia, the most recent being the organic law establishing the National Authority for the Prevention of Torture[19].

The crucial regulatory instruments, such as the Code of Medical Ethics[20], the general internal rules of hospitals[21] and the decree concerning human experimentation[22], are old instruments focused more on the organisation of the public service than on the protection of the person – the sick, the patient or the user – and featuring the principles of protection only incidentally. They are supplemented by instruments of an infra-regulatory value, such as the Patient's

(8) Art. 5 L. n° 91-63, 29 July 1991: "The public and private health facilities and establishments and structures must operate in conditions that guarantee: 1) Fundamental human rights [...]".

(9) L. n° 92-52, 18 May 1992, concerning narcotic drugs.

(10) L. n° 92-83, 3 August 1992, on mental health and conditions of hospitalization for mental health problems.

(11) L. n° 82-26, 17 March 1982, on the organisation of taking blood for transfusion.

(12) L. n° 91-22, 25 March 1991, on organ transplants and grafting of human organs.

(13) L. n° 93-2001, 7 August 2001, on reproductive medicine.

(14) Organic L. n° 63-2004, 27 July 2004, on the protection of personal data.

(15) L. n° 98-75, 28 October 1998, on the assignment of a patronymic family name to abandoned children or children of unknown descent, amended by L. n° 51-2003, 7 July 2003.

(16) Framework L. n° 83-2005, 15 August 2005, on the promotion and protection of disabled persons.

(17) L. n° 94-114, 31 October 1994, on the protection of elderly persons.

(18) L. n° 71-2004, 2 August 2004, creating a health insurance scheme.

(19) Organic L. n° 2013-43, 23 October 2013. Also a politically charged instrument.

(20) Decree n° 93-1155, 17 May 1993, embodying the MEC.

(21) Decree n° 81-1634, 30 November 1981, embodying the general internal regulations of hospitals, institutes and specialist centres under the Minister of Public Health.

(22) Decree n° 90-1401, 3 September 1990, establishing the modalities for medical and scientific testing of drugs intended for human medical use.

Charter[23], which specifically refer to principles of protection of the body[24], but whose prescriptive nature isn't obvious.

On the subject of protection of the body, it is also interesting to refer to the disciplinary decisions of the National Council of the Tunisian Medical Association sanctioning violations of the Code of Medical Ethics, as their objective is to protect the patient. However, the prescriptive nature of these decisions is limited. If punishments declared for violations by a doctor of an ethical principle are enforceable against the doctor, do they have a reference value?

The opinions of the National Medical Ethics Committee[25] refer also on principles of protection of the person and his body.

Finally, although case law (civil, criminal or administrative) has the virtue of recognising some of the principles of protection of the human body, it is disadvantaged by its rare appearance[26].

The dispersed nature of the principles of protection of the human body within different sources, whose normative force is sometimes open to question, involves a lack of visibility of these principles. It therefore appears that, while the Tunisian instruments establish, explicitly or implicitly, a number of principles of protection of the person (I), they are of a rather random nature, due to their lack of implementation and inadequate recognition (II).

I. – The statement of principles: dispersed and insufficiently visible

Providing a statement of the principles of protection of the human body in Tunisia remains a difficult exercise. What is more, no definition or delineation of their scope is given. These principles are divided into two categories, of differing significance: general principles with implications for the protection of the human body,

(23) Circular of the Minister of Public Health n° 36/2009 of 19 May 2009 concerning the Patient's Charter.

(24) "The health professionals ensure respect for the dignity of the patient": "Free, prior and informed consent of the patient to health care must be obtained , subject to the exceptions provided for by the law", for example for the Hospital Patient's Charter.

(25) The National Medical Ethics Committee was created by law n° 91-63 of 29 July 1991 on organisation of the health system and governed by decree 94-1939 of 19 September 1994, which determines its remit, composition and operating modalities.

(26) See part two.

and principles specifically relating to the protection of the human body. However, this material distinction reveals the exaggerated and almost factitious recognition of the principle of dignity (A) and the subsidiary nature of everything that is not dignity (B).

A. – *A principle of universal value: human dignity*

Tunisia has a relationship with the principle of dignity that is first and foremost political. However, it is conceivable to refer in the future to this principle in the field of biomedicine to protect the person's body, as dignity is now a principle deemed to be essential to the rule of law.

The principle of dignity was constitutionally established on two occasions in different contexts, but in both cases it related to the human being as a citizen. Its purpose and scope was purely political.

In 2002, the Constitution of 1 June 1959 innovated by pronouncing in the new article 5 the "dignity" of the person and relating it to the "human rights in their universality". This first recognition, at such a high level of the hierarchy of norms, must be seen in the political context of the time, which was authoritarian and not respectful of human rights, and which merely sought to give the impression of respecting these rights.

The Constitution of 26 January 2014 demonstrates a political ideal of recognising the individual citizen within society. It enshrines the principle of dignity more explicitly, almost redundantly. Included in the Preamble(27) and then in the country's motto(28), dignity is truly enshrined in general terms in article 23(29) of the Constitution and then more specifically in two further references to prisoners(30) and children(31).

---

(27) "Taking pride in the struggle of our people [...] to achieve the objectives of the revolution for freedom and dignity [...]".

(28) Art. 4: "The motto of the Tunisian republic is: Liberty, Dignity, Justice, Order".

(29) "The State protects the dignity of the person [...]".

(30) Art. 30: "All inmates have the right to humane treatment that preserves their dignity [...]".

(31) Art. 47: "The rights to dignity, health, care, a good upbringing and education are guaranteed to the child by its parents and the State".

This first vision of dignity, of political usefulness, is also related to the law on prevention of torture[32].

On legislative level, the principle of dignity appears mainly in the laws concerning people who are vulnerable or in a position of inferiority. Accordingly, the law on mental health and conditions for hospitalisation for mental health problems[33] states that "the hospitalisation of person for mental health problems shall be carried out with respect for individual freedoms and in conditions that guarantee human dignity" (art. 1). Likewise, the law on the protection of elderly persons states that: "The protection of the elderly persons is based on the following principles: to protect their health and uphold their dignity by helping them to overcome the difficulties confronting them in their daily lives owing to their advanced age".

Laws specific to the field of biomedicine, such as the law on reproductive medicine, link dignity to the medical act. For example, article 1 of this law states that "reproductive medicine is subject to the provisions of the present law within the framework of the guarantee of the dignity of the human person [...]".

With regard to the regulatory instruments, the Code of Medical Ethics affirms that: "A doctor asked or required to examine or treat a detainee may not, directly or indirectly, even if only by being present, facilitate or support a violation [...] or of [this person's] dignity [...]" (art. 7). With regard to advisory structures, such as the National Medical Ethics Committee in particular, their opinions must reflect "human values" and "human rights", therefore having to refer to the principle of dignity[34].

B. – *The principle of protection of physical integrity*

In addition to the principle of dignity, there are principles directly related to the protection of the integrity of the human body, *i.e.* physical integrity. However, even at this level, the principle of dignity is used as a primary reference or source of inspiration: we

(32) Organic L. n° 43-2013, 23 October 2013, on the creation of the National Authority for the Prevention of Torture.

(33) L. of 3 August 1992 on mental health and conditions of hospitalization for mental health problems.

(34) Decree n° 94-1939, 19 September 1994. See *infra*.

can therefore often see a specific link established between dignity and physical integrity.

The Constitution establishes the principle of respect for physical integrity as a constitutional principle by linking it to dignity: "[The State protects...] his [the human being's] physical integrity and prohibits all forms of mental and physical torture."

Before this enshrinement of the principle of physical integrity in the Constitution, the Tunisian Criminal Code of 1913, still in force, sanctioned the various violations of this integrity(35), although these sanctions did not fall within a perspective of support for the human being and protection of the body, but were based on the notion of protecting society against offenders.

Almost all of the laws specific to the protection of the human body refer to the principle of protection of physical integrity that leads to the prohibition of other people from violating the body of the person. Medical and biomedical procedures are regarded as permissible exceptions to this principle. This is the case with the law on organ transplants and grafts(36) and the law on reproductive medicine(37). On the other hand, the law on the use of human blood is more focused on the requirement for the free and informed consent of the person to justify the violation of the body(38) than on preserving physical integrity.

Although the Code of Medical Ethics does not refer to this principle with regard to the medical act in general, it pronounces it in the specific case of people in detention(39).

With regard to the "dead" body (the corpse), its protection is based more on public order and administrative police considerations(40) through the respect due to the corpse(41) than on a desire to ensure

(35) Art. 218, 219 and 225, Part II, Crim. C.

(36) Art. 1 of the law : "The physical integrity of the human being is guaranteed".

(37) *Id.*, Reproductive medicine "[...] is subject to the provisions of the present law within the framework [...] of the preservation of one's physical integrity".

(38) Art. 2 L. n° 82-26, 17 March 1982, referred to above.

(39) Art. 7 MEC: "A doctor asked or required to examine or treat a detainee may not, directly or indirectly, even if only by being present, facilitate or support a violation of the physical or mental integrity of this person [...] or of his dignity".

(40) Decree n° 97-1326, 7 July 1997, concerning the methods of preparing graves and setting rules for the interment and exhumation of remains or corpses forms the basis for local administration control procedures. This decree is based on law 57-3 of 1 August 1957 concerning civil status and on organic law 75-33 of 14 May 1975 concerning municipalities.

(41) A. Bouhdiba, "Perception de la douleur et de la mort dans les sociétés du Maghreb", *JIBio*, 2001/4, vol. 12, p. 51.

the protection of the physical integrity of the deceased person. Public order prevails over the protection of the person.

C. – *Other principles of protection*

The first is that of informed consent, which must be linked to the duty of the doctor to provide information and also to the principle of inviolability of the human person, which prohibits any violation of the body without the consent of the person concerned. There are numerous instruments referring to the right to information, establishing the principle of informed consent: these instruments refer to it in general terms, through the structures in which it is exercised and through certain categories of patients. This principle is affirmed for all biomedical practices[(42)].

There are other important principles for the protection of the human body: it cannot be disposed of the body with a prohibition on surrogacy[(43)], there are no property rights over the human body and its parts, a principle clearly established with regard to organ donations[(44)] and blood samples[(45)].

Beneficence and justice are diffuse principles that only emerge from a horizontal reading of all of the opinions of the National Medical Ethics Committee[(46)] concerning Assisted Reproductive

(42) Reproductive medicine, organ transplants, clinical trials, etc. See *Le principe du consentement éclairé en matière de soins et de recherches, Actes de colloque*, Tunis, 2012; see more esp. the study by S. Dabbou Ben Ayed, "Droit à l'information et principe du consentement", p. 35.

(43) Art. 15 L. on reproductive medicine.

(44) Art. 6 L. of 25 March 1991: "The removal [of organs] is prohibited [...] in return for payment or any other form of transaction".

(45) Art. 7 *id.*: "Human blood may only be taken [...] without recompense [...]" (art. 2) and "The donation of blood is free of charge".

(46) Available at: www.comiteethique.rns.tn/ethique/avis.html.

Technologies[47], caring for people with HIV-AIDS[48] or the use of stillborn foetuses or embryos[49].

With regard to the principle of freedom, which can be interpreted in various ways – control over one's body, the refusal of a particular treatment or care, etc. – it is sometimes seen as a primary principle and sometimes, to the contrary, denied. In the first case, the freedom of control over one's body is recognised by the law on organ donations[50]. In the second case, the laws relating to mandatory treatments[51] deny the person, in some cases, any freedom in order to preserve a public order deemed to be superior, giving the impression that our legal system remains frozen in a paternalist notion of the protection of the human person and his body and dominated by the idea of the protection of public health.

In overall terms, the principles of protection of the human body appear poorly defined in relation to each other, even if a certain hierarchy is emerging. That is how dignity, the founding principle of the protection of the human body, and physical integrity often come to be linked within a single legal provision[52]. Likewise, the link between dignity and no-property rights over the body is clear, although the latter is seen as a direct consequence of the former[53].

(47) Opinion of 12 December 1996 concerning Assisted Reproductive Technologies: "The respect for life is also a principle that cannot be disposed of, from a philosophical as well as an ethical, political and deontological point of view [...]. The consent of the couple and providing them with information are important [...]".

(48) Opinion of 20 September 2007 concerning the management of tissues from embryos, foetuses and stillborn babies or those who died during the neonatal period: "The ethical measures relate here to the manner in which the family must be informed and supported throughout this perinatal bereavement; they are then able to give, if appropriate, their free and considered consent in full knowledge of the facts concerning the use of the body of their child [...]".

(49) Opinion of 22 October 2007 concerning the removal or sampling of organs and tissues from corpses on medico-legal grounds. "The removal or sampling of organs and tissues with a view to transplantation must respect the fundamental ethical principles of the dignity of the human person, the integrity of the human person, benevolence and beneficence, freedom of choice, fairness, etc.".

(50) As, on the one hand, the law begins by affirming the principle of the physical integrity of the person and requires the free and express consent of the donor while, on the other hand, and for transplants from deceased donors, it requires compliance with an entire procedure during the lifetime of the donor.

(51) Transmissible diseases, drug addicts, mental patients presenting a danger to public order. See R. JELASSI, "L'hospitalisation d'office", in *La maladie et le droit. Actes de colloque*, Tunis, Groupement Latrach, 2014.

(52) As we have noted in the constitutional instrument and as is apparent in the law on reproductive medicine, "Reproductive medicine is subject to the provisions of the present law within the framework of the guarantee of the dignity of the human person and the preservation of his physical integrity" (art. 1).

(53) Particularly in the law concerning the taking of human blood samples.

Thus, numerous instruments affirm the principles of protection of the body. In practice, however, these often remain proclaimed without necessarily being implemented.

II. – The reality of the principles: a problematic enshrinement

Knowing what a person can do in case of an infringement of these principles means considering the legal nature of the principles of protection of the human body. It also brings up the link between principles and subjective rights, the latter often being the expression of the former. The granting of subjective rights[(54)] to individuals, whether by legal instruments or by the courts, is here revealed to be a crucial element in the protection of the person, as the purpose of these rights is to enable individuals who have suffered violation to obtain reparation and compensation.

The question of the basis for the violation of a principle of protection of the person is problematic: is it a failure of the author of the damage to fulfil a contractual obligation (giving rise to a contractual liability) or a violation of one subjective right of the victim? What is the legal nature of the rights conferred on the human person to protect his body[(55)]?

In Tunisia, the various laws including a protection of the human body stipulate sanctions in the case of violations, but can we state that these sanctions protect the principle in themselves[(56)]? It seems that the injured persons rarely base their legal action on the principle of protection of the body. The context of the violation here proves to be an important indicator of the protective nature of a principle[(57)].

Legal instruments and case law prove to be of little help on the subject (A). However, an analysis of the case law shows that

(54) M. Charfi, "The subjective rights are recognised by the law for the benefit of their holders to be respected or executed", in *Introduction à l'étude du droit*, Tunis, CERES, 1997, n° 439. In the opinion of the author, concerning part of the doctrine, the concept of subjective right would be a "mere technico-legal instrument", but "particularly useful" (*ibid.*, n° 446).

(55) R. Jelassi, *Le corps humain en droit civil*, Tunis, CPU, 2013.

(56) M. Charfi, *Introduction à l'étude du droit*, *op. cit.*, n° 438.

(57) See A. Khaldi, "Les responsabilités d'ordre privé existant en matière d'exercice de la médecine", in *La responsabilité médicale*, Tunis, CPU-ATDS, 2006 p. 57. *Id.*, *La place actuelle du consentement du malade à l'acte médical dans le Code des obligations et des contrats*, Centenary book of the Code of Obligations and Contracts, Tunis, CPU, 2006, p. 323.

the protection of the person's body in the context of biomedicine essentially relies on the principle of consent (B).

A. – *Confused instruments and an embryonic case law*

The instruments make no clear pronouncements on sanctions in the case of a failure to respect the principles of protection of the person's body. As a result, case law can be a useful indicator of the reality and strength of these principles. However, the judicial and administrative courts are rarely approached on the basis of a violation of the principles of protection. Only the principle of informed consent has a specific place in their judgments, due to the doctor's obligation to provide the patient with information before a treatment or surgical intervention.

However, it seems that failures to meet this obligation to inform are usually dealt more with under contract law and, more specifically, the doctor's contractual liability, than the violation of a subjective right granted to the victim to ensure his physical integrity. In the case of clinical trials(58), for example, given that concluded conventions are acts of physical disposition, they will be void if the severity of the risk incurred outweighs the expected positive results of the new drug for the community. This means that if the person taking part in the research project has not been informed of these risks, he will be protected under the terms of this failure to inform (requirement imposed by contract law) and not for the violation of a subjective right (the right to respect for his physical integrity).

The inadequate protection of the person provided by the principles is clear in the case of the participation of minors in a clinical trial or a medical act(59) where the general instruments(60) were adopted using a different line of thinking to that which led to the development of instruments specific to the protection of the person(61). The fact is that the general instruments were not

(58) *Les essais cliniques de nouveaux médicaments chez l'homme : impératifs éthiques et cadre juridique*, Papers from the 9th Annual Conference of the National Medical Ethics Committee, Tunis, 2005.

(59) See A. Aouij Mrad and S. Hamrouni, "Adolescent et acte médical en Tunisie : des reconsidérations nécessaires", *in* B. Feuillet-Liger and R. Ida (eds.), *Adolescent et acte médical : regards croisés*, Brussels, Bruylant, 2011, p. 279.

(60) Art.16 Obligations and Contracts C.

(61) Art. 154 Personal Status C.

developed with the aim of protecting the person, but as a basis for a potential civil liability action.

The instruments are of no help in the express recognition of subjective rights here, as in the event of a violation of a person's rights, it is the person who has to prove the violation and thus has the burden of proof[(62)]. It follows that, in law, the person who has the burden of proof but does not succeed in establishing it loses their case. In practice, this makes any liability action based on a violation of the person of the plaintiff difficult to win. To alleviate this state of affairs, judges are often content, in liability actions based on a violation of physical integrity[(63)], with the absence of any challenge by the defendant[(64)]. In fact, as proof of the express consent of the persons whose rights were violated is difficult to obtain, the courts settle for the doctor's silence as sufficient evidence.

B. – *Privileged application of the principle of consent*

It is on the basis of the principle of informed consent of the person that any damage caused them is assessed, which enables a move towards recognising the subjective rights of the individual. Protecting both integrity and dignity, the consent of the person[(65)] seems to open the way to a number of legal actions that remain all too rare for the time being.

Furthermore, case law is still unclear, particularly with regard to proof of consent, especially when it is not incorporated into any legal instrument, as is the case with current medical acts. For a long time, the ordinary courts were indulgent with regard to the means of proof used by doctors to establish that they had informed their patients. This case law thus reduces the protection of the principle of physical integrity and protects the medical profession.

(62) Art. 420 Obligations and Contracts C.: "The evidence of the obligation must be given by the person making the claim".

(63) Tunis CA, 16 March 1955: "[...] While the fact of not having obtained the consent of the patient or his legal representatives constitutes, apart from in an emergency, a fault of the surgeon, following the ordinary rules of fault liability, it rests upon the party invoking a fault to establish its existence"; in this case, the judges considered that the consent to the surgical intervention was tacit, as the child's mother's didn't object to the surgical intervention.

(64) Tunis CA, n° 48788, 29 April 1998. The doctor must inform the patient of the risks related to the drugs prescribed and the patient remains free to accept or refuse the treatment.

(65) See *Le principe du consentement éclairé en matière de soins et de recherche, Actes de colloque, op. cit.*

The courts considered that the refusal of care released entirely the doctor from any criminal liability[66].

Case law recently marked a turning point in the explicit granting of subjective rights to the victim of damage: a failure to provide information about the risks of a surgical intervention was recognised as constituting a civil fault giving rise to criminal liability of the doctor[67]. The freedom of consent of the patient requires the doctor to inform his patients of all existing treatments.

Although still rare, this recognition of a right to compensation[68] was recently affirmed by the Supreme Court, which gave the requirement to provide information a general character by linking it with the principle of consent: the doctor has a duty to provide information that covers all acts that he plans to carried out and all of the risks incurred. This obligation can also be associated with the principle of the dignity of the human person, as the courts make this obligation a human duty[69].

The theory of implicit consent now appears to be relevant only in emergency situations[70].

Would there be a recognition of subjective rights to protection of the person for biomedical acts that are more of a threat to the whole person, the body in particular, this recognition being apparent through the formal procedure of the consent required, itself related to the exceptional nature of the act?

The problem arose in the particular context of blood tests to establish paternity[71]. Two rights were in conflict in this situation: the protection of the physical integrity of the person on one hand, and the right for a child to know his origins, on the other hand. Is

(66) Cass. (crim.), 28 February 1966, *RTD*, 1966. As part of the duty to provide care.

(67) Cass. (civ.), 25 June 2003. Decision reported in the *Revue de la jurisprudence et de la legislation*, 2005, n° 1, p. 67. The courts now make the distinction between minor risks and major risks. Failure to provide information renders the doctor liable to sanctions.

(68) Article 275 of the Obligations and Contracts Code states that the obligation to do "results in damages and interest if non-performance [...]".

(69) Cass. (civ. ch.), 13 March 2013, n° 20241. Unpublished.

(70) Moreover, the interpretation of the Code of Medical Ethics allowed this to be affirmed a contrario: "When called to provide emergency treatment to a minor or an incapable adult, and when it is impossible to obtain the legal consent within a reasonable time, the doctor must provide the required care" (art. 35). The same applies to article 2, paragraph 2, of the law on the collection of blood, which clearly refers to emergency situations as exceptions to the requirement to obtain consent.

(71) Before the enactment of law 98-75, of 28 October 1998, paternity suits were based on blood analyses that gave rise to the same problems.

a refusal to have a blood sample taken or submit to a DNA test on the basis of the principle of the physical integrity and inviolability of the human body valid?

Case law was uncertain. It initially considered a refusal by presumed fathers to submit to such a test as constituting an implicit admission, thereby denying the principle of inviolability and even that of individual freedom(72). In 2003, however, the law on the assignment of a surname was amended(73): such a refusal is no longer considered to be an admission; it is now up to the judge to draw his own conclusions from a refusal in each individual case.

In the context of paternity suits, the uncertainty of case law is also apparent for samples taken from corpses, which relate to the principles of physical integrity and the dignity of the corpse(74).

The administrative court appears, in its rare decisions, to offer some protection to the person with regard to medicine: to incur the liability of the public hospital service, which is the only way to award compensation to the victims of damage, instead of looking for an personal fault on the part of the doctor, it settles for a failure to provide information or the provision of insufficient information, even in the absence of a fault(75). In administrative matters, the protection of the human person and his body is thus provided by the engagement of the hospital's liability. As part of the organisation and effective operation of the public hospital service, the obligation to provide specific information to hospital patients can serve as a basis for a liability action before the Administrative Court.

Conclusion

Tunisia still has a long way to go when it comes to establishing the principles of protection of the human body. The legislator has to realise that the time has come to restructure all of the laws relating

(72) Cass. (civ. ch.), 19 October 2001, n° 10020. This judgment was in contradiction to that of the previous year, Cass. (civ. ch.), 16 November 2000, n° 4182, which considered refusals to be irrelevant to the ongoing proceedings. *Rev. trim. dr.*, 2001, pp. 169 and 171, obs. M.K. Charfeddine.

(73) L. n° 51-2003, 7 July 2003.

(74) Sfax CA, n° 2694,18 April 2001, *Revue de jurisprudence et de législation*, n° 10 p. 87. However, the Court of Appeal did not at any time justify its order to submit the corpse to biological analyses, probably on the grounds that the alleged father did not object to having samples taken during his lifetime.

(75) CA, 2 March 2007, *Ruth Engelberg v. Minister of Public Health*, n° 12148, unpublished.

to biomedicine by providing a clear affirmation of certain crucial and fundamental principles on the subject. In the meantime, is it not incumbent on the courts to show some courage and forward-looking spirit in order to take the opportunity, starting now, to base their decisions on the principles of protection of the body?

THE PRINCIPLES OF PROTECTION OF THE BODY IN THE CONTEXT OF BIOMEDICINE: THE EGYPTIAN LEGAL SYSTEM BETWEEN THE LOGIC OF THE PERSON AS THE OWNER OF HIS BODY AND THAT OF THE PERSON AS THE CUSTODIAN OF HIS BODY

Hassan ABDELHAMID

Professor at the Faculty of Law University of Ain Shams, Cairo (Egypt)

Egyptian civil law is based on a fundamental division between the subject of law (the person) and the object of law (tangible or intangible goods)[1]. Egyptian legal doctrine has followed the French doctrine, itself inherited from the Roman distinction between things and persons[2]. Thus, the person is an absolutely intangible entity.

The person can therefore exist before birth. A child that has been conceived is deemed to have been born when that is in its interest[3]. It can even outlive the human being[4]. There is, for example, a presumption of the continuing existence of an absent person whose physical death cannot be proven. Conversely, a person can be declared dead when their body is still alive. In effect, a declarative judgment of absence can legally certify the death of a person who is nevertheless alive[5]. The person can also

(1) The Civil Code deals with persons in the second chapter of the General Provisions and with things and goods in the third chapter. It makes the distinction between a thing and a good (art. 81).

(2) See J.-M. Carbasse, *Manuel d'introduction historique au droit*, 2nd ed., Paris, PUF, 2003, p. 62.

(3) Art. 29, § 2, Civ. C.

(4) Art. 32 Civ. C.

(5) It therefore authorises the transmission of the inheritance to the heirs and the remarriage of the spouse. The reallocation of a legal personality to an absent person who returns is given a highly significant name: resurrection.

be a legal person[(6)], *i.e.* a subject of law representing a group of individuals (a company or an association), or even a quantity of assets (a foundation).

What is therefore the status of the body in relation to the person? In civil law, the right to physical integrity is addressed in the framework of personal rights. It is one of the non-transferable, unassignable, undistrainable and imprescriptible extra-patrimonial rights (as it has no monetary value in itself). The right to physical integrity does not provide a general theory of the protection of the body in itself. The body is protected by the general rules of protection of the person[(7)]. In the context of the Egyptian Criminal Code (offences of assault and battery[(8)]), what is done to my body is punished as a violation of my person. The body, however, cannot in itself be considered as a 'thing'. This poses a fundamental problem as, in legal terms, a thing is an object of law. It therefore becomes possible for a thing to be treated as an item of property. Therefore, since it appears difficult to apply the legal status of property to the body, it is necessary to introduce a distinction.

If no distinction is made, the desacralisation of the body can lead to the justification of slavery. If I possess my body as an item, nothing prevents me from selling it. Using the same logic, I can also sell the products or even parts of my body. Legally speaking, nothing prevents me from selling my hair. In which case, how can the prohibition on the sale of blood, sperm, a kidney or a lung be justified? How can prohibiting prostitution be justified[(9)]? Possessing my body as an object gives me the right to dispose freely of this body.

This logic of the person who is the owner of his body is different from that of the person who is the custodian of his body, which is predominant in Muslim legal thinking. In Muslim thought, the person is a body just as it is the mind, the whole body and the whole

(6) Art. 52 and 53 Civ. C.

(7) Concerning this trend in Egyptian civil doctrine, see H. ELEHWANY, *The legal problems of human organ transplants* (in Arabic), Cairo, University of Ain Shams, 1975, p. 3; H. ABDELRAHMAN, *The concept of law* (in Arabic), Cairo, Dar Alfekr Alaraby, 1979, p. 44.

(8) Art. 240, 241, 243 and 265 Crim. C.

(9) In this sense, see, P.-A. MIQUEL, "Respect et inviolabilité du corps humain", *Noesis*, n° 12, 2007, placed online on 28 December 2008, http://noesis.revues.org/1383.

mind. The person = body + mind[10]. The individual is therefore not the owner of his body. He is merely the custodian of this body and this life. The person cannot therefore have a right to dispose freely of his body. Thus, the sacralisation of the person involves at the same time the sacralisation of the body, as the person does not exist without his body. Accordingly, the body cannot be considered as an item of property.

Egyptian legal thinking wavers between these two logics. This can be seen in the perception of the principle of physical integrity. This principle is recognised by the Egyptian legal system and endowed with its constituent elements and derogations. However, this principle, which is very much focused on the individual, does not take precedence over an absolute right to dispose of one's body. The law tends to justify the principle of physical integrity out of a concern to protect society, rather than the person, by considering that the person is not the owner, but merely the custodian of his body[11]. The body thus swings constantly between individual availability and social "unavailability"[12]. In general, however, Egyptian legal doctrine is closer to Muslim logic, according to which the person is the custodian of his body and not the owner.

It is in this context of duality that the Egyptian legal system organises the protection of the human body. To present the principles of protection of this body, we need to explore the sources of this protection (I) and the possibilities of invoking the principles of protection before the courts (II).

I. – Sources of the principles of protection of the human body

According to the Constitutional High Court, international treaties have no constitutional value in the Egyptian legal system.

(10) See our article, H. Abdelhamid, "Le corps de la femme et la biomedicine dans le contexte de la culture juridique égyptienne", *in* B. Feuillet-Liger and A. Aouij-Mrad (eds.), *Corps de la femme et Biomedicine : Approche internationale*, Brussels, Bruylant, 2013, pp. 181-200, esp. p. 188.

(11) Except that it is in view of the ownership of his body that the patient has to give his consent to any medical intervention and that it is on account of his own individual 'intentionality' that the subject of law is deemed to be responsible and answerable for the uses of his body.

(12) The justification of physical integrity lies in human dignity and the social interest. Concerning this justification in Egyptian doctrine, see T. Sorrour, *Organ transplants between living persons* (in Arabic), Cairo, Dar Al-Nahda Alarabiya, 2001, pp. 89 et seq.

The Constitutional High Court confirmed this attitude during a case in 1984(13). This denial of a constitutional value to international treaties does not seem to prevent the High Court from referring to international documents relating to human rights whenever it wants to broaden the scope of the protection of the rights and freedoms of individuals, particularly if there is a link between the standards contained in these documents and the standards contained in internal constitutional instruments. Several decisions of the Constitutional High Court confirm this tendency(14).

The protection of the body is provided by legal standards (A), complemented by ethico-religious standards (B).

A. – *Legal standards*

Constitutional (1), criminal (2) and civil (3) protection is provided.

1. – *Constitutional protection*

The new Egyptian Constitution of 2014 devotes seven articles to the defence of human dignity. Article 51 affirms this principle of dignity as an inviolable human right, and its respect and protection constitute an obligation for which the State is responsible. The Constitution does not define this principle directly, but does so in an indirect manner by designating the acts that contravene it.

In this way, the human body is protected against any violation. According to article 52, torture, in all its forms, constitutes an imprescriptible crime. The principle of the inviolability of the

(13) Decision of 28 January 1984, case n° 48, 4th judicial year.

(14) Thus, in its decision of 2 February 1992, the Court declares that: "The criteria for a fair trial consist in a set of rules that constitute an integral system whose objective is the protection of the dignity of the human being and his fundamental rights. [...] The presumption of innocence falls within the context of the principle of the fair trial, as a rule imposed by the nature of the matter, and enshrined in article 67 of the Constitution, which thereby confirms the content of article 11 of the Universal Declaration of Human Rights of 1948 and article 6 of the European Convention on the Protection of Human Rights." (Judgment of 2 February 1992, case n° 13, 12th judicial year). In its judgment of 2 March 1996, the Court states that: "The right to development is, according to article 1 of the International Covenant on Civil and Political Rights, closely linked to the right to life [...] Furthermore, the declaration of the United Nations General Assembly of 4 December 1986 (Resolution 41/128) concerning development, confirmed the right to development as one of the inalienable human rights" (Judgment of 2 March 1996, case n° 34, 15th judicial year).

human body is enshrined in article 60. The human body is inviolable and any violation constitutes a crime punishable by law[15].

The Constitution also enshrines the principle of the non-patrimoniality of the body and its parts (its commercialisation is prohibited) and the principle of consent. Free and informed consent must be obtained for medical experiments and treatment according to the rules recognised by science[16].

In addition, to be able to use medicine to provide care for others, article 61 sets out the principles of solidarity and gratuitousness (the 'cost-free' or 'no payment' principle) of the body and its parts: the donation of organs and tissues is a life-preserving act. Each individual has the right to donate his organs during his lifetime or after his death, by means of a will or an expression of consent. The State is obliged to organise the removal and transplantation of the organs.

Article 89 prohibits and sanctions all forms of slavery, oppression, forced exploitation, sex trade and, more generally, any form of human trafficking.

Legal personality confers subjective rights on individuals, rights of protection of the body that are punishable by law if violated. Such rights have their own specific characteristics: they are extra-patrimonial (without any monetary value), non-transferable, undistrainable and imprescriptible. Under the terms of article 92 of the Constitution, these rights are not liable to be withdrawn or reduced.

2. – *Criminal protection*

Egyptian legal doctrine[17] makes the distinction between three categories of human substances: non-regenerable organs, regenerable organs and the residues of the human body.

With regard to non-regenerable organs, the principle of the inviolability of the human body was usually against any form of

(15) The article states that "No one shall be subjected to torture, or to cruel, inhuman or degrading treatment or punishments".

(16) On this subject under Egyptian law, see M. Aid Al-Gharib, *Medical and scientific experimentation and the principle of the inviolability of the human body* (in Arabic), Cairo, ed. Wahba, 1989; A. Mahfouz, *Medical experimentation between legality and criminalisation* (in Arabic), Cairo, Dar Al-Nahada Al-Arabiya, 2009.

(17) In this sense, see M. Najib Hossny, "The right to physical integrity and its criminal protection" (in Arabic), *L& Econ. Rev.*, n° 3, 1959, pp. 537 et seq.

removal, as such an act constitutes a definitive violation of the living person. The removal of organs has given rise to controversy. In fact, in the view of some commentators, in spite of the provisions of the Criminal Code[18] protecting physical integrity, the practice of transplantations could be allowed as it was based not on a justification, but on a state of necessity[19].

The law[20] and the decree[21] organising the removal of organs for therapeutic transplantation impose the requirement to inform the donor and obtain his consent concerning "all foreseeable physical and psychological consequences of the removal, as well as any possible repercussions resulting from this removal for the personal, family and professional life of the donor"[22].

These instruments set the general rules for the removal and transplantation of organs. However, since 1959 Egyptian law has, exceptionally, organised the removal and transplantation of the cornea[23] and the creation of cornea banks. The resources of these banks come from cornea donations, removals carried out for medical reasons, removals from deceased persons following an accident or autopsy, persons executed after a death sentence and deceased persons of unknown identity[24].

Removals are only approved "provided that the operation carries no excessive risk and that such removals do not appear to present any immediate or long-term problems for the health of the donor"[25]. A removal causing a risk to a living donor, even if it constitutes a treatment of benefit to the recipient, must not be carried out, as the desire to save the life of a person cannot justify

(18) Art. 240, 241, 243 and 265 Crim. C.

(19) According to some, only this construction could justify the removal of an organ from a living person, without serious risk, in the case of the beneficiary being unable to survive without this organ. Concerning this justification, see A. CHARAF ELDINE, "The legal framework of the legitimacy of the removal and transplant of organs" (in Arabic), *National Penal Review*, n° 1, 1978, p. 115.

(20) Egyptian L. n° 5-2010, *J.O.*, 6 March 2010.

(21) Decree n° 93-2011.

(22) Art. 7.

(23) L. n° 274-1959, *J.O.*, 26 December 1959, replaced by L. n° 103-1962, *J.O.*, 16 June 1962.

(24) The new law authorises cornea donations, but always in the context of the principle of physical integrity.

(25) Art. 7.

the removal of any organ from a living person if it is likely to violate his bodily integrity[26].

Furthermore, the proportionality rule applies and leads to a conflict between the respective interests of the donor and the recipient and to the removal being approved only if there exists a reasonable balance between the risks incurred by the donor and the benefits for the recipient[27].

The principle according to which the human body is non-commercial, or not for sale, applies to all organs, including regenerable organs. Although as these have, by their very nature, the capacity to renew themselves automatically, they may be transferred without causing objections. This traditionally refers to milk, hair and blood. However, the question is more complex in the case of eggs, sperm and embryos; in other words, to use a general term, "genetic materials". This also applies to bone marrow.

Legal doctrine traditionally gives milk and hair the same status. Nursing and cutting hair are not by nature harmful to the person, and what is more, they are intended to provide a service, bearing in mind the existing harmony between the purpose these elements serve for the individual and their purpose of meeting the needs of the third parties concerned[28].

Likewise, blood cannot be considered as an "item of merchandise" or as a medicine, in spite of the transformations it undergoes. The civil rules do not apply to it in view of its unique nature[29].

---

(26) See A. Alshahawy and M. Alshahawy, *Explanation of the law on the organisation of the removal and transplant of human organs n° 5 of 2010* (in Arabic), Cairo, Dar Alnahda Alarabiya, 2011/2012, pp. 15 et seq.

(27) See T. Sorrour, *Live organ transplants* (in Arabic), *op. cit.*, pp. 184 et seq.

(28) It was therefore possible to conclude that milk and hair had a shared status: that of a thing subject to transfer in return for a consideration. In addition, the purpose of the organ in question gives it a more or less sacred character and therefore influences its status. Hair has a purely aesthetic purpose and can without objection fall within the purview of the common contract law on moveable objects. However, milk is not an ordinary thing. The Romans considered that the purpose of the wet nurse was to provide care for the child entrusted to her and, secondarily, if she agreed, she could breast feed the child. This transfer of milk must not be at the expense of the wet nurse's child, who is primarily entitled to it, which is evidence of the fact that this not a question of an ordinary "product" (in French: "*fruit*"). Concerning this distinction, see A. Charaf Eldine, "Les prélèvements d'organe. Commentaire de la loi du 22 décembre 1976", *Rev. tr. Dr. San. et Soc.*, 1978, p. 445.

(29) Therefore, and quite rightly, a regulation intended to prevent both speculative and medical risks for the donor and recipient was developed. See Egyptian L. n° 178 -1960, *J.O.*, 12 June 1960.

With regard to "genetic materials", they are not subject to any comprehensive legal regulation. There is only one provision in the legislation concerning the donation of organs(30), under the terms of which the removal and transplantation of organs, parts of organs or tissues that could have repercussions on parentage are prohibited. It is an expression of the respect and protection of genealogical lineage and parentage. In this regard, the transfer of eggs, sperm and embryos is prohibited. It is not a matter of items falling within the category of trade, but of elements of the body containing the seed of life and intended for human reproduction.

The rest of the "genetic materials" are related to an ethico-religious structure (based on common principles: dignity and the principle of the non-patrimoniality of the body and its elements, on the one hand, and the principle of solidarity on the other) and the code of conduct.

3. – *Civil protection*

In civil law, the body is protected from unlawful violations by a third party under civil liability regulations, as demonstrated by article 164 of the Egyptian Civil Code, which states: "Any act committed by a person which causes damage to another oblige the one by whose fault it occurred to compensate it".

Thus, the person whose fault caused the damage is liable to compensate it. Material, personal, non-pecuniary, aesthetic injury, as well as diminution of enjoyment of life, must be compensated for.

At the same time, however, as a result of the autonomy, the person can allow such violations. Nevertheless, the legislature endeavours to ensure a balance between respect for public order and respect for autonomy; between individual and collective interests(31). In fact, it is in the name of an imperative ofintegrity making the body unavailable to its custodian that the transplantation of organs is contested, while it is under the principle of the greater interest

(30) Art. 2 L. n° 5-2010, on organ transplants.

(31) In fact, developments in science and technology have modulated relationships between individuals. This is why the autonomy - public order pairing is no longer sufficient to arbitrate between the divergent interests that come into conflict, as they can no longer be reduced to a simple private matter.

of living persons that its supporters justify it. The law on organ donations is based on the achievement of common interests.

Furthermore, the Egyptian legislature protects the person after his death. The principle of the inviolability of the human body persists beyond death. The Egyptian Criminal Code sanctions any indignity committed on the corpse and makes it an offence not to provide a burial place[32]. Private law enshrines the principle of the inviolability of the human body beyond death and proscribes violations of the corpse.

However, the sacred status of the dead body is put into perspective. The Civil Code affirms respect for the will of the deceased person with regard to the disposition of his body. Just as they take precedence with regard to the disposition of his assets and property through the will[33], the wishes of the deceased prevail with regard to the disposition of his corpse. Law no. 130/1946 authorises the donation of the corpse to scientific institutions or universities for scientific use, once the consent of the family of the deceased has been obtained. It is only in the greater interest or in the interest of public health that the wishes of the deceased or his immediate family are not complied with. Likewise, the Egyptian law on organ transplants, law no. 5/2010, regulates the donation and removal of organs and tissues as a result of the last will and testament[34]. The consent of the deceased donor must be given in a valid will.

In addition, the Egyptian law on the removal and transplantation of corneas[35] authorises the creation of cornea banks by the removal of corneas without a will or the consent of the family being required.

In other words, it is the legacy left by the person and the enduring social representation that must be subject to protection, as it is through these that an individual and posthumous component of human dignity is safeguarded. According to Muslim jurisprudence, a living and a dead body have the same dignity, and neither belongs to the person. It belongs to God and will return to God.

(32) Art. 160 Egyptian Crim. C.
(33) Art. 915, 916 and 917 Civ. C.
(34) Art. 8.
(35) L. n° 274-1959, *J.O.*, 26 December 1959, replaced by L. n° 103-1962, *J.O.*, 16 June 1962, see *supra*.

B. – *Ethico-religious standards*

It is in reality the ethico-religious principles that govern the other areas of bioethics since, in Egypt, there are no laws in this domain and the legal system authorises a return to the religious order. We will first consider the medical ethics (1), and then the religious principles (2).

1. – *Medical ethics*

According to the decree concerning ethics in the medical profession[(36)], the oath taken by doctors contains the following undertaking: the doctor must "preserve the life and dignity of human beings".

This decree prohibits doctors from "performing an abortion, except when necessary to protect the mother and with the testimony of two doctors"[(37)], from "disclosing the patient's secrets, except in those cases determined by law"[(38)] and from "practising euthanasia"[(39)].

The decree also stipulates the obligations of doctors with regard to a number of medical practices[(40)]. "Doctors are prohibited from performing a sex change operation. Gender correction surgery, which involves those cases where a person has both masculine and feminine genders at the same time, requires the approval of the Doctors' Union specialist committee, and these operations may only be performed after certain examinations"[(41)].

In vitro fertilisation using the husband's sperm and the wife's egg, followed by the injection of the fertilised egg into the wife's uterus, is subject to ethical rules whose purpose is the preservation of the human race and the treatment of infertility, while respecting the purity of the direct line of descent and the legal criteria stipulated by the competent authorities[(42)]. In vitro fertilisation using the husband's sperm can only be carried out while they are

(36) Enacted by the decision of the Ministry of Health n° 238-2003, 5 September 2003.
(37) Art. 29.
(38) Art. 30.
(39) Art. 36.
(40) In the third section, entitled "Medical interventions of a special nature".
(41) "Hormonal analysis and the chromosomal mapping test and after a period of psychological and hormonal treatment of at least two years" (Art. 43).
(42) Art. 44.

married. In addition, gestational surrogacy is prohibited(43), as are sperm banks and banks for fertilised eggs(44). Organ and tissue transplants are subject to the ethical criteria and legal rules that apply to them(45).

The commercialisation of organs, tissues, human cells and human genes is prohibited. Under no circumstances may a doctor participate in such commercialisation. If he does so, he will be liable to disciplinary action(46). He will be required to answer charges before a disciplinary board(47).

The decree also sets out the conditions for experimentation and the obligations of doctors(48). Thus, "The doctor must respect all ethical criteria and social and religious values imposed by the competent authorities with regard to scientific tests or trials on the human body"(49). Doctors may not conduct drug trials or test new medical techniques on humans without first obtaining the approval of the competent authorities(50). They must follow the required procedures with regard to medical experimentation and research involving human subjects(51).

In these biomedical fields, the decree complies with the religious rules. It prioritises the principle of respect for physical integrity and that of the inviolability of the body.

2. – *Religious rules*

On the basis of the Muslim outlook(52), Muslim jurists have developed an Islamic jurisprudence (*fiqh*) expanding the scope of

(43) Art. 45.
(44) Art. 46.
(45) Art. 49.
(46) He will be required to answer charges before a disciplinary council, art. 51.
(47) Art. 51.
(48) In the fourth section, entitled "Medical experiments and research on human subjects".
(49) Art. 52.
(50) Art. 53.
(51) Art. 54 to 61.
(52) In Muslim thinking, the individual is not the owner of his body. The individual is only the 'manager' of this body and this life. The individual can therefore never have the right to dispose freely of his body. However, suffering is never a benefit. All means possible must be used to fight the illness with dignity and determination, and, in this spirit, there is considerable tolerance with regard to medical practices. In fact, the Quran speaks especially of *haram* (*i.e.* what is forbidden or illegal). As a result, anything that is not forbidden is authorised. Furthermore, the preservation of life, as an objective of divine legislation, means that a person in need may contravene all of the prohibitions, provided there is no intent of rebellion or deliberate transgression.

shari'a or Islamic Law to include all aspects of public and private life. This jurisprudence is based on some general principles. Among the principles recognised by the *Ouçoul al-fiqh* (the study of the origins on which Islamic Jurisprudence is based), some relate to biomedicine(53):

- Principle of freedom: the principle of independence (*hourriya*), concerning relationships between individuals, the principle of free use (*ibaha*), which governs relationships with objects. This principle enables human beings to exercise control over themselves. This power of free human beings constitutes what Muslim jurisconsults call *walaya*; original *walaya* from which all other principles derive(54). The original *walaya* means the exercise of the free human being's power over his person. The specific *walaya* derives from this original *walaya;* in other words, the power exercised over a third party by virtue of which the third party must implement the decisions made, whether he wants to or not. The consequence of this is that decisions made by one person become enforceable with regard to another person (transitive *walaya*, as in the case of the executor of a will), and the general *walaya*, the condition under which one or more persons will be accorded a "legal capacity" (*cifa*) giving them the right to exercise a legitimate and legally effective power over all of the Faithful.
- Principle of respect for the public good (*Maslaha 'ama*). The interests of the community shape and limit the interests of the individual.
- An extreme need can lead to what is prohibited being authorised(55).
- No one may cause harm to others. The duty to help one's neighbour entitles others to assistance, solidarity and meritorious acts.

(53) We have explained these principles in our article, H. ABDELHAMID,"Le corps de la femme et la biomedicine dans le contexte de la culture juridique égyptienne", *in* B. FEUILLET-LIGER et A. AOUIJ-MRAD, *Corps de la femme et Biomedicine : Approche internationale, op. cit.*, see pp. 189 et seq.

(54) We have explained this meaning of "*walaya*" in our article, H. ABDELHAMID, "La contractualisation d'une société : la Umma musulmane et la base de l'administration des choses publiques", *in* J. BOUINEAU (ed.), *Personne et res publica*, coll. Méditerranées, vol. I, Paris, L'Harmattan, 2008, pp. 275-297.

(55) A person in state of necessity may contravene all of the prohibitions, provided there is no intent of rebellion or deliberate transgression.

- Principle of usefulness outweighing disadvantages (*maslaha*)[56].
- Principle of respect for life. Life is a gift from God. No one is entitled to take a life, either one's own (suicide) or the life of another (crime), or to propose death (euthanasia).
- A living or dead body is entitled to be treated with the same dignity. It does not belong to the individual. It belongs to God and will return to God.
- It is an obligation to care for one's body in the event of sickness: the body is a sacred gift entrusted to human beings, and it is their duty to care for it.
- Principle of respect for the individual's physical and mental integrity.
- Principle of respecting and sustaining genealogical lineage and parentage.

These principles will therefore be used as the basis to provide a solution to current bioethical issues in accordance with Muslim morality.

II. – The victim's recourse to the courts

The Egyptian legal system guarantees the victim recourse to the Constitutional Court (A), the Criminal Court (B) and the Civil Court (C).

A. – *Recourse to the Constitutional Court*

The Egyptian Constitutional Court appears to affirm the link between constitutional redress and the protection of human rights. The Constitutional High Court frequently declares that the main objective of the control it exercises over the constitutionality of laws and regulations is to impose compliance with individual rights and freedoms. Thus, in its judgment of 18 April 1994, the Court stated that: "The objective pursued by the legislature through the review of the constitutionality of laws is to ensure that this

(56) The advantages must outweigh the disadvantages caused by a practice to allow the latter.

Court can provide the satisfaction allowed for by the constitutional provisions in the event of a violation of the rights guaranteed by the Constitution [...]"[57].

In the context of a general movement towards the recognition of a "right of access to the courts", the 2014 Constitution and law no. 84 of 1979 concerning the Constitutional High Court provide three possible systems of referral that we can qualify as "ordinary".

Laws already enacted may be referred to the Constitutional High Court. Its control is not preventive. Cases are ordinarily referred to the Court in three different ways: by the defendant[58], by the jurisdiction itself or the body with jurisdictional competence[59], and finally by the Constitutional Court itself[60].

What is more, the Constitutional Court can use its own initiative to indirectly examine the constitutionality of an instrument when this examination is necessary to settle one of the cases submitted to it concerning direct individual actions in certain cases provided for by the law[61].

---

(57) Case n° 19, 15th judicial year.

(58) During a trial before a jurisdiction or a body with jurisdictional competence, a defendant may raise the unconstitutionality of a legislative or regulatory instrument to be referred to during the trial. The jurisdiction or body with jurisdictional competence must examine the nature of the exception and, if appropriate, refer it to the Constitutional Court within a period of no more than three months (art. 29-2 L. n° 48- 1979).

(59) The question of unconstitutionality can be raised by the jurisdiction itself or by the body with jurisdictional competence if, during a trial, a doubt arises concerning the constitutionality of the instrument in question. In this case, the jurisdiction must postpone the proceedings and refer the question of unconstitutionality to the Constitutional Court to rule on the issue (art. 29-1 L. of 1979).

(60) The question of unconstitutionality can be raised by the Constitutional Court itself during the exercise of one of its competences (art. 27 L. of 1979).

(61) The Court has the competence to review the constitutionality of laws (art. 175 Constit. and 25-1 L. of 1979), interpret the laws enacted by Parliament and the laws and decrees enacted by the President of the Republic, rule on conflicts of positive or negative competence between the different courts and jurisdictions (art. 25-2 L. of 1979), rule on conflicts concerning the execution of contradictory judgments given in the same cases (art. 25-3 L. of 1979) and settle disputes concerning the execution of its own orders and decisions (art. 50 L. of 1979). The Court also receives requests for interpretations from the Minister of Justice, on the initiative of the President of the Council of Ministers, the President of the People's Assembly and the President of the High Judiciary Council, in accordance with article 33 of the law of 1979 concerning the Court. As the judge of the constitutionality of the law and the judge of the interpretation of legislative instruments, the Court may not therefore be approached directly by individuals. However, individuals may refer directly to the Constitutional High Court when it is called on to rule on jurisdictional conflicts (art. 25-2 L. of 1979), on conflicts concerning the enforcement of contradictory final judgments (art. 25-3 L. of 1979), or on disputes concerning the enforcement of its own orders and decisions (art. 50 L. of 1979). These cases of referral are qualified as "direct recourse" of individuals before the Egyptian constitutional jurisdiction.

There are therefore a number of ways to refer to the Constitutional High Court. This helps to broaden the scope of this right of access to the Constitutional Court and thereby to provide defendants with a further guarantee of their rights and freedoms.

B. – *Recourse to the Criminal Court*

The conditions imposed by Egyptian law for organ transplants to be legal are as follows: the existence of a therapeutic necessity and of consent, and the absence of remuneration[(62)].

The legality of medical interventions is dependent on their compliance with legal instruments; either a general instrument, such as the law on organ transplants (no. 5/2010), or a specific instrument for cornea transplants[(63)] or blood transfusions[(64)]. In addition, the Criminal Code contains a number of provisionswhose objective is the protection of the physical integrity of the person.

With regard to organ donations, the protection of physical integrity requires the donor to be fully informed of the risks and benefits inherent to the act and to give their consent. The law on organ transplants[(65)] imposes an important formalism[(66)]. The consent of the living donor must take the form of a written agreement and be witnessed by two close family members (first degree relatives) with regard to the accuracy of this agreement. In the absence of such witnesses, the agreement must be certified before a notary (a State official). The consent of a deceased donor must be contained in a valid will. The donation of organs by children is prohibited, even with the agreement of the parents, tutor or guardian. The same applies to legally incompetent adults. Finally, up to the time of removal, the donor may withdraw his agreement without any legal repercussions.

(62) Concerning these conditions see, by way of example, M. SALAH ALE'ZA, *The protection of the human body in light of modern medical trends* (in Arabic), Alexandria, Dar al-gami'a algadida li-alnashr, 2002; A. ALSHAHAWY and M. ALSHAHAWY, *Explanation of the law on the organisation of the removal and transplant of human organs n° 5 of 2010*, (in Arabic), Cairo, Dar Al-Nahda Alarabiya, 2011/2012, pp. 15 et seq.; T. SORROUR, *Live organ transplants* (in Arabic), *op. cit.*, pp. 184 et seq.

(63) L. n° 274-1959, replaced by L. n° 103-1962.

(64) L. n° 178-1960 on the collection, storage and distribution of blood.

(65) L. n° 5-2010.

(66) Detailed in article 5 of its implementing Decree n° 93-2011.

The donor must be informed about the nature and consequences of the removal of his organs. Law no. 5/2010 and its implementing decree no. 93/2011 require an important procedure. In each authorised hospital, the law requires that a committee of three doctors not connected with the hospital informs the donor and the recipient about the nature of the removal and transplant and the potential immediate and long-term risks, and the committee must write a report of these procedures signed by both the donor and the recipient. The donor's consent must be particularly informed(67).

With regard to the absence of remuneration, the law confirms the application of the principle according to which the human body is "non-commercial", as any form of payment would be contrary to public order. The justification for non-payment is that such a violation of the human body can only be agreed to in a spirit of solidarity and, as a result, the absence of remuneration is essential(68).

The Egyptian law on organ transplants enshrines the principle of solidarity and, therefore, that of non-payment(69). The 'no remuneration' rule must be absolute. The transfer of any part of the body in return for a consideration constitutes the sale of a part of the human body, contrary to public order. Only altruism can justify such a serious violation of the human body.

With regard to regenerable elements of the body(70), financial compensation can be approved much more easily. However, this compensation and the agreement that gives rise to it must not operate according to the laws of the market and the civil rules concerning sales. Any profit must be ruled out. It is for this reason that the Minister of Public Health has to establish a pricing system that must set the remuneration in a manner which "rules out any

(67) A. ALSHAHAWY and M. ALSHAHAWY, *Explanation of the law on the organisation of the removal and transplant of human organs n° 5 of 2010*, *op. cit.*, pp. 48 et seq.

(68) Art. 4 L. Concerning this article, see A. ALSHAHAWY and M. ALSHAHAWY, *ibid.*, pp. 25 et seq.

(69) Article 6 of this law states the following: "6/1: It is prohibited to conclude an agreement concerning an organ, part of an organ or a bodily tissue, by sale or purchase or by any remuneration of any kind whatsoever. 6/2: Under no circumstances may the transplant of an organ, part of an organ or a bodily tissue be authorised if it involves a profit to the donor or one of his heirs, regardless of the nature of the profit. 6/3: The specialist doctor is prohibited from commencing the transplant operation when he knows that these rules have been violated."

(70) Like milk and blood, which are considered to be "products" (in French: "*fruits*"). For a long time, Muslim jurisconsults have accepted that milk can be subject to payment.

profit". Officially, blood is not paid for at this time, and there is no system in place with regard to the other regenerable elements.

Finally, the justification for transplants is a therapeutic necessity concerning a third party. The decree implementing this law lays down the method by which this necessity is determined. It is the responsibility of the medical team at the authorised hospital to assure themselves of its existence before proceeding with the removal and transplant[71].

Legality, therapeutic necessity, consent and the absence of remuneration are therefore the conditions imposed by Egyptian law to ensure that transplants are not crimes under the Criminal Code[72]. This instrument achieves a certain balance between the protection of the body and social solidarity.

C. – *Recourse to the Civil Court*

Egyptian law has an "objectivist" conception of civil liability. As in Muslim law[73], the notion of "risk" reaches a new level in the Egyptian Civil Code[74]. A human being is liable for the harm he causes. Thus, under the terms of article 164 of the Civil Code, a person who lacks capacity can be ordered to compensate in equitythe damage he has caused. This provision, borrowed from the German Civil Code[75], encounters an undisputed principle of Muslim law: the liability of a young child or an insaneperson is, in

(71) Article 2 of the law states the following: "2/1: It is prohibited to remove an organ, part of an organ or bodily tissue from the body of a living or deceased person for transplantation to the body of another person except in the case of a therapeutic necessity required for the preservation of the recipient's life or as treatment for a serious illness, provided that this transplant is the only way of providing this treatment and that the transplant does not cause serious harm to the body and health of the donor. 2/2: It is prohibited to transplant an organ, part of an organ, tissues or sex cells that could lead to mixing the genealogical lineage".

(72) Concerning the criminal protection of the human body in Egyptian law, see M. Salah Ale'za, *The protection of the human body in light of modern medical trends* (in Arabic), Alexandria, Dar al-gami'a algadida li-alnashr, 2002. The Egyptian Constitution, and particularly the new 2014 Constitution, has for some time contained (art. 60) a prohibition on making the human body available for scientific trials without free and informed consent and using current scientific knowledge.

(73) In fact, the general spirit dominating the subject in Muslim law is an objectivist trend. In 1949, the Egyptian legislator opted for this objectivist trend: it therefore re-joined Muslim legal thinking and regained the connection with the past.

(74) C. Chehata, "Les survivances musulmanes dans la codification du droit civil égyptien", *International review of comparative law*, vol. 17, n° 4, October-December 1965, pp. 839-853, available at: www.persee.fr/web/revues/home/prescript/article/ridc_0035-3337_1965_num_17_4_14398.

(75) Art. 829; see also art. 54 Swiss Civ. C.

fact, used in Hanafi law whenever the damage is caused by an act committed by one of these[76].

In the Egyptian legal system, the right to physical integrity is a subjective right. Civil liability should be in a position to prevent violations of the exclusiveness of subjective rights and to compensate for any prejudices suffered as a result of these violations. In fact, the victim and his body are now central, and we start with the prejudice itself rather than the causal event, with the result that correlatively, physical injury has become the be-all and end-all of the compensatory function of civil liability.

Five conditions are necessary to establish the principle of liability: the harmful event, the fault, the causal link, the damage and the unlawfulness (or the prejudice, if we bear in mind that, as distinct from damage, it can be the central issue of the requirement of unlawfulness). Nevertheless, the Egyptian legal system does not require that all of these conditions are met, as historical developments have already resulted in the contraction of some of them[77].

We can see this reasoning in the matter of medical interventions without the consent of the patient. The Court of Cassation considered that the doctor's breach of his information duty to the patient causes to this patienta damage for which the Court

(76) The theory of incapacity belongs, in principle, to the law concerning persons. In the preliminary section of the Egyptian Civil Code, chapter II is specifically dedicated to "Persons". These provisions determine the persons affected by the incapacity to exercise their rights (art. 44 to 48). However, the law of incapacity is not unrelated to the law on obligations: legal acts made by persons incapable of judgment are invalid. That is why the Egyptian Civil Code also includes articles on the incapacity to exercise rights in the chapter on contracts (art. 109 and 110). These various instruments, which constitute the basis for the law on persons incapable of judgment, are supplemented by the law on guardianship and curatorship (law enacted independently of the Civil Code in 1952) and by family law, which is strictly speaking Muslim law. See C. Chehata, "Les survivances musulmanes dans la codification du droit civil égyptien", *op. cit.*

(77) Civil liability presupposes that the victim has suffered a damage – a physical aspect of his injury that has repercussions in the legal sphere; it matters little whether these repercussions are called prejudice or illegal damage. The first criterion verifies that the victim has suffered a loss, the second, that this loss is against the law. These two criteria contract by a dual process that results in damage that appears to require compensation, as it is in violation of a fundamental right.

This dual process comprises on the one hand a tendency to believe that any violation of a fundamental right is necessarily unlawful, and on the other, the belief that any violation of a fundamental right is necessarily prejudicial or damaging. Concerning this development in French law, see C. Quézel-Ambrunaz, "La contraction des conditions de la responsabilité civile en cas d'atteinte à un droit fondamental", *RDLF*, 2012, chron. n° 27, avaiblable at: http://rdlf.upmf-grenoble.fr/?p=3028.

must ensure compensation. This jurisprudence also appears to have been an opportunity to affirm the fundamental nature of the protection of the body: instead of basing its argument on article 164 (concerning civil liability in general), the Court invoked the principles of respect for the dignity of the human person and the integrity of the human body(78).

The Court of Cassation thus describes the prejudiced interest as a personal right, detached from physical violations and accessory to the right to physical integrity. Violation of this subjective right leads to moral damage resulting of a failure to prepare psychologically for the risks incurred and the resentment experienced at the idea of not having consented to a violation of one's physical integrity. By this reasoning, the courts allow the recourse to liability, even if the risk (about which the patient was not informed) has not materialised(79).

Conclusion

The Egyptian legislature has made no pronouncement on the legal status of the human body and its parts. We can see a number of trends in the legal doctrine. According to the dominant trend, a human being has no right of ownership of his body. The body is an integral part of the person. It has no independent status. A person's use and disposition of his body are not based on any right of ownership of the body, but stem from the principle of the inviolability of the human body. However, parts detached from the human body (after their removal) become objects in the real world.

We can distinguish two groups of elements of the human body. The first includes those parts whose separation from the body has no serious consequences for the person, such as nails, hair and blood. The second includes those elements whose separation from the body, although possible during the person's lifetime, will be painful and will have serious consequences for the person's health or even life. Although the law makes no distinction between these two groups, the first is, by its nature, closer to the category of

(78) However, the solution does not change and will be the same when reference is made to the medical ethics Decree, n° 238-2003, of 5 September 2003.

(79) After analysing some of the decisions of the Court of Cassation, the doctrine has no hesitation in believing that "the only finding of a violation (of the information duty) gives a right to compensation".

objects, and third parties therefore appear to be able to acquire rights over these parts of the human body.

In spite of the absence of a clearly defined consensus on the legal status of the human body, an analysis of Egyptian doctrine and jurisprudence in certain fields reveals a “mixed normative approach” to the legal status of the human body: the legal status of the human body is based on both religious tradition (through the array of principles recognised by religion) and legal tradition (through the set of personality rights).

In Egyptian doctrine and jurisprudence, the protection of the human body (living and dead) is above all based on the principle of human dignity. However, the situation is more complex when it comes to determining the legal status of parts removed from the human body, since these are neither objects nor persons.

MEDICAL INTERVENTIONS ON THE HUMAN BODY IN TURKISH LAW

Saibe OKTAY-ÖZDEMIR

Professor at the University of Istanbul Faculty of Law (Turkey)

AND

Gülen Sinem TEK

Research fellow at Bahcesehir University Faculty of Law (Turkey)

As a result of the progress and dissemination of human rights and medical technology, the problems related to bioethics are diversifying, leading to the standardisation of bioethical rules at international level and the need to ensure that national rules conform to this standardisation. Accordingly, our study aims to evaluate the bioethical principles for the protection of the human body and their application by the Turkish courts.

I. – The existence of protection of the body

In Turkish law, any intervention on the human body is illegal and gives rise to the criminal and civil liability of the perpetrator. However, this liability cannot be invoked if there are justifying grounds, as in the case of medical intervention on the person[1].

A. – *Medical intervention on the body*

Medical intervention was defined in Turkish law for the first time during the modification of the Regulations on the rights of the patient[2]. Article 2 of the Regulations stipulates that a medical intervention is "a physical and psychological act carried out, in

(1) M.K. Oğuzman, Ö. Seliçi and S. Oktay-Özdemir, *Kişiler Hukuku*, Istanbul, 12th ed., 2012, pp. 191 seq. Consent constitutes the justifying grounds for medical intervention.
(2) *Resmi Gazete* [*Official Journal*], n° 28994, 8 May 2014.

compliance with the professional obligations and standards for the protection of health, to provide a diagnosis and treatment of diseases, by persons qualified in the medical field." This definition, which excludes aesthetic medicine, medico-legal examinations and abortion, is not without its critics and can cause practical difficulties. In addition, the Court of Cassation defined medical intervention more broadly before the regulations were modified[(3)].

According to the doctrine, medical intervention is a technical and extendable concept, the content of which can vary over time. It comprises any biological or medical intervention performed on the person[(4)]. Some examples are as follows: diagnosis, treatment, preventive intervention, prescribing medications, analyses, aesthetic surgery, psychiatric intervention, medico-legal examinations, organ and tissue transplantation, genetic tests, experiments on the human body and artificial insemination[(5)].

In fact, to qualify as a medical intervention, the following conditions must be met:

1. – *The person carrying out the medical intervention must be authorised by the official authorities*

To ensure the protection of people and society, medical interventions have to be performed by officially authorised health personnel[(6)].

The law on medical practice restricts medical acts to officially competent persons: these are doctors, orthodontists, dentists, midwives, persons practising circumcision, official healthcare personnel and nurses.

(3) In its initial decisions, the Court of Cassation listed the hypotheses for interventions by a doctor: A doctor practising medicine performs activities with the aim of ensuring the life and health of the person, such as diagnosis, prescribing medication, surgical interventions and follow-up observation of the patient: Cass. (4th Civ.), 7 March 1977, n° 6297-2541. However, in a decision in 2004, medical intervention was defined as an intervention carried out by a doctor and governed by the rules of medicine: Cass. (2nd Civ.), 14 April 2004, n° 149-8841.

(4) M. Ayan, *Tıbbi Müdahaleden Doğan Hukuki Sorumluluk*, Ankara, 1991, p. 5; H. Hakeri, *Tıp Hukuku*, 8th ed., Ankara, 2014, pp. 22 et seq.

(5) H. Hakeri, *op. cit.*, p. 33.

(6) Health personnel are people who work under the mandate of any health service. It should, however, be noted that not every health worker is qualified for medical intervention.

2. – *The intervention must have a medical purpose*

The act must be performed for the diagnosis, treatment or prevention of a disease threatening life, health, physical integrity or population planning[7]. However, the new definition set out in the patient's rights Regulations does not include all of these objectives.

3. – *The intervention must comply with the rules of medical science*

For an intervention to be medical, it must conform to the rules and techniques recognised by medical science. An intervention performed by authorised persons, but that does not comply with the rules universally approved by medical science, does not constitute a medical act. The incompatibility of the intervention must be evaluated from the most advanced scientific and technical data that medical science has validated at the time the act is carried out[8].

4. – *The patient's informed consent must have been given*

With the exception of those cases that justify a medical intervention without the consent of the person concerned[9], the person must consent to the medical intervention. The consent is a justification authorising the doctor to violate the body of the person[10]. This means that, even if the other conditions have been met, the lack of consent renders the medical intervention unlawful. For this consent to be valid, the person must have been provided with detailed information, as the consent must be informed.

(7) Such as, for example, to control birth rates. C. ÇILINGIROĞLU, *Tıbbi Müdahaleye Rıza*, Istanbul, 1993, p. 18.

(8) C. ÇILINGIROĞLU, *op. cit.*, pp. 33-34.

(9) Under the terms of article 15 of the Patient's Rights Regulation, consent does not have to be sought in case of emergency (risk to the life or vital organs of the patient).

(10) S. OKTAY-ÖZDEMIR, "Tıbbi Müdahaleye ve Tıbbi Müdahalenin Durdurulmasına Rızanın Kimler Tarafından Verileceği", in *Prof. Dr. Rona Serozan'a Armağan*, t. II, Istanbul, 2010, p. 1321.

B. – *Source of the principles of protection of the human body in the field of biomedicine*

The rules that protect the human body originate from the Constitution, international agreements ratified by Turkey, Turkish codes, specific laws, instruments and regulations.

1. – *Constitution*

The preamble to the Constitution outlines a number of fundamental rights, including the dignity of human beings. Article 10 relates to the principles of non-discrimination and equality. Article 17 sets out the principle of inviolability of the body, which prohibits any violation of the integrity of the human body, except in cases of medical intervention or other cases stipulated by law. Article 56, concerning the right to live in a healthy environment, stipulates that the State has the duty to plan, implement and control an environment in which each person can lead a physiologically and psychologically healthy life. Article 135, which refers to the disciplinary and moral codes within professional establishments, gives doctors the competence to determine their ethical and disciplinary rules.

These constitutional measures play an important role in the implementation of bioethical principles. Furthermore, the public health duty assigned to the State to ensure the protection of health demonstrates that medical activities are deemed to be a public service[11].

2. – *International agreements*

According to article 90 of the Constitution, international agreements that have duly entered into effect have the same force as the law. When there is a conflict concerning fundamental rights and freedoms between a law and an international agreement, the international agreement takes precedence over the law.

(11) Some activities of private healthcare establishments meeting the collective public needs have links with the Administration. Controlling these activities is never a simple regulatory issue. The administration has the authority to define the applicable rules and to require private enterprises to comply with them and can intervene with regard to the appointment of staff; see İ. H. Özay, *Günışığında Yönetim*, Istanbul, 2004, p. 226.

International agreements may or may not be binding. The 1964 Helsinki Declaration, the 1981 Lisbon Declaration, the 1994 Amsterdam Declaration, the second Lisbon Declaration revised in 1995, the Statute of Rome on patients' rights of 2002 and the 2003 UNESCO Declaration on the Genome and Human Rights are not binding, but influence the decisions of the professional chambers and ethical committees(12).

a. *The Convention on Human Rights and Biomedicine*

For this study, the most important binding international agreement is the Convention for the protection of Human Rights and Biomedicine of 4 April 1997. It was ratified by Turkey on 16 March 2004.

Article 1 of the Convention on Human Rights and Biomedicine states that the fundamental rights and freedoms must be protected with regard to the application of biology and medicine. Article 2 notes that the interests and welfare of the human being shall prevail over the sole interest of society or science. Article 4 requires health professionals to respect the professional rules. Article 23 guarantees appropriate judicial protection to prevent or to put a stop to an unlawful infringement of the rights, and article 24 states that the person who has suffered undue damage resulting from a medical intervention is entitled to fair compensation.

This Convention modified some rules of Turkish positive law. The Convention, which places human dignity and the fundamental human rights and freedoms at the centre of the practice of biology and medicine, highlights the concept of autonomy. In Turkish law, it is not the principle of autonomy, but the principle of protection of the person that is fundamental(13). In fact, in view of article 23 of the Civil Code and the Patient's Rights Regulation, a person can decide on his future if there is no danger to his life. There is at present no clear position with regard to priority between the principle of the right to life and the principle of human dignity. However, in a case of multiple organ transplantation(14), the doctor

(12) İ. Gülel, "Tıbbi Müdahale Sözleşmesine Uygulanacak Hükümler", in *Türkiye Adalet Akademisi Dergisi*, t. I, n° 5, 2011, p. 608.

(13) S. Oktay-Özdemir, *op. cit.*, pp. 1321 et seq.

(14) This relates to the transplantation of two arms and two legs, obtained from the same corpse. The recipient died. The hospital and the doctor stated that the patient had insisted on receiving this multiple transplant. The hospital received an administrative sanction. As

and the hospital's ethics committee have chosen to follow the patient's will in spite of the risks.

Article 5, par. 3, of the European Convention on Biomedicine, which stipulates that the person concerned may freely withdraw his consent at any time, is inconsistent with article 15 of the Patient's Rights Regulation, which states that consent is not required in an emergency situation where the patient's life or vital organs are in danger. Article 90 of the Turkish Constitution states that international agreements that have duly entered into effect have the force of law and that, if they are inconsistent with an internal law, they must take precedence over the latter. As a result, there is reason to believe that the European Convention on Biomedicine now takes precedence over the Regulation.

b. *Other international agreements*

A number of instruments, such as the European Convention on Human Rights of 1950, which protects the fundamental rights and freedoms, the 1961 European Social Charter, the 1966 International Covenant on Civil and Political Rights, the International Covenant on Economic, Social and Cultural Rights, the 1981 Convention for the Protection of Individuals with regard to Automatic Processing of Personal Data and the 1987 Convention for the Prevention of Torture, are not directly applicable, but can indirectly influence national legislation[15].

3. – *Turkish Civil Code*

Articles 23 and 24, which are the interpretation of articles 12 and 17 of the Constitution, govern the protection of the personality. The person is protected against itself and against third parties. These provisions also give the courts the right to intervene in cases of violation of the personality rights.

Article 23, par. 3 of the Civil Code stipulates that the removal of biological material is only possible with the written consent of the person concerned. The donor may withdraw his consent at any time, even if he had previously agreed, without incurring any liability.

---

the patient's family did not take legal action, it is not easy to determine the attitude of the courts with regard to the principle of autonomy.

(15) İ. GÜLEL, *op. cit.*, p. 616.

Article 24 of the Civil Code states that, in the event of an unlawful infringement of his personality rights, the victim can apply to the courts for protection against the person involved.

4. – *Other codes*

Certain provisions of the Turkish Criminal Code govern the failure to respect the conditions for medical intervention. A number of special laws (laws concerning the practice of medicine[16]; nursing[17]; population planning[18]; the removal, preservation and transplantation of organs and tissues[19]; general health[20]; private hospitals, blood and blood products[21]) also contain provisions relating to the protection of physical integrity.

5. – *Rulings and regulations*

Various rulings (for example, on medical ethics[22], medical specialisations[23] and private hospitals[24]) and the Patient's Rights Regulation[25] regulate violations of the person in the context of a medical act.

II. – Application of the rules of protection of the body

There is no specific instrument in Turkish law proclaiming the bioethical principles. However, some principles of protection of the body are recognised, in particular by case law: six major principles are accepted.

A. – *Respect for dignity and human rights*

The principle of respect for dignity and human rights is essentially established in the Constitution and in the Convention

(16) L. n° 1219, *Resmi Gazete* (*Official Journal*), n° 863, 14 April 1928.
(17) L. n° 6283, *Resmi Gazete* (*Official Journal*), n° 8647, 2 March 1954.
(18) L. n° 2827, *Resmi Gazete* (*Official Journal*), n° 18059, 27 May 1983.
(19) L. n° 2238, *Resmi Gazete* (*Official Journal*), n° 16655, 3 June 1979.
(20) L. n° 1593, *Resmi Gazete* (*Official Journal*), n° 1489, 6 May 1930.
(21) L. n° 5624, *Resmi Gazete* (*Official Journal*), n° 26510, 11 April 2007.
(22) *Resmi Gazete* (*Official Journal*), n° 10436, 19 February 1960.
(23) *Resmi Gazete* (*Official Journal*), n° 24790, 19 June 2002.
(24) *Resmi Gazete* (*Official Journal*), n° 17924, 10 January 1983.
(25) *Resmi Gazete* (*Official Journal*), n° 23420, 1 August 1998.

for the protection of human rights and Biomedicine. According to this principle, the dignity of the human being must be protected in the practice of biology and medicine.

The Patient's Rights Regulation translates this principle into reality by imposing hygiene conditions on healthcare establishments and providing patients with legal recourse[26]. The dignity of the human being is also protected by article 23 of the Civil Code. Case law defines it as respect for the humanity that resides in each person. The right to life without infringement of one's physical and mental integrity is regarded as a personality right, with torture therefore deemed to be contrary to the dignity of the human being[27]. Clinical research is considered to be in accordance with human dignity if it causes no pain, discomfort or fear and if the risks to the patient's health are minimal[28].

B. – *Principle of autonomy and principle of consent*

According to this principle, which is controversial in Turkish law[29], each individual has the right to self-determination, a right to control the disposition of his physical integrity. This means that the patient must be able to make decisions freely with regard to medical interventions performed on him. This principle forbids a doctor from carrying out an intervention without the patient's consent. The principle of autonomy is based on the principles of respect for one's private life and informed consent[30]. Health personnel have a duty to provide the patient with detailed information about the medical intervention. In addition, Article 24 of the Patient's Rights Regulation accords the disabled some autonomy by requiring healthcare establishments to inform them and obtain their consent. These regulations also stipulate that the will expressed in advance by a patient (who is no longer able

(26) Art. 1 and 39 of the Regulation.

(27) Cass. (8th Crim.), 13 December 2012, n° 29994-38227.

(28) Art. 5 of the Clinical Research Regulation, *Resmi Gazete* (*Official Journal*), n° 28617, 13 April 2013.

(29) On the doctrine that accepts the principle of autonomy in Turkish law, see H. Hakeri, *op. cit.*, p. 275, and on the contrary view, see S. Oktay-Özdemir, *op. cit.*, pp. 1321 et seq. In Turkey, people use hunger strikes as an instrument of political struggle. While a hunger strike is initially respected, a medical intervention occurs as soon as the person is in danger of death.

(30) S. Metin, *Biyo-Tıp Etiği ve Hukuk*, Istanbul, 2010, p. 125.

to express them during the medical intervention) is sufficient[31]. In accordance with international agreements, article 26 of the Regulation requires, as far as possible, the participation of the minor or the protected adult in the medical intervention.

Nevertheless, the medical act will be carried out without the patient's consent if the patient is unconscious and if he is in danger of death or if there is a serious risk of the total or functional loss of a vital organ[32]. Likewise, in these cases, the medical intervention will be carried out even if the patient is opposed to the treatment (refuses to give his consent) or wants to withdraw his consent.

In Turkish law, when a situation arises that removes the autonomous capacity of the individual or carries a danger of death, the medical act is performed in accordance with the principle of non-maleficence[33] without obtaining the consent of the person concerned. This demonstrates that Turkish law does not totally recognise the patient's self-determination[34].

The principle of consent is a corollary to the principle of autonomy. In accordance with the first one, a medical intervention is lawful when the will of the patient has been expressed[35]. The consent defines the scope of the medical intervention. A general consent for all forms of medical intervention is not valid.

The Patient's Rights Regulation stipulates the information that must be provided to the patient for an informed consent. However, article 23 of the Civil Code also requires that the objective of the medical intervention must comply with the law, morality and public order.

When a medical intervention is carried out without the consent of an unconscious patient (in the case of a danger of death or serious risk[36]), the patient's family and legal representative (if appropriate) are informed. In the same way, the scope of the

(31) On the importance of the advance will of the patient, see S. OKTAY-ÖZDEMIR, *op. cit.*, p. 1329; H. HAKERI, "Amendments to the Patient's Rights Regulation", available at: www.medimagazin.com.tr/authors/hakan-hakeri/tr-hasta-haklari-yonetmeligindeki-degisiklikler-72-64-3641.html.

(32) Art. 24 of the Patient's Rights Regulation.

(33) A. ERDEM, "Tıp Etiğinde Hasta Özerkliğine Saygı İlkesi", in *Erciyes Tıp Dergisi*, t. 25, n °2, 2003, p. 95.

(34) See n° 16.

(35) M.K. OĞUZMAN, Ö SELIÇI and S. OKTAY-ÖZDEMIR, *op. cit.*, p. 192; Ö. YENERER CAKMUT, *Tıbbi Müdahaleye Rızanın Ceza Hukuku Açısından İncelenmesi*, Istanbul, 2003, p. 193.

(36) Art. 24 of the Patient's Rights Regulation.

medical intervention can be extended without seeking the patient's consent if the medical situation requires this, e.g. the risk of total or functional loss of a vital organ. Should the patient lose the capacity of discernment as a result of the illness, the consent given when the patient was in full control of his mental faculties will be sufficient to allow a subsequent medical intervention when he is no longer in possession of those faculties.

Consent is limited in article 8 of the law on the organ or tissues removal, preservation and transplantation: such acts must not endanger the life of the donor.

The right of the individual to have control over the disposition of his own body is therefore not unrestricted. Acts that would lead to the complete negation or excessive limitation of the rights of the individual would be unlawful, regardless of the consent of the person in question. Furthermore, the patient must have the civil capacity to consent to the medical act. For this, he must be in a position to understand the significance of the violation of the body to which he has consented, and the benefit that can be achieved by the intervention on his body.

In Turkish law, consent can only make an intervention lawful within the framework of the rights the person enjoys under the terms of the law. In Turkey, as no one may waive their right to life, consent to euthanasia is not valid[(37)].

The Council of State also considered that the consent of the patient is not necessary when there is a risk of transmission to others or a threat to public health, as, in these cases, treatment is mandatory in accordance with the law in order to preserve the lives of others[(38)].

C. – *Principle of non-maleficence*

The objective of this principle is to protect people against any possible harm, mainly in the context of clinical research.

---

(37) M.E. Artuk and C. Yenidünya, "Ötenazi", in *Prof. Dr. Turhan Tufan Yüce'ye Armağan*, İzmir 2001, pp. 300 et seq.; S. Oktay-Özdemir, *op. cit.*, pp. 1319 et seq.

(38) Council of State, 1st Ch., 30 October 2008, n° 789-1091.

The civil[39] and criminal liabilities of anyone failing to comply with the conditions for medical intervention could be invoked. If the person who commits the unlawful act is a State official, the State has an objective liability.

The principle of non-maleficence also comes into play with regard to organ transplantation: organ transplants may only take place in the therapeutic interest of the recipient. The transplant is also unacceptable if it risks harming the donor. Adults can be donors if the donation poses no vital risk to them. To avoid possible abuse, particularly commercial, organ or tissue transplants from live donors are only permitted between relatives. With regard to clinical research, article 28 of the Clinical Research Regulation requires ethics committees to analyse the potential benefits and risks so as to evaluate the research application. In one of its decisions, the Council of State ruled that experimental treatments may only be implemented if there is a possibility of contributing to the patient's welfare and if the treatments will not produce a worse outcome than standard treatments[40].

D. – *Principle of equality, justice and fairness*

According to the principle of equality, medical resources must be shared fairly between individuals. Health personnel and the State must take measures to apply this principle.

The principle of justice mainly concerns intensive care units. It requires the organisation of the "fair and equitable" use of these units within society in the knowledge that there is only a limited number of them in Turkey and that these services are very expensive[41].

Likewise, the allocation of elements of the body as part of organ and tissue transplants must be accomplished while respecting the principle of justice: if the organs of a deceased person are removed,

(39) If there is the least risk of harm in the case of an intervention on the person, the doctor and the hospital will be liable for not having taken this risk into consideration and not acting appropriately. Cass. (13th Civ.), 18 September 2008, n° 4529-10750.

(40) Council of State, 1st Chamber, 30 October 2008, 789-1091, aforementioned.

(41) S. Adıgüzel, *Yoğun Bakım Ünitelerinde Aydınlatma ve Onam Alma Yükümlülüğü*, unpublished Master's thesis, University of İstanbul Institute of Social Sciences, 2011, p. 154. The author maintains that in intensive care units the treatment of patients who have no chance of recovery should be withdrawn, in the name of equal distribution of public resources.

and if a relative of this person is on the waiting list to receive an organ, this relative will be given priority.

E. – *Principle of non-commercialisation of the body*

In Turkish law, the body, parts of the body and the corpse are not goods; they cannot be the subject of a profit-making act. As a result, the transplantation of organs and tissues between living persons is only authorised when they are members of the same family.

F. – *Principle of non-discrimination*

According to this principle, all people have the same rights, which cannot be withdrawn on account of their social status, religion, language, race, gender, political opinions or faith.

In this context, although freedom of contract is a rule in Turkish law and each individual is free to accept or refuse an offer, health institutions and personnel are required to intervene in a case of emergency. Apart from such emergency cases, they are entitled to this freedom of contract and can therefore choose their contracting partners; this freedom of contract must not, however, in any circumstances be based on discrimination.

Conclusion

Turkish law admits various principles of protection of the person's body in the field of biomedicine, but the right to life is the most fundamental. Every individual must respect his own life as well as the lives of others. For this reason, no one may consent to an intervention that could endanger their life. The principle of non-maleficence thus prevails over the principle of autonomy. The practice of medicine must, above all, respect the life of the person. As a result, in Turkey the will of a person or his family is still far from being able to result in a request for death[42].

(42) S. Adigüzel, *op. cit.*, p. 170.

REFLECTIONS ON THE PRINCIPLES OF PROTECTION OF THE BODY IN THE CONTEXT OF BIOMEDICINE IN CANADA

Dominique GOUBAU

Professor at the Faculty of Law, Laval University, Quebec City (Canada)

As stated by my colleague Suzanne Philippe-Nootens[1] in the introduction to her recent work *L'intégrité de la personne et le consentement aux soins*[2] (The integrity of the person and consent to medical care), "the inviolability of the human person is and will remain a controversial subject by its very nature, as it translates the vision of each society in regard to human dignity". We might make the same observation, however not by referring to dignity, but to public order, a concept that is, all legal experts will agree, scarcely less controversial.

The following considerations do not represent an exhaustive report of the legal protection of the human body in the context of biomedicine in Canada; they are rather an outline of some of the main elements of Canadian law, selected arbitrarily in light of some recent developments in this area.

It is interesting to note, right from the start, that there is no single *Canadian* approach in biomedicine to the legal protection of the human body. In fact, Canada is a federation whose Constitution expresses a subtle share of legislative powers, thus creating multiple sources of rules on the subject. In general terms, the federal government has the major responsibility with regard to criminal law, while the provinces have most (but not all) of the authority with regard to private law and health law. It is immediately clear that this widespread diversity of jurisdictions

(1) An M.D. and a professor of law at the University of Sherbrooke, Quebec.

(2) R.P. KOURI and S. PHILIPS-NOOTENS, *L'intégrité de la personne et le consentement aux soins*, 3rd ed., Cowansville, Yvon Blais, 2012.

will affect biomedicine and the protection of the human body. Thus, to give only two examples, on one hand, germinal gene therapy is prohibited by the federal legislation on assisted reproduction, and this prohibition therefore applies to the whole of Canada; on the other hand, the removal of organs or tissues from a living or deceased human body falls within the competence of the provincial and territorial governments, on account of their jurisdiction over private law and the organisation of health care. As a result, there are as many laws on the subject as there are provinces and territories (to which must be added the federal regulations concerning the health security rules and the measures taken by ten organisations competent in the field of organ donations). In the specific case of organ donations, or the use of medical waste, a comparative analysis of the legislation leads some to state that there is a common overall approach (an approach that emphasises the principle of autonomy, through the requirement for explicit consent), but the fact remains that there are some significant differences from one province to the other with regard to the specific conditions for the donation or use of tissues removed from a patient. The reasoning could be applied to the right to respect of one's privacy: each province has its own laws on the subject and there are a very large number of them. We are therefore a long way from achieving a common approach to the law on biomedicine in Canada. The system for the protection of physical integrity is therefore characterised by the diversity of its sources. There is no equivalent of the bioethics laws (as in France) that embrace most of the legal standards concerning biomedicine. There is instead a multitude of specific laws on issues ranging from organ donations to consent for medical care for 'incapable' persons, and from the organisation of biomedical research ethics committees to the protection of personal data in the public and private sectors, etc.

This legislation covers different aspects of the protection of the human body and expresses some of the major principles on which this protection is based. Although no hierarchy has been established for these principles, we can nevertheless state that the right to self-determination (including the right to respect for the residual autonomy of incompetent persons[3]) increasingly

(3) In Canadian law, the principle of respect for the residual autonomy of incompetent persons is well established and indicates that the degree of legal incompetence is constantly balanced according to the degree of incompetence of the individual in question. Thus, even

appears to be the key principle concerning numerous aspects of protection. However, this legislation does not cover, far from it, all of the legal questions raised by biomedicine. For example, while the creation of embryos for research purposes is officially prohibited in Canada, experimentation on foetuses and embryos is not specifically covered by the law. This gap leaves the door open for ethical regulations. A number of observers consider that ethical principles are preferable to obligations imposed by law in some fields, particularly that of genetic research and the establishment and use of biobanks (population-based or others). This is currently the case, since genetic and genomic research are essentially regulated by simple policy statements, such as the *Statement of principles on the Ethical Conduct of Human Genetic Research Involving Populations*(4) or the *Statement of principles for genetic research involving children*(5) by the Network of Applied Genetic Medicine of the Quebec Health Research Fund. On the other hand, others believe that a legal framework is now useful or even essential, due in particular to the development of research in the private sector which is usually subject to less stringent ethical rules.

The ethical rules are established by the government funding bodies and the omnipresent research ethics committees which, of course, are largely inspired by international consensus. For example, the *Tri-Council Policy Statement: Ethical conduct for research involving humans* of 2010, which is the joint policy of the three major federal research bodies(6), pronounces rules on the removal and use of human biological material and human genetic research. This statement clearly refers to international documents such as the *International ethical guidelines for biomedical research*

if the person is subject to a very strict protection regime (*i.e.* guardianship, which implies total and permanent incompetence), the fact remains that in the field of consent for medical care, the medical staff must confirm whether or not the person is actually competent to understand the implications and consequences of the proposed medical intervention. When appropriate, the person's consent will be necessary, just as his refusal of care must be respected, regardless of whether or not there is a protection regime (*Institut Philippe Pinel v. A.G.*, [1994], *R.J.Q.* 2523).

(4) Network of Applied Genetic Medicine, statement of principles: *Research in human genomics, 2000 version*, available at: www.rmga.qc.ca/fr/documents/Enoncedeprincipesrechercheengenomiquehumaine_fr_000.pdf.

(5) J. Samuël, D. Avard and B.M. Knoppers, *Réseau de médecine génétique appliquée*, 2007, available at: www.rmga.qc.ca/fr/documents/FINALERMGA-Enoncedeprincipessurlarechercheaveclesenfants_000.pdf.

(6) The Canadian Social Sciences and Humanities Research Council, the Natural Sciences and Engineering Research Council and the Canadian Institutes of Health Research.

involving human subjects from the Council for International Organisations of Medical Sciences(7) or the *Helsinki Declaration* by the World Health Organisation(8). With regard to publicly funded research, the *Tri-Council Policy Statement* now represents an important source of norms to be added to the numerous policy statements by the provincial governments and to legal standards: see for example those imposed by the Quebec Civil Code.

In Quebec the law was extended in 2013 to include an obligation to seek approval from an ethics committee for all research with competent research subjects. Until that date, such approval was only sought for research involving incompetent adults and minors. This reform shows tensions between the principle of respect for individual integrity and the requirements of scientific research by allowing both minors and incompetent adults to be enrolled in research involving serious health risks. The Civil Code states simply that the risk incurred may not outweigh the benefit reasonably expected. In evaluating such risk, one should consider both the child or the incompetent's state and health condition(9). The expanded scope of this reform is sizable, although it must be recognised that research cannot continue if the person concerned, objects, provided this person, in spite of his/her young age or incompetence, understands the nature of the research project.

The law's omission on a number of issues also results in moving certain debates on biomedicine to the judicial arena. Case law thus becomes an important source of norms with regard to the protection of physical integrity in Canada. It was originally the courts that stated that patient's autonomy, *i.e.* the patient's right to make decisions concerning his body and his life, prevails over any other consideration, including the benevolent intentions of doctors(10). The Canadian Supreme Court recently revisited this

(7) The Council for International Organisations of Medical Sciences, *International Ethical Guidelines for Biomedical Research Involving Human Subjects*, CIOMS, Geneva (2002), available at: www.recerca.uab.es/ceeah/docs/cioms.pdf.

(8) Helsinki Declaration – Ethical Principles for medical research involving human subjects (2008), available at:
www.wma.net/fr/30publications/10policies/b3/index.html.

(9) Although, in the context of research on a group of patients, the benefit for a single person is not the purpose.

(10) *Nancy B. v. Hôtel-Dieu de Québec*, [1992] R.J.Q. 361 (C.S.); *Manoir de la Pointe Bleue v. Corbeil*, [1992] R.J.Q. 712, EYB 1992-74873 (C.S.); *Centre hospitalier de Chandler v. C.C.*, [2000] R.J.Q. 1159, REJB 2000-17538 (C.S.); *Carrefour de la santé et des services sociaux de la St-Maurice v. Cadieux*, [1999] R.D.F. 292, REJB 1999-10538 (C.S.); *Centre Hospitalier affilié universitaire de Québec v. L.B.*, 2006 QCCS 1966.

principle, stating, in a judgment from 18 October 2014 that "the law is now clear that treatment may not be administered without consent, irrespective of the ethical imperative that physicians may feel"(11). The law (and in particular the Quebec Civil Code) now accepts the principle of the absolute right of the patient to refuse care(12), whatever the nature of the care and consequences of the refusal. With regard to incompetent patients, all of the Canadian provinces have legislated to ensure their protection by means of mechanisms for obtaining substituted consent(13). However, in view of the omission of the law regarding the right of a proxy (guardian or other) to request the continuation of care that the doctors consider futile it is left to the courts to establish the norms. There are numerous examples of intervention by judges with regard to the protection of the body in the context of biomedicine(14).

The importance of the case law in the field of the protection of the human body is clearly emphasised in Canada by the fact that since the 1970s, and very evidently since 1982, the year in which the Canadian Charter of Rights and Freedoms, (which is an integral part of the Constitution) was adopted, the courts were granted the power to check the constitutionality of laws and, in the broader sense, of State interventions(15). Simply put, Canada has an American-style legal system, qualified by some as "government by the judges". The courts can now declare that a law is inapplicable *erga omnes*(16) and, in some cases, require the legislature to rewrite

(11) *Cuthbertson v. Rasouli*, 2013 CSC 53.

(12) Art. 10 and seq. C.c.Q.

(13) E.g., Law of 1996 on consent to health care, L.O. 1996, c. 2, Annex A (Ontario); *Care Consent Act*, SY 2003, c 21, Sch B (Yukon); Health Care (Consent) and Care Facility (Admission) Act, RSBC 1996, c. 181 (British Columbia); Consent to Treatment and Health Care Directives Act, RSPEI 1988, c C-17.2 (Prince Edward Island).

(14) Some examples from the case law of the Supreme Court of Canada: *Cuthbertson v. Rasouli*, 2013 CSC 53 (cessation of life-maintaining treatment of a person in a neuro-vegetative state); *E. (Mrs)* v. *Eve*, [1986] 2 R.C.S. 388 (the question of the forced sterilisation of mentally handicapped persons); *A.C. v. Manitoba (Director of Children and Family Services)*, 2009 CSC 30 (the extent of the right of a 15-year-old child to refuse a blood transfusion on account of his/her religious beliefs).

(15) In the Canadian legal system, any State acts in the broadest sense (*i.e.* general acts such as laws or regulations, as well as acts with a more restricted scope, such as granting a permit; this concerns all public entities, whether Ministries, municipal authorities, public bodies, etc.) must respect the freedoms and fundamental rights granted by the Charters of rights and is subject to verification of its compliance by the courts.

(16) This is how, for example, in *R.* v. *Morgentaler*, [1988] 1 R.C.S. 30 the Supreme Court came to invalidate the provision of the Criminal Code concerning therapeutic abortion. The Court concluded that the conditions imposed on women to obtain an abortion did not comply with their right to security granted by the Canadian Charter of Rights. Consequently the contested provision was invalidated by the Supreme Court. Since 1988, all political

the law. Therefore, these Charters of rights have made a hierarchy of the rights related to biomedicine making them fundamental rights, whether it is the right to physical integrity, the right of respect for one's privacy, the right to life and security or the right to freedom. Violating a right guaranteed by the Charters results in sanctions whose nature depends on the type of violation. If it is the result of a legal rule, for example when a legal provision violates a fundamental right, the court can invalidate such provision. If the violation results from a specific decision[17], the person wronged can obtain the cessation of the violation (whether by the annulment of the offense or by an injunction, *i.e.* a prescriptive court order[18]). The victim can also obtain damages and interest in accordance with the rules of tort law. In addition, to take the example of the Quebec Charter, when it can be demonstrated that a violation of a guaranteed right is intentional, a court may impose punitive damages on the offending party, based on both the principle of compensation and that of exemplarity[19].

The constitutional or quasi-constitutional Charters do not specifically deal with bioethics or biomedicine. They pronounce, the rights and freedoms in general terms, in their application to the context of biomedicine. The courts have always refused to establish an *a priori* hierarchy of rights and freedoms guaranteed by the Charters and they continue to make *ad hoc* rulings when two rights are in conflict. The Supreme Court has thus already established that the competent patient's right to autonomy takes precedence over the constitutional principle of respect for life, although when the patient is a minor, the principle of protection usually, but not always, takes precedence over the minor's rights to freedom (freedom of religion, for example)[20].

The protection of the right to freedom extends, in the words of the Supreme Court, "to the right to an irreducible sphere of personal autonomy wherein individuals may make inherently private choices free from State interference", which involves, "by

attempts to legislate on the subject have failed. With the result that Canadian law imposes no restrictions on the right to abortion, as a direct consequence of the 1988 decision in the case of Doctor Morgentaler.

(17) For example, the refusal of a public administration to grant a permit.

(18) Thus, in the example of the refusal to grant a permit, the injunction could contain an order to issue the permit within a given period.

(19) Charter of human rights and freedoms, L.R.Q. c. C-12, art. 49.

(20) *A.C. v. Manitoba (Director of children and family services)*, 2009 CSC 30.

their very nature, basic choices going to the core of what it means to enjoy individual dignity and independence"(21). Until now, however, the Supreme Court has refused to extend this sphere of autonomy to include the right to euthanasia(22). Nevertheless, at the beginning of 2014, the Quebec legislature passed its law on end-of-life care, the result of work by the Parliamentary Commission on Death *with dignity*(23). This law, which came into force on 10th of December 2015, introduces a legislative framework for "physician-assisted dying" and defines the requirements that must be satisfied to ensure the binding nature of advance medical directives in Quebec(24) (as is already the case in several Canadian provinces). The law's first article states that its aim is to provide persons in the final stages of life with care that is respectful of their dignity and autonomy(25). This reference to the concept of dignity is evidence of the importance of this principle. In fact, the right to dignity has a special place in the Charters of rights and freedoms. Furthermore, an analysis of the case law of the Canadian Supreme Court over the last twenty-five years reveals that, put simply; the purpose of the Charters is to ensure respect for the "inherent dignity of the human being"(26). In the opinion of the Supreme Court, dignity is the underlying value of all rights guaranteed by the Canadian Charter. A parallel can also be drawn with the field of ethics, whose principles are often presented as serving human dignity. For example, the *Biobanks Ethics and Governance Framework* of the organisation "Génome Québec" sets

(21) *Godbout v. Longueuil (Ville)*, [1997] 3 R.C.S. 844, § 66.

(22) *Rodriguez* v. *British Columbia (P.G.)*, [1993] 3 R.C.S. 519. This issue is, however, likely to return to the headlines as on 15 June 2012, a British Columbia court ruled that paragraph 241b) violates articles 7 and 15 of the Canadian Charter (*Carter v. Canada [Attorney General]*, 2012 BCSC 886) and the Supreme Court currently has the case, which will enable it to revisit the position it adopted in the *Rodriguez case* more than twenty years ago.

(23) Quebec National Assembly, Special Commission on the question of dying with dignity, Report 2013, available at:www.assnat.qc.ca/fr/travaux-parlementaires/commissions/CSMD/mandats/Mandat-12989/index.html.

(24) An act respecting end-of-life care, L.Q. 2014, c. 2.

(25) The wording of article 1 is worth quoting in full: "The purpose of this Act is to ensure that end-of-life patients are provided care that is respectful of their dignity and their autonomy. The Act establishes the rights of such patients as well as the organization and framework for end-of-life care so that everyone may have access, throughout the continuum of care, to quality care that is appropriate to their needs, including prevention and relief of suffering. In addition, the Act recognizes the primacy of freely and clearly expressed wishes with respect to care, in particular by establishing advance medical directives regime."

(26) C. BRUNELLE, "Les domaines d'application des Chartes des droits", *in* Barreau du Québec, *Droit public et administratif*, coll. Droit - Barreau du Québec, vol. VII, Cowansville, Yvon Blais, 2013, p. 29.

out ten ethical principles that govern biobank interventions (good governance, a scientific approach, representativeness, justice, beneficence, respect for privacy, protection of confidentiality, non-maleficence, respect for autonomy and responsibility), stating that these "serve the dignity of patients"(27).

The Quebec Charter goes even further in the protection of human dignity since it officially raises this concept to the rank of a "right", stating that "every person has the right to the saveguard of his dignity"(28). In this way, dignity goes from the status of a principle to that of a right, opening the way to claims for damages and interest as well as punitive damages. In a celebrated judgment on a joint claim on behalf of patients with intellectual disabilities who had been deprived of basic hygiene care for more than a month during an illegal strike by the employees of a hospital, the Supreme Court found that there had been a violation of the right to protection of the dignity of these patients. The Court stated that this right is specifically protected and that this protection "addresses interferences with the fundamental attributes of a human being which violate the respect to which every person is entitled simply because he or she is a human being and the respect that a person owes to himself or herself"(29). The Supreme Court thus puts forward an objective interpretation of the concept of dignity, giving it a content that is the same for every person, whatever his particular situation. Of course, the principle (like the other principles providing protection of physical integrity) is not defined in law, and the courts, once again have the task of defining it on a case-by-case basis. The *Tri-Council Policy* defines the respect for dignity through three core principles: respect for individuals, concern for well-being and justice(30).

In addition, the prohibition of any commodification of the person, as the legal expression of human dignity, explains the absolute nature of the cost-free principle in Canadian laws, whether this concerns gametes donations, gestational surrogacy or participation

(27) Available at: www.genomequebec.com/DATA/TEXTEDOC/BB_Cadre-FR.pdf.

(28) Charter of human rights and freedoms, L.R.Q. c. C-12, art. 4.

(29) *Syndicat national des employés de l'Hôpital St-Ferdinand (C.S.N.) v. Québec (Curateur public)*, [1996] 3 R.C.S. 211.

(30) *Énoncé de politique des trois conseils: Éthique de la recherche avec des êtres humains*, 2nd ed., 2013, available at: http://ethique.gc.ca/fra/policy-politique/initiatives/tcps2-eptc2/Default/.

in medical research, for example[31]. However, it is also in the name of human dignity that some commentators in Canada support the idea that participants in research studies, surrogate mothers and gametes donors deserve a fair reward for their valuable services[32].

These reflections help us to understand the number and complexity of the sources in Canada of the principles of protection of the human body in the biomedical context. The federal constitutional system, the combined influences of Common law and Civil law, government by the judges and the proliferation of bodies responsible for ethics are all factors that explain this complexity.

---

(31) Article 25 of the Quebec Civil Code sets out the "cost-free" principle in this way: "The alienation by a person of a part or product of his body shall be gratuitous; it may not be repeated if it involves a risk to his health. A person's participation in research that could interfere with the integrity of his person may not give rise to any financial reward other than the payment of an indemnity as compensation for the loss and inconvenience suffered." In addition, the *Assisted Human Reproduction Act*, L.C. 2004, c. 2, which is a federal law, prohibits payment of the surrogate mother as well as advertising and soliciting in the context of gestational surrogacy.

(32) In June 2014, a Member of Parliament tabled in the Canadian House of Commons a draft law intended to lift the prohibition on the payment of surrogate mothers: *Law amending the Assisted Human Reproduction Act (surrogate mothers)*, Draft law C-607, 2nd sess., 41st Legislat., 62-63 Él.II, 2013-2014.

IT'S MY BODY AND I'LL DO WHAT I WANT TO: THE U.S. PERSPECTIVE ON PROTECTION OF THE PERSON

Marsha GARRISON[(*)]

Suzanne J. & Norman Miles Professor of Law Brooklyn Law School, Brooklyn, New York (USA)

Back in the 60s, Lesley Gore sang, "It's my party", and the Animals declaimed, "It's my life". The obvious predicate of "my", both agreed, was "I'll do what I want to"[(1)]. Today, a quick internet search reveals literally dozens of reprises on the equation of "my" with "do as I want". Many, if not most, relate to the body: The "it's my body" anthem serves as justification for personal choices ranging from overeating and tattoos[(2)] to unprotected sex and prostitution[(3)].

In the United States, the law governing individual choices about the body and its medical care has gone a long way toward accepting the equation of "my" with unfettered personal choice. Although U.S. legislatures and courts do impose restrictions on individual choice, these are typically justified as necessary to avoid harm to others or to protect incompetents. There is a strong presumption is in favor of individual control, and a range of legal doctrines aim to ensure that an individual's personal goals and values determine the treatment and use of his body, even after loss of competence or life.

(*) Research for this chapter was supported by the Brooklyn Law School Faculty Fund.

(1) See www.lyrics.net/lyrics/%22It%27s%20my%20party%22; www.lyrics.net/artist/The%20Animals/3555.

(2) See www.pinterest.com/natdupuis/it-s-my-body-i-ll-do-what-i-want/ (tattoos).

(3) See www.facebook.com/...Ill-do-what-I-want/121260944584431?v (unprotected sex); https://answers.yahoo.com/question/index?qid=20131119062523AAtXJ9l (prostitution).

I. – American culture and individualism

The equation of "my" with "do what I want to" has deep roots in American culture. In his early, and now classic, study of life in the United States, de Tocqueville noted that the American refusal to accept aristocratic privilege led to a social equality in which "more and more people [...] owe no man anything and hardly expect anything from anybody. They form the habit of thinking of themselves in isolation and imagine their whole destiny is in their own hands"(4).

Popular culture in the United States has long been pervaded with images of rugged individualism: Paul Revere rode, alone, to warn the colonists of British troop movements; Daniel Boone (and countless other pioneers) set off, alone, to conquer the wilderness; Thomas Edison invented, alone, the electric light bulb; and Steve Jobs pioneered, alone, the personal computer. Of course, in reality, all of these iconic figures worked with others. But their mythic stature in American culture comes from the sense that each marched – stubbornly and successfully – to his own drummer. It is no accident that the longest-running and perhaps most successful of U.S. advertising campaigns featured a lone cowboy(5).

In keeping with this notion of rugged individualism, both the U.S. Constitution and its legal tradition invariably treat rights as *negative*, *i.e.*, as ensuring freedom from interference by the state or other individuals. The "Bill of Rights" contained in the U.S. Constitution does not contain a single positive pronouncement; instead, it enjoins state interference with protected individual rights and liberties.

When Justice Cardozo famously announced that "[e]very human being of adult years and sound mind has a right to determine what shall be done with his own body"(6), he was thus saying what, to the typical American, was obvious. Cardozo's 1914 pronouncement has been quoted and affirmed by U.S. courts on literally hundreds of occasions. The views Cardozo expressed both influenced the

(4) A. de Tocqueville, *Democracy in America*, Richard D. Heffner (ed.), New York, New American Library, 1956, 194 p.

(5) The "Marlboro man" ad campaign endured from 1954 to 1999; in the two years after its introduction, Marlboro sales increased 300%. See www.nytimes.com/books/first/k/klein-logo.html; http://www.bbc.co.uk/news/world-us-canada-11963364.

(6) *Schloendorff v. Society of New York Hospital*, 211 N.Y. 125, 105 N.E. 92 (1914).

development of the common law doctrine of informed consent and provided a foundation for the U.S. Supreme Court to declare that refusing "an unwanted medical treatment" is a "liberty interest" protected by the United States Constitution(7).

II. – Basic principles: property, liberty, and federalism

The American bioethics literature invariably describes both the informed consent doctrine and the liberty interest recognized by the U.S. Supreme Court as manifestations of an ethical principle protective of individual autonomy(8). But the Supreme Court and lower courts that have developed the informed-consent doctrine do not, in fact, rely on an autonomy principle; typically, they fail to even use the word autonomy. Nor does "autonomy" appear in the United States Constitution or any of the statutory rules the federal government and the various states have established to protect the right to refuse an unwanted medical treatment.

Legally, both the constitutionally protected right to refuse an unwanted medical treatment and the broader, more nebulous claim that "it's my body, I'll do what I want to" are better described as manifestations of property rights or liberty interests. Doctrines and rules governing the disposition of the body and its parts are typically grounded in some notion of property right. Doctrines and rules that relate to medical decision making typically are grounded in some notion of individual liberty. (The exception is decision making about reproduction, where the Supreme Court has relied on individual privacy as a basis for restricting state law making).

Although property and liberty concepts typically ground U.S. law, it is important to keep in mind that there are often fifty different laws or, on some issues, no law at all. The United States has rarely entered into international covenants relating to medical care and decision-making(9). And, although the U.S. Constitution binds the national government and the states, the Supreme Court

(7) See K. Orfali, *infra*.
(8) See K. Orfali, *infra*; T.L. Beauchamp and J.F. Childress, *Principles of Biomedical Ethics*, 4th ed., Oxford, Oxford University Press, 1994, pp. 120-188.
(9) The United States is not a party to either the U.N. Convention on the Rights of the Child or the Convention on the Elimination of Discrimination against Women. In 2008, the U.S. Food and Drug Administration adopted a "Good Clinical Practice Code" and eliminated all reference to the Declaration of Helsinki in its rulings and standards. See L. J. Burgess et D. Pretorius, "FDA Abandons the Declaration of Helsinki: The Effect on the Ethical Aspects

has issued very few opinions on individual choice about medical care and the body outside the abortion context. Moreover, most of its decisions, while recognizing the right of a competent individual to make medical decisions, have ultimately upheld challenged state restrictions on individual choice, typically because the restriction, in the Court's view, is appropriately designed to protect public health[(10)], safeguard incompetents[(11)], foster informed decision making[(12)], or protect the desperate and dying from risky or possibly coerced personal choices[(13)]. In many of these cases, the Court has deferred to legislators' and regulators' judgments about risk; it has also, although not always explicitly, been responsive to historical norms[(14)]; patients who sought the right to physician-assisted suicide lost, in part, because state rules barring this type of medical practice had a long history and were supported by the medical profession[(15)].

The fifty states have fifty different constitutions that may supplement the rights provided under the U.S. Constitution. Some state high courts have utilized these constitutions to expand the sparse guidance provided by the Supreme Court. But many state high courts have not been confronted with cases in which they have had the opportunity to "flesh out" the scope of individual rights in this area or have chosen not to do so. Moreover, with a couple of notable exceptions, statutory law governing medical decision making and control of the body is made at the state instead of the federal level.

---

of Clinical Trial Conduct in South Africa and Other Developing Countries", *SAJBL*, vol. 5, n° 2, 2012, pp. 87-90.

(10) See *Gibbons v. Ogden*, 22 U.S. 1 (1824) (upholding quarantine rules); *Jacobsen v. Massachusetts* (upholding vaccination requirements).

(11) *In re Cruzan*, 497 U.S. 261 (1990).

(12) See, *e.g.*, *Planned Parenthood v. Casey*, 505 U.S. 833 (1992).

(13) *Rutherford v. United States*, 442 U.S. 544 (1979) (upholding FDA rule denying terminally ill patients access to unapproved drugs); *Washington v. Glucksberg*, 521 U.S. 702 (1997) (upholding state law criminalizing physician-assisted suicide); *Vacco v. Quill*, 521 U.S. 793 (1997) (same). See also *Abigail Alliance for Better Access to Developmental Drugs v. Von Eschenbach*, 495 F.3d 695 (D.C. Cir. 2007) (*en banc*) (upholding FDA rule denying terminally ill patients access to experimental drugs) (*en banc*: U.S. appellate courts typically hear and decide cases in three-judge panels. But a losing party may request a hearing by the entire appellate court. If the court agrees to hear the case, it issues a decision *en banc*, *i.e.* by the entire court).

(14) *United States v. Oakland Cannabis Buyers' Cooperative*, 532 U.S. 483 (2001) (upholding laws criminalizing marijuana use even when intended as a pain reliever).

(15) See *Washington v. Glucksberg*, 521 U.S. 702 (1997); *Vacco v. Quill*, 521 U.S. 793 (1997).

The large role of state courts and legislatures ensures substantial variation in the law from one state to the next. This is true even of basic principles like the informed consent doctrine. Although the informed consent principle has been accepted in all of the states, its source and scope vary substantially from one state to the next. Some states have statutory formulations of the informed consent doctrine; others do not. About half the states permit the patient to recover whenever a reasonable, prudent patient would want the information the physician failed to disclose; the other half require the patient to show that the doctor failed to conform with custom among like physicians in failing to disclose the information that is the subject of the patient's lawsuit(16). The scope of the informed consent claim also varies widely. Some states exclude or limit its applicability, for example, in regard to disclosure of physician inexperience(17) or diagnostic tests(18), while others do not.

This pattern of interstate variation is pervasive. There are few areas of medical choice where rules are uniform across the United States.

Perhaps because much of U.S. law derives from cases instead of statutes, it is also likely that there is a gap between the law in the books and the law in action. For example, in responses to a case vignette published in the Journal of the American Medical Association, two noted medical experts opined (for different

---

(16) In 2007, 25 states and the District of Columbia utilized the patient-oriented standard, and 23 used the professional-custom standard; in two states (Colorado and Georgia), the approach could not be readily classified. See D.M. STUDDERT *e.a.*, "Geographic Variation in Informed Consent Law: Two Standards for Disclosure of Treatment Risks", *J. Empirical Legal Stud.*, vol. 4, 2007, pp. 103 et seq, esp. p. 114. See also L.B. FRANTZ, Annot., "Modern Status of Views as to General Measure of Physician's Duty to Inform Patient of Risks of Proposed Treatment", 88 ALR 3d 1008.

(17) Some courts have permitted the patient to sue when the physician failed to disclose his lack of experience. See, *e.g.*, *Johnson v. Kokemoor*, 545 N.W.2d 495 (Wis. 1996); *Wlosinski v. Cohn*, 713 N.W. 2d 16 (Mich. App. 2005); *Degennaro v Tandom*, 873 A.2d 191 (Conn. App. 2005). Other courts have allowed such claims only when the patient has explicitly asked for information about the physician's experience. See, *e.g.*, *Duttry v. Patterson*, 771 A. 2d 1255 (Pa. 2001); *Lucas v. Awaad*, 830 N.W. 2d 141 (Mich. App. 2013).

(18) For example, § 31-9-6.1 Ga. Code permits use of the informed consent doctrine in a diagnostic context only when the patient has undergone an "amniocentesis diagnostic procedure or a diagnostic procedure which involves the intravenous or intraductal injection of a contrast material." Other state statutes contain no such limitation. See, *e.g.*, Wis. Stat. § 448.30. And while most courts that have considered the issue have rejected the claim that the informed-consent obligation requires disclosure of diagnostic tests the doctor does not recommend (see *Hall v. Frankel*, 190 P. 3d 852 [Colo. 2008]; *Pratt v. Univ. of Minn. Affiliated Hosps. & Clinics,* 414 N.W. 2d 399 [Minn. 1987] ; *Linquito v. Siegel,* 850 A. 2d 537 [N.J. App. 2004] ; *Binur v. Jacobo,* 135 S.W. 3d 646 [Tex. 2004]), some have disagreed. See, *e.g.*, *Jandre v. Wisconsin Injured Patients and Families Compensation Fund*, 813 N.W. 2d 39 (Wis. 2012).

reasons) that family members had the right to order the removal of a pacemaker from a demented 85-year-old man based on his relatives' perception that the patient "wouldn't have wanted to live like this"[19]. None of the limited case law confers such a right on an incompetent patient's family, however. Indeed, under each and every one of the state high court decisions on related issues, the family members would have lost[20].

In sum, U.S. law respecting choices about the body and medical care is typically grounded in one or another property right or liberty interest. These rights are invariably negative; they protect the actor against state or private interference with individual choice but do not convey any positive entitlements. Because the Supreme Court has not issued a large number of rulings in this area, the precise scope of individual rights is often unclear. The extensive role of the states in formulating both statutory and case law has created a patchwork of variable rules, and on many issues there is little or no law. It is thus possible that U.S. medical practice not infrequently deviates from the dictates of U.S. law.

III. – My body, my property

The "it's my body, and I'll do as I want" perspective is evident in a variety of contexts. U.S. courts have, by and large, refused to recognize a property interest in body tissues and excised cells[21]. However, virtually all of the states recognize a "right of publicity" that protects the individual's right to control use of his name and likeness; a number of states have extended the publicity right beyond death[22]. And more than one federal court has recognized that a decedent's next-of-kin has a property interest in the decedent's body[23].

(19) See J.A. Rhymes *e.a.*, "Withdrawing Very Low-Burden Interventions in Chronically Ill Patients", *JAMA*, vol. 283, n° 8, 2000, pp. 1061 et seq.

(20) See *infra*, at notes 66-72.

(21) See *Moore v. Regents of University of California*, 793 P.2d 479 (Cal. 1990); *Greenberg v. Miami Children's Hospital*, 264 F. Supp. 2d 1064 (S.D. Fla. 2003), 121 ALR 5th 687.

(22) See A. Hicks, Note, "The Right to Publicity After Death: Postmortem Personality Rights in Washington in the Wake of Experience Hendrix v. HendrixLicensing.com", *Seattle Univ. L. Rev.*, vol. 36, 2012-2013, pp. 275 et seq.

(23) *Brotherton v. Cleveland*, 923 F.2d 477 (6th Cir. 1991); *Newman v. County of Los Angeles*, 287 F. 3d 786 (9th Cir. 2002), cert. denied 537 U.S. 1029 (2002).

The "it's my body, and I'll do as I want" perspective is most striking in U.S. law governing transfer of body parts and capacities. This body of law has developed largely in response to new medical technologies that permit the division of gestation from genetics and the transfer, in vivo and post-mortem, of body parts and products ranging from sperm to lungs and livers. Unsurprisingly, U.S. law makers have responded to these new technologies with rules that strongly emphasize individual choice and control.

The individual-control philosophy is particularly evident in the law governing the transfer of reproductive material and capacity where, in contrast to the norm in other nations with advanced medical systems, U.S. law imposes almost no restrictions on individual choice. One U.S. court has permitted a testator to will his stored sperm to a girlfriend, over the opposition of the testator's children(24). Some have authorized a parent, as next-of-kin, to obtain and direct the use of a decedent child's sperm(25). The sale of reproductive material is legal in all fifty states, and although the American Society for Reproductive Medicine (ASRM) has issued an "ethical statement" urging that "sums of $5,000 or more require justification and sums above $10,000 go beyond what is appropriate" for ova purchase(26), a 2010 study found that a quarter of egg "donation" advertisements culled from more than sixty college newspapers offered egg donors sums in excess of the ASRM $10,000 ceiling(27). Sperm providers earn considerably less than ova providers on a per-donation basis, but may nonetheless earn substantial sums(28). Gestational services are also freely saleable in much of the United States. Although the vast majority

(24) *Hecht v. Superior Court (Kane)*, 16 Cal. App. 4th 836, 20 Cal. Rptr. 2d 275 (1993).

(25) See S.D. James, "Sperm Retrieval: Mother Creates Life After Death", 23 February 2010, available at:
http://abcnews.go.com/Health/Wellness/mother-murdered-son-hopes-create-grandchild-post-mortem/story?id=9913939; B. Spielman, "Pushing the Dead into the Next Reproductive Frontier: *Post Mortem* Gamete Retrieval under the Uniform Anatomical Gift Act", *J. Law Med. & Ethics*, vol. 37, 2009, pp. 331 et seq. (describing cases).

(26) Ethics Committee of the American Society for Reproductive Medicine, "Financial Incentives in Recruitment of Oocyte Donors", *Fertility and Sterility*, vol. 88, 2007, pp. 305 et seq.

(27) See A.D. Levine, "Self-Regulation, Compensation, and the Ethical Recruitment of Oocyte Donors", *Hastings Center Report,* vol. 40, 2010, n° 2, p. 25.

(28) For example, the California Cryobank, one of the nation's largest, currently invites potential sperm providers to "be your own boss" and advertises the possibility of earning as much as $1,200 per month through sperm "donation"; see: www.spermbank.com/why-donate/sperm-donor-pay.
See also: www.nwcryobank.com/sperm-donation/.

of states have outlawed surrogacy agreements when the mother is genetically related to the child she bears[29], state courts have typically not applied these statutory prohibitions to so-called "gestational surrogacy," in which a woman agrees to carry to term a fetus produced with the intended mother's ova or ova the intended mother has purchased[30]. Agencies seeking gestational surrogates currently offer the opportunity to earn as much as $50,000 for a completed pregnancy[31].

Nor do couples who make use of reproductive technology confront legal restrictions on the manner in which they do so. ASRM has issued ethical guidelines on issues ranging from preembryo gender selection to the use of IVF by older women[32] but, again, these guidelines are not binding, and the available evidence suggests that medical providers do not always follow them[33]. The federal government requires fertility centers to report basic statistics, including success rates, but has no substantive law on the use of reproductive technology, and the states have not filled the regulatory vacuum.

The transfer of organs is subject to a much larger body of regulatory requirements; organ transfer is also subject to a ban on compensation. The Uniform Anatomical Gift Act (UAGA), one version or the other of which has been enacted in all fifty states, forbids the sale of "all or a part of a human body to take place after the donor's death"[34]. And, since 1984, the federal government has forbidden the exchange of "valuable consideration" for any "human

(29) There is a small number of states in which all types of surrogacy agreements are legal. However, when the gestational mother is also the genetic mother, these states allow her to rescind the contract within a statutorily specified time period after conception. See, *e.g.*, N.H. Rev. Stat. § 127.287 (allowing contract rescission within 72 hours of child's birth); Va. Code Ann. §§ 20-156 et seq. (authorizing rescission of surrogacy contract within 180 days of conception).

(30) See "U.S. Surrogacy Laws by State", available at: www.thesurrogacyexperience.com/surrogates.cfm?sc=23&p=99.

(31) https://sandiego.craigslist.org/csd/etc/4520634535.html.

(32) The full set of ASRM Ethical Statements is available at:www.asrm.org/EthicsReports/.

(33) For example, the ASRM Ethical Statement on using preimplantation genetic diagnosis for the sole purpose of sex selection "should be discouraged," (ASRM, *Fertility and Sterility*, vol. 99, 1999, pp. 595 et seq, esp. p. 598), but a 2012 news account estimated that 4,000 such procedures are now performed every year and that "[f]ertility doctors foresee an explosion in sex-selection procedures on the horizon." J. Sidhu, "How to Buy a Daughter", *Slate*, 14 September 2012, available at: www.slate.com/articles/health_and_science/medical_examiner/2012/09/sex_selection_in_babies_through_pgd_americans_are_paying_to_have_daughters_rather_than_sons_.html.

(34) Unif. Anatomical Gift Act § 10 (1987); Rev. Unif. Anatomical Gift Act § 16 (2008).

organ", at any time; human organ is defined to include bone marrow, cornea, eye, bone, and skin but not reproductive material or blood(35). Classic bone-marrow extraction has now largely been replaced by stem-cell apheresis, in which stem cells are removed directly from the blood stream; a federal court has held that this methodology is so close to that employed in blood donation that the "valuable exchange" prohibition cannot be applied(36). A non-profit organization thus plans to begin compensating stem-cell donors with "a small scholarship, housing allowance or [...] a gift to another charity in their honor"(37).

However, except for the "valuable consideration" ban, U.S. organ transfer law follows the model used in reproductive medicine; its primary concern is ensuring individual control. All versions of the UAGA mandate consent by the individual during his lifetime or, post-mortem, by his designated agent or next of kin. The most recent version of the UAGA also specifies that the donation decision of an individual made during his lifetime take precedence over the wishes of his agent/next of kin *post mortem*(38). This provision was aimed, at least in part, at the tendency of organ procurement personnel to defer to the wishes of decedents' relatives; surveys had found that less than 12% of Organ Procurement Offices were "very" or "pretty" likely to procure when the decedent's wish to donate, specified during his lifetime in a donor card, were opposed by the decedent's relatives(39). It is not yet clear whether this legislative shift has had any impact on organ procurement rates.

What is clear is that the gap between the supply of donated organs and the demand for those organs continues to grow; in 2014, more than 120,000 Americans were awaiting an available organ(40). This shortfall grows every year(41), and it has spurred

(35) 42 U.S.C. § 274(e).

(36) *Flynn v. Holder*, 684 F.3d 859 (9th Cir. 2011), cert. denied 131 S.Ct. 1556 (2011). The U.S. Department of Health and Human Services has issued a proposed interpretive rule that would overrule *Flynn*. 78 Fed. Rptr 60812 (2 October 2013).

(37) See http://moremarrowdonors.org/about-us/.

(38) Rev. Unif. Anatomical Gift Act § 8 (2008).

(39) See D. Wendler and N. Dickert, "The Consent Process for Cadaveric Organ Procurement: How Does It Work? How Can It Be Improved?", *JAMA*, vol. 285, 2001, pp. 329 et seq.

(40) See www.organdonor.gov/index.html.

(41) Between 1988 and 2006, for example, the number of U.S. organ transplants more than doubled, but the wait list grew roughly sixfold. See D. Orentlicher, "Presumed Consent to Organ Donation: Its Rise and Fall in the United States", *Rutgers L. Rev.*, vol. 61, 2009, pp. 295 et seq., esp. p. 298.

a range of legal reforms aimed at increasing donation rates. One state, Texas, experimented with a "mandated choice" regime under which citizens were *required* to sign a form in which they consented, or refused to consent, to post-mortem organ retrieval. Proponents of mandated choice had urged that such a regime would increase donation rates because, in surveys, the vast majority of Americans say that they support organ donation even though much smaller numbers actually fill out organ donation forms. But the experiment failed, abysmally. Almost 80% of Texans either refused to respond or refused to donate[(42)].

Some transplant centers have also pioneered new methods of addressing the shortage. One is "paired exchanges"; in a paired exchange, a living donor who wishes to benefit Patient A, but whose blood type is not compatible with A, donates instead to Patient B; Patient B's intended donor, whose blood type matches A but not B, donates to A. Paired exchanges can be simple, as in this example, or more complex; a number of four-way swaps have been reported. Paired exchanges undeniably violate the ban on valuable consideration, however. But in 2008, Congress amended NOTA to make clear that its consideration prohibition did not apply to paired donation[(43)]. Since this amendment, paired organ exchanges have expanded to include so-called "domino" and "ongoing organ chains" in which any number of individuals are involved[(44)].

Despite the continuing shortfall, there has been no serious U.S. movement toward the adoption of a presumed consent regime for organ donation, however. More than two-thirds of the states, at one time or another, did apply presumed consent to one, limited-donation scenario[(45)]. The typical statute authorized a medical examiner (coroner) who was performing an autopsy to presume consent to the retrieval of corneas and other eye tissues; some states authorized coroners to remove organs as well. The basis for this approach seems to have been that, "[s]ince these people would be undergoing an autopsy to determine the cause of death, their bodies already would be subjected to a major intrusion"[(46)]. The

(42) See L.A. Siminoff and M.B. Mercer, "Public Policy, Public Opinion, and Consent for Organ Donation", *Cambridge Q. Health Care Ethics*, vol. 10, 2001, pp. 377 et seq.

(43) 42 U.S.C. § 274e (A)-(E).

(44) See Living Kidney Donor Network, available at: www.lkdn.org/paired_kidney_exchange.html.

(45) See D. Orentlicher, *supra*, at 299 n° 17.

(46) D. Orentlicher, *supra*, at 299.

1987 version of the UAGA probably reinforced state enthusiasm for this approach by recommending presumed consent for the donation of any organ or tissue from cadavers under the control of a medical examiner(47).

State courts that reviewed lawsuits by disgruntled family members initially found that these presumed consent statutes did not violate any constitutional right(48). But federal courts have been much more receptive to the claims of decedents' families. Two federal appellate courts have held that family members have a constitutionally protected interest in the disposition of their loved one's remains(49). In the words of the Ninth Circuit Court of Appeals, which struck down California's presumed consent statute:

> "Under traditional common law principles, [...] the parents had exclusive and legitimate claims of entitlement to possess, control, dispose, and prevent the violation of the corneas and other parts of the bodies of their deceased children. With California's adoption of the UAGA, it statutorily recognized other important right of the parents in relation to the bodies of their deceased children – the right to transfer body parts and to refuse to allow their transfer. These are all important components of the group of rights by which property is defined, each of which carried with it the power to exclude others from its exercise [...] Thus, we hold that the parents had property interests in the corneas of their deceased children protected by the Due Process Clause of the Fourteenth Amendment"(50).

As a result of this line of cases, it is unclear whether any presumed consent scheme would pass constitutional muster in the United States. In 2006, this legal uncertainty led the drafters of the UAGA to eliminate the provision authorizing presumed consent by a medical examiner, and few states have retained these provisions(51).

(47) Unif. Anatomical Gift Act § 4 (1987).

(48) *Tillman v. Detroit Receiving Hosp.*, 360 N.W.2d 275, 277 (Mich. Ct. App. 1984); *Ga. Lions Eye Bank v. Lavant*, 335 S.E.2d 127, 128-29 (Ga. 1985); *State v. Powell*, 497 So. 2d 1188 (Fla. 1986).

(49) *Brotherton v. Cleveland*, 923 F.2d 477 (6th Cir. 1991); *Newman v. County of Los Angeles*, 287 F. 3d 786 (9th Cir. 2002), cert. denied 537 U.S. 1029 (2002).

(50) *Newman*, at pp. 797-798.

(51) See Rev. Unif. Anatomical Gift Act § 22 (2008); D. Orentlicher, *supra*.

IV. – Unwanted medical care: rights, their promotion, and their limits

As one would expect, U.S. courts have long recognized the right of a competent individual to avoid unwanted medical treatments. Even before the Supreme Court had held that this right had constitutional dimensions, state courts had upheld treatment refusals even when such a refusal was certain to lead to the patient's death(52). Many, probably the majority, of these state cases focus on whether the patient is competent. Although competence standards vary somewhat from one state to the next, all are based primarily on cognitive ability(53). The patient who is "capable of appreciating the nature and consequences of her act" is typically deemed competent to decline life-saving treatment even when the patient is confused(54), depressed(55), or in despair(56).

Under U.S. law, even incompetent patients have limited treatment-refusal rights. The Supreme Court has held that the state may not confine a mentally ill patient against his will unless there is clear and convincing evidence that he is a danger to himself or others(57). Lower courts, both federal and state, have also held that a psychiatric hospital may not treat a mentally ill patient with antipsychotic drugs he does not want unless the safety of the patient or others is at stake and the state provides him with appropriate procedural safeguards(58); some state courts have enacted fairly elaborate procedures to ensure that mentally ill patients are treated against their will only in cases of real necessity. These procedural hurdles almost never result in a decision against treatment, but they may delay treatment for substantial periods(59).

(52) See, *e.g.*, *Bouvia v. Superior Court*, 225 Cal. Rptr. 297 (Calif. Ct. App. 2d Dist. 1986); *Georgia v. McAfee*, 385 S.E. 2d 651 (Ga. 1989); *Lane v. Candura*, 376 N.E. 2d 1232 (Mass. App. Ct. 1978).

(53) See M. Garrison et C.E. Schneider, *The Law of Bioethics: Individual Autonomy and Social Regulation*, 2nd ed., 2009, pp. 473-475 (surveying state laws).

(54) See *Lane v. Candura*, supra.

(55) See M. Garrison and C.E. Schneider, *supra* at p. 482 (summarizing research showing that vast majority of depressives pass U.S. competence tests).

(56) See *McKay v. Bergstadt*, 802 P.2d 617 (Nev. 1990).

(57) *O'Connor v. Donaldson*, 442 U.S. 564 (1975); *Addington v. Texas*, 441 U.S. 418 (1979).

(58) *Washington v. Harper*, 494 U.S. 210, 226 (1990).

(59) See M. Garrison and C.E. Schneider, *supra*, at pp. 553-554.

The right to refuse medical care logically extends to a right to refuse participation in medical research, and on this issue, uniquely, there is a large body of federal regulations. These regulations were developed during the 1980s and codified as a "common rule" that applied across federal agencies in 1991. This regulatory initiative followed a series of widely publicized revelations of research misconduct; in all of the cases, medical researchers subjected the participants to serious risks without their consent(60). The federal government, through the National Institutes for Health, funds a substantial portion of medical research conducted in the United States and, for many years, the regulations applied only to federally funded research. Recent amendments have expanded their applicability to a wide variety of "human subject research," however(61).

The basic principle on which the federal regulations rely is that of informed consent. But, in contrast to the relatively vague standards applicable to state informed-consent tort actions, the federal rules are extensive and detailed: they lay out eight different types of disclosures applicable in all cases, and an additional six that may be required(62); yet more requirements apply to consent by guardians for minors or incompetents(63), and the rules require, in all cases, extensive documentation of the consent process(64).

In keeping with the tradition of a limited federal role in health care, the enforcement of these extensive regulatory requirements is largely decentralized. The rules require research institutions to establish "institutional review boards" (IRBs) to review research requests and determine that federal requirements have been met(65). The federal government itself occasionally reviews the work of IRBs, and it may deny federal funding when an institution's IRB is found to have done a bad job of applying the federal requirements. But this enforcement mechanism is not utilized frequently.

Human subject research is also the only aspect of medical decision making in which the federal government has played the dominant law-making role. State legislatures and courts have developed most of the law governing medical decision making;

(60) See K. ORFALI, *infra*.
(61) 45 C.F.R. § 46.101.
(62) 45 C.F.R. § 46.116.
(63) 45 C.F.R. § 46.408.
(64) 45 C.F.R. § 46.117.
(65) 45 C.F.R. §§ 46.103-46.115.

most of this law-making effort has aimed at ensuring that personal values continue to control an individual's care even when that individual has lost the capacity to direct care himself.

Much of the case law focuses on ensuring that the patient's guardian or next-of-kin does not curtail life-saving care that the patient would have wanted. The Supreme Court has held that the states may require clear and convincing evidence of the incompetent's wishes as a predicate to terminating life-sustaining treatment[66], and a number of state courts have found that the gravity of the termination decision, combined with the state's interest in ensuring the patient's wishes have been accurately assessed, requires not only clear and convincing evidence, but other procedural safeguards.

Perhaps the most frequently cited state decision is *In re Conroy*, in which the New Jersey Supreme Court confronted a request to remove a nasogastric feeding tube from an 84-year-old bedridden woman who had "serious and irreversible physical and mental impairments", but who was not terminally ill or in a persistent vegetative state. The *Conroy* court held that life-sustaining treatment could not be withheld or withdrawn unless: 1) there is clear and convincing evidence that "the particular patient" would have made this choice; or 2) there is "some trustworthy evidence that the patient would have refused the treatment, [and] it is clear that the burdens of the patient's continued life with the treatment outweigh the benefits of that life for him," or 3) "the net burdens of the patient's life with the treatment clearly and markedly outweigh the benefits that the patient derives from life"[67]. The *Conroy* Court also specified that "burden," under the second and third decision-making standards, is largely synonymous with physical suffering: "we mean that the patient is suffering, and will continue to suffer throughout the expected duration of his life, unavoidable pain, and that the net burdens of his prolonged life (the pain and suffering of his life with the treatment less the amount and duration of pain that the patient would likely experience if the treatment were withdrawn) markedly outweigh any physical pleasure, emotional enjoyment, or intellectual satisfaction that the patient may still be able to derive from life"[68]. And in the case of Claire Conroy,

(66) *In re Cruzan*, 497 U.S. 261 (1990). See also K. Orfali, *infra*.
(67) 486 A.2d 1209, (1985).
(68) *Id.*

the court found that none of these tests had been satisfied. Her nephew's uncontradicted statements that Conroy "feared and avoided doctors", "had never visited a doctor until she became incompetent", and "would not have allowed [the nasogastric tube] to be inserted in the first place" did not, in the court's view, provide clear and convincing evidence of Mrs. Conroy's wishes to terminate treatment, and neither the second or third tests were satisfied because no doctor testified that she was in pain[69].

The high courts of California (*In re Wendland*) and Michigan (*In re Martin*) have similarly required clear and convincing evidence of patient preferences in cases involving minimally conscious patients[70]. Both found that the available (in one case, very extensive) evidence was inadequate to meet that standard[71]. And the California court, faced with a state statute that unequivocally required only a "preponderance of the evidence" as support for the substitute decision maker's medical choice, went so far as to rewrite the statute. The Court ruled that, unless the substitute decision maker (called a conservator under California law) had been designated by the patient while competent, a clear and convincing evidentiary standard was mandated:

> "The ultimate decision is whether a conservatee lives or dies, and the risk is that a conservator [...] will make a decision with which the conservatee subjectively disagrees and which subjects the conservatee to starvation, dehydration, and death. This would represent the gravest possible affront to a conservatee's state constitutional right to [...] freedom from unwanted bodily intrusions and to life"[72].

These state-court decisions place restrictions on the decision-making rights of conservators and other substitute decision makers to ensure that incompetent patients are not deprived of life-saving treatments that that they would have wanted; both the federal and state governments have played an active role in legislating to foster

(69) *Id.*

(70) In contrast to a persistent vegetative state (PVS) in which the patient evidences no consciousness or cognitive capacity, a patient in a minimally conscious state (MCS) is conscious, can feel pain, and has some level of cognitive capacity. See J.J. FINS *e.a.*, "The Minimally Conscious State: A Diagnosis in Search of an Epidemiology", *Arch. Neurology*, vol. 64, 2007, pp. 1400 et seq.

(71) *In re Martin*, 538 N.W.2d 399 (Mich. 1995), *cert. denied* 516 U.S. 1113 (1996); *Conservatorship of Wendland*, 28 P. 3d 151 (Cal. 2001).

(72) Conservatorship of Wendland, *supra*.

the capacity of competent individuals to express their treatment wishes in a form that will bind their doctors and substitute decision makers should the individual become incompetent. Today, all of the states have legislation authorizing individuals to name the individual who will make decisions on their behalf in the event of incapacity; these state laws also empower individuals to execute "advance directives," sometimes described as "living wills," that aim to provide guidance to physicians and substitute decision makers about the individual's treatment preferences.

Opinion polls invariably show that most Americans favor advance directives. But that general enthusiasm has not led the majority of Americans to actually execute them. In 1990, hoping to increase use of advance directives, the federal government enacted the Patient Self-Determination Act (PSDA), which requires hospitals to "provide written information" to all patients about their right "to make decisions concerning [...] medical care [...] and the right to formulate advance directives," document the execution of an advance directive in the patient's record, and to provide "education for staff and the community on issues concerning advance directives"(73).

Although vast sums of money were spent(74), and the evidence suggests that "hospitals have generally complied with the PSDA and do inform patients of their right to complete an advance directive"(75), the statute has "generally failed to foster a significant increase in advance directives' use"(76). Record surveys conducted by the federal Agency for Healthcare Research and Quality continue to find that the majority of "severely or terminally ill patients,"

(73) 42 U.S.C. §1395cc.

(74) One study estimated the cost of implementing the PSDA at "1,038 bed, inner city, tertiary care, teaching facility serving indigent patients [...] as well as referral patients." The start-up costs were $114,528. In addition, the hospital incurred "on-going incremental costs including document copying, file folders, audits, and personnel. It also has on-going total costs including continued training and physician education regarding advance directives". J. Sugarman *e.a.*, "The Cost of Ethics Legislation: A Look at the Patient Self-Determination Act", *KIEJ*, vol. 3, 1993, pp. 387 et seq.

(75) T.M. Pope, "The Maladaptation of Miranda to Advance Directives: A Critique of the Implementation of the Patient Self-Determination Act", *Health Matrix*, vol. 9, 1999, pp. 139 et seq.

(76) See E.D. Morrell *e.a.*, "The Do-Not-Resuscitate Order: Associations with Advance Directives, Physician Specialty and Documentation of Discussion 15 Years After the Patient Self-Determination Act", *J. Med. Ethics*, vol. 34, 2008, pp. 642 et seq. See also J.L. Yates and H.R. Glick, "The Failed Patient Self-Determination Act and Policy Alternatives for the Right to Die", *J. Aging & Social Policy*, vol. 9, 1997, pp. 29 et seq.

have no advance directive in their medical files[77]. Similarly, in a retrospective survey of more than a thousand critically ill cancer patients admitted to an intensive care unit between 2006 and 2008, only 15.7% had an advance directive[78].

Even when patients execute advance directives, researchers have found that they are frequently ignored, either because they are unavailable, fail to address the medical decision at hand, provide insufficient guidance, or simply because family members and the patients' physicians decide that another course of action is preferable[79]. Although all states have laws authorizing advance directives, these laws do not require medical providers to comply with them; typically health care providers may decline to comply "for reasons of conscience" or because the care mandated under the advance directive is "contrary to generally accepted health-care standards" or "ineffective"[80].

A wide range of research reports also suggest that advance directives may not capture patient preferences well most of the time. Patient preferences seem to shift substantially even over relatively brief periods[81], and patients seem to be swayed, quite dramatically, by the way choices are presented in an advance directive form[82].

Because of the infrequency and limitations of advance directives, new models for protecting patient preferences are emerging. The best known and most rapidly growing is Physician Orders for Life Sustaining Treatment, generally abbreviated as POLST. A POLST is an immediately actionable medical order, signed by the patient's health care provider as well as the patient. It is brightly colored and designed to travel with the patient[83]. Perhaps most importantly, the POLST is designed for a targeted population with clear and immediate health care choices, not the general population. Most POLST patients are in their last year of life; the most common

(77) See www.ahrq.gov/research/findings/factsheets/aging/endliferia/endria2.html#2.

(78) See N.A. Halpern *e.a.*, "Advance Directives in an Oncologic Intensive Care Unit: A Contemporary Analysis of their Frequency, Type, and Impact", *J. Palliative Med.*, vol. 14, 2011, pp. 483 et seq.

(79) See M. Garrison and C.E. Schneider, *supra*, at pp. 298-307.

(80) Unif. Health Care Decisions Act § 7.

(81) See M. Garrison and C.E. Schneider, *supra*, at pp. 301-302 (summarizing research).

(82) See S.D. Halpern *e.a.*, "Default Options In Advance Directives Influence How Patients Set Goals For End-Of-Life Care", *Health Affairs*, vol. 32, 2013, pp. 408 et seq.

(83) T. Pope and M. Hexum, "Legal Briefing: POLST: Physician Orders for Life-Sustaining Treatment", *J. Clinical Ethics*, vol. 23, 2012, pp. 353 et seq.

triggers for a POLST are beginning hospice care, being admitted to a skilled nursing facility, or being discharged from a hospital where a DNR order had been entered(84).

Introduced without much opposition or attention, the majority of states have now adopted POLSTs. As of 2013, only seven states and the District of Columbia did not have a POLST program in some stage of development. All states require a medical provider to sign a POLST. In most, the signer must be a physician, though some states allow other medical personnel, such as nurse practitioners, to sign one. Most states also require the signature of the patient or a designated surrogate but some, such as Oregon and New York, do not(85). Some of these programs are legislative, but many are still informal.

Although the research data are still sparse, initial findings are encouraging. One study, for example, found that patient preferences noted on POLST forms matched the actual treatment (or non-treatment) in 94% of surveyed cases(86). But at this point we really do not know how frequently doctors offer POLSTs to appropriate patients, how well patients understand POLSTs, and how well POLSTs capture actual patient choices. It is possible that the POLST is solving some of the problems that have plagued advance directives, but it is also possible that it is not.

V. – U.S. LAW IN PERSPECTIVE – WHAT DOES IT ACHIEVE?

We have seen that U.S. law on the body and its medical treatment is strongly grounded in the ideal of personal control. Policy makers have undertaken a number of legal initiatives designed to ensure that individual goals and values guide medical treatment even after loss of competence or life. But many of these initiatives have had very limited success: Advance directives, for example, are everywhere available, but they infrequently guide treatment decisions and we have every reason to believe that they poorly capture patient preferences. Similarly, the evidence

(84) See S.D. Halpern, *supra*; T. Pope and M. Hexum, *supra*.

(85) See M. Ollove, *New End-of-Life Measure Quietly Sweeps the Nation*, Stateline, June 2013, available at: www.pewstates.org/projects/stateline/headlines/new-end-of-life-measure-quietly-sweeps-the-nation-85899484943.

(86) See S.E. Hickman *e.a.*, "The Consistency Between Treatments Provided to Nursing Facility Residents and Orders on the Physician Orders for Life-Sustaining Treatment Form", *J. Am. Geriatric Soc.*, 2011, n° 1.

suggests that the extensive informed consent process mandated by federal law for medical research often serves as little more than a formalistic exercise. Even in cancer research, where patients have urgent reasons for understanding their choices and the high level of risk has produced extensive study of patient understanding, research subjects often fail to grasp the most basic information(87). In one typical study, for example, "[m]any did not realize that the treatment being researched was not proven to be the best for their cancer, that the study used non-standard treatments or procedures, that participation might carry incremental risk, or that they might not receive direct medical benefit from participation"(88).

Many U.S. legal requirements could thus be described as elaborate – and expensive – exercises in formalism. In some areas, there are also costs to patient well-being. The field of mental health law offers a particularly gloomy example. Courts have often required elaborate procedures courts to "protect" individuals from unwanted treatment. But as many as 99% of mental health treatment refusals are, ultimately, overruled(89); these formalities thus accomplish nothing more than treatment delay, even though experts unanimously agree that treatment works best when it is begun early on(90). Similarly, the procedural barriers to mental health commitment erected in service to choice often prevent those who desperately need treatment from getting it at all. More Americans with serious mental illnesses are now confined in U.S. jails than in mental hospitals; those who elude the law often subsist – precariously – on the streets(91).

In sum, the "do as I want to" policy value that underlies much of American law on medical choice provides the appearance of extensive individual control over one's medical destiny. But the frequent reality is that choice is hollow, and the emphasis on choice may lead to neglect for the patient's real medical needs.

(87) See O. Ben Shahar and C.E. Schneider, "The Failure of Mandated Disclosure", *U. Pa. L. Rev.*, vol. 159, 2010, n° 647, pp. 667-670 (reviewing evidence).

(88) S. Joffee *e.a.*, "Quality of Informed Consent in Cancer Clinical Trials: A Cross-Sectional Survey", *Lancet*, vol. 358, 2001, pp. 1772-1777, esp. p. 1775.

(89) See M. Garrison and C.E. Schneider, *supra*, pp. 544-545 (summarizing relevant research).

(90) See *id.* at pp. 536-537; pp. 539-542.

(91) See E. Torrey Fuller *e.a.*, *More Mentally Ill Persons are in Jails and Prisons than Hospitals: A Survey of the States* (Nat, Institute of Corrections 2011), available at: http://community.nicic.gov/blogs/mentalhealth/archive/2011/01/28/more-mentally-ill-persons-are-in-jails-and-prisons-than-hospitals-a-survey-of-the-states.aspx.

FROM THE NOTION OF PRIVACY TO THE PRINCIPLE OF AUTONOMY: THE RULES GOVERNING THE BODY IN AMERICAN BIOETHICS AND MEDICINE

Kristina ORFALI

Associate Professor of Bioethics Columbia University, New York (USA)

Introduction

There is no explicit reference in the American Constitution to a right to one's physical integrity or to privacy or to any specific limit to state interference on one's body. The Supreme Court, however, has broadly read the "liberty" guarantee of the Fourteenth Amendment to guarantee a fairly broad right of privacy that has come to encompass decisions about child rearing, procreation, marriage, and termination of medical treatment. A woman's right to have an abortion in *Roe v. Wade* (1972) alludes also to the right of privacy. In the *McFall v. Shimp*, the trial court in Pennsylvania ruled that it is unacceptable to force another person to donate body parts (bone marrow), even in a situation of medical necessity. This case if often quoted in maternal-fetal conflicts, emphasizing the pregnant woman's rights over her own body. No one can force a person to submit to an intrusion of his/her body.

The notion of *privacy* is in the USA almost as ambiguous as dignity in other countries. The right to *privacy* includes a protection which extends to the body, to contraception, reproduction and abortion... but the word encompasses also rights concerning an individual's intimacy. *Privacy* is in a way a subjective domain, difficult to define, from the "right to be let alone"[1] to "a domain

(1) S. Warren & L. Brandeis, "The Right to Privacy", *Harvard Law Review*, vol. 4, n° 5, 15 Dec. 1890, p. 193-220.

free from any external interference"[2]. *Privacy* alludes to a zone immune to any external control and in a way a protection of one's liberty in the American sense of freedom from government tyranny[3]. The body belongs of course to this zone and has strongly been defended in the reproductive area (but not really regarding for example pornography). It is worth noting that *privacy* alludes to an individual right while dignity alludes to the broader realm of human rights.

A central dimension of privacy is *prima facies* the principle of individual autonomy. Self-determination defined as the right to be free from any external influence and to decide over one's own life has become the prevailing principle in bioethics and in medical practice. It is probably less a principle of *protection* over one's own body as viewed in a European perspective and more a principle which emphasizes moral agency and an individual's control over one's own body[4]. The shift from *privacy* to the more pragmatic principle of autonomy in the world of medicine will be triggered by both the contemporary bioethics movement (born in the US) and the law through the numerous cases which will shape jurisprudence. Yet informed consent which is the primary method to respect this patient's autonomy, his values and preferences was already quoted in 1905 and famously by Judge Cardozo in 1914, "every human being of adult years and sound mind has a right to determine what shall be done with his own body and a surgeon who performs an operation without his patient's consent commits an assault for which he is liable in damages"[5]. By consenting, the individual expresses the permission given to intervene on his body. The first references are linked to surgery, which usually is intrusive; they stem from English Common Law regarding battery. The views Cardozo expressed both influences the development of the common law doctrine of informed consent and provided a foundation for the US Supreme Court to declare that refusing "an unwanted medical treatment" is a "liberty interest" protected by the

(2) F. Rigaux, "L'élaboration d'un 'Right of Privacy' par la jurisprudence américaine", *RID comp.*, vol. 32, Issue 4, pp. 701-730.

(3) J.Q. Whitman, "The two western cultures of privacy: dignity versus liberty", *Yale Law Review Journal*, vol. 113:1151, 2004.

(4) "The autonomous individual acts freely in accordance with a self-chosen plan, analogous to the way an independent government manages its territories and establishes its policies", T.L. Beauchamp and J.F. Childress, *The Principles of Biomedical Ethics*, 6th ed., Oxford, Oxford University Press, 2009, p. 99-100.

(5) *Schloendorff v. Society of New York Hospital*, 211 N.Y. 125, 105 N.E. 92 (1914).

United States Constitution. The notion of informed consent[(6)] will become central first in the domain of research on human subjects, then in medical practice. Informed consent cannot be dissociated from patient autonomy in the American perspective. It has less to do, at least in the US with any reference to the inviolability of the human body or the dignity of a person and more to do with the patient's self-determination. In fact the reference to human rights which is so strong in international law, is less prevalent in a country so entrenched in defending individual rights. Yet it is not really a property right *per se* over one's body[(7)], as even in the US, one cannot dispose freely of one's organs but still can sell reproductive material.

Two different perspectives within the modern bioethics movement should be distinguished here: one stems from the tradition of human rights (what should be protected in that perspective is the fact of belonging to the human condition; the body is viewed as a 'usufructuary' body as in Rousseau's conception) more prevalent in European countries. The other perspective is strongly influenced by individual liberties which emphasizes the body as belonging to the private individual's domain. These two views seem to co-exist but at the same time they have to be differentiated as they each will emphasize either dignity or autonomy in an opposed way, sometimes both at the same time.

In the US, the emergence and development of modern bioethics in the 60's and 70's will give priority to patient's autonomy over any other principle in the biomedical world. Among the many structural and cultural factors which explain the emergence and prevalence of the autonomy paradigm, P. Wolpe (1998)[(8)] quotes the role of medicine, of law and of the philosophical, social and theological debates within the bioethical field. In fact, by understanding first the development of the bioethics movement, one can comprehend why autonomy has become a core principle in American bioethics and medical practice despite the fact that after all the norm of autonomy was a priori alien to medical tradition. Yet how come that autonomy has triumphed despite its imperfections? We will

(6) First appearing in *Salgo v. Leland Stanford Jr., University Board of Trustees* in 1957.

(7) R. Rao, "Property, Privacy and the Human Body", *Buffalo University Law Review*, n° 80, 2000, p. 359.

(8) P. Wolpe, "The Triumph of Autonomy in American Bioethics", *in* R. DeVries and J. Subedi (eds.), *Bioethics & Society*, Prentice Hall, 1998.

analyze how informed consent and autonomy have come to prevail both theoretically and in practice regarding any rules governing the body. While the law does not often explicitly refer to the word of autonomy, bioethics and medical practice have made autonomy their core principle.

I. – The emergence of autonomy in the USA

A. – *Bioethics as a social movement*

We need to distinguish between the two (sometimes overlapping) components of the movement to understand the specificity of American bioethics: research ethics focused on human experimentation on the one hand and healthcare or bedside ethics on the other hand. Modern bioethics, starting with the doctrine of informed consent and the codes for human experimentation and protection for research subjects so prevalent in modern bioethics, are often said to be rooted in the Nuremberg trials of the Nazi doctors. The Nuremberg code, promulgated in 1947, is viewed generally as the first authoritative statement of consent requirements in biomedical ethics or more precisely in research ethics, followed by the Helsinki Declaration (1964). However, Rothman (1991) notes that, de facto, the Nuremberg code had little, if any, impact on American medical practice. Between 1945 and 1966, the National Institute of Health (NIH) funded more than 2,000 research projects and none of them used informed consent!

So how did the autonomy principle come to prevail in the US? It clearly is the result of the development of modern bioethics(9). Most narratives emphasize the specific context of the 60s with the civil unrest and popular rebellion linked to anti-authoritarian movements (Vietnam War, civil rights movements, feminism etc.) to explain a legitimacy crisis in the US. Yet there were other similar movements elsewhere (end of the decolonization; in France May 1968; Germany; Prague Spring etc.) which did not affect directly medical practice. Modern bioethics emerged as a response to questionable practices in human experimentation in the US context with debates within the field of medicine and in other disciplines such as philosophy and theology. Dr. Henry Beecher, a scientist

(9) K. Orfali and R. DeVries, "A sociological gaze on Bioethics", *in* W. Cockerham (ed.), *The New Companion to Medical Sociology*, Wiley-Blackwell, 2010.

created a scandal in the field of medical research in 1966 when the New England Journal of Medicine published an exposé of the abuse of human subjects taking place during research procedures. Beecher's exposé, together with additional revelations about other instances mistreatment of research subjects – the most infamous of which were the abuse of poor black men in the Tuskegee syphilis study (NY Times, 1972)[10] and the Willowbrook study involving injecting retarded children with hepatitis B in order to test a vaccine – led to the creation of administrative structures for the regulation of research. In the 60s and 70s, human experimentation became an identified public problem. Both the state and the medical establishment's abuses were denounced (1966-1973). This led to the establishment of the National Commission for the Protection of Human Subjects of Biomedical and Behavioral in 1973, after strong resistance against any outside public or governmental scrutiny for researchers (Rothman 1991). In 1979, the Commission issued "The Belmont Report"[11] which made the informed consent process the essential component for the protection of human research subjects.

As a consequence, in medical research[12], Institutional Review Boards (IRB) were created to control that medical experiments were carried out with the patients' explicit informed consent and that research protocols followed ethical standards. Federal regulations 45 CFR 46, known as the "common rule", stipulate that all federally funded research involving human subjects be reviewed by a local IRB[13]. IRBs are today interdisciplinary committees involving the scrutiny of volunteer members recruited from the research institution and from the local community over medical research.

Interestingly, this regulation – a distinctive American feature – will be extended to all federally funded academic or industrial research taking place in the US, even if they are non- medical[14].

(10) For forty years the US Public Health Service had conducted a study on 600 black men, mostly poor and uneducated to study the natural history of syphilis in the untreated patient even when a therapy became available.

(11) The Belmont Report, available at: http://ohsr.od.nih.gov/guidelines/belmont.html.

(12) First limited to medical research funded by federal grants, IRB's now control all research going on in the US.

(13) (IRB), Institutional Review Board committee that has been formally designated to approve, monitor, and review biomedical and behavioral research involving human research subjects which are now extended to all academic research. *Belmont Report* in 1979.

(14) The IRB requirements tend today to extend to any international research involving US academics.

Following the American model, many countries have implemented new ethical regulation for human experiments[15] within scientific and medical research but rarely beyond these fields. The previous narrative describes how, despite much resistance, what is now known as the American model of bioethics prevailed, shaping scientific and medical research worldwide. Equally remarkable was the process that led to the extension of the scope of the new requirements introduced by bioethics, from research practice to the situation of ordinary patient in the clinic. After all how come physicians came to accept the norm of autonomy which a priori was so alien to their tradition? While the analysis of the different factors contributing to this radical transformation is beyond our scope[16], informed consent in research extended to inform consent regarding all medical practice becoming the legal, ethical norm to protect the patient from any unwarranted intrusion on his/her body[17]. The principal characteristic of the American Bioethics socio-cultural movement is perhaps that a radical transformation of modes of accountability and oversight took place not only within the context of research but also in the more private world of care; medical practice itself deeply changed, switching from professional and self- regulated peer accountability to accountability to the patient and to lay people. Strikingly, this evolution was mostly an American specificity; while, as mentioned above, the emergence of research ethics became a global phenomenon, it did not generate outside the US a similar drastic transformation within the care setting which still remains largely pervaded with paternalism.

The first development of American bioethics emphasized the *protection* of the vulnerable human subjects in research (some subjects were considered more vulnerable than others such as children, pregnant women or minorities); the second phase will stress the more active role of the patient as a decision-maker, rebelling against the implicit "assent" norm of paternalistic benevolence. The law[18] has certainly played an influential role in the shaping of Bioethics and in the promotion of "a right to decide

(15) See M. GARRISON, "It's my body and I'll do what I want to: the US perspective on protection of the person", *op. cit.*, previous chapter in this book.

(16) See K. ORFALI and R. DEVRIES, "A sociological gaze on bioethics", *op. cit.*

(17) The term "informed consent" will be mentioned for the first time in a legal text in 1957 (*Salgo* v. *Leland Stanford Jr*). This will be the first time a court will impose on physicians a duty to inform the patient before any bodily intervention.

(18) G.J. ANNAS, *Standard of care: the Law of American Bioethics*, New York, Oxford University Press, 1993.

rather than in terms of the right thing to do". It is no longer only informed consent that comes into play but the *autonomy* of the individual first and above all. Physicians suddenly had to deal not only with the patient's permission given to intervene on his/her body but with an active decision-maker on equal feet with the expert to define his own best interest. In a way federal regulations are aimed at protecting more decision making rights than bodily integrity *per se*.

B. – *"Principlism"*

While bioethics as a social movement was becoming a distinct discipline, there was a need to find a theoretical framework and a common ground to operate, and choose the best possible option in cases of ethical dilemmas. The American Bioethics is a practical discipline in which exemplars of high theory (e.g., consequentialist utilitarianism, Kantian deontology, rights-based theories, natural law, etc.) are directly "applied" to practical problems. The Belmont Report first defined three core principles (respect for autonomy, beneficence and justice) but Beauchamp and Childress, in an influential book published in 1979[(19)], developed the four principles that form today the core of modern bioethics. "Principlism" has evolved into a practical approach for ethical decision-making that focuses on the common ground moral principles of autonomy, beneficence, non-maleficence, and justice. These four principles despite criticism, have withstood challenge for more than three decades. However, even if in the mind of their originators, none of these principles are more important than another, the principle of autonomy has become the prevailing norm in bioethics, research and medicine in the US. In reality these principles can compete with each other: individual liberalism for example is difficult to reconcile with the notion of common good. Respect for autonomy challenges beneficence when Jehovah's Witnesses refuse a much needed blood transfusion. Autonomy and justice can clearly conflict. In fact, in the 80's, autonomy was considered as a reaction against paternalism as mentioned in R. Veatch's (1984) article "The temporary triumph of autonomy". But in 1990, E. Pellegrino considered the ascendency of autonomy over beneficence as one of

(19) T.L. BEAUCHAMP and J.F. CHILDRESS, *Principles of Biomedical Ethics*, New York, Oxford University Press, 1979.

the most radical reform (and probably irreversible) of medicine. In 1998, the sociologist P. Wolpe's paper "The triumph of autonomy" analyzed how America endorsed one of the most remarkable evolutions of bioethics and medical practice. Since the mid 80's, medical and nursing codes in the US have come to include rules explicitly based on the respect for autonomy.

Why did after all, the principle of autonomy win over all the other ethical principles? Again it was an unfamiliar concept in medicine and it was as foreign to medical practice in the US as anywhere else. Benevolence was a more traditional notion, fitting the medical ethos, sparing the patient from bad news and dismal prognosis... The physician's duty' is after all to increase the patient's welfare not to promote his decision making capacity. We must therefore consider how revolutionary this notion of patient autonomy was within medical practice even in the US. In England for example, from which Common Law originates, other values are taken into account such as the professional obligations of the physician over patient autonomy[20]. Only the US (and maybe Canada) makes patient autonomy the core principle for ethical decision-making.

Several factors have played a role in this promotion of autonomy. The shift from acute care to chronic illness has increased the presence of a more powerful lay voice into medicine, advocating for a more symmetrical partnership. Among the constellation of issues that triggered debates in the 60s, from fertility control to human experimentation and from abortion to death and dying most were linked to technological advances in medicine – such as dialysis, organ transplant or respirators. From defining death (a matter of clinical, philosophical, theological and legal expertise) the issue became linked to the more practical clinical problem of discontinuing life support and who should decide. Yet among the factors leading to the development of the Bioethics movement, which we briefly quote here, many- as mentioned above- are not specific to the American context. P. Wolpe (1998) gives an account of how autonomy became the central and most powerful principle in medical decision making, showing its practical value in

(20) In a famous case in UK medical law, (referred to colloquially as 'Bolam'), a judge ruled that doctors would not be found guilty of medical negligence if they had acted in a way that was "accepted by a responsible body of medical men", K. Mason and G. Laurie, *Mason and McCall Smith's Law and Medical Ethics*, 8th ed., Oxford, Oxford University Press, 2013. p. 148.

decision-making particularly in a society with no universal health coverage. Callahan (1999)[21] emphasizes how much autonomy is linked to a right-centered society, while other authors[22] point out to the fact that the dominant US version of informed consent is grounded on principles of patient/consumer autonomy and seems to enhance market choice. The resistance met by the Obamacare shows in a way how much the principle of autonomy and self-determination (against any authoritative interference) is deeply rooted in American culture and not necessarily the principle of justice, a more egalitarian and European notion.

Individual autonomy as expressed in informed consent is easy to apply and allows anyone to have a control over their therapeutic choices. This notion can collide with the state's general interest in protecting life. Yet autonomy and individual choice are mainstream culture in America and they often position themselves precisely against state interference. The respect for patient autonomy has become the respect for patient's decision making. As stated by sociologist Renee Fox: "From the outset, the conceptual framework of bioethics has accorded paramount status to the value-complex of individualism, underscoring the principles of individual rights, autonomy, self-determination and their legal expression in the jurisprudential notion of privacy"[23].

II. – The primacy of autonomy

A. – *Defining autonomy*

In the *Belmont Report,* the prevailing principle of autonomy was meant to ensure the protection of those who were vulnerable. Authors such as McCullough & Wear[24], define autonomy as the right to be protected from decisions imposed by any external authority. The opposition to paternalism explains the negative

(21) D. Callahan "The Social Sciences and the Task of Bioethics", *Daedalus, J. of the American Academy of Arts & Sciences*, 1999, 128, pp. 275-294.

(22) G.J. Annas and F.H. Miller "The Empire of Death: How Culture and Economics Affect Informed Consent in the US, the UK and in Japan", *Am. J. of Law & Medicine*, 1994, 20(4), pp. 357-394.

(23) R. Fox, "The evolution of American Bioethics: A sociological Perspective", *in* G. Weisz (ed.), *Social Science Perspectives on Medical Ethics*, Philadelphia, University of Pennsylvania Press, 1990, p. 206.

(24) L.B. McCullough and S. Wear, "Respect for autonomy and medical parternalism reconsidered", *Theoretical Medicine*, n° 6, 1985, pp. 295-308.

nature of the definition. It is also in a way linked to the notion of *privacy,* mentioned above, which pervades the American culture. Some authors allude to this principle as stemming from Kant and Mill while others mention Locke who was in fact concerned by protecting the individual rights against precisely the State's interference. There are inalienable rights possessed by individuals such as the right to life, to health, to liberty and property. Only the individual's explicit authorization can allow any authority to violate these rights. (The social contract between citizens will allow only punishment and coercion to be performed by the state). In a way, the moral characteristics of the liberal state define much more than the Kantian philosophy, the meaning of the principle of autonomy. The autonomy principle of American bioethics (as included in the *Belmont Report*), is a negative liberty such as defined in classic liberalism: to protect the individual against any unwanted intervention. There is a continuum in that sense with the notion of *privacy*. The privacy tradition of non-interference has emphasized autonomy as the core principle of bioethics as much as the respect for individual liberty.

It is surprising however that community values[(25)] did not play a greater role in such a religious and multicultural country as United States, prioritizing after all these values above the individual's rights. In certain cultural groups such as in Asian communities, the family is considered the patient's best decision-maker, not the patient himself, with the goal of shielding the ill from unwarranted stress. Disclosure of a terminal illness directly to the patient is far from being accepted among all ethnic and religious subcultures even in the US. End of life issues are also strongly linked to religion. Yet the bioethics movement in the US has become increasingly secular with no unifying meta-social principle such as "human dignity" for example. This is probably due to the cultural and religious pluralism of American society; this pluralism has to be translated into one voice, on equal foot with any other voice. Autonomy becomes the easiest principle to apply to respect all the different and competing cultural or religious values.

Yet there is a paradox in such emphasize on autonomy in medicine when precisely scientific innovations and technological advances have created situations in which so many patients can

(25) See the discussion by L. TURNER, "Bioethics in pluralistic societies", *Medicine, Health Care and Philosophy*, n° 7, 2004, pp. 201-208.

be kept alive yet have no autonomy, hooked up to machines and unaware of being alive! While the medical world has evolved towards the greater recognition of patient's autonomy (at least theoretically), the reality today is the reverse. People often die comatose, people age with Alzheimer; people linger in a vegetative state... Chronic illness makes people dependent more than ever to medical technology; from dialysis to ECMO machines, patients are bound to medical devices. Yet the prevailing ethos is patient autonomy when the reality is more often a fiction of autonomy. In fact in many situations, the patient cannot consent, leading to difficult ethical dilemmas.

While in most countries worldwide (at least legally) when a patient has capacity, the patients' right to self-determination is recognized, things get more unsettled when the patients can no longer consent, when they are unconscious or too ill, when old age dementia has deprived them of reason(26). However in the US, the law will ensure ways of prolonging the self-determination enjoyed by the competent patient, should that same patient become incapacitated. The basic idea is that the incapacitated patient should in fact have the same rights as the patient with full capacity. The same right of self-determination that underpins the doctrine of informed consent provides legitimacy for the use of advance directives; that is, the patient's right to choose a course of action remains after he or she loses decision making capacity. Likewise, provisions should be made to respect the patient's wishes even after competence is lost. American bioethics most influential role has probably been the promotion of autonomy even in situations in which such autonomy is questionable(27), in which consent can only be a surrogate decision. While autonomy and informed consent remain the prevailing norm ruling over bodies, they are also highly problematic in many medical settings.

B. – *The role of the law*

Many widely held ethical practices have been transformed into law such as disclosure of risks during the informed consent process

(26) B. Feuillet-Liger, K. Orfali and T. Callus (eds.), *Families and End of Life Decisions. An International Perspective*, Brussels, Bruylant, 2013.
(27) C.E. Schneider, *The Practice of Autonomy: Patients, Doctors and Medical Decisions*, New York, Oxford University Press, 1998.

or offering patients the opportunity to make advance directives such as living wills or appointing a healthcare proxy. The law (Annas, 1993) in a way emphasized the American Bioethics shift from questions of substantive content of right and wrong, more attuned to philosophical and theological discourse or as J. Evans[(28)] expresses from "thick" rationality (debates over ends) to "thin" rationality (formal) as it focused more strongly on who should decide, promoting thus the autonomy paradigm more clearly than ever even in cases in which the patient could not decide. Both case law (judge-made law expressed in court decisions) and statutory law (federal and state statutes and their accompanying regulations) set standards for science, medicine and healthcare and these sources have deeply influenced bioethics. Case law has established important precedents that provide material for reflection on both legal and moral issues. Prominent examples include judicial decisions about informed consent and ending life sustaining treatment.

1. – *Informed consent*

The right of an adult patient to consent to receive or refuse a medical treatment has now long been recognized by common law and in the courts. The necessity to respect the private choices regarding one's own health has created a specific legal duty for doctors to inform the patient about all options. The doctrine of informed consent- articulated by a California court as early as in 1957, elaborated in numerous judicial decisions and statutes over several decades has resulted in an increase in information to the patients and a transformation in the doctor-patient relationship.

This concept is derived from the United States constitutional right to privacy and the common law right of an adult person to control his or her person. For example, touching a person without his or her consent is a battery, a crime against that person under the common law[(29)]. Because battery is a crime, physicians and healthcare providers obtain written consent from patients prior to treatment. This legal concept is similar to the ethical principle of patient autonomy, that a patient has a right to make informed

(28) J.H. Evans, *Playing God? Human Genetic Engineering and the Rationalization of Public Bioethical Debate*, Chicago, University of Chicago Press, 2002.

(29) W. Keeton *e.a.*, *Prosser and Keeton on Law of Torts*, 5th ed., West Group, § 9, 1984, pp. 39-42.

decisions about receiving or refusing medical care (AMA Code of Medical Ethics, Opinion 10.01). Thus, although a patient has a right to make decisions about care, a state is also permitted to enact requirements that must be met when a patient refuses care or seeks withdrawal of treatment. Most states have laws supporting the right of adult patients to refuse care and to provide directives about end-of-life (EOL) care when the patient can no longer make decisions for himself or herself. Yet there are notable variations[30] in the law from one state to another.

Several court cases and the law will ensure ways of prolonging the self –determination enjoyed by the competent patient, should that sane patient become incapacitated. The *Quinlan* case and later the *Cruzan* case (1990) and finally the Patient Self-determination Act can be viewed as the legal milestones of the bioethical enterprise enacting the right to refuse life sustaining treatments even when one lacks competency. An arsenal of diverse means from the durable power of attorney to living wills were created to ensure that patient's autonomy as a decision maker could be respected even when- as in fact in most of today's end of life cases- that patient no longer was competent.

2. – *The Quinlan case*[31]

In 1976, a father of a young girl in coma petitioned the court to be her guardian to be allowed to disconnect her from the respirator that kept her alive for years. The hospital refused and Quinlan's physician argued that because she was not brain dead, both medical standards and ethics required him to continue treating her, with the respirator being part of that treatment. The government also intervened, arguing that the state's interest in protecting the sanctity of life must be protected and that removing the respirator was tantamount to criminal homicide.

The New Jersey Supreme Court rejected both arguments, deciding that Quinlan's right to privacy, protected by the Constitution, was violated when her physician and the hospital refused to remove the respirator. Although the court recognized that the state had an interest in preserving life, it found that interest weakened and the individual's right to privacy grew as the

(30) See chapter M. Garrison.
(31) *In Re Quinlan*, 70 N.J. 10, 355 A.2d 647 (1976).

degree of bodily invasion increases with a very dismal prognosis. The court also rejected the idea that the medical profession was required to use all means at its disposal to keep patients alive. As to who could make the decision to remove life supports because Quinlan was unable to, the court held that it could be her father. Practically, according to the court, Quinlan's right to privacy would be rendered meaningless unless her father could exercise it on her behalf. Central to the court's decision was its belief that Quinlan's father was of "high character" and very "sincere, moral, ethical, and religious." The court rejected the argument that her father's emotional state would distort his decision-making process, making him unable to make life-and-death decisions concerning his daughter. Karen Ann was removed from the respirator but continued to receive artificial nutrition and hydration. She lived until 1985.

The law also – in the *Quinlan* case- by turning to a hospital ethics committee "to find a clear and convincing evidence" of what Karen Quinlan would have wanted had she been aware, gave bioethics the legitimation at the very bedside it lacked until then. In a way the law validated a new bioethical expertise[32] more than any medical expertise and triggered the extensive institutionalization of the field with the adoption by the JCA of Healthcare Organizations of the requirement of clinical ethics committees for hospital accreditation.

3. – *The Cruzan case*[33]

Nancy Cruzan trapped in a vegetative state and no longer on a respirator, was kept alive by feeding tubes. Despite the parents and guardian ad litem in agreement over terminating artificial nutrition and hydration, the case was taken to state supreme court because it was without a precedent. The legal battles around this case addressed matters such as a right to privacy and the state's interest in life and not in quality of life for fear of treading a slippery slope. The United States Supreme Court recognizes that the due process clause of the Constitution gives competent

(32) A.M. Capron, "What contributions have social sciences and the law made to the development of policy on bioethics?", *Daedalus, J. of the American Academy of Arts & Sciences*, 1999, 128, pp. 295-325.

(33) *Cruzan by Cruzan v. Director, Missouri Department of Health*, n° 88-1503, 497 U.S. 261 (1990).

adults an interest in refusing unwanted medical treatment. In that case, the United States Supreme Court discussed the constitutional implications of a situation in which a patient is unable to communicate his or her wishes. This case established the right of a patient or patient representative to refuse treatment but recognized the state's interest in establishing parameters before such decisions can be made[34]. In fact the Cruzan case became the center piece of a bitter debate about how and when families can decide to withdraw not only medical treatment but also hydration and nutrition to bring the death of an incapacitated loved one. It also emphasized the importance of documenting patient's previous wishes. Nutrition and hydration thus were considered as medical treatment that could be withdrawn and finally Nancy Cruzan was allowed to die (12/26/1990).

The ruling in the Cruzan[35] case spurred enormous interest in living wills and advance directives and who should make decisions for a patient if he became incapacitated. Various states not bound by the Constitution to be as protective of an individual's right to have life sustaining treatment withdrawn as New Jersey under *Quinlan* or as protective of human life in all its form as Missouri under *Cruzan* took a number of different paths in their right to die jurisprudence. It went from empowering guardians and other surrogates to make life and death decisions for incompetent individuals without judicial oversight to requiring a judicial proceeding and clear and convincing evidence before allowing medical treatment to be withdrawn. That was the case in *In re Conroy*[36] in which such criteria was deemed insufficient by the court to allow the family to request removing a nasogastric feeding

(34) The law "[...] rejected the argument that her parents were entitled to order the termination of her medical treatment, concluding that no person can assume that choice for an incompetent in the absence of the formalities required by the Living Will statute or clear and convincing evidence of the patient's wishes. [...] The clear and convincing standard of proof has been variously defined in this context as 'proof sufficient to persuade the trier of fact that the patient held a firm and settled commitment to the termination of life supports under the circumstances like those presented'". In U.S. Supreme Court, *Cruzan v. Director*, Mdh, 497 U.S. 261 (1990), 497 U.S. 261, Cruzan, By Her Parents And Co-Guardians Cruzan Et Ux. V. Director, Missouri department Of Health, Certiorari To The Supreme Court of Missouri, n° 88-1503. Argued 6 December 1989, decided 25 June 1990, footnote 11.

(35) "Reasoning that an incompetent person retains the same rights as a competent individual 'because the value of human dignity extends to both', the court adopted a 'substituted judgment' standard whereby courts were to determine what an incompetent individual's decision would have been under the circumstances", *Cruzan by Cruzan v. Director, Missouri Department of Health*, n° 88-1503, 497 U.S. 261.

(36) See chapter M. Garrison.

tube from their bedridden 84 year old loved one. Thirty years later the Schiavo case(37) very similar in substance to the Cruzan case involved also family rift, demonstrating how unsettled end of life issues can be.

A jurisprudence of medical dying was taking place, giving bioethicists a greater role than ever not only in philosophical debates or in research ethics but also within the private world of the clinic. The law played in the US a role as an instrument of accountability in health care unparalleled in other societies. As mentioned by Beauchamp and Walters(38) in their introduction, "Bioethics in the United States is currently involved in a complex and mutually stimulating relationship with law". American society is strongly committed to "due process" and formal legal equality (and an unwillingness to defer to expert authority). This translates into a strong reliance on the courts, making the law a major shaping force in Bioethics development and in the promotion of autonomy as a core principle for the protection of the person.

So finally does this principle of autonomy promote a real control over one's own body or has it become a clinical (legal) category translated only into formal rituals of informed consent that ignore the often dependent relationship between patient and doctor? Informed consent can certainly be an important ethical tool that protects subjects from overt coercion but it can also be a fiction leading to so-called "empty ethics"(39).

(37) This case (1998-2005) strongly parallels a current unresolved French case, *Vincent Lambert*. Physicians had decided not to continue artificial nutrition and hydration with the wife's agreement but despite his parents opposition. The *Conseil d'État* used the same arguments as the Cruzan case, deeming that: "M. Lambert had several times before his accident (in 2008) clearly expressed his wish not to be maintained artificially under such treatment".

(38) T.L. Beauchamp and L. Walters, *Contemporary issues in Bioethics*, 6th ed., Thomson Wadsworth, 2003.

(39) O. Corrigan, "Empty ethics: the problem with informed consent", *Sociology of Heath & Illness*, vol. 25, issue 7, 2003, pp. 768-792.

THE PROTECTION OF THE HUMAN BODY IN BRAZILIAN LAW: RECONCILING HUMAN DIGNITY AND BODILY AUTONOMY

Maria Claudia CRESPO BRAUNER

Professor at the Federal University of Rio Grande

Associate researcher at the CNPq (Brasil)

AND

Anderson CAVALCANTE LOBATO

Professor at the Federal University of Rio Grande (Brasil)

The human body in the context of biomedicine has no specific legal status in Brazilian law, except with regard to certain biomedical practices such as organ transplants(1). However, the human body is protected in general terms by the personality rights set forth in the Brazilian Civil Code that came into force in 2002(2). Previously, bodily integrity was protected by the application of civil liability(3) rules and criminal law (violations of the person)(4).

The possibilities currently offered by medicine to meet people's expectations to have control over their own bodies have resulted, in legal terms, in a gradual erosion of the principle of the "non-availability" of the body. There is therefore a growing need in Brazil, for the fundamental principle of a legal protection of the human body to be reconciled with the possibility for the individual to have control over his body, subject to there being no violation of his dignity.

To protect the person and define the parameters of a legal status for the human body, Brazilian law relies on two complementary

(1) L. nº 9.434, 4 February 1997, on the donation of organs for transplants.
(2) By art. 11 to 21 Civ. C. of 2002.
(3) Art. 186 and the single paragraph of article 927 of the Civil Code of 2002.
(4) Articles121 to 136 of the Criminal Code punish violations of life, physical integrity, honour and freedom.

principles: the inviolability and the fact that the body cannot be the subject of a property right.

In Brazil, the protection of the human body relies on a set of standards (I) that define the principles of protection, a violation of which is punishable (II).

I. – The system of protection of physical integrity

In Brazil, the protection of the human body is based on ordinary law, in particular on constitutional law[5], the Civil Code[6] by means of the personality rights, and the Criminal Code[7], which punishes violations of physical integrity. However, alongside this legal arsenal, protection is also provided by the Code of Medical Ethics[8], the resolutions issued by the Federal Medical Council in a number of areas such as surgery carried out on transsexuals[9], assisted reproductive technologies (ART[10]), or by the National Health Council with regard to human research[11].

However, the protection of the body is also based on international standards. Indeed, Brazil has signed a number of international legal instruments, in particular the International Convention on the Rights of the Child of 1989, UNESCO's Universal Declaration on the Human Genome of 1997, the Universal Declaration on Bioethics and Human Rights of 2005, the International Declaration on Human Genetic Data of 2003 and the Ibero-Latin American Declaration on Ethics and Genetics[12]. These standards concerning human rights have constitutional status[13] and are taken into consideration by case law and to fill the legal voids.

(5) Federal Constit. of 1988.
(6) Civ. C. of 2002.
(7) Crim. C. of 1940.
(8) 2009 MEC.
(9) CFM resolution n° 1955-2010.
(10) CFM resolution n° 2013-2013.
(11) CNS resolution n° 466-2012.
(12) Manzanillo Declaration of 1996.
(13) In accordance with the provisions of paragraph 3 article 5 of the 1988 Federal Constitution.

A. – *The constitutional protection of the human body*

The protection of the person is provided by the Federal Constitution of 1988 through the principle of human dignity[14], the right to life[15] and the prohibition of torture[16].

This constitutional protection applies to the "living" body and the "dead" body, as well as the tissues, organs and elements separated from the body, which cannot be subject to commercialisation. This protection starts at birth and continues after death. A special law covers organ removal[17].

Likewise, constitutional law recognises the right to free access to family planning based on the principles of human dignity, freedom and responsible parenthood[18]. This means recognising the autonomy of the person with regard to his/her body and the prohibition of any infringement of reproductive rights[19].

B. – *The protection of the body by the personality rights in the Civil Code*

The primacy of the human person remains the cornerstone on which the 2002 Civil Code is built. In this way, the legislature has established the personality rights as subjective rights[20] with the intention of strengthening the effective protection provided to the person[21]. Nevertheless, this reinforcement of the personality rights must not result in any erosion of the inviolability of the body or regarding the limits to acts of disposal after death[22].

The law permits the free disposal of the body or its elements after death for scientific purposes[23]. At the same time, however, if a body has not been claimed from the authorities within thirty

(14) Art. 5, III, Federal Constit.
(15) Art. 5 *id.*.
(16) Article 5, III, *id.*
(17) L. n° 9.434-97 on organ donation for transplants.
(18) Art. 226, § 7, Constit.
(19) Abortion, however, remains prohibited and punishable by the Criminal Code of 1940.
(20) Through the influence of French and German doctrine, the category of personality rights was established in Brazilian law.
(21) According to the law, the violation of a subjective right opens the way to legal action.
(22) Art. 13 to 15 Civ. C. of 2002.
(23) In accordance with art. 14 Civ. C. of 2002.

days of the death, it can be allocated to medical schools for the teaching purposes or for scientific research[24].

The protection of physical integrity ensures respect for life and feeding and is intended to cover not only the body as a whole, but also those parts separated from the body[25].

The personality rights constitute the basic protection of the body. Since the Federal Constitution of 1988, human dignity has become a fundamental principle from which all other rights of protection of the body follow.

C. – *The Criminal Code and violations of physical integrity*

All offences committed against life are subject to criminal law protection of the human body, as a death resulting from an offence is only a violation of a person's vital organs.

The Brazilian Criminal Code punishes violations of life and physical integrity by making the individual responsible for his conduct if he causes death or damage to the biological, anatomical, physiological or psychological functions of another person (the victim[26]).

Criminal law punishes threats to life and bodily integrity[27], honour and freedom, in such a way as to protect not only the body of the human person, but also his/her moral integrity. The Criminal Code also sanctions any violation of the corpse[28]. With regard to bodily harm, the legislature has not laid down an action that can be the cause of the offence in question, but has settled for a causality link between the action of the perpetrator and the actual violation of the person's physical integrity. Although the violation of a person's physical integrity theoretically requires an action, it is accepted that the perpetrator can also be held liable when he refrains from doing something in a case where the law

(24) Art. 13 Civ. C. and in accordance with art. 2 L. n° 8.501-92.

(25) M.-H. Diniz, *Curso de Direito Civil Brasileiro. 1. Teoria Geral do Direito Civil*, São Paulo, Saraiva, 2007, p. 119.

(26) Art. 129 Crim. C.

(27) The Criminal Code (Special Part - *crimes against the person*, art. 121 to 129) punishes the various forms of homicide, abortion and battery.

(28) Articles 209 to 212 of the Criminal Code punish violations of respect for the dead.

imposes a legal obligation to ensure the physical integrity of the victim, in other words when he commits a crime by omission[29].

D. – *Protection of the body through medical ethical norms*

In Brazil, the first regulations relating to experimentation on human beings were in ethics and were established by the National Health Council in order to ensure respect for human rights[30]. The resolution currently in force covers all research involving human subjects.

The National Health Council (NHC) also follows the guidelines of the Nuremberg Code[31], the Declaration of Helsinki[32], and the International Guidelines for Biomedical Research Involving Human Subjects[33] and the Brazilian Code of Medical Ethics of 2009[34], which are a reference for researchers and legal experts.

The Code of Medical Ethics[35] sets out the obligations and prohibitions for doctors in order to ensure the protection of the physical and psychological integrity of patients. They are required to respect the dignity of the patient, they may not commit any form of discrimination toward the patient[36], they have to obtain the patient's informed consent (or that of his/her legal representative[37]) and provide information about care and they must abide to the patient's freedom of choice concerning his/her person and well-being[38].

Doctors are further required to report any act of torture or degrading, inhumane or cruel treatment practised on their patients. Likewise, they may not be the perpetrator of such actions or an accomplice by providing the means, instruments, substances or knowledge required for such acts to take place[39].

(29) In accordance with art. 12, § 2 Crim. C.

(30) Resolution n° 01-88 of the National Health Council, which was subsequently amended by Resolution n° 466 of 10 October 2012.

(31) Nüremberg C. of 1947.

(32) Helsinki Declaration of 2013.

(33) International Ethical Guidelines for Biomedical Research, CIOMS, 2003.

(34) Code of Medical Ethics (MEC) of 13 April 2009.

(35) MEC – CFM Resolution n° 1931-2009.

(36) Art. 23 MEC.

(37) Art. 22 MEC.

(38) Art. 24 MEC.

(39) Art. 25 MEC.

They are compelled to respect the voluntary hunger strike of any physically and mentally capable person and cannot force feed this person although they must inform him of the likely complications arising from prolonged fasting and, in the event of a risk of imminent death, they must provide treatment[(40)].

A doctor may not jeopardise the physical and mental integrity of the patient by using methods that could influence the patient's personality or conscience during a police enquiry or a procedure of a similar nature[(41)]. That is the case with the use of drugs to force someone to tell the truth (drug serum[(42)]). Likewise, doctors may not hospitalise a person without his consent, except when the law stipulates otherwise. Any act that can harm the physical or mental health of a patient in the care of a doctor must be reported to the competent authority and the Regional Medical Council. Such acts can give rise to disciplinary action as well as legal proceedings.

II. – Principles of protection of the human body and compensation for physical harm

The principles of protection of the human body recognised by Brazilian law can be listed in the following order: the principle of human dignity, the principle of inviolability of the human body, the principle of the non-property rights over the body, the principle of autonomy and consent. The content of these principles are not defined by the law. Their scope is defined by the doctrine influenced by bioethical discussions concerning the risks of violations of the human body related to the practice of medicine.

A. – *Principle of the dignity of the human person*

According to one author[(43)], human dignity constitutes the quality acknowledged to be intrinsic to every human being, which makes him worthy of respect and consideration on the part of

(40) Art. 26 MEC.
(41) Art. 27 MEC.
(42) For example, the drug Pentotal, which was used during the military dictatorship in Brazil.
(43) I.W. Sarlet, "As dimensões da dignidade da pessoa humana: uma compreensão juridico-constitucional aberta e compatível com os desafios da biotecnologia", *in* I.W. Sarlet, G.S. Leite, *Direitos Fundamentais e Biotecnologia*, São Paulo, Método, 2008, p. 37.

the State and the community; it generates a set of fundamental rights and duties that protect the person against any degrading and inhumane act and guarantee the minimum living conditions required for a healthy life.

This principle was established as a fundamental principle in the Constitution, which means it takes precedence over other constitutional principles. Therefore, as a focal point in the constitutional order, the principle of human dignity will always take precedence over the other constitutional principles in the event of a conflict between them[44].

Although in theory there is no hierarchy among the constitutional principles, the principle of human dignity must necessarily give priority to any principle that best protects the dignity of the human being[45].

However, the scarcity of decisions based on the principle of dignity must be mentioned. This appears to be explained by the concern of the courts regarding applying such an abstract principle that could be used to defend dogmatic positions. It is, in fact, very difficult to reach an agreement on the content of such a principle in a multicultural society like Brazil, as demonstrated by the debate concerning certain biomedical practices (abortion, research on embryos, euthanasia, surrogacy, etc.).

B. – *Principle of inviolability of the body*

At first sight, this principle can be interpreted as a simple rule: that of not violating the body of a person. However, the principles of protection can be a matter for debate concerning their content. The complexity of the definition of the fundamental rights is particularly significant with regard to the protection of physical integrity. In fact, this right is linked to the protection of the body, as well as to the desire of the individual to have control over their body and its parts (particularly after death[46]).

(44) Art. 5, III, Federal Constit.

(45) W.O.L. Bernardo, "Princípio da dignidade da pessoa humana e o novo direito civil: breves reflexões", *Revista da Faculdade de Direito de Campos*, Ano VII, n° 8, June 2006, p. 252.

(46) The protection of physical integrity is covered in article 13 of the Civil Code.

A living person is authorised for therapeutic purposes for the benefit of others, to donate organs if it does not cause any harm to himself. In accordance with the law, it is perfectly possible to dispose of regenerative parts of the human body with no compensation, such as bone marrow, eggs, sperm, a kidney or part of the liver, in order to save the life of another person or for scientific purposes[(47)]. Any such donation must be authorised in writing.

The principle of the inviolability of the human body allows anyone to refuse to submit to a violation of one's body. This means that the respondent in a paternity suit cannot be ordered by the court to undergo a DNA test. Nevertheless, the judge can draw his own conclusions from such a refusal in making a decision on the paternity of the man in question[(48)].

It is therefore important to reflect on the significance of acts of intervention on the body. Under the terms of article 13 of the Civil Code[(49)], except in the case of a medical emergency, the law forbids any invasion of the bodily integrity or when it is "contrary to morality"[(50)].

Things are not, however, that simple. The situation of transsexuals reflects this. Previously, sex change operations performed on transsexuals were prohibited under the terms of article 13 of the Civil Code, as practices violating the integrity of the human body and human dignity. Later, these medical acts were recognised as having a therapeutic purpose and being a means to promote the protection of the physical and mental health of the patient. Finally, the Federal Medical Council authorised sex change surgery in proven cases of transsexualism[(51)]. This practice, which was originally considered to be unlawful (immoral), therefore ended up being an approved solution for gender identity disorders.

---

(47) Art. 9 L. n° 9.434-97.

(48) In accordance with art. 2 L. n° 12.004/2009. *Habeas corpus* n° 71.373- 4, Rio Grande do sul.

(49) Art. 13 Civ. C.

(50) For example, the practice of body modification or 'wannabe' (want to be) cases of people seeking the amputation of an undesirable part of their body. These goings on generate a threat to physical integrity beyond the authorised purposes. Apotemnophilia is characterised by the desire of a person to have one or more body parts amputated. G.P. Jorge Leite, *Considerações sobre personalidade, pessoa e os direitos da personalidade no direito civil brasileiro*, available at:

www.ambito-juridico.com.br/site/index.php?n_link=revista_artigos_leitura&artigo_id=1287.

(51) CFM Resolution n° 1652-2002.

An increasing number of agreements relating to experiments, tissue and organ donations and sex change surgery are allowed in accordance with the conditions defined by the law or by case law.

C. – *Principles of autonomy and consent*

The individual's autonomy over his own body, based on the bioethical principle of self-determination imposes physicians with the obligation to respect the patient's opinion, which reflects his moral, religious and ethical values. Nevertheless, the doctor must ensure that the patient has such total control over his body, his life and his mind, and that nothing can harm the dignity and integrity of the patient.

Even in life and death cases, no one can force a patient to undergo a medical treatment or a surgical operation. Therefore, in serious cases, doctors may only take action after seeking the patient's express consent. Failure to pursue this course of action will result in the doctor's civil liability being engaged. Indeed, with the exception of an emergency intervention performed in an intensive care unit in order to save the life of a seriously ill patient, the doctor can take no action without the patient's consent.

The debate about the rights of the person with regard to his/her body in the context of medicine relies on the principle of the autonomy of the patient, who alone can decide what care and treatment he will receive. The consent of a capable adult patient is required. A minor or an incapable adult must be represented by the parents or legal representative in accordance with the provisions of the Civil Code(52).

It is necessary to link respect for autonomy with informed consent as key elements in the doctor/patient relationship. This applies to any medical act, including organ transplants, the use of assisted reproductive technologies, therapeutic or cosmetic surgery or basic genetic tests. The informed consent of the patient, which expresses the patient's autonomy, is mandatory for all forms of medical intervention.

(52) Article 15 of the Civil Code stipulates the requirement for the unprompted and informed consent of the patient or his legal representative if he is a minor or incapable to authorise any surgery or medical treatment.

By virtue of this principle of autonomy, Brazil allows surrogacy, which is regulated by the Federal Medical Council(53). A woman (only one who is related to the 4th degree to the infertile couple) can decide to "lend" her womb to a couple who are unable to have children. This possibility is open to both heterosexual and homosexual couples. Payment is prohibited in all such cases in accordance with the constitutional principle of the non-commercialisation of the body.

Human research is authorised subject to consideration of the respect for the dignity and autonomy, as well as the protection of the vulnerability of the research subject. One of the means of providing the various guarantees is the free and informed consent of the research subject or, if appropriate, his legal representative. The consent must in particular be protected when given by vulnerable persons or those in the care of an authority, such as students, military personnel, or persons confined in institutions or religious centres or associations(54).

While the autonomy of the person is essential, there remains the question of its limitations in practice. As an example, the courts authorised a doctor to intervene in spite of the refusal of a patient who was a Jehovah's Witness(55). Although the patient's consent is theoretically necessary, the doctor will be required to take action in the event of a risk of death. The debates taking place in Brazil on the freedom of a person to decide whether or not to agree to a medical treatment have nevertheless resulted in changes with regard to the refusal of care(56) and the advance directives(57), at the behest of the Federal Medical Council. On the

(53) CFM Resolution n° 2013-2013.

(54) H.H. Barboza, "Responsabilidade civil em face das pesquisas em seres humanos: efeito do consentimento livre e esclarecido", *in* J. Martins-Costa and L. Ludwig-Moller, *Bioética e responsabilidade*, Rio de Janeiro, Forense, 2009, p. 221.

(55) Ação de obrigação de não fazer cumulada com pedido de antecipação de tutela n° 0014859-61.2014.402.5101, 26ª Vara Federal/RJ. (Rio de Janeiro, 2014).

(56) CFM Resolution n° 1805-2006 permits, with regard to caring for the patient and respecting his wishes, in the terminal phase of serious and incurable diseases, the limitation or withdrawal of medical treatment and procedures to prolong the life of the patient, while providing pain relief.

(57) CFM Resolution n° 1995-2012 defines the advance directives as all of the wishes previously and specifically expressed by the patient concerning the care and treatment he does or does not wish to receive when incapable of giving consent independently. The doctor must take these directives into consideration.

other hand, euthanasia and assisted suicide, as positive actions to end life, remain prohibited[58].

D. – *Principle of non-property rights over the body*

Traditionally, Brazilian law considers that, as the human body does not come under the legal category of property due to the fact that the body cannot be disposed of and as such it falls into the category of "persons". The body therefore becomes the subject of a personality right.

The Constitution expressly prohibits the commercialisation of blood and organs within the context of transplants[59] in such a way as to prohibit any form of commercialisation of the living body[60]. The parts of the body (living or dead) form an integral part of the person and therefore cannot be disposed of in return for payment[61].

When these different principles of protection come into conflict, doctrine and case law recommend finding a balance between them by referring to a principle of constitutional value, the principle of proportionality.

E. – *Compensation for violations of bodily integrity*

The notion of compensation for the damages suffered, inherent to civil liability law, has long been predominant, regarding violations of physical integrity. The preoccupation was based on the need to make reparation for the prejudice incurred. This notion has evolved within the framework of private law. Besides the view centred on the compensation, the idea of protection of the human being and certain values has come to be considered. As a result, a violation of the body can give rise not only to compensation for physical injury under the terms of civil liability rules, but also to penalties on the basis of the violation of the human being.

For example, sanctions in the case of any injury to a person who has agreed to participate in a biomedical research experiment

(58) According to article 122 of the Criminal Code.
(59) Art. 199 Constit.
(60) The law prohibits the sale of embryonic stem cells. Art. 5, § 3, L. n° 11.105-2005.
(61) Art. 199, § 4, Federal Constit. and art. 1 L. n° 9.434-97.

is no longer a civil liability issue alone for any damages linked to human research experiment but also a breach of the principles of protection of the person. Payment of damages then becomes automatic in accordance to the principle of solidarity and protection of the human person[62]. The principle of full reparation is applied.

As a result, in all areas of human life, any violation of human dignity must cease or, if this has been achieved, there has to be an automatic application of sanctions, although in practice they will often be of financial nature[63].

The person is at the centre of the legal system. It therefore appears quite clear that this person's rights are protected against threats in a systematic and unrestricted manner, in accordance with the Constitution[64].

If we really want to make these protective rights truly subjective rights, the person must not only be protected against violations, but also be able to have the full use and free disposal of these rights[65].

Conclusion

Brazilian law aims in protecting the human body while respecting the freedom of persons to dispose of their own bodies, the ultimate limit being the prohibition of any commercialisation of the body. The protection of the dignity of persons requires setting limits to the principle of autonomy. Furthermore, to provide the best possible protection for the person within the context of biomedicine, the legal protection must not only continue to cover the human body as an integrated whole, but also the individual parts of the body.

(62) H.H. Barboza, "Responsabilidade civil em face das pesquisas em seres humanos: efeito do consentimento livre e esclarecido", *in* J. Martins-Costa and L. Ludwig-Moller, *Bioética e responsabilidade*, *op. cit.*, p. 217.

(63) In accordance with art. 12 Civ. C.

(64) In particular by civil liability and criminal law actions, the *mandado de segurança*, the *mandado de injunção*, *habeas corpus* and *habeas data*.

(65) G. Tepedino, *Temas de Direito Civil*, 2nd ed., Rio de Janeiro, Renovar, 2001, p. 26.

THE BODY AND ITS PROTECTION: THE PRINCIPLES OF CHILEAN LAW

Carmen DOMINGUEZ HIDALGO

Professor of Civil Law

Director of the CU Family Centre

Pontifical Catholic University of Chile (Chile)

Today in Chile, the primary function of the law is to protect the person. This is a priority for the law; the protection of the person is binding on it. The protection of a person's physical integrity must therefore fall within the first group of rights protected by the law, so that each individual may benefit from the respect for the basic protective human rights. Not only does the law pronounce on the protection of the physical integrity of the person (I), but it also ensures it is respected (II).

I. – The recognition of the principles of protection

Protection of the body of the person is provided not only by ordinary law, by laws specific to biomedicine but also by ethical rules.

A. – *The recognition of the right to physical integrity by ordinary law*

Chilean legislation guarantees every individual, as a first fundamental right, the right to life, including that of the unborn child[1], and then, as a second fundamental guarantee, the right to physical and psychological integrity[2]. This protection of the

(1) Art. 19, n° 1, Constit. of 1980.
(2) Art. 19, n° 2, *id.*

person is based on a set of legal standards taken from different levels of the legislative hierarchy.

First of all, the Constitution covers the principles and rights formulated in international law(3). In fact, international treaties are considered to constitute part of Chilean law, although there is no consensus on how these international treaties rank in the legislative hierarchy: at the constitutional level or simply the legal level? The legal protection afforded to the physical integrity of human beings by the international treaties ratified by Chile forms part of the law, in particular that part guaranteed by the UN International Covenant on Civil and Political Rights of 1966.

Next, alongside the Constitution and the international treaties, a number of laws originating in different branches of the law protect the body of the person. First and foremost, are punishable under criminal law, the homicide and violations of the body, and, in the field of health, medical professional malpractice is an offence(4). This latter sanction is based on the importance of life and physical integrity and shows the legislator's intention to distinguish this malpractice from other forms of professional negligence.

Secondly, civil law also protects the body by means of various rules. The civil code lays down the principle that it cannot be disposed of the body by stipulating that any act whose purpose is outside of legal trading shall be incurably void: the body is one of the principal illustrations(5). The civil code also prohibits the waiver of rights of public policy(6). This means that a patient may not waive in advance his right to compensation following medical negligence or his right to be informed of the risks related to the proposed medical interventions(7).

All of these rules are general and not intended to apply only to bioethical issues. The principles of protection set out in these rules

(3) Art. 5 *id.*

(4) Medical negligence is penalised by article 491 of the Criminal Code, which stipulates that: "Any doctor, surgeon, pharmacist and midwife who causes harm to a person through negligence in the exercise of his or her profession incurs the penalties set out in the previous article."

(5) Art. 1464, n° 2 and 1682 Civ. C.

(6) According to article 12 of the Civil Code, the rights conferred by law can only be surrendered when they are of individual interest and if such a waiver is not prohibited by law.

(7) Informed consent is a right guaranteed to each patient in articles 10 and 14 of Law 20.584 of 13 April 2012, on the patient's rights and duties.

apply in cases related to biomedicine submitted to the Chilean courts.

All of these rules contain a number of major principles concerning the protection of the body.

The first is respect for the dignity of every human being. It is more than a principle as it constitutes the foundation of all of Chilean law. It is also provided for in article 1 of the Constitution. According to the doctrine, all the guarantees or fundamental rights provided by the Constitution stem from this principle[(8)].

The second principle is that of personal autonomy, which applies in a certain number of fundamental rights, particularly with regard to the body, in the right to life and physical and psychological integrity[(9)]. It can also be found in the right to respect for the honour[(10)] and privacy of the person[(11)], a right that plays an important role in terms of health[(12)].

These rights and principles apply in the field of biomedicine. In particular, they were very useful prior to the adoption of laws specific to biomedical practices[(13)] and they are still important today in this field.

---

(8) Article 19 of the Constitution of 1980 sets out the fundamental rights guaranteed to every human being.

(9) Art.19, n° 2, Constit.

(10) Article 19, n° 4, *id.* "The Constitution guarantees all human beings: 4.- The respect and protection of the privacy and honour of the person and his family."

(11) *Ibid.*

(12) Thus, article 12 of Law n° 20.584 on the rights and duties of medical staff states that the information featuring in the medical records, studies or other documents relating to medical treatment undergone by the patient must be considered as sensitive information as defined in article 2 of Law n° 19.628. This means that such information belongs to the person concerned. Article 13 of the same Law establishes as a general principle that only health professionals involved with the patient may have access to this information. See the judgments of the Concepción CA, 22 April 2014, Rol n° 1705-2014 and Concepción CA, 29 November 2012, Rol n° 1226-2012.

(13) For example, the supremacy of the right to life was used by the courts to rule on the question of the refusal of blood transfusions by Jehovah's Witnesses. As a first step, the courts used this principle to prohibit the refusal of a blood transfusion by the patient (*Revista Fallos del Mes*, n° 402, Santiago, May 1992, pp. 227-231, also Rancagua CA, confirmed by the Supreme Court on 22 August 1995 [*Revista Gaceta Jurídica*, n° 50, p. 76, Santiago, 1995], Supreme Court *Revista Gaceta Jurídica*, n° 232, Santiago, October 1999, pp. 107-108), Santiago CA, 1 December 1995, confirmed by the Supreme Court on 18 January 1996. Secondly, certain decisions allowed the possibility for a person to refuse a blood transfusion on the grounds that the principle of the right to life is only intended as protection of the person when his life is threatened by a third party and not when that person decides not to avail himself of this right to life, as no individual can be forced to invoke a right. (See Santiago CA, *Hospital San José v. J.C.*, Rol n° 806-96, , which refused a hospital the option of forcing the patient to submit to a blood transfusion. Along the same lines, Talca CA,

B. – *The recognition of the principles of protection of the body in the specific bioethics rules*

In recent years, a number of legal rules have been added to the general rules previously adopted, and these are slowly beginning to form a health law. They are embedded in the law on organ removal and transplantation, revised in 2013[(14)], in the law on scientific research on the person[(15)] and in the law on patients' rights and duties[(16)].

These laws have incorporated the major principles of protection approved by ordinary law.

Thus, the principle of respect for the dignity of the patient is pronounced and is even applied in the field of medicine. A provision of the law on patients' rights stipulates that people have the right to dignity: the health care professional must notably, at all times and in all circumstances, use appropriate and comprehensible language, act with courtesy and kindness, and ensure that the patients are addressed by name[(17)].

2011, Rol n° 60069-01. Thirdly, some judgments distinguished the refusal of care by an adult for religious reasons when his will is clearly expressed, which can be upheld, and the refusal by parents of a transfusion for their child, which must be rejected. See Iquique CA, 2002, Rol n° 39.162 and Rancagua CA, 2007, Rol n° 1034-2007, which decided that: "On the conscientious objection of the parents [...] it must not be forgotten that the latter are separate persons from their son, who is a unique and autonomous human being, and that in the case of a conflict between them, and if the life of the child is at stake, the Court has a duty, in accordance with the International Convention on the Rights of the Child, to act in the best interest of the child, in particular to ensure the lawful right for this child to receive the timely medical treatment required to continue to live." Along the same lines, the judgment of the Valdivia CA , 14 May 1999, en Vivanco, "Negativa de un menor de edad y de su familia a que este reciba una terapia desproporcionada o con pocas garantías de efectividad. Apelación de medida de protección otorgada por la jueza de familia de Valdivia. Judgment of the Valdivia Court of Appeal, 14 May 2009", in *Revista Chilena de Derecho*, 2009, vol. 36, n° 2, available at: www.scielo.cl/scielo.php?script=sci_arttext&pid=S0718343720090002000O8&lng=es&nrm=iso&tlng=es#65. When the refusal of care relates to adults, some Courts have allowed it (San Miguel CA, Rol n° 104-2008). For more details on the evolution of the case law on this subject, see A. Zuñiga, "Derechos del paciente y eutanasia en Chile", *Revista de Derecho (Valdivia)*, 2008, vol. 21, n° 2, pp. 127-128.

(14) L. n° 19.451, 10 April 1996, on organ transplants and donations amended by L. n° 20.673, 29 May 2013.

(15) L. n° 20.120, 22 September, on scientific research on humans, the genome and human cloning.

(16) L. n° 20.584, 1 October 2012, on the individuals' rights and duties relating to medical acts.

(17) Art. 5 L. n° 20.584.

Likewise, an entire chapter of the law is aimed at guaranteeing the principle of the person's autonomy in healthcare[18]. The law requires informed consent for any medical practice and guarantees that the individual has full autonomy in deciding on any medical treatment[19], organ donation or submitting to any kind of scientific research[20].

Some exceptions to this principle have nevertheless been provided for. With regard to organ removal from deceased persons, after an amendment to the law in 2013[21], any person over the age of 18 is considered to be an organ donor after death, unless he or she has, while alive, expressly stated his or her will to the contrary before a notary[22]. Furthermore, persons in the terminal phase of life cannot refuse the support measures required to maintain the life of a person[23].

The principle of respect for the honour and privacy of the person is given additional support in the medical field. All recordings, photos or films without the written consent of the patient or his legal representative are prohibited[24]. Likewise, access by third parties to medical records are very strictly controlled, as described above[25]. The confidentiality of a person's genetic information is also guaranteed[26].

C. – *The protection of the body by ethical rules*

In Chile, a number of biomedical practices are not regulated by the law, but are governed by ethical considerations. That is the case with assisted reproductive technologies (ART), which have not always been subject to a law due to the deep divisions that exist in the political sphere on issues concerning the status of the embryo, and in the absence of interest from medical establishments and hospitals for a regulatory system, as they prefer to operate with total freedom.

(18) Art. 14 et seq., § 6, L. nº 20.584.
(19) Art. 10 *id.*
(20) Art. 14 *id.*
(21) L. n° 19.451, 10 April 1996, amended by L. n° 20.673, 29 May 2013.
(22) Art. 2 *bis* L. n° 19.451.
(23) Art. 16 L. n° 20.584.
(24) Art. 5 L. n° 20.584.
(25) Art. 13 *id.*
(26) Art. 12 L. n° 20.120.

All of the questions relating to the protection of the person (and therefore the body) that arise within the framework of ART are entirely concerned with the ethics of doctors and the ethics committees of each medical institution. The protection of the person's body is therefore dependent on the ethics of doctors, and this phenomenon is all the more important as individuals who have access to these techniques do not understand the legal issues that arise (in particular the question of who can access ART, which techniques can be used, the anonymity of the donor, etc.).

II. – Respect for the principles of protection of the body

In order to ensure the effectiveness of all of the principles of protection, Chilean law provides for a number of actions to ensure that they are respected.

The first is a protective action, similar to *habeas corpus* in Chilean legislation, which enables anyone, when certain fundamental guarantees covered by the Constitution are being threatened, to request their regional Court of Appeal to order measures to guarantee these rights[(27)]. This is therefore an action to prevent the imminent violation of a fundamental right by means of a simple and very fast procedure.

This action is undertaken to ensure respect for physical integrity in diverse situations where a person's life is in danger: hunger strikes[(28)], the refusal of patients to receive blood transfusions[(29)],

(27) The protective action, similar to the French proceedings, is laid down in article 20 of the Constitution. The procedure has been established by the Supreme Court.

(28) In its judgment of 9 August 1984, the Santiago Court of Appeal ordered the end of a hunger strike of a group of students protesting against the expulsion from the University of another group of students. Santiago CA, 9 August 1984, *Revista de Derecho y Jurisprudencia*, vol. 12, 1985, p. 148. See commentary by E. Soto Kloss, in the *Revista de Derecho y Jurisprudencia*, vol. 12, 1985, p. 150 and *id.*, "Right to life and access to protection", *Puntolex*, Santiago, Chile, 2010-04-28, 14:58:42.783525-04. More recently, the action of protection exercised by the local authority of the los Legas Region on behalf of two secondary school pupils, aged 16 and 19, who were on hunger strike was approved by the Puerto Montt Court of Appeal. The Court ordered the Director of the Health Service of the Province where the children lived to take all necessary measures to ensure their right to life, including the use of public force if necessary. Puerto Montt CA, 9 September 2011, Rol n° 215-2011.

(29) The Rancagua Court of Appeal ordered the doctors lodging the appeal to carry out a blood transfusion on a 20-year-old man who had refused on the grounds of being a Jehovah's Witness, Rancagua CA,, 22 August 1995, *Revista de Derecho y Jurisprudencia*, t. XCII, nº 3, September- December 1995, section 5. Along the same lines, in the case of a newborn baby, Concepción CA, 5 December 2011, Rol n° 1156-2011. *Contra*, the Antofagasta Court of Appeal rejected the protective action on the grounds that the freedom of conscience and beliefs

the commercialisation or delivery of the morning after pill[30], the refusal of essential care[31].

The second approach is the criminal action leading to the penalising of a violation of or threat to life and physical integrity, in particular that set out in article 491 of the Criminal Code (the offence of medical negligence). This punishment has a significant deterrent effect in practice.

The third approach is civil action: claims for damages before a civil court that provides compensation for any material or moral damage caused to the patient[32]. In fact, as Spanish doctrine has certainly observed, this liability is a "general guarantee of protection of the person"[33], as it only requires the person to be affected in any way, financially or in these extra-pecuniary rights, for the liability of the perpetrator of the prejudice to be engaged. This reasoning is also the basis of medical civil liability which, since the 20th century, has given a patient who has suffered a prejudice caused by the negligence of a doctor the right to compensation. Before 1994, Chilean case law considered that medical liability was non-contractual. After a Supreme Court judgment in 1994[34] that opened the way to compensation for mental suffering, medical

guaranteed by article 19, n° 6, of the Constitution and the personal freedom guaranteed by article 19, n° 7, took priority over the right to life. In this case, a woman, a Jehovah's Witness, had stated before a notary before becoming ill her will to refuse a blood transfusion in the event of illness. For the Court, this constituted the exercise of her personal freedom and conscience. Antofagasta CA, 3 October 2008, Rol n° 557-2008.

(30) In its judgment of 30 August 2001, the Supreme Court upheld the protective action exercised by a group of people to have the supply of the morning after pill declared illegal, and ordered that the sale of this pill be prohibited. The Court considered that the possible effect of interrupting the embedding of the embryo violated the right to life guaranteed by article 19, n° 1, of the Constitution. Cass., Rol n° 2186-2001.

(31) Article 14 of Law n° 20.584, on the individuals' rights and duties relating to medical acts, grants any individual the right to refuse care, subject to certain limits: such a refusal must not give rise to an accelerated death, euthanasia or assisted suicide and, in accordance with article 16, while the terminally ill person can refuse any treatment intended to prolong life by artificial means, he or she cannot refuse measures to maintain life.

(32) As with most civil rights codified in the 19th century, compensation for prejudices has, in Chilean law, two founding principles: that of tortious or non-contractual liability, which orders compensation for any prejudice caused under the terms of articles 2314 and 2329 of the Civil Code, and that of contractual liability provided for in articles 1556, 1557 and 1558 of the Civil Code.

(33) J.J. López Jacoiste, *Transformaciones y paradojas de la responsabilidad extracontractual*, Madrid, Real Academia de Jurisprudencia y Legislación, 1994, pp. 17-30.

(34) In a judgment of 20 October 1994, the Supreme Court approved for the first time compensation for moral damage in a contractual matter.

liability was recognised as being contractual(35). This case law has subsequently been confirmed on a number of occasions(36).

Conclusion

Chilean law recognises, due to a substantial legal arsenal, not only principles for the protection of the person, but also protective ideas or concepts. Nevertheless, the rarity with which they are referred to in legal proceedings means that it is not always possible to clearly identify these principles of protection of the body. Perhaps things will change in the future?

(35) On the evolution of moral damage in Chile and in comparative law and on contractual moral damage, C. Dominguez Hidalgo, *El daño moral*, t. I and II, Editorial Jurídica de Chile, Santiago, 2003; "La reparación del daño moral derivado del contrato en el derecho civil chileno: realidad y límites", *Cuadernos de Análisis Jurídico*, Universidad Diego Portales, Colección de Derecho Privado, Temas de contratos, n° 3, 2006, pp. 227-244.

(36) Cass., 11 May 2001: The Court once again ordered compensation for the moral damage caused to the victim following a breach of the contract. In this case, a person had been diagnosed as being HIV positive, whereas two years later, this diagnosis was shown to be incorrect. The victim claimed damages from the laboratory for moral damage, and the Supreme Court approved this claim.

PRINCIPLES OF PROTECTION OF THE BODY IN JAPAN: PRINCIPLES RELATED TO THE TRADITIONAL BELIEF IN A UNITY OF THE BODY AND THE SPIRIT

Ryuichi IDA

Graduate school of global studies Doshisha University, Kyoto (Japan)

Before the vast edifice of the principles of protection of the human body of European origin, the Asian peoples, and in particular the Japanese, seem a little uneasy, as the spiritual tradition places importance not only on the body, but also on the soul. The body and the soul are inseparable. As a result, referring only to the body and not to the soul or the spirit in a discussion about bioethical issues would not give an accurate overview of the principles of protection adopted in Japan. That is why the analysis of these principles will be presented alongside the consideration of the particular relationships that the body and the soul maintain in Japan.

The principles of protection of the body do not in any way ignore the importance of the soul, and this observation must always be taken into account in the Asian, and particularly Japanese, context. When these principles are put under the microscope, it is important to be able to interpret them with the spiritual element of the context in mind.

I. – Japan's regulatory framework

A. – *The biomedical standards concerned*

Biomedical "law" in Japan is based on binding legal rules and non-bonding ethical standards, knowing that most biomedical standards are non-binding or ethical. In Japan, the legal standards for biomedicine can be classified into three categories: the medical rules (in the narrow sense of the term; *i.e.* standards for clinical application), the rules concerning biomedical research, and the pharmaceutical standards. The first category is composed of two major laws, one relating to doctors, which determines the authorisations, examinations and obligations[(1)], and one governing medicine, which is principally aimed at healthcare facilities[(2)]. In addition to these, particular laws relating to specific areas such as organ transplants[(3)] or epidemics[(4)] have been adopted. The second category of rules, which is related to biomedical research, is made up of non-binding guidelines. There is no legislation covering research, except in a few specific areas such as research on human cloning[(5)] or regenerative medicine[(6)]. The third category contains the "Law on pharmaceutical matters"[(7)] which has a general scope and is explained in the ministerial regulations ("ICH-GCP").

Thus, the principles of protection of the human body stem either from substantive law or from non-binding ethical standards[(8)]. However, it is important to explain that the majority are not defined in the legislation, rules and guidelines specific to the field of medicine, but more broadly cover the field of the life and health sciences and technologies (research and treatment).

B. – *Traditional Japanese thinking*

According to Japanese thinking, the body and the soul are inseparable.

In Japan, the principles of protection of the human body stem from the respect for the human being and the human rights laid down in the Constitution. Article 13 of the Constitution states that "All citizens must be respected as individuals. Their rights to life, freedom and the pursuit of happiness, provided that does not harm the public well-being, remain the supreme concern of the legislature and other government officials."

(1) L. of 30 July 1948 on doctors.
(2) L. of 30 July 1948 on medical treatments.
(3) L. of 16 September 1997 on organ transplants.
(4) L. of 2 October 1998 on the prevention of epidemics and to patients of epidemics.
(5) L. of 6 February 2000 on the regulation of human cloning technologies.
(6) L. of 27 November 2013 on regenerative medicine.
(7) L. of 10 August 1960 on quality insurance, the effectiveness and safety of pharmaceutical products and medical devices, revised on 27 November 2013.
(8) In Japan, medical law includes both hard law and soft law. See S. HAYAKAWA.

With violations of the human body being regarded in Japan as the negation of the human being, we might deduce that the principles of protection of the human body implicitly stem from the Constitution. As the protection of the human body therefore has a constitutional value, it is not necessary to develop specific legislation.

Likewise, Japan does not have general legislation on the protection of the rights of the human being, since human rights are protected by the article 11 of the Constitution[(9)].

While the principles of protection of the human body are not subject to any specific pronouncement in the law, they have a specifically Japanese connotation. It is therefore interesting to research the origins of these principles and the reasons why they do not appear explicitly in the Japanese biomedical legal system.

The highest value is awarded to the human body in the traditional culture of Japan. The respect of the Japanese for certain acts practised on the body illustrates this. In Japanese tradition, suicide by "Harakiri" is a supreme act of samurai dignity. Likewise, at the end of World War II, the suicide of soldiers to avoid capture was considered to be an honourable act. The so-called "Kamikaze" act (suicide attacks by fighter planes carried out by young pilots) is another example of this. The Japanese Criminal Code includes the death penalty, which is considered by the Japanese to be an honourable way for the accused to pay for the crime he has committed. For example, if he has committed murder, the perpetrator must pay by this ultimate violation of his body, just as he violated the life of another person.

Of course, these examples have nothing to do with biomedicine. Nevertheless, faced with the silence of Japanese legislation and guidelines on the meaning of the "protection of the human body", they give an understanding of how the Japanese perception of respect for the body (and therefore, ultimately, for life) can differ from that of Westerners.

In Japan, the body is linked to the soul. To be persuaded of this, it is worth exploring another example, also far from the field of biomedicine. It relates to a Japan Airlines plane which crashed in the

(9) Art. 11: The people shall not be prevented from enjoying any of the fundamental human rights. These fundamental human rights guaranteed to the people by this Constitution shall be conferred upon the people of this and future generations as eternal and inviolate rights.

Mount Osutaka area in August 1985. Only four passengers survived. Following this crash, the families and friends of the passengers carried out searches in an attempt to recover the bodies, or parts of the bodies, of their relatives or friends. This search continued over a number of years. This type of reaction is typical of the Japanese attachment to the body of the deceased. There is a popular belief that the deceased person cannot "rest in the peace of Buddha" if the body cannot be recovered, or if the body is in imperfect condition. This shows that the body and the soul are inseparable, that the worth of the human body is as important as that of the soul and the spirit. It is therefore quite natural for the Japanese to recognise the principles of protection of the human body.

Nevertheless, certain practices or beliefs could put this idea of protection of the body into perspective. Buddhism approves the act of self-sacrifice, as in the cases of "Harakiri" among the Samurai or in the lesson of the Buddhist priest who allowed himself to be eaten by a female tiger tempted to eat her own offspring in a time of famine. These examples could lead one to think, at least in the first instance, that the human body has little value. That is far from the case. On the contrary, it is crucial to understand that in these cases, the value of the human body is so high that the sacrifice of the body represents a gesture of extreme respect for the other.

II. – System for the protection of persons

A. – *Legislation*

The principles of protection of the human body are not specifically provided for in the different standards governing medicine, and they never appear as such in Japanese biomedical law, except in one specific legislation concerning the protection of the mother's body[10].

However, this protection of the human body seems to stem from a number of general legal instruments. Firstly, it appears to be based on certain principles contained in the Constitution: the prohibition of slavery[11], the right to a minimum level of material

(10) Mother's Body Protection Act of 2006 (previously "Eugenic Protection Law of 1948"), which governs sterilisation and abortion in order to protect the life and health of the mother.

(11) Art. 18: No person shall be held in bondage of any kind. Involuntary servitude, except as punishment for crime, is prohibited. (English translation of the Japanese Constitution

and cultural life(12), the prohibition of exploitation through work(13), the prohibition of torture and cruel punishment(14).

Furthermore, the Criminal Code sanctions a series of offences against people by imposing corporal punishments, including the death penalty(15). Crimes against people, such as murder and assault, are two examples of this. The law also provides protection for the corpse. The dissection and preservation of the corpse must be carried out with the respect due to a (dead) human being, subject to punishment under criminal law(16). This means that the human body, even after death, has a value as it does during the lifetime of a person. However, the most explicit legislation on the protection of the body is the *Mother's Body Protection Act*. The aim of this law is to protect the life and health of the mother(17). It states that a doctor may perform an abortion if the continuation of the pregnancy or childbirth risks causing serious harm to the health of the mother for physical or financial reasons(18).

Finally, the Civil Code provides for compensation for physical injuries(19).

Although legislation relating to medicine is rarely aimed at the medical acts and the violations of the human body that can result from them(20), that which governs biomedical research on

is taken from the Cabinet Office website, see http://japan.kantei.go.jp/constitution_and_government_of_japan/constitution_e.html. The Japanese original is the official source document.

(12) Art. 25: All people shall have the right to maintain the minimum standards of wholesome and cultured living.

(13) Art. 27: All people shall have the right and the obligation to work. Standards for wages, hours, rest and other working conditions shall be fixed by law. Children shall not be exploited.

(14) Art. 36: The infliction of torture by any public officer and cruel punishments are absolutely forbidden.

(15) Art. 199 Crim. C.: A person who kills another shall be punished by the death penalty, life imprisonment or imprisonment for a period of not less than 5 years.

(16) Art. 23 L. of 10 June 1949 on the dissection and preservation of the corpse.

(17) Art. 1 of the Mother's Body Protection Act of 13 July 1948.

(18) Art. 14 *id.*

(19) Art. 710 Civ. C..

(20) The Law relating to doctors of 30 July 1948 (revised on13 June 2014) determines the qualification of the title of doctor of medicine. The Law relating to medical services of 30 July 1948 (revised on 27 June 2014) mainly concerns the conditions required of hospitals and clinics. The Law concerning pharmaceutical matters of 10 October 1960 (completely revised on 27 November 2014 and now called the "Law relating to the quality insurance, effectiveness and safety of pharmaceutical products and medical instruments") regulates the procedures and the administration of pharmaceutical products. In addition there are the regulations for best clinical practices (ICH-GCP). Other legal instruments, however, also regulate the biomedical field.

the human body or a part of it, particularly the guidelines, has the clear objective of guaranteeing the safety of those persons who agree to be subject to such research, particularly when they are ill. This implies that providing such safety results in a guarantee of the protection of the human body and constitutes the corollary to the principles of protection of the body. The recent legislation on regenerative medicine(21), which states in article 1 that its objective is to guarantee the safety of people who agree to undergo trials and that it takes account of bioethical considerations, is an example of the recent trend to refer to "bioethical" principles in the legislation.

B. – *Case law*

It is very rare for the courts to refer expressly to the protection of the human body. However, the elements protecting the person in general(22), such as dignity, autonomy, consent and non-commercialisation, are used by the courts to provide protection for the body. In particular, the protection is invoked when the human being (and consequently his body) is the subject of various prejudices. As the human body has a supreme value in Japanese tradition, the principle of protection constitutes a peremptory rule (*a jus cogens*) that remains non-specific to allow judges the discretion to interpret it and apply it to practical cases.

III. – Principles guaranteeing the real protection of the human body

A. – *Human dignity*

Dignity is provided for in the Japanese Constitution(23). This concerns the dignity of individuals and not human dignity in terms of the dignity that exists in each person.

The concept of human dignity has been the subject of discussions concerning the prohibition of reproductive cloning, particularly

(21) The Law, adopted in 2013 and which came into force in November 2014, called the "Act on the safety of regenerative medicine". This law on the cellular therapies governs, in particular, trials using embryonic, adult or iPS stem cells. The therapy called regenerative medicine, above all that using iPS stem cells, is currently allowed only in clinical trials and not yet in medical treatment and is therefore not covered by social security.

(22) See *infra*.

(23) Art. 13 Constit.

within the National Bioethics Committee, and an analysis of the opinion of this National Committee shows that the protection of the body is linked to the principle of dignity. Indeed, the Committee shows that three consequences of reproductive cloning (the use of someone's body, offending the identity of the person[24] and undermining the concepts of family and humanity) constitute a violation of human dignity. Therefore, the censure of the use of someone's body, the basis of the violation of dignity, leads to the provision of protection for the human body. In fact, the Committee censures the cloning that results not only in the use of the female body (the uterus) used to give birth to the human clone, but also of the body of the clone who, once born, may be considered to be a source of organs or body parts that can be used to treat the cloned person. Thus, this example shows that the Committee is basing its opinion on a principle of interdiction of the use of someone's body, *i.e.* as a principle of protection of the body.

B. – *Autonomy*

The term "autonomy" is often used in civil law, particularly with regard to contract law. The validity of a contract depends in theory on the consent of the parties to the act; a consent that is testament to a principle of autonomy of the person. In the field of biomedicine, autonomy constitutes the right of the person to self-determination. That is why the principle of informed consent is at the heart of autonomy.

The protection of the body is therefore included in this general concept of autonomy. Nevertheless, autonomy does not mean that one has complete freedom of decision with regard to one's body or a part of it.

C. – *Consent*

Consent is required by the *Medical Service Law*: the doctor must make every effort to provide suitable explanations and ensure

(24) Offending the identity of the person, as the person born as a result of a cloning operation would be the identical reproduction of another person (the person who provided the nucleus of one of his cells), whereas the individual identity guarantees the individual a unique existence in the world.

that the patient understands[25]. This instrument lays down the obligation to obtain the informed consent of the patient. As the terms of the law are very general and the instruments lack precise instructions, nothing specific is imposed on the doctor.

The notion of informed consent is defined in the non-binding guidelines on biomedical research[26]. As these standards tend to be practical, they provide explanations about the doctor's obligation to provide information. For example, the Ethical Guidelines for Medical and Health Research Involving Human Subjects list in twenty one sub-paragraphs the elements to be presented to the person consenting to be a research subject, including the objectives and significance of the research, the method and time, the possibility of compensation in case of harm caused by the research, the clinical researcher's investigative options and information about the intervention of an ethics committee[27].

However, it is important to note that in law, informed consent is not regarded as a patient's right. It is consequently difficult to conclude that it guarantees the protection of the human body. It is therefore important that the protection of the body of the patient or research subject is ensured within the framework of patients' rights or human rights in general. If this is not done, the protection of the person provided by the consent rule remains limited.

IV. – Protection of the body within the framework of specific medical practices

A. – *Organ transplants*

The Organ Transplant Law of 16 July 1997 (revised on 17 July 2009) stipulates that no one may receive, request or promise a financial contribution for the donation of an organ[28]. This instrument sets down a principle of non-commercialisation of

(25) Art. 1.4 L. of 30 July 1948 on the Medical Service, revised in 2014.

(26) These are Guidelines on clinical and epidemiological research, research on embryonic stem cells, clinical research using stem cells, research concerning the analysis of the human genome and genes, research on certain types of embryo and medical research on human subjects.

(27) Ethical Guidelines for Medical and Health Research Involving Human Subjects of 22 December 2014. (See Chap. 5, Sect. 12, Subpara. 3) English translation, available at: http://www.lifescience.mext.go.jp/files/pdf/n1500_01.pdf.

(28) Art. 11 of the Law.

organs, a principle that guarantees the protection of the human body.

B. – *Use of the corpse*

The Law of 10 June 1949 states that anyone responsible for the dissection or storage of a corpse or part of a corpse must ensure that the body is treated with respect[29]. In this way the law ensures that the body is protected after death.

C. – *Abortion*

The Mother's Body Protection Act of 13 July 1948 (revised in 1988) authorises abortion in two cases: rape and serious risk to the health of the *mother's body*[30]. This instrument is the only specific legislation that refers literally to the principle of protection of the body.

D. – *Biomedical research*

Biomedical research is regulated, not by legislation or regulations, but by legally non-binding guidelines. There are no provisions relating to the protection of the human body. The body and body parts may be the subject of research. Nevertheless, protection is provided in practice by the requirement for informed consent. Furthermore, the fact that there must be no payment associated with the research is clearly stipulated in all the guidelines concerning the different types of authorised biomedical research. A principle of cost-free stems from this.

Conclusion

This analysis of Japanese law and guidelines shows that while the protection of the body is not guaranteed by specific principles pronounced in the field of biomedicine, it is provided in practice by the general principle of protection of the person. While my own experience in the preparation of various specific legislations

(29) Article 20 *id.*
(30) Article 14 *id.*. Literal translation of the article.

and ministerial guidelines is testimony to the fact that there has never been an explicit reference to the protection of the human body, it is undoubtedly contained in Japanese biomedical law: it is, however, unwritten and implied. It is in fact provided by the general principles of protection of the person contained in the legal and bioethical fields. The reasons behind this lack of the clear and unequivocal development of the protection of the human body are principally that in Japan the body and the soul are inseparable, and it is therefore not necessary to emphasise the importance of the human body, as this derives from the importance of the soul, and therefore of the person himself.

Although there is no question that protection of the body exists in Japan, its scope varies from one field of activity to another. Indeed, the protection of the human body can sometimes come into conflict with other principles, such as the principle of autonomy of the person: the freedom to decide what happens to one's body can lead to violations of the body and be at variance with the protection of the body. However, Japan is not the only country to have difficulty reconciling values...

THE PROTECTION OF THE HUMAN BODY IN JAPAN: THE LACK OF A COMPREHENSIVE LEGAL SYSTEM OF PROTECTION

Shinichiro HAYAKAWA

Professor at the University of Tokyo (Japan)

Japan has no specific law governing the protection of the human body. As a result, such protection is not provided by a comprehensive and coherent legal system, but by applying here and there rules found in the prevailing norms.

I. – Rules for protection of the body

There are two categories of rules governing the protection of the body: "hard law" and "soft law"(1).

A. – *Legal rules*

A number of different rules included in the Constitution, the Civil Code, the Criminal Code and laws relating to specific fields of interest, cover the protection of the human body.

The Japanese Constitution, in article 13(2), endows all citizens with the right to the pursuit of happiness. Although this article does not refer specifically to the body, it constitutes the basis of the protection of the body.

The Japanese Civil Code contains some articles that can be used to guarantee the protection of the body.

(1) Hard law is a rule officially established by the public authority, which is legally binding for all citizens. Soft law, on the other hand, is a rule that that is not legally binding.

(2) Article 13 of the Constitution stipulates that: "All of the people shall be respected as individuals. Their right to life, liberty, and the pursuit of happiness shall, to the extent that it does not interfere with the public welfare, be the supreme consideration in legislation and in other governmental affairs."

First, in accordance with the rules relating to offences[3], a violation of the body of a third party can constitute an offence (an unlawful act) leading to compensatory damages. Second, a transaction made in regard to a body part, for example a sales agreement for an organ, would be punishable under the terms of article 90 of the Civil Code[4], which states that agreements and contracts contrary to public order or morality are null and void. The wording of this article therefore pertains to the protection of the body.

The Criminal Code, by its very nature, contains rules that ensure the protection of the body, particularly article 204, which sanctions assault and battery[5] and article 190, which refers to violations of the body[6].

Alongside these rules of general law, there are some laws specific to certain biomedical practices that provide some protection. Under the terms of the law of 1997 on organ transplants, the removal of organs from the body of a deceased person is only possible with the prior consent of the donor given during his lifetime and provided that it is not vetoed by the family, or with the consent of the family, assuming there is no prior veto by the donor[7]. Likewise, the sale of organs is liable to criminal penalties[8].

Other specific laws, such as the law of 1949 on autopsies and the preservation of corpses[9] and the law of 2000 on the regulation of human cloning, contribute to protecting the human body.

(3) Article 709 of the Civil Code states that: "Anyone who, deliberately or by negligence, violates a right or a legally protected interest of another person shall be liable to compensate for any resulting damage." Article 710 of the Civil Code states that: "Anyone who, by virtue of the provisions of the previous article, is required to pay damages with interest, is also required to make reparation for any non-financial damage he has caused, irrespective of whether the violation inflicted was of the body, liberty or reputation of a person, or if it was related to his property rights."

(4) Article 90 states that: "Legal acts whose object is to cause a violation of public order or morality are null and void."

(5) Article 204 of the Criminal Code stipulates, in the case of assault and battery, a maximum sentence of fifteen years' imprisonment and a fine of 500,000 Yen.

(6) Article 190 of the Criminal Code stipulates a maximum sentence of three years' imprisonment for a violation of a corpse.

(7) Article 6 of the law.

(8) Article 11 *id.*

(9) With the most recent amendment in 2012.

B. – *Soft law*

In the absence of a widespread system of hard law rules in Japan, soft law plays an extremely important role with regard to the protection of the human body.

Soft law is made of so called "Guidelines" drawn up by the government and of "Opinions" from professional bodies. Among these Guidelines for the protection of the body, two are particularly important: the ethical guidelines for clinical research[(10)] and the ethical guidelines for epidemiological research[(11)]. With regard to the Opinions of the professional bodies, those of the JSOG (Japan Society of Obstetrics and Gynaecology) on the use of assisted reproductive technologies[(12)] ensure some kind of protection for the female body.

II. – Main characteristics of the protection of the body

Two characteristics of the system for the protection of the body in Japan deserve to be highlighted: the lack of any coherent structure of principles on this topic and the primacy of the principle of self-determination.

There is no comprehensive and coherent declaration of the principles of protection of the human body due to the lack of any specific law or code covering the protection of the body. This, in turn reflects the failure of any in-depth national debate on the subject of such protection. The lack of specific legislation is all the more significant as the prevailing soft law guidelines, play a very important role in Japan; such rules have been prepared and produced by a variety of different actors in the field, both public and private, with no real coordination. This has resulted in a failure to create a coherent system for the protection of the human body.

The tendency to give an absolute priority to the principle of self-determination is the result of rules that are specific to certain medical practices and to the "Guidelines" and the "Opinions" of

(10) Pronounced in 2003 by the Ministry of Health, Labour and Welfare, available at: http://www.mhlw.go.jp/general/seido/kousei/i-kenkyu/rinri/0504sisin.html (in Japanese).

(11) Pronounced in 2002 jointly by the Ministry of Health, Labour and Welfare and the Ministry of Education, Culture, Sports and Technology, see www.niph.go.jp/wadai/ekigakurinri/index.htm (in Japanese).

(12) See: www.jsog.or.jp/ethic/index.html (in Japanese).

professional bodies. Indeed, in the absence of a well thought-out legal system for the protection of the human body, the medical and ethical authorities responsible for developing "para-legal" rules have met no resistance in imposing their tendency to prioritize the principle of self-determination. This chapter appears to show, however, that a comprehensive study and debate concerning the protection of the body in Japan is strongly needed.

Overview

THE PRINCIPLES OF PROTECTION OF THE BODY, A SHARED REFERENCE WITH MULTIPLE PERSPECTIVES

Brigitte FEUILLET-LIGER

Professor at the Rennes Faculty of Law (IODE, UMR 6262)

Member of the Institut Universitaire de France

Addressing the question of the principles of protection of the human body in seventeen countries around the world[1] is not only the focus of a comparative law study, but also provides the opportunity to understand the cultures of these countries. Indeed, behind these principles of protection lie the different views that the States have of the human being, and more specifically the body. In fact, the body is a reality that changes from one society to another and the politics around it adapts to the philosophy of the moment. As Pierre Lecoz demonstrates, the political corollary of the theological dogmatism of the Middle Ages was the criminalisation of the uses of the human body (prostitution, homosexual relations) and, from the time of Descartes, a long journey towards the autonomy of the individual (and therefore of the body) has been under way[2].

Even now, philosophy still provides us with different perceptions of the body. The deontological moral advocated by Kant considers that the human body cannot only be "means to some other need"[3]. Alongside this, the utilitarian theory[4], based on the greatest happiness of the largest number, considers government intervention as necessary only when the acts violate the bodily integrity of others, granting individuals broad control over what happens to

(1) Germany, Belgium, Brazil, Canada, Chile, Egypt, Spain, France, Greece, Hungary, Italy, Japan, United Kingdom, Switzerland, Tunisia, Turkey, USA.

(2) See *supra*, P. Lecoz, p. 33.

(3) Kant, *Fondements de la métaphysique des mœurs*, trans. Delbos, ed. Electronique, 1785, see http///perso.club-internet.fr/folliot.philippe/fondem.htm, 2006, p. 39.

(4) J.S. Mill, *L'utilitarisme*, Champs classiques, trans. G. Tanesse, 1988.

their body. Finally, the more recent *libertarian*[(5)] movement, which sets moral limits purely on the basis of not causing harm to others, advocates the unlimited ownership of the human body[(6)]. There are significant differences between these three approaches, and consequently the perceptions of different governments also vary considerably.

However, the study carried out as part of this work highlights a kind of unity transcending cultural differences: some principles of protection of the human body are recognised everywhere, although this simple statement covers a number of different realities. Respect for physical integrity, under a variety of names, is shared by all of the countries studied. Indeed, in all of these countries, if a person suffers a violation of his body, he can have the perpetrator punished, although the scope of this protection can vary from one country to the other, depending on the context in which the violation is carried out[(7)]. Furthermore, this general protection can be applied with regard to biomedicine. The notion of principles of protection is generally recognised everywhere (I). Indeed, in numerous countries, the protection of the body is based on a variety of principles ranging from respect for physical integrity, human dignity, and autonomy or the non-commercialisation and non-property rights over the body. However, our study reveals the disparate nature of these principles (II).

I. – THE WIDESPREAD RECOGNITION OF THE PRINCIPLES OF PROTECTION OF THE BODY

In all the countries studied, the body benefits from protection (A) guaranteed by principles (B).

(5) Not to be confused with the "*mouvement libertaire*" – the right wing of the libertarians often referred to as anarchists – which can still be found today, but also existed in ancient times. See *supra*, P. LECOZ.

(6) See *supra*, P. LECOZ, p. 47.

(7) For example, in some countries, violations of the body (blood tests, genetic tests, etc.) ordered by a judge can be permitted. Likewise, with regard to medicine, the powers of a doctor over a person's body vary from one country to another.

A. – *Widespread protection of the human body*

While reading through this work emphasises a shared recognition of the notion of protection of the body, it also provides an opportunity to define this statement. In most of the countries, the protection of the body is not specific, but follows the individual's protection. *A priori*, this is not a surprise since the body is, indeed, the individual's. It is a person's 'mortal coil'. Dean Carbonnier referred to the "substratum of the individual"(8) and Dean Cornu of a "reality that exists before the mind becomes strong and remains even after the mind has deteriorated"(9). Roman law considered human unity, avoiding any differentiation between the body as a separate object from the person thus avoiding the issue of the human body by hiding behind an abstraction: the legal person(10). Person was not a person without the body.

Most international legal instruments also refer only to the person. The European Convention on Human Rights of 4 November 1950 pronounces rights and freedoms without specifically referring to the body. That is also the case with the European Convention on Biomedicine of 4th April 1997(11). The explanation for this lies in the fact that the first of these conventions is intended to protect the person in its relationships with the state, and the second is aimed at the human being as both an individual and a member of the human race. The individual, rather than the body, is therefore given precedence, and there is no direct reference to respect for physical integrity(12). For that matter, the few international instruments relating to the body consider the integrity of the individual(13).

Analysis of the different positive rights shows that, in all these States, a principle of respect for the physical integrity of

(8) J. Carbonnier, *Droit civil, les personnes*, Paris, PUF, 2004, p. 19.

(9) G. Cornu, *Droit civil. Les personnes*, 13th ed., Paris, ed. Montchrestien, p. 29.

(10) O. Thozan, "La réification du corps humain en droit civil français", *in* O. Thozan (ed.), *Jure corporis ou la réification du corps humain*, Les Cahiers de droit de la santé du Sud-Est, n° 2, PUAM, 2004, p. 12.

(11) This document is important internationally as, under the terms of article 34, this Convention can be signed by States that are not members of the Council of Europe.

(12) Nevertheless, a number of the rights and freedoms contained in these conventions, such as the right to life, the prohibition of inhumane and degrading treatment and slavery, and the right to freedom, can in practice guarantee the protection of the body. See *infra*.

(13) Art 3 of the Charter of Fundamental Rights of the European Union of 18 December 2000, the European Declaration in Bioethics of 19 October 2005 (which is only aimed at the integrity of vulnerable persons).

the individual[14] is recognised. The protection of the body is one element of the protection of the individual. In practice, it follows the ordinary law of those States, in other words, the civil law and criminal law governing offences against people[15]. In civil law, the foundations are different: protection can be based on the "law of persons" through a theory of personality rights[16], or simply on civil liability law providing recourse to legal action to seek compensation for any harm sustained[17]. Nevertheless, even in those countries that have not adopted the civil law approach of the personality rights, these prerogatives are often recognised as fundamental rights in constitutional texts[18] or are laid down by the courts.

Only France has opted, in 1994, for a specific set of legislation concerning the protection of the body[19] by means of two laws: one general law laying down the principles of protection[20], and the other applying them to a number of biomedical practices[21].

Prior to this reform, the body was absent from the French Civil Code[22]. The Napoleonic Code had situated the essence of the individual in the will rather than in the body. The purpose of

(14) Some countries use the reference to "bodily integrity" (Hungary, Switzerland). H. Gaumont-Prat, in *Lamy, Droit de la santé*, étude 160, "Droits fondamentaux de la personne : le droit à la vie, à l'intégrité corporelle", étude 160-7, "Respect de l'intégrité physique de la personne". B. Feuillet, "Droit au respect de l'intégrité physique" *in* D. Chagnollaud and G. Drago (eds.), *Dictionnaire des droits fondamentaux*, D, 2006, p.497. On the content of this right, see *infra*.

(15) Murder, assault and battery, violence, sexual assault, illegal confinement, etc. In Germany, see Art. 211, 229 and 216 Crim. C., and Art. 823 Civ. C.

(16) Belgium, Brazil, Chile, Spain, France, Egypt, Greece, Hungary, Italy, Quebec, Switzerland, Tunisia, Turkey. These personality rights are usually upheld by the courts.

(17) This is the case in most Anglo-Saxon countries (see *supra*, M. Garrison, p. 293), and Canada (except in Quebec). In English law, the right to physical integrity is recognised through the concept of consent (see *supra*, T. Callus, p. 209). In Japan, these rights are not included in the law but are recognised in practice (See above R. Ida, p. 349).

(18) See *supra*, D. Goubau.

(19) Italy has also passed a number of laws providing this protection of the body, although these instruments have not introduced general provisions on the protection of the body into the Civil Code. See *supra*, C.M. Mazzoni, p. 185. As for the other countries, they have not developed an autonomous protection of the body, although a number of them have introduced measures protecting the body in laws specific to certain medical practices.

(20) L. n° 94-653, 29 July 1994, on respect for the human body brought the body into the Civil Code by creating a new chapter on "Respect for the human body" (art. 16 to 16-9 Civ. C.). Y. Buffelan-Lanore and V. Larribau-Terneyre, *Droit civil. Introduction. Biens. Personnes. Famille*, 18th ed., Sirey, 2013, p. 338.

(21) L. n° 94-654, 29 July 1994, on the donation and use of elements and products of the human body, medically assisted procreation and prenatal diagnosis.

(22) J.M. Auby, "L'autorité judiciaire gardienne du corps humain ?", in *L'unité du droit. Mélanges en l'honneur de Roland Drago*, Economica, 1996, p. 353.

providing the body with protection in a specific legal instrument was not apparent. Case law and legal doctrine were able to compensate for this shortcoming. The protection of physical integrity was provided by means of ordinary law, and principally criminal law[23]. In addition, legal provisions on procedures which individuals undergo in relation to their body (employment or medical agreements/contracts) offered some practical solutions. Finally, in the absence of any identifiable specific principles of protection in the current law, the judges included these provisions in their rulings[24]. However, there was a move in the French legislature. In fact, the new powers of medicine led the legislator to take action[25]. Today, doctors deal with the body not only for therapeutic reasons but also to ensure the individual's well-being (cosmetic surgery, assisted reproductive technology, etc.) or even to treat other people[26]. However, the principal factor prompting the legislature to take action was undoubtedly the increasingly common act of making parts or elements of the body available, sometimes to the point of exploiting them commercially[27]. Therefore French authorities thought it a good idea to introduce specific legislation protecting the body as such.

By taking this position, the legislature has turned the body into a separate legal category[28]. It even makes distinctions within the protection of the body. Some principles are specific to the body as a whole[29], some are common to the body and its elements[30], and others are common to all of the organs, although they do not apply to mere "products of the body"[31]. In this way, we move from the protection of the physical integrity of the individual to that of the

(23) For a long time, the law was concerned with regulating violence against the body.

(24) The Court of Cassation introduced the principles of the inviolability and unavailability of the human body to cases involving a surrogate mother; see Cass. plen. Ass., 31 May 1991, *D.*, 1991, p. 417, note D. Thouvenin.

(25) J.-P. Baud, *L'affaire de la main volée. Une histoire juridique du corps*, Paris, Seuil, 1993.

(26) Alongside medical acts in the interests of the patient, medical acts in the interests of others (donations of elements of the body, research on human beings, surrogacy) are also developing.

(27) See *supra*, D. Le Breton (p. 21) and P. Lecoz (p. 33).

(28) S. Hennette-Vauchez, *Disposer de soi ? Une analyse du discours juridique sur les droits de la personne sur son corps*, L'Harmattan, 2004, p. 29.

(29) Art. 16-1, subpara. 2, Civ. C. (principle of inviolability).

(30) Art. 16-1, subpara. 3, 16-2, 16-5, 16-6 Civ. C. This is also the case in Germany (the law on transplantation covers the human body elements and products).

(31) G. Cornu, *Droit civil. Les personnes*, *op. cit.*, p. 32.

body[32], and therefore from a right of the individual as a person to a right of the body.

Although this approach remains singular for the time being, there is every reason to believe that it will be taken up mainly by the western countries; where the social structures are individualistic and where only the person is taken into account and has autonomy, and that it will be less common in traditional societies where "the body is not designated as separate from the man"[33]. In fact, with legislation specific to the body, it is no longer the person that is the subject, but the individual.

The question then becomes whether this legislation specific to the body has an impact on the protection itself. Physical integrity has always been protected by the law, since long before the emergence of new biomedical procedures. So what are the benefits of a specific form of protection? There is good reason to ask such a question. Indeed, such a development should *a priori* be for the purpose of improving the safeguards. However, that does not appear to be the case. Didn't the traditional connection made by the law between the person and the body make violations of the body more difficult? By distinguishing between them, the body is separated from the person, and this 'external' factor allows us to distance ourselves from the (embarrassing?) idea of a violation of the individual; the latter being always more psychologically burdensome than a violation of the body alone. The knowledge that these "new therapies" are precisely the ones intended to provide an element of well-being (assisted reproductive technologies, cosmetic surgery, etc.), which have resulted in the differentiation between the body and the individual, suggests a further in-depth examination. Doesn't isolating the body, – promised to be more protective of the individual – hide in reality a way of facilitating violations in the unstated interests of other people (in particular commercial interests)? All this achieved in the name of greater freedom for the individual over his body.

In any event, this reflection demonstrates the ambivalence of medicine as well as its evolution. The changes in medical law are moving towards a greater recognition of the patient as a person.

---

(32) On this distinction between the person and the body in Belgium, see below G. Schamps, p. 79.

(33) See *supra*, D. Le Breton, p. 23.

Likewise, the individual is increasingly relegated to second place after the body because, as has just been pointed out, the evolution referred to seems to require the body to be regarded as separate from the person in the interest of greater protection. Is it not, however, the connection (of the patient or only of the patient's body) to the individual that affords the greater protection? Indeed, the reference to the person inevitably leads us to question the freedom of the individual in regard to his body[(34)] and not the availability of an autonomous body; the latter would be more firmly based on the ownership of the body by a person than on the exercise of a freedom[(35)].

Whether we think in terms of protection of the individual or protection of the body alone, our study has revealed that respect for physical integrity is universally recognised. It has also highlighted that other principles, from one country to another, supplement this protection. These principles include that of respect for the dignity of the individual, respect for the body, and the inviolability, also the fact that the body cannot be disposed of and no property rights over the body[(36)]. Before defining these principles, it is important to consider first the concept of "principles of protection", which is also shared by all the countries studied.

B. – *The widespread recognition of the principles of protection*

The study of comparative law carried out in this work shows that the concept of "principles" of protection is recognised everywhere[(37)], although this common reference does not cover precisely the same reality in every country, due to the polysemy of the term[(38)].

(34) Because the person has (is) a body, he must be able to enjoy protection of the body and must be able to express his freedom through the body. This freedom to control what happens to one's body is recognised in all the countries studied, although its scope varies considerably between countries (from a freedom limited to access to "traditional" medical procedures to a genuine principle of self-determination of the individual; see *infra*).

(35) This is even greater when we consider the different elements of the body.

(36) See *infra*, II. A range of principles of protection.

(37) On the notion of principles in general see P. Morvan, "Principes", in D. Alland and S. Rials (ed.), *Dictionnaire de la culture juridique*, PUF, Lamy, 2003, p. 1203; S. Caudale (ed.), *Les principes en droit*, Economica, Étude juridique, 2008; R. Alexy, *Theorie der Grundrechte*, Frankfurt am Main, BD, 582, 1986; L. Prieto Sanchis, *Sobre principios y normas. Problemas del razonamiento juridico*, coll. Cuadernos y debates, vol. 4, Madrid, 1992; M. Atienza, J. Ruiz Manero, *Las piezas del derecho. Teoria de los enunciados juridicos*, Barcelona, Ariel, 1996; P. Morvan, *Le principe de droit privé*, éditions Panthéon Assas, 1999.

(38) A. Jeammaud, "De la polysémie du terme *principe* dans les langages du droit et des juristes", in *Les principes en droit*, *op. cit.*, p. 53.

* The assertion according to which the idea of "principles of protection" is shared everywhere stems from a simple observation: none of the contributors to this research project concluded that this notion did not exist in their own country.

At first glance, such an observation may seem surprising. In fact, the principles seem to be derived more from codified legal systems and, more specifically, civil law systems based on the recognition of general and abstract data[(39)] than from Anglo-Saxon systems, of a more jurisprudential type, where the general nature of the regulations has no place as the law is based on the facts[(40)]. Yet this work seems to refute these foregone conclusions, as the widespread existence of the legal (albeit sometimes informal) recognition of the principles of protection has been confirmed[(41)]. In all of the countries studied, the concept of a principle is either specifically provided for by the legal instruments[(42)] and/or by the courts[(43)], or simply referred to by legal doctrine on the basis of the rights and freedoms featuring in the legal instruments, or recognised in practice[(44)]. In the USA, the principles have always been recognised[(45)] in the field of ethics, and while they have not been laid down as formal legal rules, they achieve this status by being taken into consideration by the judges in the cases referred to them. Indeed, by ruling against a doctor who has violated the body of an individual who has not consented, the judges implicitly accept a principle of respect for physical integrity.

While the explicit recognition of this concept of "principles" is not currently the generally accepted rule in the countries studied[(46)],

(39) F. ZENATI-CASTAING, "Les principes généraux en droit privé", in *Les principes en droit*, *op. cit.*, p. 257.

(40) It is indeed difficult for a Common Law jurist to find a solution from an abstract standard.

(41) Except in Belgium, where this reference to the idea of "principle" seems to be excluded. See *supra*, G. SCHAMPS, p. 75.

(42) In general instruments or those specific to certain biomedical practices.

(43) A judge may discover these principles, even in the absence of legal instruments, from elements that already exist in the legal system. In the United Kingdom, the development of principles from facts, see *supra*, T. CALLUS, p. 209.

(44) See *supra*, R. IDA (p. 349) and S. HAYAKAWA (p. 359).

(45) Especially with the emergence of *principlism* (theorisation of moral principles by T.L. BEAUCHAMP and J.F. CHILDRESS, *Principles of Biomedical Ethics,1977; Les principes de l'éthique médicale*, French translation by M. FISBACH, coll. Médecine & Sciences humaines, Paris, Les Belles Lettres, 2008: *principlism* is a system of ethics on which decisions can be based). See *supra*, K. ORFALI, p. 313.

(46) The governments are still extremely attached to the notions of rights and freedoms, although legal doctrine generally has a tendency to talk of principles when referring to these rights and freedoms. For Belgium, see *supra*, G. SCHAMPS, p. 75.

it seems to be the approach adopted by the international forums. Indeed, the non-legal international declarations, developed by medical NGOs or ethics committees, have always referred to the concept of principles[(47)]. With regard to international legal instruments, the earliest restricted themselves to pronouncing the rights and freedoms and did not refer to the concept of principles[(48)], although the most recent do so expressly. All the following instruments refer to the notion of "principles"; from the Universal Declaration on the Human Genome and the European Convention on Biomedicine[(49)] adopted in 1997 to the Universal Declaration on Bioethics of 2005[(50)], via the Charter of Fundamental Rights of the European Union of 7 December 2000[(51)]. Finally, the European Court of Human Rights also appears to concern itself with the notion of "general principles" as a new autonomous source of protection of the individual[(52)].

Governments have not yet taken this path and appear to remain firmly attached to the idea of rights and freedoms. In practice, however, legal doctrine everywhere recognises this concept of principles of protection of the body.

The fact remains, however, that such widespread recognition cannot be taken for granted. Indeed, the concepts of person and body rely on value judgments that are deeply ingrained in a culture and that can vary from one legal system to the next. The fact that the countries studied share all the idea of principles of protection is interesting, as it would seem to show that the law does not simply follow customs but can also include norms with an "objective foundation". Let us explore more specifically why, in all these States, the concept of "principles of protection of the

(47) The Helsinki Declaration drawn up by the World Medical Association in June 1964, amended on numerous occasions, contains general ethical principles concerning research.

(48) The UDHR of 10 December 1948, the ECHR of 4 November 1950.

(49) In this Convention, the reference to the concept of "principles" remains nevertheless unassertive, as the text does not refer to it explicitly when it speaks about the rights protecting the body, but does so only in Chapter VIII on "Infringements of the provisions of the Convention" (art. 23).

(50) See the last sentence of the Preamble, the last paragraph of article 2 defining the aims of this declaration, as well as the statement of the articles.

(51) This instrument alludes to "principles" in the last sentence of the Preamble and then talks of rights and liberties.

(52) The Court frequently refers to "general principles", considerations of a general nature stemming from its case law and relative to a provision of the European Convention on Human Rights or recognised by civilised nations. It has even referred to the existence of cross-cutting general principles (ECHR, 28 August 2012, *Simons v. Belgium*, n° 71407-10, *JCP*, 2012, n°1221, p. 2052, note K. Blay-Grabarczyk).

body" is used. Is it because, with regard to respect for the person (and therefore his body), there remains an area considered by all of these countries to be essential: these "principles" constitute the basis for a way of acting[(53)] which protects the human being? This idea is even more prevalent in Germany, due to the memory of the abuses committed by the Nazis. The term "principle" refers to a norm considered to be fundamental. Furthermore, in terms of etymology, the word principle, from the Latin *principium* derived from *princeps*, means "first man, or chief leader". This fundamental character stems from the close relationship these principles have with values deemed to be fundamental[(54)]. Principles, adopted by States, allow preserving the values considered as most important by each of them.

J. Rawls showed the importance of the principles of social justice. In his opinion, they stem from a general agreement, as they are based on objective criteria[(55)]. However, this argument has its critics[(56)]. Our study nevertheless certainly seems to show that the idea of principles (in this case of protection of the body) is shared because there is, within all of the countries and irrespective of their culture, a system of strong and objective arguments (since it concerns the protection of the human being) in favour of accepting these principles. In fact, the general recognition of these principles is based on an axiological rationale, and more specifically, that theorised by Raymond Boudon[(57)]. According to him[(58)], value judgments are based on reasons that are viewed strongly by the social subject and are therefore shared between individuals.

This means that underlying the principles of protection, there would be a universal line of argument – namely the need to protect

(53) H. JONAS, *Principe de Responsabilité*, Paris, ed. du Cerf, 1979.

(54) A. JEAMMAUD, *op. cit.*, p. 72: "There is, in this concept of principles, an ideological dimension...".

(55) Criteria enabling an objective judgment of the validity of certain rules. *A Theory of Justice*, Cambridge, 1971.

(56) For a critical examination, see B. BARRY, *The liberal theory of justice – A critical examination of the principal doctrines in A theory of justice by J. Rawls*, Oxford, Clarendon, 1973. Relativism stems from the idea that the law can only be a reflection of morals.

(57) R. BOUDON, "Penser la relation entre le droit et les mœurs", in *L'avenir du droit, Mélanges en hommage de François Terré, D.*, 1999, p. 11.

(58) R. BOUDON shares the axiological rationale initiated by Max WEBER (value judgment "X is good or bad" is accepted because it respects or contradicts a principle. The rationale is based on the balance or non-balance between a state of affairs and certain principles); see the aforementioned article, p. 17.

a person's bodily integrity[(59)]. That is undoubtedly the reason why, although the notion of "principle" has particularly developed along with the emergence of modern natural law[(60)], when it is considered within the framework of the protection of the body; it is recognised by all systems, even the positivist ones, as this concept concerns the human being.

* However, above and beyond this observation of a widespread recognition of the concept of "principles of protection of the body", the study shows that this concept must be nuanced due to the vague nature of this notion.

Numerous works devoted to the "principles" in law are somewhat imprecise in nature[(61)]. All the countries refer to "principles of protection" without us knowing what this reference to the concept of "principle" really means. This lack of precision inevitably has consequences for the effectiveness of these principles: as a result, they are themselves also imprecise. Indeed, reading this work shows that these principles of protection of the body all differ in their scope from one country to the next, but also from one principle to the next. Nevertheless, three lessons can be drawn from it.

First of all, there is an axiological component of the principle of respect for physical integrity apparent in all the States. The protection of the individual's body is a truth accepted by all of the countries studied, although the actual content of this principle varies between States.

Next, as a consequence of the first lesson, the principles of protection of the body, whether they are legally binding or simply ethical guidelines, carry a certain "weight"[(62)].

---

(59) While the axiomatic content of principles (truth accepted by all) is worthwhile for the idea of "principles of protection of the human body" and, more precisely, for the principle of protection of the physical integrity of persons, it is open to question when we consider the other principles of protection of the body as the principles of dignity or non-ownership. See *infra*.

(60) The philosophy of the school of modern natural law, which emerged in the 17th century, viewed "principles" as a key concept. Natural law is not made up of rules, but of general principles applicable everywhere and at any time because of their universal nature. See J. Boulanger, "Principes généraux du droit et droit positif", in *Mélanges Ripert*, Paris, LGDJ, 1950 p. 69.

(61) S. Caudale, "Rapport introductif" in *Les principes en droit, op. cit.*, p. 4; R. Alexy, *Theorie der Grundrechte, op. cit.*; L. Prieto Sanchis, *Sobre principios y normas. Problemas del razonamiento juridico, op. cit.*; M. Atienza, J. Ruiz Manero, *Las piezas del derecho. Teoria de los enunciados juridicos, op. cit.*

(62) A. Jeammaud, *op. cit.*, p. 74.

Finally, there is quite a margin of variability regarding the authority of the principles. Indeed, an analysis of the different contributions leads us to conclude that the principles of protection are, at the very least, "guidelines" or "guiding norms" and, at their maximum level of authority, norms generating subjective rights. This maximum authority is given to the principle of respect for physical integrity, as in all countries a violation of the body can result in legal proceedings. On the other hand, this is not the case with all the other principles of protection. The principle of non- commercialisation (or 'gratuity') of the body[(63)] does not appear to confer a subjective right allowing the victim to obtain compensation for a failure to comply with this principle, unless the law (criminal or civil) expressly states otherwise. As for the principle of respect for dignity, acknowledged in most of the countries, it is not systematically endowed with a legal scope: it only confers a subjective right in certain countries, although at the same time, it is generally considered to be the foundation for all the other principles[(64)].

The authority of the principles of protection stems from a number of elements. The law (the bill itself or case law) can define it specifically. The scope of the principle will often depend on its source, although this rule must be carefully evaluated. As an example, principles contained in numerous Constitutions are not routinely combined with subjective rights enabling the person to take legal action in the event of a violation.

These principles often take the form of norms[(65)], and sometimes mere observations[(66)] or "guidelines" that do not confer any prerogative, but that can lead to the development of legally binding standards[(67)]. From one country to the next and one principle to the next, principles pronounced as a foundation of values to be defended and principles that give prerogatives, and sometimes subjective rights[(68)], can be seen side by side. The role of the judge (even outside of the common law countries) is therefore of particular

(63) See *infra*, p. 385, the study of this principle.
(64) See *infra*, p. 379, *id.*
(65) A. JEAMMAUD, "La règle de droit comme modèle", *D.*, 1990, chron., p. 199.
(66) See *supra*, V. SAN JULIAN, p. 121.
(67) On the qualification of these principles as "extra-positive principles", see A. JEAMMAUD, p. 70.
(68) In Germany, the principles contained in the Basic Law are recognised as directly applicable rights (art. 1, subpara. 3, BL).

significance, as it is usually the judge who, in practice, will endow these principles with an authoritative power[69]. Detailed analysis of the different principles of protection of the body provides evidence of this.

II. – A RANGE OF PRINCIPLES OF PROTECTION

Except France, which opted for specific principles of protection of the body, other countries protect the body using principles of protection of the individual. Nevertheless, some States have specified the principles of protection of the body in the context of specific biomedical procedures (assisted reproductive technologies, the removal of organs or other elements of the body, etc.).

Our study reveals that some of these principles are often formally laid down, while with others this is less common or only in specific fields of medicine.

A. – *Principles most frequently referenced*

One principle, accepted by all the countries, is specific to the protection of the individual's body. Two others (respect for dignity and the autonomy of the individual) are general, but have an impact on the protection of the body.

* Respect for physical integrity is guaranteed everywhere, although in some countries (United Kingdom, USA and Japan) this principle is not laid down as such, but is merely the consequence of a legal rule[70]. In those countries where it is specifically referred to in legal instruments or by the courts, some refer to respect for physical integrity[71], some to the inviolability of the body[72],

(69) According to R. DWORKIN, a differentiation can be made between principles and rules according to how they are applied: the former (unlike the latter) have no legal consequences automatically resulting from them (R. DWORKIN, *Prendre les droits au sérieux*, coll. Léviathan, Paris, PUF, 1977, p. 82).

(70) In the Anglo-Saxon countries, it is recognised through the rule of consent, which applies to any procedure performed on an individual's body (see *supra*, T. CALLUS, p. 209, and M. GARRISON, p. 293). In Japan, this principle is not specifically recognised by the law, but is recognised in practice through the application of the civil liability rules. See *supra*, S. HAYAKAWA, p. 359.

(71) Chile, Canada, Spain, Tunisia.

(72) France (although art 16-3 Civ. C. refers to the notion of integrity), Italy, Turkey.

and others to both principles[73], but the basic principle is always the protection of the body. In those states that do not specifically pronounce this principle but translate it in practice, the foundation is respect for freedom. Indeed, violations of the body are punished because they have been carried out without the person's consent[74] or in breach of a right to privacy. Indeed, the concept of privacy that is aimed at the protection of the individual also includes the protection of the body[75].

An overview of this study shows that, in all countries, this principle of respect for physical integrity allows for compensation to anyone who has suffered a violation of a "principle of inviolability of the body": no one may cause harm to the body of another person[76]. On the other hand, the content of this principle varies from one country to another. In common parlance, the term "integrity" comes from the Latin *integritas* which means "something that is sound, whole, that has not been altered in any way". In some countries, the positive rights are viewed in the broadest terms, similar to the Charter of Fundamental Rights of 7th December 2000, for which the integrity of the individual in the biomedical area imposes compliance with the informed consent rule, the prohibition of eugenic practices and making a profit from the body or its parts[77]. In Germany, this principle encompasses the right of access to health care. Additionally, in the name of this principle, Germany declares more often that requiring transsexuals to have surgery before they can legally change sex, is unconstitutional[78]. A German judge has even ruled that piercing the ears of a child must be subject to criminal sanctions[79].

---

(73) Brazil, Canada, Egypt, Greece, Switzerland (which also refers to the intangibility of the human body). Inviolability and integrity are generally thought of as synonyms (J.-R. Binet, "Protection de la personne. Le corps humain", *JCP*, art. 16 to 16-13, Fasc. 12, n° 78), although the right to integrity could theoretically take precedence over inviolability (B. Feuillet, "Intégrité physique", in *Dictionnaire des droits fondamentaux*, p. 498).

(74) See *supra*, M. Garrison, p. 293.

(75) See *supra*, K. Orfali, p. 313.

(76) However, the principle of inviolability is not absolute and there may be exceptions. It is possible to violate the body of a person in the person's best interest (especially in a medical emergency) or even in the interest of the individual committing the violation (state of necessity, self-defence). EC 25 November 2001, *RFDA*, 2002, p. 164: the constitutional principle of the protection of health can outweigh that of the inviolability of the body.

(77) Art 3-2 of the Convention. Switzerland also takes a broad view (see *supra*, D. Manaï, p. 221).

(78) BVerfG, 11 January 2011, BVerfGE 128, 109.

(79) See *supra*, F. Furkel, p. 51. Likewise, German case law requires a person to submit, by force if necessary, to tests to determine parentage!

Respect for integrity may be extended to cover the integrity of the entire human race[(80)].

The axiological aspect of this principle[(81)] results in it having a different meaning in different countries, depending on each culture. Indeed, the basis of this principle, which is to protect the body itself or to protect the freedom of the individual in regard to his body, has an impact on its scope. By using freedom and consent as a basis, US law includes the idea of almost a property right over the body[(82)], thereby limiting the number of possible scenarii in which a violation of the individual's physical integrity is likely to be invoked.

* Respect for human dignity and the principle of autonomy (or self-determination[(83)]) are principles that have been widely, although not unanimously, recognised by different countries[(84)].

The principle of dignity is recognised by many countries[(85)], even the Anglo-Saxon countries as Canada acknowledges it and the United Kingdom refers to it[(86)]. Many of these States have even used it to create a framework of the other principles of protection of the body[(87)].

Dignity is not defined in any national or supranational legal instrument and is generally seen as a vague concept[(88)]. The

(80) The French *bioethical laws* of 1994 enshrined a special provision concerning respect for the human species within the framework of the protection of the body (art. 16-4 Civ. C.).

(81) This principle certainly relates to the area of values.

(82) On the limits to the recognition of a right of ownership, see *supra*, K. ORFALI, p. 315, note 7.

(83) This principle, in spite of its dual terminology (autonomy and self-determination), can appear in the expression of another principle, the principle of consent (consent is required in order for a procedure to be performed on the body). See *infra*.

(84) The Universal Declaration on Human Rights of December 1948 considers dignity and equality to be the basis for freedom and justice. The Universal Declaration on Bioethics of 2005 began by referring to respect for the dignity and freedom of persons before devoting articles to the principles of autonomy and consent.

(85) Germany (dignity has a supra-constitutional value, art. 79 BL), Belgium (Constitution), Brazil, Canada, Chile, Egypt, Spain, France, Greece, Hungary, Italy, United Kingdom, Switzerland, Tunisia, Turkey. In international terms, this principle features in the United Nations Charter of 26 June 1945, the Universal Declaration of Human Rights of 10 December 1948 (§ 1 of the preamble), the European Convention on Biomedicine (art. 1) and the Charter of Fundamental Rights of the European Union of December 2000 (Chap. 1).

(86) See *supra*, T. CALLUS.

(87) Germany, Brazil, Egypt, Spain, Greece, Tunisia, Chile, United Kingdom, Switzerland and France (B. MATHIEU, "Pour une reconnaissance de principes matriciels en matière de protection constitutionnelle des droits de l'homme", *D.*, 1995, Chr., p. 211).

(88) C. GIRARD and S. HENNETTE-VAUCHEZ (dir.), *La dignité de la personne humaine. Recherche d'un processus de juridicisation*, coll. Droit et Justice, Paris, PUF, 2005; P. PEDROT

European Court of Human Rights tends to rely on a subjective notion of dignity, considering that individual will determines the parameters of dignity, while in France, the Court of Cassation and the Council of State, together with legal doctrine, seem to opt for an objective idea(89). Nevertheless, all the States that have adopted it believe this principle guarantees a protection of the body, although this protection appears to vary considerably from one country to the next(90). From the statement of a philosophical principle without any real legal weight(91) to the granting of a subjective right enabling people to take legal action in case of violation(92), the scope of this principle is not identical in various States. In Germany, the human body is considered sacred and dignity is intangible(93). On the other hand, the principle of dignity has not been enshrined in law and has little significance in the USA and Japan(94).

The second general principle accepted by all of the countries to guarantee the protection of the body is autonomy. It is based on personal freedom, and more specifically on the freedom of the individual to control what happens to his body (the freedom

---

(dir.), *Éthique, droit et dignité de la personne, Mélanges Christian Bolz*, Economica, 1999; B. Mathieu, "La dignité de la personne humaine : du bon (et du mauvais) usage en droit positif français d'un principe universel", *in* Cl. Neirinck (ed.), *Le droit, la médecine et l'être humain, propos hétérodoxes sur quelques enjeux*, Marseille, PU Aix-Marseille, 1996; M. Fabre-Magnan, "La dignité en droit : un axiome", *in* A.M. Dillens and B. Van Meenen (eds.), *La dignité aujourd'hui. Perspectives philosophiques et théologiques*, Brussels, Publications Facultés Universitaires Saint-Louis, 2007, p. 53; B. Edelman, "La dignité de la personne humaine", *D.*, 1997, chron., p. 185.

(89) See *supra*, F. Kernaleguen, p. 149.

(90) A recent study by the Réseau Universitaire International de Bioéthique (http://rui-bioethique.univ-rennes1.fr/) on the application of this principle in some twenty countries of different cultures has just been completed and demonstrates this. See *La réalité du principe de dignité. Approche internationale*, B. Feuillet-Liger and K. Orfali (eds.), Bruylant, to be published in 2016.

(91) In Switzerland, dignity has considerable legal effect: sometimes a guiding principle of the government, sometimes a subjective right (see *supra*, D. Manaï, p. 221).

(92) Germany, Brazil, Canada, Egypt, Spain, Greece.

(93) See *supra*, F. Furkel, p. 51.

(94) On recognition of this principle in these countries and in China, see B. Feuillet-Liger and K. Orfali (eds.), *La réalité du principe de dignité. Approche internationale*, *op. cit.*

to dispose of one's body)[(95)], as well as on respect for privacy[(96)]. There are only a few States that have established the principle of "the freedom to dispose of one's body"[(97)], although none of them has expressed any principle of responsibility[(98)]. The principle of autonomy is recognised in all of the countries[(99)], expressly or simply, by means of a statement of the principle of consent[(100)].

However, the impact of this principle varies considerably from one country to the next in accordance with the degree of freedom each government allows individuals regarding their bodies: some allow total ownership over the body[(101)], while others limit

---

(95) S. HENNETTE-VAUCHEZ, *Disposer de soi ? Une analyse du discours juridique sur les droits de la personne sur son corps, op. cit.*; M. T. MEULDERS-KLEIN, "Le droit de disposer de soi-même, étendue et limites en droit comparé", in *Licéité en droit positif et références légales aux valeurs*, X[e] journée d'études juridiques Jean Dabin, Brussels, Bruylant, t. XIV, 1982, p. 215; ROMAN D., "Libre disposition de soi et santé", *in* J.-M. LARRALDE, *La libre disposition de son corps*, Brussels, Bruylant, 2009, p. 199.

(96) In the USA and Spain, where the right to privacy includes the body (see *supra*, V. SAN JULIAN, p. 121).

(97) In Switzerland this freedom is one of the personality rights (art. 28 Civ. C.), see *supra*, D. MANAÏ, p. 221. In the USA, this freedom has been established by case law; See *supra*, M. GARRISON, p. 293.

(98) Indeed, the idea of freedom suggests that of responsibility. However, the Universal Declaration on Bioethics of 2009 refers to autonomy and individual responsibility (and not to freedom).

(99) Belgium, Chile, Canada (case law), Spain (Constitution), Greece, United Kingdom, USA (ethical principle). On the distinction from the principle of self-determination, see Japan article (ethical principle). Germany and Switzerland also refer to this concept of self-determination.

(100) This principle of consent stems from the requirement to obtain the individual's consent in order perform a medical act. Brazil, Greece, Tunisia, Egypt (principle adopted with regard to assisted reproductive technologies), Japan (accepted for organ donations), France (art 16-3 Civ. C.), Hungary (accepted for the removal of elements of the body and for research). In Italy, legal doctrine is aimed at autonomy and the laws relating to biomedical practices refer to consent, see *supra*, C.M. MAZZONI, p. 185. Canada refers to the right to freedom (see *supra*, D. GOUBAU, p. 283). In Germany, the BGB considers any medical act without the patient's consent to be a violation of bodily integrity and assimilates it with assault and battery (§823BGB).

(101) On the adoption of this right by the European Court of Human Rights, see ECHR, 29 April 2002, *Pretty v. United Kingdom*, n° 13, *JCP*, 2003, II n° 10062, N. C. GIRAULT. On the extent of its scope (with regard to sadomasochistic practices), see ECHR, 17 February 2005, *KA and AD v. Belgium*, n° 312: an individual may, in accordance with a right to personal fulfilment, "take part in activities perceived to be physically or morally damaging or dangerous for his person", and M. FABRE-MAGNAN, "Le sadisme n'est pas un droit de l'homme", *D.*, 2005, chron., p. 2973. On the freedom of a woman to own her body, see B. FEUILLET-LIGER and A. AOUIJ-MRAD (eds.), *Corps de la femme et Biomédecine. Approche internationale*, Brussels, Bruylant, 2013; B. FEUILLET-LIGER, K. ORFALI and T. CALLUS (eds.), *The Female Body: A Journey Through Law, Culture and Medicine*, Brussels, Bruylant, 2013.

autonomy to the requirement for consent in order to carry out a medical act[(102)].

In the USA, this autonomy means that the principle of non-commercialisation or the principle of a body that cannot be disposed of have little influence[(103)] in order to bestow a substantial freedom over one's body. This principle of autonomy is also central in some other countries, such as Germany[(104)], Belgium[(105)], Greece[(106)], Canada[(107)] and Japan. It is also interesting to note that Japan is the only country to give priority to a "right to happiness", which helps us understand the importance given to freedom in that country[(108)]. By referring in its Constitution and at a similar level, to personal well-being[(109)] and to dignity[(110)], Spain gives a consequent significance to the principle of autonomy in the context of biomedical practices, although that country still remains under the considerable influence of the Catholic Church.

However, this freedom with regard to the body is not absolute and includes some exceptions[(111)]. Even in the USA, certain limits are defined on a case by case basis by the judge and by the laws of some states, especially with regard to informed consent[(112)]. In the United Kingdom, the individual's consent is not sufficient: the medical act must not run counter to public order[(113)]. In other States, the scope of the principle of autonomy remains extremely

(102) In Turkey, the principle of non-maleficence considerably limits the scope of the principle of autonomy; see *supra*, S. Oktay-Özdemir and G. S. Tek, p. 271. In Egypt, an individual does not have control of what happens to his body, which belongs to God, see *supra*, H. Abdelhamid, p. 251.

(103) The body or its elements can be the subject of contracts, and even of formal commercial agreements (the sale of elements of the body, payment of the surrogate mother. etc.). See *infra*.

(104) In Germany, this right of self-determination, generated in part by Kantian philosophy, is particularly widespread. It does not, however, mean complete ownership of one's body.

(105) See *supra*, G. Schamps, p. 77.

(106) However, the limit is gratuity; see *supra*, P. Agallopoulou, p. 195.

(107) Although the legal system is mixed, as it combines Common Law and Civil Law, freedom (the principle established by case law) seems to be predominant: see *supra*, D. Goubau, p. 283.

(108) See *supra*, S. Hayakawa, p. 359.

(109) This general principle applies to health. See *supra*, V. San Julian, p. 130.

(110) On the argument caused by this, see *supra*, V. San Julian, p. 130.

(111) For Belgium, see *supra*, G. Schamps, p. 77.

(112) The principle of informed consent generated by medical practice and ethics (see *supra*, K. Orfali), before being enshrined by the courts (see *supra*, M. Garrison, p. 293), allows limits to be set on an individual's freedom to control what happens to their body.

(113) See *supra*, T. Callus, p. 209.

limited on the grounds that the body cannot be used freely for religious reasons[114].

This principle of autonomy also covers the elements of the body. In numerous countries, it is provided for in specific pieces of legislation (donations of organs, gametes or other body products). Disposing of elements of the body often appears to be much easier than controlling what happens to the body as a complete unit. Yet in Switzerland, the law encompasses a right to bio-material self-determination that provides less protection than that concerning the body. In fact some products of the body can, exceptionally, be used without consent[115]. In the USA, the sale of some body parts is allowed in some states.

Although both of these principles (dignity and autonomy) are recognised, at least *de facto* and sometimes simply *a minima* by all of the countries studied, the importance of one often depends on that accorded to the other[116]. In fact, respect for dignity can result in the restriction of an individual's freedom over their body[117]. In Brazil, for example, this freedom must not result in a violation of physical integrity or be contrary to the moral order, the instruments giving thus physicians control over acts harmful to dignity or integrity[118]. In Germany, the non-commercialisation s and sometimes the unavailability of the body are considered to be the unwritten rules protecting human dignity, and thus limiting an individual's freedom in regard to his body[119].

Behind the relationships between dignity and freedom lies the crucial issue of protecting the individual from himself[120]. Is the duty of the law (especially criminal law) restricted to protecting

(114) See *supra*, H. ABDELHAMID, p. 251.

(115) See *supra*, D. MANAÏ, p. 221.

(116) On this question, see B. FEUILLET-LIGER and K. ORFALI (eds.), *La réalité du principe de dignité. Approche internationale*, *op. cit.*

(117) In France, see CE ass, 27 October 1995, *D.*, 1996, p. 177, note. D. LE BRETON: the judges prohibited, in the context of a fair, the tossing of a dwarf (who claimed this freedom), as that was a violation of human dignity. The principle of respect for dignity has nevertheless lost, in France, the uninfringeable nature accorded to it by the Constitutional Council in 1994; see Const. Ct. 27 June 2001, n° 2001-446 DC, *J.O.*, 7 July 2001.

(118) See *supra*, M.C. CRESPO-BRAUNER and A. LOBATO, p. 329.

(119) See *supra*, F. FURKEL, p. 51.

(120) On the exclusion of legal intervention in the "self-to-self" relationship, although this ability to harm oneself does not constitute a right or a freedom, see M. FABRE-MAGNAN, "Le domaine de l'autonomie personnelle, l'indisponibilité du corps humain et justice sociale", *D.*, 2008, p. 31; see also D. ROMAN, "À corps défendant, la protection de l'individu contre lui-même", *D.*, 2007, p. 1284.

the individual against others, or should it extend to protecting the individual against himself? The issue lies in the debates around different moral theories, which is hardly surprising as these concepts of dignity, consent and freedom and autonomy vary according to their social context and stem from moral choices[121].

Alongside these principles set down in all of the countries studied, others appear in one country or another.

B. – *Other Principles*

The principle of respect of the body is only expressed in French law[122] and in the United Kingdom[123]. In France, it should not be confused with respect for physical integrity, because it encompasses not only the inviolability but also the non-commercialisation of the body[124]. By developing a specific protection of the body in the Civil Code, the legislature introduced this intermediate principle. It is in fact one of the applications of the higher principle of dignity to the body[125] although it covers two other principles considered crucial by French law in the protection of the body: inviolability and no property rights over the body.

Despite an encompassing and "rhetorical" function, this right to respect for the body does not appear to constitute a subjective right; it is not capable of conferring – like the principle of respect for privacy from which it was developed[126] – a right for the victim to obtain any compensation in the case of a violation[127]. Unlike the inviolability of the human body, which is a prohibition, the right to respect for the body appears to have the flexibility of a positive precept whose content remains undefined and applicable in different ways[128]. However, one could examine the possibility

(121) See *supra*, D. Le Breton, p. 21.

(122) See *supra*, F. Kernaleguen, p. 149.

(123) See *supra*, T. Callus, p. 209.

(124) Article 16-1, Paragraph 1, of Civil Code is devoted to the principle of respect for the body (a sort of preamble), the following two paragraphs concern inviolability and non-ownership. During the preparatory work for the law, these last two principles were presented as the consequences of the general principle of respect for the body.

(125) The principle of dignity is set out in the previous article (art. 16 Civ. C.).

(126) Article 16-1 of Civil Code is written in the same terms as article 9 Civil Code, which confers a subjective right (respect for privacy).

(127) Criminal law does not impose any sanction on the non-respect of the body, although it includes specific offences to protect the body (art. 511-2 to 511-14 Crim. C.).

(128) On this subject see, G. Cornu, *Les personnes*, *op. cit.*, p. 31.

of citing a violation of this principle in order to secure a conviction for a failure to act (such as not providing a restoration of the body after organ removal) resulting in the non-respect of the body. The obligation to provide the "best possible restoration" of the body after an organ removal, as expressed in the French Public Health Code[(129)] introduces that.

Another principle established in a number of positive rights is that of the non-commercialisation of the body, which prohibits making any financial agreement concerning the body. In the countries studied, it is sometimes included in the legislation (general[(130)] or relating to specific biomedical practices[(131)]), sometimes stated in accordance with contract law, which requires the subject of an agreement to be "legally negotiable"[(132)], or simply accepted in practice[(133)].

On the other hand, another principle with a close link to the unavailability of the body is more often referred to: the non-ownership of the body[(134)] or gratuity[(135)] or the non-commercialisation of the human body[(136)]. Italian law uses the name "gratuity" for the concept of "not for sale", the lack of compensation and the

(129) Art. L. 1232-5 Pub. Health Code.

(130) Brazil (art. 13 Civ. C.), Greece, Chile (Civ. C.). In Italy, the Civil Code states that the body is unavailable if the legal act carried out on the body risks leading to permanent reduction in physical integrity or if the act is against the law, or contrary to public order or morals; see *supra*, C.M. MAZZONI, p. 185.

(131) In Tunisia, the principle is used to prohibit surrogacy; see *supra*, A. AOUIJ-MRAD, p. 235.

(132) Germany, France (this principle was established by case law, but was not included in the Civil Code).

(133) In Germany, the unavailability of the body (like non-ownership) is an unwritten rule for the protection of human dignity. In Japan, this principle stems from the application of the civil liability rules; see *supra*, S. HAYAKAWA, p. 359.

(134) The principle is sometimes stated in general terms (Germany, France, Greece) or in instruments relating to certain biomedical practices (Egypt, Greece with regard to surrogacy, Tunisia for the removal of organs and blood; Turkey: the law on the removal, preservation and transplantation of organs and tissues clearly refers to the non-ownership of the human body).

(135) Germany (principle stated in the medical directives on the use of assisted reproductive technologies), Belgium, Canada (laws on the removal of organs, surrogacy and research), Spain (laws on the elements of the body), Greece (laws concerning surrogacy), United Kingdom, Switzerland (included in the Constitution for the removal of organs and in the laws for other elements of the body). In Italy, this principle stems from the application of contract law, see C.M. MAZZONI, p. 185. Hungary refers to the lack of financial compensation; see *supra*, J. SANDOR, p. 178.

(136) The United Kingdom refers to this principle with regard to the use of assisted reproductive technologies and surrogacy (see *supra*, T. CALLUS, p. 213) and the Swiss refer to it for germinal material (see *supra*, D. MANAI, p. 226). The German law on transplantation prohibits trading in organs and tissues (see *supra*, F. FURKEL, p. 71).

prohibition of financial gain(137). Swiss law appears to distinguish between the concepts of "gratuity" and non-commercialisation, as the sanctions for a violation are not the same(138). The European Convention on Biomedicine of 4 April 1997, an instrument specific to biomedicine, refers to the prohibition of making the body or its elements a source of financial gain(139).

Whatever the statement the aim of this principle is to prohibit not only any payment but to avoid putting a price tag on the body or body parts: It is also to prohibit any commodification of the body(140). In fact, non-commercialisation goes hand in hand with the principle of autonomy in preventing that an individual's control over their body results in a property right of the body(141).

This principle also applies to the elements of the human body. Indeed, the review of the legislation shows that legal systems differ: the principle of non-property rights sometimes applies to the body and its elements (or only to some of them(142)), and sometimes only to the body and not to the elements.

Although non-commercialisation rules out any idea of payment it is interesting to note that in most countries advocating this principle, compensation is provided for in the biomedical research context for the human research subject and/or for the provision of elements of the body. In Spain, the concept of a "justified payment" is used(143). This reconciliation between non-property rights and the payment of compensation is also included in the European Parliament Directive of 31 March 2004(144). So in practice, this possibility provided by the legal instruments can lead to the provision of actual payments(145). This observation highlights a reality that is not (or barely) consistent with the idea of the absence of profit, and highlights the complexity of this principle. According

(137) See *supra*, C.M. Mazzoni, p. 191.

(138) See *supra*, D. Manaï, p. 226.

(139) Art. 21.

(140) See *supra*, V. San Julian, p. 138.

(141) See *supra*, F. Kernaleguen, p. 155.

(142) In Egypt, the principle of the non-ownership of the human body does not apply to its regenerative elements; see *supra*, H. Abdelhamid, p. 251.

(143) See *supra*, V. San Julian, p. 138.

(144) Directive 2004/23/EC of 31 March 2004 of the European Parliament and of the Council on setting standards of quality and safety for the donation, procurement, testing, processing, preservation, storage and distribution of human tissues and cells. This instruments states that compensation can be paid to cover the expenses and inconvenience related to a donation.

(145) See *supra*, F. Furkel, p. 71.

to the countries, the non-commercialisation rule can be seen as the most significant translation of the principle of dignity applied to the body[146] or, just the opposite: a meaningless principle in view of the freedom of the individual over his/her own body[147], or yet as a principle whose exceptions (or misuse) could, in practice make it useless. We need to explore further the principle of no-property rights over the body and its parts before considering the very delicate issue of the relationship between the body and money[148].

The right to life is also referred to by a number of States as a principle of protection of the body[149] in cases in which a violation can result in the person's death[150]. In Chile, this principle is the leading fundamental right[151]. However, it is not enshrined in French legislation specific to the protection of the body[152].

Another principle sometimes considered is that of anonymity[153]. However, this is less related to the protection of the body itself and more to the individual's identity since the principle of anonymity leads to protecting the donor's identity and even non-identifying information[154].

(146) In Switzerland and Germany (in Germany, the prohibition of commercialisation is based on the prohibition of acts that are contrary to public morals; see *supra*, F. FURKEL, p. 70).

(147) This is the case in the USA where the sale of elements of the body is permitted in a number of states. See *supra*, K. ORFALI, p. 313.

(148) Such an international (covering twenty countries) and multidisciplinary study, under the direction of B. FEUILLET-LIGER and S. OKTAY, has been scheduled by the *Réseau Universitaire International de Bioéthique* in 2015 and will be published at the end of 2016, on "The reality of the principle of the non-ownership of the body".

(149) Germany (absolute principle included in Basic Law), Belgium, Brazil, Canada, Chile, Egypt, Spain, Greece, Hungary, United Kingdom, Switzerland. In Turkey, this right limits the principle of autonomy; see *supra*, S. OKTAY-ÖZDEMIR and G.S. TEK, p. 271.

(150) The ECHR, in the aforementioned *Pretty* case, considered that this right to life could be interpreted as creating a right to death. B. MATHIEU, "La vie en droit constitutionnel comparé. Éléments de réflexions sur un droit incertain", *RIDC*, 1998-4, p. 1031.

(151) Before the principle of respect for physical and mental integrity; see *supra*, C. DOMINGUEZ-HIDALGO, p. 341.

(152) The *bioethical laws* of 1994 do not refer to it. Although it does not feature in the Civil Code and the Constitution, it is nevertheless guaranteed by the existence of numerous offences contained in the Criminal Code (art. 221-1 to 221-11).

(153) Canada, France, Greece, Italy. In Germany this is only allowed for organ donations.

(154) On the diverse positions adopted by the countries on this issue, see B. FEUILLET (ed.), *Procréation médicalement assistée et Anonymat. Panorama international*, Brussels, Bruylant, 2008; B. FEUILLET, K. ORFALI and T. CALLUS (eds.) *Who is my Genetic Parent? Donor Anonymity and Assisted Reproduction: A Cross-Cultural Perspective*, Brussels, Bruylant, 2011.

The principles of beneficence, maleficence and justice are rarely referred to in the context of the legal protection of the body[(155)], and when they are, it is in relation to ethics[(156)]. However some countries refer to the legal principle of "patient's best interests"[(157)] which appears to be a legal interpretation of the principle of beneficence[(158)].

To conclude this review of the different principles of protection of the body, it is important to note the emergence of a new global phenomenon regarding the abuses observed related to the elements of the human body (mainly the organs): the fight against human trafficking. However, none of the contributions, except those concerning Belgium[(159)] and Hungary[(160)], has noted this trend, although it is related to the protection of the body. Although the condemnation of slavery is included in the general international instruments on human rights[(161)] and although it is mainly intended for activities on the body (forced labour, prostitution), "modern" slavery and human trafficking also concern the use of the body itself. The European Directive adopted in 2011 on human trafficking[(162)] gives a broad definition by incorporating the exploitation of others for the removal of organs, which constitutes a serious violation of human dignity and physical integrity. French law and Greek law have incorporated this directive nationally[(163)]. The principle of the prohibition of slavery and human trafficking is generally recognised in a number of countries, and constitutes

(155) Canada, Spain, Hungary (the principle of non-maleficence is used with regard to organs), Switzerland, Tunisia, USA. The principle of non-maleficence appears to play a major role in Turkey in limiting the autonomy of the individual; see *supra*, S. OKTAY-ÖZDEMIR and G.S. TEK, p. 280. In France, it is not used with regard to the protection of the body, but to guarantee the protection of vulnerable persons.

(156) *Principlism* (T.L. BEAUCHAMP and J.F. CHILDRESS, *Principles of Biomedical Ethics, 1977 ; Les principes de l'éthique médicale, op. cit.*) has highlighted four principles whose implementation allows the establishment of moral judgments on concrete cases: autonomy, non-maleficence, beneficence and justice. See *supra*, K. ORFALI.

(157) Spain, Switzerland, United Kingdom.

(158) See *supra*, V. SAN JULIAN (p. 137) and D. MANAÏ (p. 231).

(159) See *supra*, G. SCHAMPS, p. 84.

(160) See *supra*, J. SANDOR, p. 172.

(161) In particular, art. 4 of the 1950 ECHR.

(162) Directive 2011/36/EU of the European Parliament and of the Council of 5 April 2011 on Preventing and Combating Trafficking in Human Beings and Protecting its Victims.

(163) L. n° 2013-711, 5 August 2013, on a variety of adaptation measures in the field of justice, in accordance with European Union law and the international commitments of France (*JORF*, n° 0181, of 6 August 2013, p. 13338). M. FABRE-MAGNAN, "Les nouvelles formes d'esclavage et de traite, ou le syndrome de la ligne Maginot", *D.*, 2014, p. 491. This is also the case in Greece (L. n° 4198-2013) and Switzerland.

a tool the States can use to sanction all organ removals leading to human trafficking.

There is a wide range of principles contributing to the protection of the body. In the event of a failure to comply with these legally enshrined principles, criminal, civil, administrative and disciplinary sanctions are imposed. In a number of countries, however, in spite of the recognition of these principles, they remain only marginally effective as so few legal proceedings have been initiated(164).

All or some of these principles of protection also apply to the dead body, as the protection of the body continues to be provided after death(165). In France, the courts even considered that the basic ethical principles should apply to the corpse, even though this is not stipulated in the legal instruments(166). In Germany, in the name of *post-mortem* dignity, numerous funeral rites are prohibited. However, the death of the individual does mean that the protection is sometimes less important than for a living person. In Brazil, if the corpse is not claimed after death, it is given to a medical school(167)! Additionally some countries consider protecting the corpse based not only on a desire to protect the integrity of the body itself, but also for public order and administrative police considerations(168).

In all the countries studied, when the different principles come into conflict and there is no legally defined hierarchy(169), it is usually up to the judge to decide. This does not challenge the validity of these principles, but forces the judges "to take the relative weight of each of them into consideration"(170) in accordance with the principle of proportionality, and to reconcile the different

(164) See *supra*, A. Aouij-Mrad, p. 245.

(165) Germany, Brazil, Egypt (inviolability), Spain, France, Greece, Switzerland, Turkey (the Turkish Criminal Code provides for the protection of the corpse and the Council of State refers to *post-mortem* dignity).

(166) CE, 2 July 1993*, Milhaud case*, *JCP*, 1993, n° 22133. Since this decision, the legislature has intervened and adopted a number of provisions expressly protecting the corpse; see *supra*, F. Kernaleguen.

(167) See *supra*, M.C. Crespo-Brauner, p. 332.

(168) See *supra,* D. Manaï and A. Aouij-Mrad, p. 241.

(169) Nevertheless, in most of the countries studied, dignity and freedom are the principles on which all the other principles are based. On the hierarchy for these principles, see *supra*, V. San Julian, p. 121.

(170) R. Dworkin, *Prendre les droits au sérieux*, coll. Léviathan, Paris, PUF, 1977, p. 85.

values they represent. The major problem seems to be the conflict between dignity and freedom[171].

CONCLUSION

On completion of this summary, it appears that the principles of protection adopted by the different countries represent the view, conservative or liberal, that different States have of the individual and the individual's relationship with his body. The conservative viewpoint is based on the idea that the individual is only the custodian of his body, which belongs to God or to nature, while the liberal viewpoint is based on the autonomy of the individual, which is the ultimate value[172]. The study also reveals how much the State intervenes or distances itself regarding the protection of the body. Underlying all of these considerations, the issue of the importance and extent of the individual's freedom is paramount. The answer given by each State seems to be based not only on the pre-eminence within the country of the individual or the collective, but also on the importance given by the State to the principle of dignity, which always (and inevitably) constitutes a mechanism for limiting freedoms.

However, apart from this question of the scope given to individual freedom, our study demonstrates the importance of another question, too often avoided or at least undervalued: that of the freedom of vulnerable persons, and more specifically of financially vulnerable persons. Indeed, a large number of scenarios involving control over what happen to the body (research, surrogacy) or elements of the body (various removals) concern in fact low income people. Although freedom should and must *a priori* be given to vulnerable people, just as it is to every individual, this assertion needs to be further analysed. It seems important to take into account the context in which this freedom is exercised. Is the freedom not sometimes (often?) undermined by social inequalities, and does it not then risk becoming a tool for a system pursuing financial gain? The defence of this freedom is a precious and essential aim, as is the protection of vulnerable people who are victims of trafficking.

(171) In Canada, the reconciliation between freedom and dignity is complex, for while freedom appears to be dominant, the influence of civil law gives dignity a certain importance; see *supra*, D. GOUBAU, p. 283.

(172) See *supra*, D. LE BRETON, p. 23.

In this respect, alluding to the ideas of slavery or human trafficking is an interesting path to follow, when all the conditions included in the legal instruments have been met. All the studied countries approve of fighting against all of these humtrafficking scenarios. The truly biggest issue lies elsewhere: in reconciling the freedom of financially vulnerable people with the framework of a market-based system, an undeniable fact in our world. The idea that some people have a better chance of gaining access to modern medicine by selling their kidneys or blood than by being care for is a reality[173]. However, should the state (the law) also intervene when people have this opportunity to be treated and thus to benefit from medical advances, and decide freely to sell elements of their body? Setting boundaries is far from easy. The work carried out for this study shows that the issue around the protection of the body is not only dependent on the extent of an individual's freedom but has also to take into account the evaluation of freedom in a scientific and market-oriented context. Freedom can lead to exploit the poorest members of society[174] in an underhand way. The States have an especially challenging task, as it falls within an area where morals and traditions play an important role. Let us wager that the principles of protection of the body are and will in essence be, like human rights, a promise for the future[175] to provide people with real protection.

(173) See *supra*, D. Le Breton, p. 31.
(174) See *supra*, D. Le Breton (p. 21) and P. Lecoz (p. 33).
(175) Concerning human rights, see D. Gutmann "Les droits de l'homme sont-ils l'avenir du droit", in *L'avenir du droit*, *op. cit.*, p. 329.